T0214160

Lecture Notes in Computer Science   11151

Commenced Publication in 1973
Founding and Former Series Editors:
Gerhard Goos, Juris Hartmanis, and Jan van Leeuwen

More information about this series at http://www.springer.com/series/7409

Yuhua Luo (Ed.)

Cooperative Design, Visualization, and Engineering

15th International Conference, CDVE 2018
Hangzhou, China, October 21–24, 2018
Proceedings

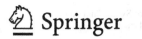 Springer

Editor
Yuhua Luo
University of Balearic Islands
Palma de Mallorca
Spain

ISSN 0302-9743 ISSN 1611-3349 (electronic)
Lecture Notes in Computer Science
ISBN 978-3-030-00559-7 ISBN 978-3-030-00560-3 (eBook)
https://doi.org/10.1007/978-3-030-00560-3

Library of Congress Control Number: 2018954067

LNCS Sublibrary: SL3 – Information Systems and Applications, incl. Internet/Web, and HCI

This Springer imprint is published by the registered company Springer Nature Switzerland AG
The registered company address is: Gewerbestrasse 11, 6330 Cham, Switzerland

Preface

The 15th International Conference on Cooperative Design, Visualization, and Engineering, CDVE 2018, was held in Hangzhou, which is a famous scenic city in China and the base of the booming internet business miracle.

The papers presented in this proceedings book reflect important trends in research and development hot topics such as robotics, artificial intelligence, cloud technology, big data, block chain technology, etc. We are excited to see that cooperative applications are playing an increasingly important role in technological development and social services.

In the field of cloud technology, particularly cloud storage for cooperation, some papers address how to facilitate multiple user information sharing in the cloud, while retaining concurrent access. Some discoveries are reported from applying comprehensive suites of concurrency benchmarking to major cloud storage systems, such as Microsoft OneDrive, Google Drive, and Dropbox, etc. A strategic heuristic-oriented management and organizational strategy is proposed to navigate the complex cloud storage landscape. The strategy is centered around the probabilistic graphical model which, according to the authors, can increase tractability and efficiency in cloud storage management.

Papers about extending the distance and range of cooperation by allowing cross-platform devices and editors to work together are presented.

A web-based tiled display wall capable of supporting collaborative activities among multiple remote sites is reported. The system introduces a key feature, the virtual display area, as a method for handling various display configuration environments with different physical resolutions and aspect ratios. This enables ad hoc participation from multiple sites to facilitate remote collaboration and cooperative work. Similarly, there are papers explaining how to create heterogeneous co-editing systems to potentially solve the long existing war among different editors.

A higher level of automation for cooperative design, such as architecture design, is sought in some papers. Visual language of design elements, graph rewriting, and rule schemes are used for automatic creation of new architecture components or fitting new architectural objects into existing design contexts.

Recently, robotics has become a very hot topic in research and social life. This fact is reflected by some of the papers in the volume. A couple of the papers presented at the conference address robot-robot cooperation and human-robot cooperation. Cloud computing is often involved in robot control, as an important element in such systems.

A very interesting topic is presented in one paper, i.e., that of emotion communication between humans and robots. In a typical scenario, the robot reads the emotional states of the user and relies on the cloud to determine the most appropriate action. Since this process generally involves several interactions before the user's comfort is achieved, timeliness becomes a critical issue. The author uses a Markovian representation for the emotional state sequence.

From the application point of view, some papers presented in this volume convincingly show that cooperative technology is one of the key elements to solving many daily social issues.

One example is about how to solve or minimize the effect of a city traffic jam. One paper presents an urban traffic interactive visual analytic system. The volume of the transportation tracking system is unbelievably large. These data are keys for unveiling human mobility patterns, transportation system utilization, and urban planning. Their system is demonstrated with a real-world taxi GPS and meter data sets from approximately 15,000 taxis running for one whole month in Cheng-du, a huge Chinese city of over 10 million people. The system shows the advantage of being easy to use, efficient, and scalable to visualize and explore transportation data. This will greatly help the traffic-control city-planning administrators in their work. At the same time, it can be used in real time for the drivers to optimize their travel plans by avoiding congestions.

Another suggestion for solving social problems is the proposal in one paper to use block chain technology. As the aging population increases, the care services of many countries are facing a crisis. The authors propose an incentive-based system to promote citizen to citizen collaboration. A method for trading care services using crypto credit is suggested to facilitate such collaboration. Based on block chain technology, citizens can trade crypto credits for care services with each other.

In the field of education, one social problem has attracted the attention a group of researchers. High school students often experience high pressure in relation to their learning and social activities, which can increase their worries and anxiety. Giving students access to relevant information and teaching them how to manage anxiety are important for their school performance and wellbeing. Given the wide use of smart phones, the group helped the local community organizations to develop an anxiety self-regulation and education application for high school students.

In summary, the papers in this volume show the more practical aspects of cooperative design, visualization, and engineering that contribute to the advancement of technology and social services. We believe that the demand for technology is a truly pushing power for research and development in our field.

As the editor of this volume, I would like to express my sincere thanks to all the authors for submitting their papers to the CDVE 2018 conference and for their contribution to technological development and their service to society.

The success of this conference is a result of the cooperation and hard work of all our volunteer reviewers, Program Committee members, and Organization Committee members. My special thanks goes to our Program Committee chair, Prof. Dieter Roller at the University of Stuttgart, Germany, for his longtime work and unconditional support over the past fifteen years. My special thanks also go to the members of our local Organization Committee, as well as, the Organization Committee chair, Prof. Wanliang Wang, and co-chairs, Yan-Wei Zhao, and Li-Nan Zhu, at the Zhejiang University of Technology, China. The success of this year's conference would not have been possible without their generous support.

October 2018   Yuhua Luo

Organization

Conference Chair

Yuhua Luo — University of the Balearic Islands, Spain

International Program Committee

Program Chair

Dieter Roller — University of Stuttgart, Germany

Members

Conrad Boton
Winyu Chinthammit
Jose Alfredo Costa
Alma Leora Culén
Peter Demian
Susan Finger
Sebastia Galmes
Halin Gilles
Figen Gül
Shuangxi Huang

Tony Huang
Claudia-Lavinia Ignat
Ursula Kirschner
Jean-Christophe Lapayre
Pierre Leclercq
Jang Ho Lee
Jaime Lloret
Kwan-Liu Ma
Moira C. Norrie
Manuel Ortega

Niko Salonen
Fernando
    Sanchez Figueroa
Chengzheng Sun
Thomas Tamisier
Huifen Wang
Nobuyoshi Yabuki
Jianlong Zhou

Organization Committee

Chair

Wanliang Wang — Zhejiang University of Technology, China

Co-chairs

Yan-Wei Zhao — Zhejiang University of Technology, China
Li-Nan Zhu — Zhejiang University of Technology, China

Members

RongRong Chen
Xiao-Su Yang
Xin-Xin Guan
Hao Yan

Wen-Bo Zhu
Tomeu Estrany
Alex Garcia
Sebastia Galmes

Pilar Fuster
Takayuki Fujimoto
Jaime Lloret
Guofeng Qin

Reviewers

Xiaojuan Ban
Marwan Batrouni
Weiwei Cai
Takayuki Fujimoto
Pilar Fuster
Henri-Jean Gless
José Guerrero Sastre
Tony Huang
Claudia-Lavinia Ignat
Ursula Kirschner

Jean-Christophe Lapayre
Pierre Leclercq
Jang Ho Lee
Jaime Lloret
Kwan-Liu Ma
Mary Lou Maher
Moira C. Norrie
Manuel Ortega
Vijayakumar Ponnusamy
Guofeng Qin

Niko Salonen
Fernando Sanchez
   Figueroa
Chengzheng Sun
Thomas Tamisier
Huifen Wang
Nobuyoshi Yabuki
Didry Yoann
Yanwei Zhao
Jianlong Zhou

Contents

TranSeVis: A Visual Analytics System for Transportation Data Sensing and Exploration

Rui Gong, Zhiyao Teng, Mei Han, Lirui Wei, Yuwei Zhang, and Jiansu Pu$^{(\boxtimes)}$

CompleX Lab, Web Sciences Center, Big Data Research Center,
University of Electronic Science and Technology of China,
Chengdu 611731, People's Republic of China
rui.gong_gr@foxmail.com, nonolily@163.com, hanmei1993@126.com,
lirui_wei@163.com, yuweizhang623@gmail.com, jiansu.pu@uestc.edu.cn
http://www.labcomplex.org

Abstract. With increasing availability of location-acquisition technologies, huge volumes of data tracking transportation system have been collected. These data are highly valuable for unveiling human mobility patterns, transportation system utilization, and urban planning. However, it is still highly challenging to visualize and explore transportation data. In this paper, an interactive visual analytic system, *TranSeVis* has been proposed. It has two visualization modules, one named region view provides geographical information and effective temporal information comparison, the other named road view provides detailed visual analysis of mobility factors along routes or congestions spots. Besides, two case studies have been used to evaluate the visualization techniques and real-world taxi data sets have been used to demonstrate *TranSeVis*. Based on the results, *TranSeVis* offers transportation researchers an easy-to-use, efficient, and scalable platform to visualize and explore transportation data.

Keywords: Visual analysis · Urban traffic · Congestion analysis
Spatio-temporal data

1 Introduction

Nowadays massive amount of humans and vehicles transportation data have been produced by advanced sensing technologies and computing infrastructures in urban spaces. From the perspective of city management and urban planning, transportation data are highly valuable not only for unveiling human mobility patterns, but also for assisting authorities, operators, and individuals to better understanding of the transportation system and possibly improved utilization and planning. In most Chinese cities, taxi cabs have contributed most of the collected transportation data for city authorities to manage. With the widespread use of vehicle Global Positioning System (GPS) and road-side sensors, taxi data

© Springer Nature Switzerland AG 2018
Y. Luo (Ed.): CDVE 2018, LNCS 11151, pp. 1–10, 2018.
https://doi.org/10.1007/978-3-030-00560-3_1

now are able to be recorded in real-time with moving paths sampled as a series of positions associated with vehicle attributes over urban road networks. Massive taxi data including their movement patterns contains abundant knowledge about cities and urban life which has been widely used for urban authorities to understand the traffic situations. Hence, studying the knowledge about taxi diaspora and behaviors extracted from these GPS data is also valuable and highly beneficial to both individuals as well as to the entire city.

Exploratory visual analytic systems are demanded to study transportation data through taxi records with efficient user interaction and instant visual feedback. However, developing visual analytics methods to meet this goal is a highly challenging task due to increasing complexity of the data. In order to design efficient methods for analysts to visualize and explore transportation data and extract valuable information, we developed *TranSeVis*, an interactive visual analytic system, integrated with two visualization modules: region view for geographical information and effective temporal information comparison, road view for detailed visual analysis of mobility factors along routes or congestions spots. The region view projects all statistical information into several parallel radial representation, maximizing the visualization of mobility related data along with clear spatial information. In this view, the speed distribution of selected areas in the city are also provided by smooth interaction and to be able to query taxis by individual or groups. And a chord diagram is presented to show the flow among different districts. Moreover, we devise road view with interactive visual query methods for users to easily explore the dynamics of transportation data over road and vehicles. The road view allows analysts to pick out interested cars or roads to explore the detailed traffic situation. Besides the Place of Information (POI) view is designed to help experts quickly navigate and explore some interesting spots extracted from statistical or mining results.

Lastly, we also demonstrate *TranSeVis* on real-world taxi GPS and meter data sets from approximately 15,000 taxis running for one whole month in Chengdu, a huge Chinese city of over 10 million people, and evaluate our visualization techniques with assorted case studies with the transportation researchers. Based on our extensive empirical experiment results, *TranSeVis* offers us an easy-to-use, efficient, and scalable platform to visualize and explore transportation data in making traffic policies and city planning, as well as for people to optimize their travel plans to avoid congestions.

In summary, we have made the following contributions. (1) We have developed a system to study large-scale transportation data, integrating visualization and data analytics methods, and propose techniques to improve efficiency and scalability. (2) We report our experience and observations in building *TranSeVis*. (3) We demonstrate and test our system by using real-life data sets for real-world applications.

2   Related Work

Geovisualization. Geo-visualization provides interactive visual tools for exploration and analysis of data with geographical information. Due to limited space, we summarize a few representative papers. Mehler et al. [10] represent news sources as datamaps to show the geographic popularity of an entity, and any possible geographic bias. Wood et al. [14] discussed geo-visualization mash-up techniques including tag clouds, tag maps, data dials, and multi-scale density surfaces for exploratory visual analysis of large spatial-temporal datasets. Fisher presented heatmap [6] to represent aggregate activity and draw users' attention to the map. One geographic visualization challenge lies in visual thinking and user interaction, such as how human vision perceives maps and images and how it finds patterns. Chang et al. [4] presented legible cities to display large collections of data for urban contexts with different levels of abstractions. Growth Ring Maps [3] is proposed to represent spatial-temporal data by plotting a number of non-overlapping pixels.

Movement Data Visualization. Andrienko et al. [1] discussed various characteristics of spatio-temporal data and categorized visualization techniques into three major categories, including direct depiction, summarization and pattern extraction. Direct depiction techniques present movement directly. Traditional methods [8] generally plot trajectory paths directly in 2D/3D according to the geographical context. This type of techniques also includes plotting paths as polylines [1] or stacked bands [12], representing origin and destination of trajectories as points [5], and depicting spatial and temporal information together with space time cube [2]. Summarization techniques present data based on statistical calculations and concerns changes of information in space and time, so that analysts can get an overall understanding of the tendencies and investigate aggregated patterns. This type of techniques includes density map [13], multivariate glyph [15], and flow map [7]. Pattern extraction techniques present extracted patterns of movement to analysts for interpretation and further investigation. Many patterns, such as the interchange pattern [16], have been studied.

The spiral layout can make periodic data trends easily apparent when the correct period is chosen. It is a well-known solution that reveals periodic pattern of temporal data along a spiral time axis by careful parameterization on recent visual designs. Liu et al. [9] display a circular time axis enclosing a road map to encode temporal information about trajectories, but the design is limited in the number of roads that can be viewed. Necklace Maps [11] project thematic mapping variables onto intervals and display them in a circular curve that surrounds the map regions. Zhao et al. [17] presented Ringmap which visualizes multiple cyclic activities over time while preserving geographical information. These approaches are perhaps most similar to our visual design. However, our system can simultaneously provide visual analytics from multiple aspects of visualizations of spatial, temporal and multi-dimensional perspectives that are linked together, helping users better explore, compare, and understand evolving transportation data.

3 System Design

In this section, *TranSeVis* is presented in detail. Our system has two major parts: the data processing part and the visual representation part. In data processing part the raw GPS data are cleaned, indexed, and computed based on their vehicle related attributes. After that, in visual representation part, different visualization techniques are integrated to provide the interactive region view and the road view respectively. With this system, the analysts can explore the spatial and temporal features of traffic flow from both region and road level interactively.

3.1 Data Processing

Taxi GPS records are used to demonstrate *TranSeVis* in this work. The raw data is collected by GPS and covers the whole city area of Chengdu, China. There are 14,931 taxis in this dataset and the sampling rate varies from a few seconds to minutes. Each record contains the taxi ID, taxi position (the latitude and longitude), the time (in seconds), and the taxi's service status. The computed transportation data is visualized on Chengdu's administrative divisions map. The first step of data processing is cleaning the data by wiping out the outliers from spatial and temporal aspects. We filtering the dataset by selecting all the points inside longitude ranging from 103.92 to 104.22 and latitude ranging from 30.75 to 30.79 to keep our case studies focused on central area of Chengdu. To highlight the spatial information of the taxi data, we categorize the data points and paths from the overall perspective into the five administrative divisions of Chengdu city, namely, Jinniu district, Jinjiang district, Qingyang district, Wuhou district, and Chenghua district. A path here is formally defined as a line segment composed by two consecutive data points from a specific taxi. In addition, system offers the temporal information comparison of the movement data by encoding all the data points into radial layout in 7 day × 24 h slots. With the above methods, we can obtain the flow matrix from the paths and the speed matrix for visualization to further help the analysts to explore the overall traffic features as well as the taxis' mobility patterns.

3.2 Visual Representation

With the spatial and temporal data prepared, we design the interactive region view and the road view to present the mobility patterns of the taxis from overall and individual level respectively.

Region View. *The Region View* (See Fig. 1(1–4)) presents the spatial and temporal distributions of the taxis' positions within five districts ranging for 24 h periods A chord diagram design (Fig. 1(3)) is used to encode the traffic flow between different districts. This view also provides the "movement area"s, which are generated by k-means clustering and can be selected in panel Fig. 1(1). More insights can be obtained from comparing such results and the administrative divisions' representation. In this view, the "flower" and the "chord" designs are applied. The "flower" design is composed of outer "petal"s and an inner ring for displaying the taxis' spatial and temporal distribution for each district as well as the traffic between the specific district and its neighbors. In fact, the "flower" design is formed by radical bar chart of temporal distributions for the points. The inner ring represents the ratio of paths between a specific district and the neighbor districts. The encoding details are illustrated in Fig. 2(a):

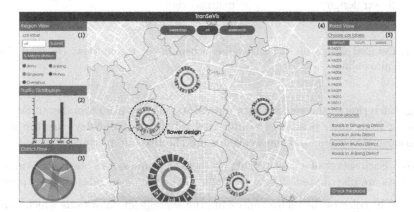

Fig. 1. System overview: (1) the control panel for the region view. (2) The traffic load distribution. (3) The district flow chord diagram. (4) The main view of *TranSeVis*. (5) The control panel for the road view.

Petal. The petal is the basic element of the "flower" design. It is a bar from the radical bar chart. Each bar on the flower represents a time slot of one hour and the height encodes the total number of spatial points within related specific district.

Sector. A sector is the basic element of the inner ring, which means the ratio of taxis travel to other districts.

Color. Color used in this view is to categorize, which is appropriate to distinguish five different districts. Here we use green to encode Jinniu district, orchid for Jinjiang district, orange for Qingyang district, medium purple for Wuhou district, and light steel blue for Chenghua district.

Road View. *The Road View* is proposed to show the mobility related factors' visualization such as taxi speed distribution for a road segment being encoded as a 7 day × 24 h radical color matrix. And the corresponding color of each sector represents the speed, where green means higher speed than red. The speed of a taxi is calculated by averaging the total mileage during the specific hour within a week. Figure 2(b) shows the detailed design:

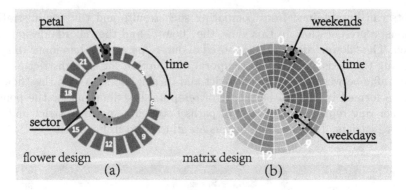

Fig. 2. Detailed design of visual encoding schemes: (a) region view; (b) road view. (Color figure online)

Ring. Each ring of the color matrix represents one day from Monday to Sunday mapping from inner position to outer rings. Thus, the weekdays are the inner five concentric circles, and the weekends are the two outer layers.

Sector. Each sector of a specific ring presents the time slot of one hour. And the time slots are distributed clockwise. Color of the sector encodes the taxi speed.

Color. The color of the sector represents the average speed of taxis which scales from green (high speed) to red (low speed). It is based on the color encoding of the traffic light signaling.

4   Case Study

In this section, we provide two case studies to demonstrate the effectiveness of *TranSeVis*. Among them, the "Overview Analysis" is taken as an example to demonstrate how this visual analytics system present the holistic traffic status of Chengdu city. The "district clustering analysis" analyzes the differences between the administrative divisions and the "movement center"s obtained from the k-means algorithm. Last but not least, the "road traffic analysis" highlights the advantages of this system in presenting and analyzing the spatial and temporal road level traffic status. The two case studies not only demonstrate the efficacy of *TranSeVis*, but also show the potentials of this system in mining the spatial and temporal traffic data.

4.1   Case 1: Overview Analysis

The main view of *TranSeVis* offers three charts as illustrated in Fig. 3: the movements district distributions ("flower" chart), the traffic connections (chord diagram), and the spatial distribution of the traffic load (bar chart). By comparing different "flower" charts for different districts, we can easily observe that Wuhou district has the largest amount of traffic load. The total amount of traffic

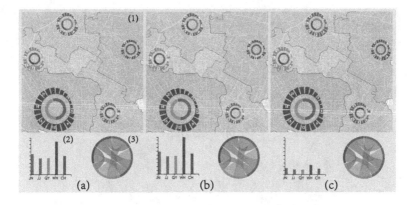

Fig. 3. Case study 1: overview analysis.

is shown in the bar chart. The taxi paths connecting different districts can be explored from the overall level in the chord diagram, and from the district level in the inner ring of each "flower" for a specific district. From the main view, we can find out that Wuhou and Chenghua have more flows with Jinjiang than others. We suggest that more attention should be paid in improving the transportation facilities of Wuhou which is the area near the city center. Besides, by comparing the bar charts, we found that the total time taxis spend at weekends is much less than that on weekdays. According to our previous work and the further exploration results of the road view, an observation could be come out that more traffic jams happens at weekends than on weekdays. Considering the traffic restriction, we thought possible because more citizens may choose to drive instead of taking a taxi on weekends, which made the congestions more serious. From this point of view, we could advice urban citizens especially those live or like to be near the city center on weekends choose public transportation system. And the government could improve the convenience of public transportation system through many ways such as increasing metro lines and improving bus routes.

4.2   Case 2: Road Traffic Analysis

Our system *TranSeVis* also provides the road view to help the analysts to grasp the spatial and temporal features of the traffic of roads. Four roads are taken as examples in Fig. 4, and they are West Jinli Road (1), Middle Jinli Road (2), East Jinli Road (3), and Renmin West Road (4). As illustrated in Fig. 4, Road 4 is in the downtown center, and the taxis here always travel at a low speed, especially on weekends and in the afternoons. Road 1, Road 2, and Road 3 are directly connected nose to tail, nevertheless, the taxi speed drops from Road 1 to Road 3, the reasons are complex and they can be inferred as: (1) the closer the road is to the north to south trunk road of the city (vertical dashed line), the more crowed it will be; (2) the closer the road is to the famous POIs (Point

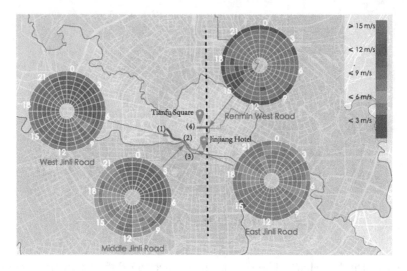

Fig. 4. Case study 2: road traffic analysis.

Of Interest, like Tianfu Square and Jinjiang Hotel), the slower the speed will be. The holistic spatial and temporal patterns of these four color matrices are that the traffic is worse in daytime and weekends for most of the roads, and the central downtown will always be in congestion. So the suggestions for people are that: reserve enough time if you have to go through the central areas or at rush hours.

5   Conclusion

In this paper, we have proposed an interactive visualization system, *TranSeVis*, in order to present the traffic situation and analyze the mobility patterns in big cities by using taxi trajectory data. This work is still in progress and many features should be developed in the future. Our system consists of two major modules at present including region view and road view. Of the two, the former allow users to observe the temporal and spatial patterns of the taxis in the city in order to give some advice on traveling around the city, while the latter shows the speed of some certain cars during 24 h on the roads users have chosen, which can tell them some information of the traffic congestion. We have paid most attention to the global situation instead of specific points to help analysts get knowledge of the condition of the whole city, but the citizens may need some information of the places they usually go. Therefore, in the future, we plan to design a new module so as to analyze the traffic situations of some POIs and provide some practical suggestions and possible routes for those who want to visit some certain place.

References

1. Andrienko, G., Andrienko, N., Bak, P., Keim, D., Wrobel, S.: Visual Analytics of Movement. Springer, Heidelberg (2013). https://doi.org/10.1007/978-3-642-37583-5
2. Andrienko, G., Andrienko, N., Schumann, H., Tominski, C.: Visualization of trajectory attributes in space-time cube and trajectory wall. In: Buchroithner, M., Prechtel, N., Burghardt, D. (eds.) Cartography from Pole to Pole. LNGC, pp. 157–163. Springer, Heidelberg (2014). https://doi.org/10.1007/978-3-642-32618-9_11
3. Bak, P., Mansmann, F., Janetzko, H., Keim, D.: Spatiotemporal analysis of sensor logs using growth ring maps. IEEE Trans. Vis. Comput. Graph. **15**(6), 913–920 (2009). https://doi.org/10.1109/TVCG.2009.182
4. Chang, R., Wessel, G., Kosara, R., Sauda, E., Ribarsky, W.: Legible cities: focus-dependent multi-resolution visualization of urban relationships. IEEE Trans. Vis. Comput. Graph. **13**(6), 1169–1175 (2007). https://doi.org/10.1109/TVCG.2007.70574
5. Ferreira, N., Poco, J., Vo, H.T., Freire, J., Silva, C.T.: Visual exploration of big spatio-temporal urban data: a study of new york city taxi trips. IEEE Trans. Visual. Comput. Graph. **19**(12), 2149–2158 (2013). https://doi.org/10.1109/TVCG.2013.226
6. Fisher, D.: Hotmap: looking at geographic attention. IEEE Trans. Vis. Comput. Graph. **13**(6), 1184–1191 (2007). https://doi.org/10.1109/TVCG.2007.70561
7. Guo, D., Zhu, X.: Origin-destination flow data smoothing and mapping. IEEE Trans. Vis. Comput. Graph. **20**(12), 2043–2052 (2014). https://doi.org/10.1109/TVCG.2014.2346271
8. Kapler, T., Wright, W.: Geotime information visualization. Inf. Vis. **4**(2), 136–146 (2005)
9. Liu, H., Gao, Y., Lu, L., Liu, S., Qu, H., Ni, L.M.: Visual analysis of route diversity. In: 2011 IEEE Conference on Visual Analytics Science and Technology (VAST), pp. 171–180, October 2011. https://doi.org/10.1109/VAST.2011.6102455
10. Mehler, A., Bao, Y., Li, X., Wang, Y., Skiena, S.: Spatial analysis of news sources. IEEE Trans. Vis. Comput. Graph. **12**(5), 765–772 (2006). https://doi.org/10.1109/TVCG.2006.179
11. Speckmann, a., Verbeek, K.: Necklace maps. IEEE Trans. Vis. Comput. Graph. **16**(6), 881–889 (2010). https://doi.org/10.1109/TVCG.2010.180
12. Tominski, C., Schumann, H., Andrienko, G., Andrienko, N.: Stacking-based visualization of trajectory attribute data. IEEE Trans. Vis. Comput. Graph. **18**(12), 2565–2574 (2012)
13. Wang, Z., Lu, M., Yuan, X., Zhang, J., van de Wetering, H.: Visual traffic jam analysis based on trajectory data. IEEE Trans. Vis. Comput. Graph. **19**(12), 2159–2168 (2013)
14. Wood, J., Dykes, J., Slingsby, A., Clarke, K.: Interactive visual exploration of a large spatio-temporal dataset: reflections on a geovisualization mashup. IEEE Trans. Vis. Comput. Graph. **13**(6), 1176–1183 (2007). https://doi.org/10.1109/TVCG.2007.70570
15. Wu, W., Zheng, Y., Qu, H., Chen, W., Gröller, E., Ni, L.M.: BoundarySeer: visual analysis of 2D boundary changes. In: 2014 IEEE Conference on Visual Analytics Science and Technology (VAST), pp. 143–152, October 2014. https://doi.org/10.1109/VAST.2014.7042490

16. Zeng, W., Fu, C.W., Arisona, S.M., Qu, H.: Visualizing interchange patterns in massive movement data. In: Proceedings of the 15th Eurographics Conference on Visualization, EuroVis 2013, pp. 271–280. The Eurographs Association & #38; John Wiley & #38; Sons Ltd., Chichester (2013). https://doi.org/10.1111/cgf. 12114, https://doi.org/10.1111/cgf.12114
17. Zhao, J., Forer, P., Harvey, A.S.: Activities, ringmaps and geovisualization of large human movement fields. Inf. Vis. **7**(3–4), 198–209 (2008). https://doi.org/10.1057/ palgrave.ivs.9500184. http://ivi.sagepub.com/content/7/3-4/198.abstract

ChOWDER: An Adaptive Tiled Display Wall Driver for Dynamic Remote Collaboration

Tomohiro Kawanabe[1][✉][iD], Jorji Nonaka[1][iD], Kazuma Hatta[2], and Kenji Ono[1,3][iD]

[1] RIKEN Center for Computational Science, Kobe, Japan
{tkawanabe,jorji}@riken.jp
[2] IMAGICADIGITALSCAPE Co., Ltd., Tokyo, Japan
kazuma-h@digirea.com
[3] Research Institute for Information Technology, Kyushu University, Fukuoka, Japan
keno@cc.kyushu-u.ac.jp

Abstract. Herein, we propose a web-based tiled display wall (TDW) system that is capable of supporting collaborative activities among multiple remote sites. Known as the <u>C</u>ooperative <u>W</u>orkspace <u>D</u>river (ChOWDER), this system introduces the virtual display area (VDA) concept as a method for handling various display configuration environments with different physical resolutions and aspect ratios. This concept, which is one of ChOWDER's key features, allows ad hoc participation among multiple sites to facilitate remote collaboration and cooperative work.

Keywords: Web-based · Remote collaboration · Cooperative work

1 Introduction

Today, thanks to the commoditization of high-resolution displays and high-performance graphics processing units (GPUs), multi-display systems have become increasingly commonplace, not only as large systems for multiple viewers, but also for personal use. The multi-display functionality of modern graphics cards, such as the NVIDIA MOSAIC and AMD Eyefinity, make it possible to configure the desktop screen of a single personal computer (PC) across as many as 16 high-resolution 4K displays without any special software.

Additionally, since the technical obstacles for building small and medium-size TDW systems have mostly been overcome, their costs have declined and display systems composed of 8K or 16K resolution screens are currently being built. This indicates that TDW systems designed to facilitate collaboration among multiple sites may become popular in the near future. Meanwhile, with advancements in network performance and web technologies such as HTML5 and WebRTC, web browsers now have sufficient levels of performance to function as the front end of software applications designed to facilitate collaboration among multiple remote sites.

© Springer Nature Switzerland AG 2018
Y. Luo (Ed.): CDVE 2018, LNCS 11151, pp. 11–15, 2018.
https://doi.org/10.1007/978-3-030-00560-3_2

The <u>Co</u>operative <u>W</u>orkspace <u>Driver</u> (ChOWDER) system proposed in this paper is a web-based TDW structure that enhances collaboration among multiple sites over the Internet. Employing the virtual display area (VDA) concept, it can dynamically change the size of a display area, as well as the magnification ratio of the display contents, without being hampered by the resolution limitation constraints of the physical display devices. For example, in a case where one VDA is shared among multiple sites, ChOWDER can adjust the display magnification ratio on the VDA at each site, even if all sites use TDWs with different resolutions or aspect ratios. Additionally, ChOWDER was designed to allow for dynamic participant changes, which means that remote participants can dynamically add their physical displays to the VDA while multi-site collaboration is ongoing. The authors believe that by introducing this concept and its related features, ChOWDER can offer increased functions as a remote collaboration environment.

Although a number of different software technologies for large high-resolution displays have been proposed to date, an extensive survey [1] conducted by Chung et al. in 2014 found that most of those systems were not designed for multi-site collaboration. Meanwhile, web-based applications, such as Skype and appear.in have emerged as practical services that enable multi-site discussion and content sharing.

To the best of our knowledge, SAGE2 [2], which is the successor of SAGE [3], is the only environment that combines a TDW system with web-based multi-site collaboration. SAGE2 has made significant contributions to establishing a software ecosystem that is accessible to large numbers of users and their corresponding software applications. Furthermore, since it is a web-based system, the SAGE2 software configuration is similar to that of ChOWDER. However, ChOWDER is unique thanks to its VDA concept and its peer-to-peer (P2P) streaming function, which will be discussed later. The VDA concept was first unveiled in 2015 during the development of the ChOWDER [4]. During that process, we referred picowalls [5], which consist of multiple small projectors, to build our TDW system.

2   Virtual Display Area Concept

A VDA is a logical two-dimensional (2D) display space in which the position and magnification ratio of physical display devices can be set arbitrarily. For example, if we assume a case in which Site A has an 8K resolution display system that consists of a set of 2×2 4K physical displays and Site B has only one 4K physical display, if the display magnification ratio of Site B is set to 0.25 on the VDA, it is possible to display the entire display 8K area at Site B (Fig. 1). In SAGE2, the display area shared between the sites is determined based on the physical resolution of the display devices. For instance, when Site A is using an 8K resolution display, successful display mirroring requires Site B to have an 8K display as well. Additionally, it should be noted that the VDA allows both the registration and deletion of physical displays to be performed dynamically during system operation. In other words, ChOWDER allows users to add or remove sites while discussions on among multiple sites are ongoing. In contrast, it is impossible to dynamically add new sites when SAGE2 is in operation because those operations require changes to the SAGE2 server configuration file, which then requires a server restart.

To allow for more widespread use of TDW systems in collaborative work, we believe it is important to alleviate this constraint. More specifically, we believe that it would be preferable to give more flexibility to TDW system construction, which could be best accomplished by allowing each remote site to choose their most optimal TDW configuration based on their individual requirements.

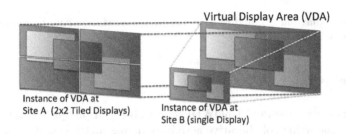

Fig. 1. VDA overview

3   System Architecture, Features, and Use Case

As shown in Fig. 2, ChOWDER consists of three software components: controller, display, and server. The controller works on the web browser with the user interface (UI), which controls the display and the displayed contents. The contents the users want to display can be registered by drag-and-drop operations to the controller window. Acceptable static data such as images and texts are delivered to the display via the server while videos, webcam data, and screen captures are P2P-streamed via WebRTC to the target display. Since the display is simply a web browser window, it is used in the full-screen mode so that the entire physical display can be used as the content display area.

The server, which was developed as a Node.js application, manages the VDA information and the metadata to determine the positions and magnification ratio to be used on the VDA of each display as well as the displayed contents. It also performs as a WebRTC signaling server at the beginning of P2P streaming. Figures 2 (2) and (3) demonstrate a use case of remote collaboration between Sites A and B, respectively. Site A uses 2×2 tiled displays consisting of four 4K liquid crystal displays, while Site B uses a 1×4 tiled projection display consisting of four high definition projectors for a combined 3200×1280 resolution. User will find that the VDA enables them to share the same contents between Sites A and B, despite their different magnification ratios.

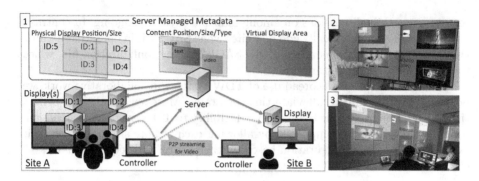

Fig. 2. System diagram (1), and remote collaboration between Kyushu University (2) and RIKEN R-CCS (3)

4   Conclusion

In this paper, we presented ChOWDER, a web-based, adaptive TDW system capable of supporting collaborative activities among multiple sites. This system uses the VDA concept to flexibly connect various display configuration environments with different physical resolutions and aspect ratios. It currently supports several kinds of content types such as image, text, and video as well as webcam and screen capture data. Of these, video, webcam, and screen capture data are directly streamed from the controller to the display (via P2P) using WebRTC technology. We evaluated ChOWDER for remote collaboration between Kyushu University and the RIKEN Center for Computational Science in order to validate its practical usability. Although ChOWDER is still under development, it has already been released as an open source software via GitHub [6].

Acknowledgements. This research has supported by a grant from the Council of Science, Technology and Innovation (CSTI) through the Cross-ministerial Strategic Innovation Promotion Program (SIP).

References

1. Chung, H., Andrews, C., North, C.: A survey of software frameworks for cluster-based large high-resolution displays. IEEE Trans. Vis. Comput. Graph. **20**(8), 1158–1177 (2014)
2. Marrinan, T., et al.: SAGE2: a new approach for data intensive collaboration using scalable resolution shared displays. In 2014 International Conference on Collaborative Computing: Networking, Applications and Worksharing (CollaborateCom), pp. 177–186. IEEE (2014)
3. Renambot, L., et al.: SAGE: the scalable adaptive graphics environment. In: Proceedings of WACE (2004). https://www.evl.uic.edu/luc/Research/papers/WACE2004.pdf

4. Ono, K., et al.: 2015 Annual Report - RIKEN AICS Advanced Visualization Research Team (2016). http://www.r-ccs.riken.jp/en/wp-content/uploads/sites/2/2017/06/aics_annualreport_fy2015.pdf
5. Knoll, A., Hammock, C., Wozniak, J., Mendoza, N., Navrátil, P., Westing, B.: Picowalls: portable tiled display walls from pico projector arrays. In: Proceedings of VISTech 2013, 22 November 2013
6. ChOWDER. https://github.com/SIPupstreamDesign/ChOWDER. Accessed 26 Apr 2018

Usability of Information Seeking Tools in 3D Mobile Interaction with Public Displays

Mayra Donaji Barrera Machuca[1(✉)], Winyu Chinthammit[2],
and Weidong Huang[3]

[1] SIAT, Simon Fraser University, Surrey, BC V3T 0A3, Canada
mbarrera@sfu.ca
[2] School of Technology, Environments and Design, University of Tasmania,
Launceston, TAS 7248, Australia
winyu.chinthammit@utas.edu.au
[3] Department of Computer Science and Software Engineering,
Swinburne University of Technology, Melbourne, VIC 3122, Australia
weidonghuang@swin.edu.au

Abstract. We designed a 3D mobile interaction technique that utilizes mobile devices as 3D user interfaces to facilitate the use of the user's natural skills to control public displays. To achieve this, we provide three layers of interaction, where users can see and share content at the same time. Another feature of our user interface is that it provides different tools for information seeking, such as new content creation. In this paper we present a study that examined how these tools were being used in three different scenario-based case studies. The results of this study indicate that participants found these tools useful.

Keywords: Public displays · Mobile devices · 3D user interfaces
Augmented reality

1 Introduction

Public displays are screens located in public places that show information related to that place useful to the people around them. Nowadays, public displays have become increasingly ubiquitous and can be found in spaces, such as bus stations, public theaters, airports and roadsides [5]. Public displays serve specific purposes depending on their location, for example, a display near the entrance of a shopping mall is for customers to explore the mall to find a specific store. On the other hand a display at a theater is to inform viewers of the latest shows. To fulfill these purposes, some of the challenges of interactive public displays are how to motivate users to start an interaction with the display, and once the interaction starts, how to keep users engaged [1, 5, 9].

In an attempt to address these challenges, we developed a 3D mobile interaction technique that allows users to collaboratively interact with the public display for information seeking purposes [2, 3]. Our 3D mobile interaction technique uses the screen of mobile devices to give individual users a unique and private perspective of the information on the public display. To achieve this, we utilize augmented reality (AR) [6, 11, 12] to allow users to see private 2D and 3D content imposed on the public

Y. Luo (Ed.): CDVE 2018, LNCS 11151, pp. 16–23, 2018.
https://doi.org/10.1007/978-3-030-00560-3_3

display. We have implemented a prototype and conducted a user study evaluating the usability of our interaction technique. The results of the study found that users were satisfied with the proposed technique and that this technique met our design objectives [3].

As part of the implemented technique, our prototype also provides various information tools for users to use on their screens, i.e. look for specific information. In this paper, we report on the results related to the usage of these individual tools. These results were collected on the evaluation of our interaction technique, but we have not reported them elsewhere. From this data, we examined how different mobile interaction tools are being used in three different scenario-based case studies. The results indicate that users found these tools useful.

The rest of this paper is organized as follows: the next section describes the information tools of the tablet interface. Section 3 presents the design of the usability study and results. Finally, Sect. 4 presents our conclusions and future work in this area.

2   3D Mobile Interaction

Our 3D mobile interaction technique is based on AR technologies, where a user utilizes a mobile device to interact with the public display [4, 7, 8, 10]. Having two screens creates a multidimensional interaction space consisting of 3 layers: *public*, where public 2D content is displayed; *virtual*, where public and private 3D content exists outside the public display, and *private*, where private 2D content is displayed. This approach allows users to focus on both screens at the same time, thus increasing the space available to display content. A thorough description of the system can be found in Barrera et al. [2, 3]. In this paper, we focus on the tools designed for the private layer, where users see personalized information. The information showed on this layer is considered private and secure. The reason for this is that it can only be seen and accessed from the screen of each individual user mobile device.

2.1   Interactions

In our user interface design, we focused on giving users a clean screen. This would enable them to interact with the content of the public display without having to overlay information on the mobile device screen. See Fig. 1, for an example of a user interface designed for hiking. In our prototype the main interaction zone, the input area, is in the middle of the screen. Here users utilize touch gestures to interact with the content. The available interaction methods are: one finger selection and translation, and two finger scaling and rotation. Using these gestures users can select information on the public layer and bring it to the virtual and private layers. Once a user selects an object, he/she can manipulate it independently of the other users' actions. The second interaction zone, the more input button, is at the bottom right of the screen. When users click this button, it changes the information each user sees in the virtual layer, which is displayed on top of the public display. The specific information tool, the third interaction zone, is in the left side of the screen. Here users can see written information of the selected content. Finally, at the top right corner, there is the private information zone, which shows private information taken from the mobile device. As stated before, our prototype was adapted to a hiking scenario, Table 1 shows the information added in each interaction zone:

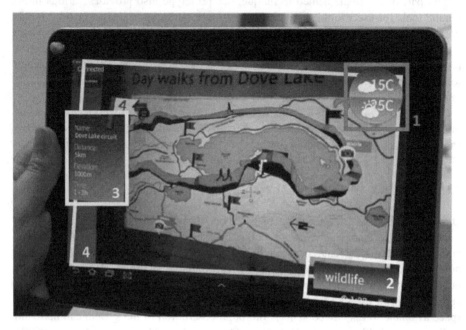

Fig. 1. A user interface showing the private information (1); more info button (2); specific info tool (3); and the input area (4).

Table 1. Use of each interaction zone in our prototype.

Name	Interaction zone	Action
Wildlife	More info button	It shows pictures of what type of wildlife have been sighted on that position
Landscapes	More info button	It shows pictures of the possible view from that position
Notes	More info button	It shows comments other hikers could have left
Weather	Private information	It shows the current weather
Trail name and extra info	Specific info tool	It displays extra information about the selected 3D model
3D Model	Input area	It shows a 3D model of the selected trail

2.2 Prototype

The prototype uses a 21.5 in monitor as a public display and an Android Tablet as a mobile device. We implemented the prototype using Unity and C#. The core tracking capabilities are taken from an AR software library (Vuforia).

3 Experiment

In our experiment participants were asked to role play as two tourists planning a day hike to Dove Lake at Cradle Mountain National Park in Tasmania, Australia. The experiment was conducted over three scenario-based circumstances. We briefly described these three scenarios and our evaluation design in the next two sub-sections, followed by the evaluation results on how individual information seeking tools were used. For more details on the evaluation design, see [3].

3.1 Scenarios

Scenario 1: Participants role-played as a couple of advanced hikers who looked to challenge themselves by choosing a trail from two available trails that has the shortest distances to the pre-selected destination even though it could be more challenging (e.g. steeper slope). The weather was set to be cloudy on the day and the starting time of the hike was at 10:00am.

Scenario 2: Participants role-played as a couple of old-aged hikers who had to consider at a half-way point of the trail whether to continue (in a clockwise direction) and complete the trail or turn around and return to where they started. The couple wished to avoid steep slopes and too hot weather. The weather was set to be hot on the day and the starting time of the hike was at 1:00 pm.

Scenario 3: Participants role-played a couple of young casual hikers who looked for a location that was relatively leveled so that they could relax and have lunch. The selected location must have a good view of the national park, which was located at higher altitude. The weather was set to be windy on the day and the starting time of the hike was at 9:00am.

3.2 Evaluation Design

The evaluation was conducted in a controlled room at the HIT Lab AU in the University of Tasmania, Newnham campus. A total of 40 participants (22 males, 18 females; age range 19–58; mean age 24.5 years) participated in the study. Most of the participants were computer science students, but some were also community members interested in the study. The participants were asked to come with a friend, and each pair was randomly assigned to either the traditional group (which used a static public display) or the mobile group (which used the proposed 3D mobile interaction proto-type). In this paper we present and discuss the results of the usability of the information seeking tools. We use the information of how each participant used the tools available on their mobile device to achieve this. The mobile application has a built-in data logging capability to capture the interaction activities on the mobile tools made by the users. And we also distributed questionnaires to collect user feedback.

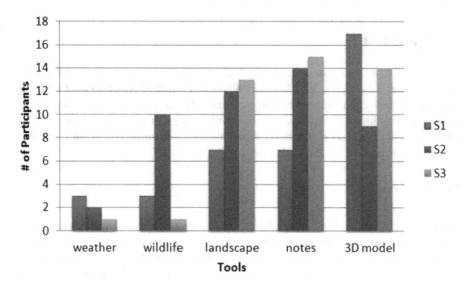

Fig. 2. Mobile group tools used.

3.3   Results and Discussion

Scenarios Comparisons. We recorded the number of times each tool was used (Fig. 2) and the number of tools used. We then used this information to see how engaged the participants were with the interaction, as the scenarios were designed to only need one or two tools to answer them. We hypothesize that participants who are more engaged with the interaction would use a greater number of tools. Analyzing the obtained results, participants rely on the tools that help them augment information on top of the map, such is the case of landscapes and notes. However, they complemented that information with the 3D model tool, which showed the slope of the trail and brought the extra information to the screen. One meaning of this is that the 3D models are useful when comparing two spots on the same trail, as it helps to differentiate them. For example, in scenario 2 that compares two spots on a trail, the most used tools were notes and landscape. However, in scenario 1 that compares two trails, the most used tool was the 3D model.

Interaction Usability. This data is related to the participant's opinion of each tool in the proposed 3D mobile interaction prototype and how useful they found that tool. It is important to analyze this data because it will help to better design the user experience of future prototypes. As shown in Table 2, in general participants thought that the information is clear enough to be able to understand it (5 in a 7 points Scale). Below we describe the results of each tool individually.

Table 2. Usability scores for each tool

Tools	Usability score (7 points scale)
Weather	4.5
Wildlife	5
Landscape	6
Notes	7
Specific info	6
3D info	6

Weather Tool: As explained before this tool mimics personal and private information taken from the mobile device. In the experiment the weather tool complemented the information given in the scenario about the type of day, i.e. sunny, windy, etc. From our 20 participants, 10 participants never used this tool during the session and for the other 10 participants the median answer was 4.5 from 7 points. These results show that participants did not find this tool useful. Some of the reasons for this conclusion are the following: the participants were already given information about the weather in the scenario description, and the weather was a mockup and not the real data.

Wildlife Tool: As explained before, this tool was one of the options in the more information button. Once users selected this option, it augmented the map on the public layer with positions where sightings of wildlife have occurred. In the experiment the wildlife tool was used in an extra scenario thought for the traditional group to use the 3D mobile interaction prototype. Mobile group participants also did this scenario. Based on this usage each group participant answered a usability question about the wildlife tool. From the 20 mobile group participants, 1 did not use the wildlife tool at all. For the rest of the participants the median answer was 5 from 7 points. These results mean that most users used the wildlife tool, and that participants found this tool useful.

Landscape Tool: This tool is also one of the options available in the more information button. Once users selected this option, it augmented the map on the public layer with pictures of possible views from that positions. From the 20 mobile group participants, all used the landscape tool, with a median answer of 6 from 7 points. This means that the landscape tool is very useful and that all participants used it for answering the scenario questions. Especially as these questions were related to information available on the landscape tool.

Notes Tool: This tool is also one of the options available in the more information button. Once users selected this option, it augmented the map on the public layer with notes left by previous hikers. From the 20 mobile group participants, all used the notes tool, with a median answer of 7 from 7 points. These results mean that all participants found the notes tool very useful for answering the scenarios questions. This result goes accordingly to the scenarios proposed, as scenarios 2 and 3 had information related to them on the landscape tool.

Specific Info Tool: This information was displayed after the participants selected a trail from the public display. It showed the following extra information about the trail: name, distance, elevation and estimated time. From the 20 mobile group participants, 4 did not use the specific info tool. From the rest of the participants the median answer was 6 from 7 points. These results mean that the specific info tool is very useful, but that its information could be found somewhere else.

3D Info: This information was the 3D model of each trail displayed in the virtual layer after the user had selected the trail in the public display. From the 20 mobile group participants, all used the 3D info, with a median answer of 6 from 7 points. These results mean that the 3D info is very useful.

4   Conclusions

In this paper we present the information tools designed as part of our 3D mobile interaction technique for public displays. This interaction merges the advantages of using mobile devices' screens to display content together with the natural skills of 3D user interfaces. Specifically the information tools we present augment the public screen with private information. Based on the interaction design, we developed a prototype to show the proposed 3D mobile interaction using Unity3D and C#.

We test this prototype in a usability study of 20 pairs of participants. In our study participants solved three case-based scenarios. In this paper we report and discuss the usability of each information tool and how it affects each scenario. In general participants found more useful the tools that augment the public display information with private content, i.e. pictures of the view of a position on a trail, and 3D models that allow them to see 3D information, i.e. the 3D model of a trail. This finding helps sustain that private information and 3D information can be useful for users of public displays.

In the future we will test the proposed 3D mobile interaction in other scenarios to identify how our proposed tools work.

References

1. Hosio, S., Kukka, H., Goncalves, J., Kostakos, V., Ojala, T.: Toward meaningful engagement with pervasive displays. IEEE Pervasive Comput. **15**, 24–31 (2016)
2. Barrera Machuca, M.D., Chinthammit, W., Yang, Y., Duh, H.: 3D mobile interactions for public displays. In: SIGGRAPH Asia 2014 Mobile Graphics and Interactive Applications (SA2014), 4 p. ACM, New York (2014). Article 8
3. Barrera Machuca, M.D., Chinthammit, W., Huang, W., Wasinger, R., Duh, H.: Enabling symmetric collaboration in public spaces through 3D mobile interaction. Symmetry **10**, 69 (2018)
4. Baldauf, M., Lasinger, K., Fröhlich, P.: Private public screens – detached multi-user interaction with large displays through mobile augmented reality. In: Proceedings of the 11th International Conference on Mobile and Ubiquitous Multimedia, p. 27. ACM, New York (2012)

5. Brignull, H., Rogers, Y.: Enticing people to interact with large public displays in public spaces. In: Human-Computer Interaction INTERACT 2003: IFIP TC13 International Conference on Human-Computer Interaction, pp. 17–24. IOS Press, Zurich (2003)
6. Huang, W., Alem, L., Livingston, M.A.: Human Factors in Augmented Reality Environments. Springer, New York (2013). https://doi.org/10.1007/978-1-4614-4205-9
7. Hyakutake, A., Ozaki, K., Kitani K., Koike, H.: 3-D interaction with a LargeWall display using transparent markers. In: Proceedings of the International Conference on Advanced Visual Interfaces. ACM, New York, pp. 97–100 (2010)
8. Lucero, A., Holopainen, J., Jokela, T.: MobiComics: collaborative use of mobile phones and large displays for public expression. In: Proceedings of the 14th International Conference on Human-Computer Interaction with Mobile Devices and Services (MobileHCI 2012), pp. 383–392. ACM, New York (2012)
9. Parra, G., Klerkx, J., Duva, E.: Understanding engagement with interactive public displays: an awareness campaign in the wild. In: Proceedings of The International Symposium on Pervasive Displays (PerDis 2014), p. 180, 6 p. ACM, New York (2014)
10. Huang, W., Alem, L., Tecchia, F.: HandsIn3D: supporting remote guidance with immersive virtual environments. In: Kotzé, P., Marsden, G., Lindgaard, G., Wesson, J., Winckler, M. (eds.) INTERACT 2013. LNCS, vol. 8117, pp. 70–77. Springer, Heidelberg (2013). https://doi.org/10.1007/978-3-642-40483-2_5
11. Azuma, R.T.: A survey of augmented reality. Presence: Teleoper. Virtual Environ. 6(4), 355–385 (1997)
12. Alem, L., Huang, W.: Recent Trends of Mobile Collaborative Augmented Reality Systems. Springer, New York (2011)

Coordinating User Selections in Collaborative Smart-Phone Large-Display Multi-device Environments

Paul Craig[✉] and Yu Liu

Xian Jiaotong Liverpool University, Suzhou, Jiangsu, China
p.craig@xjtlu.edu.cn

Abstract. This paper evaluates alternative view coordination methods for linked smart-phone large-display multi-device environments and proposes an approach whereby selections made using different displays can be coordinated in order to facilitate different degrees of autonomous and collaborative working. This involves different types of selection made by users on individual private mobile devices being combined on the main public display with individual users having the option to press a button and retrieve another user's selection from the main display. Our proposed method is developed and evaluated using the HotelFinder application which runs on several smart-phone devices connected to a large-display and allows users to find a hotel using coordinated map and scatter-plot views showing hotel location, price and review statistics.

Keywords: Information visualization · Collaborative visualization

1 Introduction

Face-to-face collaboration is an important component of most human activities. Whenever collaboration isn't absolutely necessary, it generally helps us to do a better job or have a better experience. Up until now, however, technological limitations have meant that the most common form of computer assisted working is that of one-device one-user with people normally working on their own. When people do work together they either use separate machines or one person has total control of the machine with the other looking over his or her shoulder. In either case users are not collaborating as effectively as they could do if they were able to spend more time face-to-face and focus more on interpersonal communication rather than a computer screen [1,2].

A new development that promises better support for co-located collaboration is the rise of ubiquitous computing and the development of new advanced mobile computing technologies for the burgeoning smartphone market. Key components are mobility, touch control, improved display technologies and improved connectivity. Mobile devices mean that computing is no longer tied to a physical location so that people can move to meet each other and carry their data

© Springer Nature Switzerland AG 2018
Y. Luo (Ed.): CDVE 2018, LNCS 11151, pp. 24–32, 2018.
https://doi.org/10.1007/978-3-030-00560-3_4

with them [3], large displays facilitate better face-to-face communication [4,5], and better network connectivity means that data and resources are more easily transferred and shared between devices and users [6,7].

Despite the technical advances that facilitate better combined functionality for connected large-displays and mobile devices, interfaces for multi-device co-located collaboration linking large-displays and mobile devices are still rather limited [1]. This can be attributed to device limitations such as screen space and input peripherals [8], social factors [9,10], and the complication that every aspect of an interface (interaction, security, display etc.) has to be operable by multiple users at the same time [10]. Natural sharing of control and display space together over multiple devices is an important consideration that has not been addressed adequately by current research [11]. On the other hand we have seen that information visualization techniques show great promise for overcoming device limitations [12,13] and managing collaborative working with multiple users [14–16].

This paper builds on our previous work where we investigate the feasibility of adapting information visualization techniques for co-located synchronous collaboration on large-displays connected to hand-held mobile devices [17] by evaluating different methods for coordinating selections made on mobile hand-held devices with large wall-mounted displays in a collaborative multi-device environment.

2   User Requirements Analysis

A focus group with twelve potential users (aged twenty-one to twenty-five) allowed us to gain some insights into user expectations of how a multi-device collaborative information visualization with multiple mobile devices linked to a single large display should work. The case-study used for this study was the HotelFinder application designed to run on a large-display or display-wall with connected mobile devices allowing users to find a hotel using coordinated map and scatter-plot views showing hotel location, price and review statistics. Users have a common broad objective and different knowledge to bring to the problem with varying ideas of how to find a solution. This allows us to consider different degrees of autonomous and cooperative working with different users' attention shifting between different screens, and each other, as the task progresses.

Toward the end of our focus group session after introducing and discussing the overall concept of the HotelFinder application, we asked our user group to help us identify the most important factors that would be likely to affect their experience with this type of system. This discussion allowed us to compile a list of seven factors the users considered important for multi device collaboration. These were Communication (how well the interface facilitated communication within the group), Harmony (avoiding negative disruption or irritation between group members), Inclusion (how well the interface included all group members in the task), Learnability, Ease-of-Use, Effectiveness, and Satisfaction. Of these factors, three related specifically to collaboration and four related to general usability.

While learnability and ease-of-use can also be considered important factors for usability in general [18], our potential users told us they considered them to be particularly important when multiple users worked together on the same interface. Our potential users especially didn't want to be made to feel foolish if they couldn't operate the interface or be distracted by too many options while trying to communicate with the rest of the group. These feelings are consistent with the findings of other researchers who specify that interaction with this type of interface should be fluid and seamless [19] and that mobile interfaces should feel natural and focus on interaction with the data rather than including too many menus and options [20].

3   View Coordination

Having determined the user requirements for our HotelFinder mobile-device and large-display multi-device environment, the next stage was consider the different options for coordinating selections on different device displays. The result of a selection, also known as a data-brush, can either highlight, label or filter elements of the data. The different options considered for coordinating selections between devices used in our HotelFinder application are as follows.

Independent Displays. Meaning that devices are not coordinated and each device responds independently to its own user interaction. This would support independent working on individual devices, but if a user wanted to share a selection made on their own device they would need to repeat the selection on the main display.

Complete Coordination. This means that any selection made by any user on any device would automatically appear on all connected devices. Effectively the connected devices would act like a single device with fully coordinated views on multiple screens.

Automatic Coordination on Main Display (AS). This would mean selections made on mobile devices being automatically sent to the main device but not other mobile devices. Users would be able to view the other users' selections on the main display but not on their own personal mobile device. The main device would act as a shared space showing either the latest user selection or the union of all user selections.

Manual Send and Retrieve (MS-MR). A forth option is provide users some action by which they are able to send selections to the main device or retrieve selections from the main device onto their personal devices. This has the disadvantage of adding an additional step for each user if they want to share a selection. The advantage is that it offers more control over the timing and content of view coordination events.

Automatic Send and Manual Retrieve (AS-MR). The final option considered is for user selections to be sent to the main display automatically with an explicit action to retrieve selections from the main display. This option should work like Automatic Coordination on the Main Display allowing the user move quickly between independent working on their private device and collaborative working on the main device, with advantage that they are able to move selections made by the other user to their own device through the large shared display.

These different options are implemented in our prototype HotelFinder application and evaluated according to the metrics derived from our user requirements analysis.

4 Prototype Design

The prototype HotelFinder application is shown in Figs. 1, 2. The interface runs on a large display with any number of connected mobile devices. The smartphones can be connected to the large display by scanning a QR code to initiate an android Socket connection which facilitates communication over a shared Wi-Fi connection.

The mobile display of our prototype (see Fig. 1) is designed according to the guidelines for interactive mobile visualization presented by Craig et al. [13]. The interface uses a horizontal orientation so that the device can be held in both hands with the user selecting items with their thumbs. When items at the edge of the display are selected to be labelled, labels are displayed toward the center of the display so they are not obscured by the user's thumbs. Buttons aligned along the right hand side of the display allow the user to choose interaction tools (to label or select hotels), switch between the scatter-plot and the map view, or retrieve other users' selections from the main display.

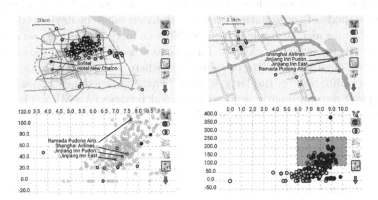

Fig. 1. Mobile device interface with the map zoomed out to show all of Shanghai with the labelling tool (top-left) and zoomed in to show the airport (top-right), and with the scatter-plot used to label (bottom-left) and select hotels (bottom-right).

Our large-display view is shown in Fig. 2. This uses multiple-linked views of the data with a map view on the left zoomed into the current user selection.

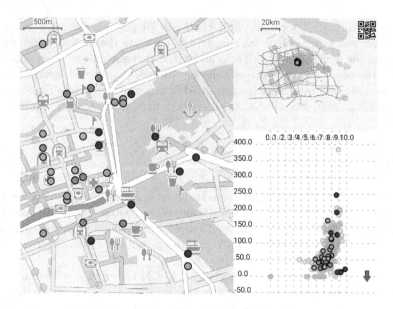

Fig. 2. Large-display interface.

A smaller map in the top right corner provides an overview of the data. A scatterplot view of hotel room-rate against hotel-rating is shown in the bottom right of the large-display view to give the user an indication of factors such as hotel quality and value-for-money.

Having previously considered the relative advantages and disadvantages of different methods of coordinating user selections on different devices (discussed in Sect. 3) we decided to implement four different methods in order to evaluate them to determine which works best for potential users. These are no coordination between devices, complete coordination (where all selections appear on all devices), coordination on the large display (where all selections appear on the large display) and automatic send with manual retrieve (AS-MR). The results of the evaluation are discussed in Sect. 5.

5   Evaluation

In our evaluation we tested the overall utility of the proposed method and compared four different methods for of coordinating user selections on different devices as discussed in Sect. 3. This involved a task-based analysis session followed by a questionnaire and interview session based on the factors our potential users considered important for multi device collaboration as described in Sect. 2.

The evaluation involved twenty-four users in total and did not include any of the users included in our original requirements analysis. The users were divided into four groups each with three members. The sample included sixteen males and eight females all between ages of twenty and twenty-five. Each group was asked to find a suitable hotel with a different type of view coordination and according to a different criteria (such as attending a football match, sight-seeing, or attending a business conference). Each group used the different types of coordination in a different order spending approximately 15 min testing each configuration making up around 1 h 30 min in total for testing (including the time taken for instructions as well as time taken to fill out the questionnaire and a short group discussion). Task criteria and methods for view coordination were randomized so that no set of criteria would be used with the same view coordination more than one time.

The methods for coordinating views were rated according to the users' response to questions asking them how much they agreed with a statement related to each factor considered important for multi-device collaboration. The seven statements were as follows.

- **Communication.** The environment facilitates communication within the group.
- **Harmony.** Interaction between group members is harmonious.
- **Inclusion.** The interface encourages all members of the group to be involved.
- **Learnability.** The interface is easy to learn.
- **Ease of Use.** The interface is easy to use.
- **Effectiveness.** The interface helped us to find the right hotel.
- **Satisfaction.** I would be encouraged to use this type of interface again.

In order to analyze the results each answer was given a numeric value. A score of -2 was given for a response of *strongly disagree*, -1 for *disagree*, 0 for *no opinion*, 1 for *agree* and 2 for *strongly agree*. The average value for each type of interaction was calculated from these values and the results tabulated.

It can be seen from the collated results (Table 1) that coordination on the main display, with and without manual retrieval of selections from the large display, tends to score higher for the metrics determined by our focus group. AS-MR scores slightly higher for the metrics related directly to collaboration but slightly lower for learnability as it took the users some time to familiarize themselves with the retrieve button. Overall effectiveness and satisfaction were highest for the AS-MR method. Ultimately the users felt that this method allowed them to switch between independent and collaborative working most effectively. It was felt to make working more efficient and less disruptive when the interest of different users diverged.

The complete coordination method scored badly for most metrics apart from communication. This is perhaps because having all the devices fully coordinated compelled the users to work together as if they were working on the same device. The users did not however feel that this type of working was particularly effective or satisfying. The devices running without view coordination scored reasonably for most factors apart from communication and satisfaction, the users felt that they could certainly achieve the task this way but they didn't feel that the working this way was particularly easy or satisfying and it certainly wasn't considered conducive to teamwork. It is notable that no-coordination is considered preferable to complete coordination but not as good as coordination only on the main display either with or without being able to manually retrieve another users selection.

Table 1. Different view coordination methods rated according to factors considered important for multi-device collaboration

Factor	None	Complete	Main display	AS-MR
Communication	−1.00	1.08	1.33	1.50
Harmony	0.17	−0.33	1.42	1.42
Inclusion	−0.42	−0.83	1.17	1.25
Learnability	0.25	−0.25	0.58	−0.08
Ease of Use	0.08	−0.50	0.50	0.25
Effectiveness	0.75	−0.67	0.83	1.33
Satisfaction	−0.25	−0.75	1.25	1.33

6   Conclusion

This study has allowed us to develop and evaluate alternative view coordinate methods for linked smart-phone and large-display multi-device environments. Critically, we discovered how selections made using different displays can be coordinated in order to facilitate different degrees of autonomous working when user-selections are disjunct, and closer collaboration when the users' area of interest overlaps. This involves different types of selection made by users on individual private mobile devices being combined on the main public display with users also having the option of pressing a button to retrieve another user's selection from the main display in order to collaborate by refining the selection on their mobile device. We called this the automatic-send manual-retrieve method (AS-MR) and would recommend this for similar applications.

In general our results demonstrate the power of multi-device information visualization to facilitate collaborative working in a multi-user multi-device environment. In the future we plan to further develop our methodology by looking at different methods for showing different user selections in the main display and working with different applications (with different numbers and types of users) using the same mobile-device and large-display set-up.

References

1. Scott, S.D., Graham, T., Wallace, J.R., Hancock, M., Nacenta, M.: Local remote collaboration: applying remote group awarenesstechniques to co-located settings. In: Proceedings of the 18th ACM Conference Companion on Computer Supported Cooperative Work & Social Computing, pp. 319–324. ACM (2015)

2. Ens, B., Eskicioglu, R., Irani, P.: Visually augmented interfaces for co-located mobile collaboration. In: Gallud, J., Tesoriero, R., Penichet, V. (eds.) Distributed User Interfaces. HCIS, pp. 169–176. Springer, London (2011). https://doi.org/10. 1007/978-1-4471-2271-5_19

3. Satyanarayanan, M.: Mobile computing: the next decade. In: Proceedings of the 1st ACM Workshop on Mobile Cloud Computing and Services: Social Networks and Beyond, p. 5. ACM (2010)

4. Isenberg, P., Fisher, D., Paul, S.A., Morris, M.R., Inkpen, K., Czerwinski, M.: Co-located collaborative visual analytics around a tabletop display. IEEE Trans. Vis. Comput. Graph. 18(5), 689–702 (2012)

5. Seifert, J., et al.: MobiSurf: improving co-located collaboration through integrating mobile devices and interactive surfaces. In: Proceedings of the 2012 ACM International Conference on Interactive Tabletops and Surfaces, pp. 51–60. ACM (2012)

6. Huang, X., Craig, P., Lin, H., Yan, Z.: SecIoT: a security framework for the internet of things. Secur. Commun. Netw. 9(16), 3083–3094 (2016)

7. Sun, Y., Bie, R., Thomas, P., Cheng, X.: Advances on data, information, and knowledge in the internet of things (2014)

8. Salim, S.S.: A systematic review of shared visualisation to achieve common ground. J. Vis. Lang. Comput. 28, 83–99 (2015)

9. Gutwin, C., Greenberg, S.: The mechanics of collaboration: developing low cost usability evaluation methods for shared workspaces. In: Proceedings of IEEE 9th International Workshops on Enabling Technologies: Infrastructure for Collaborative Enterprises, (WET ICE 2000), pp. 98–103. IEEE (2000)

10. Scott, S.D., Carpendale, S.: Theory of tabletop territoriality. In: Müller-Tomfelde, C. (ed.) Tabletops - Horizontal Interactive Displays. HCIS, pp. 357–385. Springer, London (2010). https://doi.org/10.1007/978-1-84996-113-4_15

11. Gomes Sakamoto, S., de Miranda, L.C., Hornung, H.: Home control via mobile devices: state of the art and HCI challenges under the perspective of diversity. In: Stephanidis, C., Antona, M. (eds.) UAHCI 2014. LNCS, vol. 8515, pp. 501–512. Springer, Cham (2014). https://doi.org/10.1007/978-3-319-07446-7_49

12. Kennedy, J.B., Mitchell, K.J., Barclay, P.J.: A framework for information visualisation. ACM SIGMOD Rec. 25(4), 30–34 (1996)

13. Craig, P.: Interactive animated mobile information visualisation. In: SIGGRAPH Asia 2015 Mobile Graphics and Interactive Applications, p. 24. ACM (2015)

14. Craig, P., Roa-Seïler, N., Cervantes, A.D.O., Velasco, M.P.T., García, M.R.: Information visualization for the collaborative analysis of complex data. In: 1st Conference on Research and Partnership for Development (2013)

15. Craig, P., Cannon, A., Kennedy, J., Kukla, R.: Pattern browsing and query adjustment for the exploratory analysis and cooperative visualisation of microarray time-course data. In: Luo, Y. (ed.) CDVE 2010. LNCS, vol. 6240, pp. 199–206. Springer, Heidelberg (2010). https://doi.org/10.1007/978-3-642-16066-0_30

16. Craig, P., Kennedy, J.: Concept relationship editor: a visual interface to support the assertion of synonymy relationships between taxonomic classifications. In: Visualization and Data Analysis 2008, vol. 6809, p. 680906. International Society for Optics and Photonics (2008)

17. Craig, P., Huang, X., Chen, H., Wang, X., Zhang, S.: Pervasive information visualization: toward an information visualization design methodology for multi-device co-located synchronous collaboration. In: 2015 IEEE International Conference on Pervasive Intelligence and Computing (PICOM), pp. 2232–2239. IEEE (2015)

18. Nielsen, J., Molich, R.: Heuristic evaluation of user interfaces. In: Proceedings of the SIGCHI Conference on Human Factors in Computing Systems, pp. 249–256. ACM (1990)
19. Roberts, J.C., Ritsos, P.D., Badam, S.K., Brodbeck, D., Kennedy, J., Elmqvist, N.: Visualization beyond the desktop-the next big thing. IEEE Comput. Graph. Appl. **34**(6), 26–34 (2014)
20. Lee, B., Isenberg, P., Riche, N.H., Carpendale, S.: Beyond mouse and keyboard: expanding design considerations for information visualization interactions. IEEE Trans. Vis. Comput. Graph. **18**(12), 2689–2698 (2012)

Intelligent Cloud Storage Management
for Layered Tiers

Marwan Batrouni[1(✉)], Steven Finch[2], Scott Wilson[2], Aurélie Bertaux[1],
and Christophe Nicolle[1]

[1] University of Burgundy, Dijon, France
Marwan_Batrouni@etu.u-bourgogne.fr,
{aurelie.bertaux,cnicolle}@u-bourgogne.fr
[2] Vertafore Corp, Bothell, USA
{sfinch,swilson}@vertafore.com

Abstract. Today, the cloud offers a large array of possibilities for storage, with this flexibility comes also complexity. This complexity stems from the variety of storage mediums, such as, blob storage or NoSQL tables, and also from the different cost tiers within these systems. A strategic thinking to navigate this complex cloud storage landscape is important, not only for cost saving but also for prioritizing information, this prioritization has wider implications in other domains such as the Big Data realm, especially for governance and efficiency. In this paper we propose a strategy centered around probabilistic graphical model (PGM), this heuristic oriented management and organizational strategy allows more tractability and efficiency, we also illustrate this approach with a case study applied to the insurance field.

Keywords: Cloud · Tiered storage · Bayesian Network (BN)
Insurance

1 Introduction

In ancient Egyptian mythology, the Osiris deity is said to have been resurrected to life after having been killed, partitioned into many pieces, then buried in many locations by his evil brother Seth. This ability to be buried for a long time, partitioned then resurrected, parallel in many ways the life cycle of a document in today's organizations. However, unlike in the story of Osiris, content storage costs organizations money, the advent of cloud storage, helped quite a bit in alleviating the financial burden associated with storing contents. However, the explosion of contents on the one hand and the lifespan increase for data in organizations, on the other hand, are contributing to offset the cloud storage cost advantages. For instance, this is illustrated by the exponential growth of the Internet Of Things (IOT), which is widely regarded as the number one of top ten technologies that will change the world in the next ten years [3,12].

© Springer Nature Switzerland AG 2018
Y. Luo (Ed.): CDVE 2018, LNCS 11151, pp. 33–43, 2018.
https://doi.org/10.1007/978-3-030-00560-3_5

Fortunately, the cloud is becoming more mature, and costs are dropping across the board [6]. Also cloud providers have introduced a sophisticated tiering system for different types of storage. Tiered storage is defined as a storage networking method where data is stored on various types of media based on performance, availability and recovery requirements[1]. This is the case of Amazon AWS© which proposes a *cold* tier named Infrequent Access tier (IA) and a *super cold* tier named Glacier[2]. However, to take full advantage of the growing flexibility of cloud storage, a smart and parsimonious approach to manage across tiers is primordial. In this paper we explore one such strategy, which is heuristic and probability driven, the key to this approach is the use of the Probability Graphical Models (PGM), which are a family of methodologies that use the synthesis of probability theory and graph theory [10]. They include a wide family of methods such as Bayesian Networks (BN), Markovian systems and Kalman filters. Bayesian Networks are one of the most effective method used to capture the relational structure of a set of key variables. The main reason for BN popularity is there tractability and flexibility. Our choice of this probabilistic strategy differs from other tiering strategies such as [7]. Therefore, to set the context, in the first part of the paper we present an overview of Bayesian Networks, the second part presents our strategy to apply BNs to solve the tiering management problem, the third part illustrates this with an example applied to the insurance domain.

2 Bayesian Networks Overview

Thomas Bayes (1701–1761) was an English mathematician and presbyterian minister; his work was published posthumously and presented to the Royal society by his friend Richard Price [2].

The key insight of Bayes is that our knowledge and beliefs are continuously updated with new evidence, the mathematical translation of this principal is captured in Bayes Eq. 1.

$$P(A|B) = \frac{P(B|A)P(A)}{P(B)} \tag{1}$$

Where:

- P(A) is the probability of an event A occurring.
- P(B) is the probability of an event B occurring.
- $P(A|B)$ is the probability of an event A occurring given that B occurred.
- $P(B|A)$ is the probability of an event B occurring given that A occurred.

Equation 2 presents Bayes equation in its generalized form:

$$P(A_j|B) = \frac{P(B|A_j)P(A_j)}{\sum_{i=1}^{n} p(B|A_i)P(A_i)} \tag{2}$$

---

[1] https://www.webopedia.com/TERM/T/tiered_storage.html.
[2] https://aws.amazon.com/s3/pricing.

Equation 2 assumes:

- $A_1...A_n$ and B are events from a sample space Ω
- $P : \Omega \to [0, 1]$ is a probability distribution on Ω
- $A_i \cap A_j = 0$ for all $i \neq j$
- P(B) > 0 and $P(A_j) > 0$ for all j.

Overtime the Bayesian approach became more than just an equation, but a whole way of thinking, which is applied to solve difficult problems. In this context when the field of AI faced its major crisis in the late seventies [4] as a response Judea Pearl introduced Bayesian networks in his book *Probabilistic Reasoning in Intelligent Systems* [11].

A Bayesian Network, is a type of graphical model represented as a Directed Acyclic Graph (DAG) [1,8]. They aim to model causal relations between variables; these causal relations are represented as the edges in the DAG graph. Figure 1 shows a very simple example of a Bayesian network, it reads as: (B) and (C) are conditionally independent given variable (A), where "Conditional" independence means that this independence hinge on (A) and it may change if (A) changes.

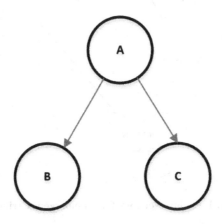

Fig. 1. Simple Bayesian Network

The uncertainty in the causal relationship is represented at the node X_i level by the Conditional Probability Table (CPT) and $P(X_i|\pi_i)$ where π_i is the parent node set of X_i.

Under a conditional independence assumption, the graphic structure of BN allows an unambiguous representation of interdependency between variables, which leads to one of the most important feature of BN: the joint probability distribution of $X = (X_1, ..., X_n)$ can be factored out as a product of the CPTs in the network named *the chain rule of BN* (Eq. 3) [5]:

$$P(X = x) = \prod_{i=1}^{n} P(X_i|\pi_i) \qquad (3)$$

Typically Bayesian networks are used to determine causality or to make inferences. To illustrate with a simple example, let's say we have a car with an installed emergency system like the OnStar© system, the system is triggered in case of emergencies such as an accident or somebody -like a child for instance-accidentally push the emergency button, triggering a false alarm. Figure 2 shows the network for a *Car emergency system* diagnostic, there are two competing reasons to explain the *Trigger* event: it is either the result of an accident or an accidental button-push. However, if bad weather is detected then the *emergency* hypothesis would gain a lot more credence and the *accidental push* hypothesis is said to be "explained away".

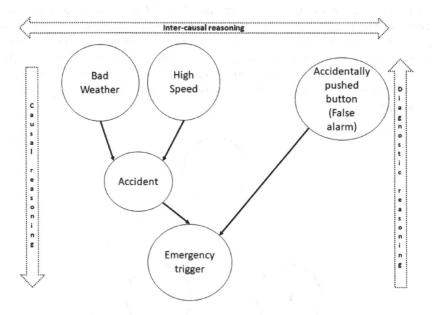

Fig. 2. Bayesian Network for an emergency trigger

To illustrate an inference exercise in our example let's say we want to know: *what is the probability that there's a high speed given that a trigger activity is detected?*

The result of this query is given in Eq. 4 (calculated using Eqs. 2 and 3).

$$P(S|T) = \frac{\sum_{w,b,a \,\in\, \{true,false\}} P(W, S = 1, B, A, T = 1)}{\sum_{q,f,p,s \,\in\, \{true,false\}} P(W, S, B, A, T = 1)} \tag{4}$$

Where $P(W, S, B, A, T) = P(W) * P(A) * P(B) * P(S|W, A) * P(T|B, A)$ (5)

In this section, we have made an introduction to Bayesian Networks (BN). Our goal from this introduction is to help to us elucidate the probabilistic Bayesian approach. In the next section, we use this approach to propose a solution to the tiered cloud storage management, applied to the insurance sector.

3   Case Study for Tiered Storage in Insurance Space

Documentation plays a central role in the insurance space. At every level of the insurance business, storing and manging documents are crucial to the success of the business. Documents, such as marketing material, policy information or claim reports are central to the day to day activity of insurance entities, whether carriers, agencies or MGA (Managing General Agent)[3].

In order for us to apply the Bayesian Network approach for our tiering solution, we need first to go through few preparatory steps. These steps are summarized as follows

1. Define variables influencing the access to a document
2. Build the DAG graph to determine the causal relationships among influencing variables (identified in step 1)
3. Define the configuration values for the variables
4. Build Variables distributions
5. Make the decision on whether a document is candidate for migration to a cheaper tier and which one.

The next section explores these steps in more details.

3.1   Steps for a Tiered Insurance Document Space

Our approach to define the influencing variables is to start with an intuitive model based on organizational experience, this approach can be enhanced further by adopting data mining operation on existing insurance databases to accomplish clustering and classification categories. Table 1 describes the set of variables in our model.

The variables in Table 1 are discretized and coarse-grained categories. The reason is that using continuous and many values for variables would make the graph intractable and explodes the number of Cartesian combinations. The resulting Directed Acyclic Graph (DAG) of the influencing variables is represented in Fig. 3.

Once we build the DAG, another important step is to define the discretized variables values. Table 2 illustrates this definition for the variable document size, such configuration is done for all the variables based on a fuzzy evaluation of the business. while keeping in mind that these values can change and evolve over time.

The step to build the variables distributions involves a statistical analysis of the organization databases to determine the frequency and distribution of these variables such as the example in Table 3, which illustrates how the end result might look like.

Algorithm 1 captures the steps needed to decide whether a document is a candidate for a tier migration and which one.

---

[3] http://www.naic.org/consumer_glossary.htm.

Table 1. Bayesian Network variables for insurance documents cloud tiering

Factor	Categories/Range	Description
Document size	XLarge, Large, Medium, Small	Simple size, can be expressed in Megabyte (MB)
Past access frequency	NoAccess, LowAccess, MediumAccess, HighAccess, ExtremelyHighAccess	How many times per hour the document had been accessed since its creation? For instance if a document is 1 year old and was accessed 30 times since its creation the value would equal $0.0035 = 30/(8760 = $ h per year)
Last access date	VeryRecent, Recent, LongTimeAgo, VeryLongTime	When is the last date/time the document was accessed or saw activity? this can be a good predictor if it went to "sleep" or not
Document type	Policy, Claim, Image, PoliceReport, RatingEstimate, GenericInsuranceDocument	Various document types can have impact on how many times are in demand, the categorization needs a collaborative and a statistical effort to define
Customer type (Agency, Property casualty, Life and annuity, MGA...etc)	AgencyPropertyCasualty, MGA, AgencyLifeAndAnnuity, Carrier, Other	The categorization of customers should follow industry standards while trying no to explode the number of categories
Customer size	XLarge, Large, Medium, Small	Here the categorization will be based on a business defined criteria such as number of employees, size of business etc.
Future access frequency	NoAccess, LowAccess, MediumAccess, HighAccess, ExtremelyHighAccess	Same as PAF with the difference however that the frequency is determined based on a fixed time interval (one week for instance or 168 hours) this time interval will be defined/configured by a business rule and eventually reevaluated

- Let OT_{fc} be the old tier fixed cost and OT_{vc} the old tier variable cost
- Let NT_{fc} be the new tier fixed cost and NT_{vc} the new tier variable cost and NT_{rc} the new tier residual cost

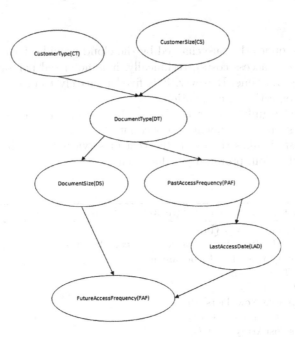

Fig. 3. Bayesian Network for document access variables

Table 2. Example of a discretized configuration of document size variable values

Qualitative value	Numerical value (MB)
XLarge	5000+
Large	1000–4999
Medium	500–1000
Small	<500

Table 3. Example of a probability distribution for discretized values

Customer type (CT)	P(CT)
AgencyPropertyCasualty	0.5
MGA	0.1
AgencyLifeAndAnnuity	0.2
Carrier	0.1
Other	0.1

– Let OT_{MinTTL} be the minimum amount of time a document is left a tier
– Let PT_{FAF} be the probability value threshold for a document to be examined

Where

- *Fixed cost* signifies the rate charged by the cloud provider for certain service (like storage or access costs), technically, it is not fixed per say since these rates change overtime. However, it is fixed relatively to other variables and from the perspective of calculation.
- *Variable cost* signifies the rate charged by the cloud provider in function parameters such as document access count.
- *Residual cost* signifies the estimated cost of services responsible for making the tiering decision, prorated per document.

Algorithm 1. Document Tier Migration Decision

Require: OT_{MinTTL}, PT_{FAF} {Input}

   $P_{FAF} \leftarrow$ Using the Bayesian network graph calculate the Future Access Frequency (FAF) probability value for the document

   if $P_{FAF} > PT_{FAF}$ **then**

      $OT_{tc} \leftarrow OT_{fc} + OT_{vc}$

      for all Available New Tiers **do**

         $NT_{tc} \leftarrow NT_{fc} + NT_{vc} + NT_{rc}$

         NewTiersCostArray $\leftarrow NT_{tc}$

      end for

      Sort NewTiersCostArray

      if NewTiersCostArray[0] $< OT_{tc}$ **then**

         Move Doc To Tier [0]

      end if

   end if

3.2 Efficiency of the Sampling Strategy

Implementing a tiering strategy requires a close evaluation. A follow through implies a continuous reassessment of the result of our decision to move the documents. This can be done by sampling a number of documents that we have moved and determine the efficiency of such a move over time. The sample needs to follow standard statistical sampling techniques to ensure that the sample is representative and includes all categories of documents. In a nutshell, we need to answer the question: given a sample of migrated documents (moved to lower tiers) is the total current cost (of the sample) lower than if they stayed where they were (higher tier)? For our purpose we use a simple sampling technique[4] with the Eq. 6

$$ n = \left[\frac{Z_{\frac{\alpha}{2}} \times \sigma}{E} \right]^2 \tag{6} $$

---

[4] https://www.isixsigma.com/tools-templates/sampling-data/how-determine-sample-size-determining-sample-size/.

Where:

- n is the sample size
- $Z_{\frac{\alpha}{2}}$ is known as the critical value, the positive value that is at the vertical boundary for the area of $\frac{\alpha}{2}$ in the right tail of the standard normal distribution.
- E is the error or the maximum difference between the population mean μ and the sample mean σ is the standard deviation

To illustrate with an example, say we have 1,000,000 documents that had been moved to non-primary tiers, and we want to determine the sample size to check if moving these files made sense economically. Therefore we need to answer if the cost for one week in the new tier(s) is lower than one week (could be more, just an example here) in the old tier(s). Assume the standard deviation for the cost per week of the population is 30 cents and assume we want a 95% confidence level that our sample mean is within 2 cents of the population mean. A 95% confidence corresponds to alpha $= 0.05$ ($1-0.95 = 0.05$) which is 0.025 for $\frac{\alpha}{2}$ (area under curve $= 0.475$) with using a statistical table we find the value for Z for $\frac{\alpha}{2} = 1.96$ Then using Eq. 6 to plug these numbers we obtain the result for the sample size we need, we obtain $\approx$864. This means we need to sample 864 documents selected at random from one million to obtain a meaningful result.

Sampling documents to determine the migration algorithm efficiency is one step, another important step is required to close the feedback loop, this step is explained in the next section.

3.3   Tiering Efficiency Evaluation

An approach to evaluate the efficiency of our tiering implementation would involve first collecting data points over time. This process collects the sample data as outlined in previous sections on sampling, This collection must assume and ensure:

- Same collection technique (regardless which sampling technique we decide upon, it needs to be same throughout to ensure an apple-to-apple comparison).
- Regular and same time interval (the period depends on business decisions, for instance, each month or quarter).
- Ensure that the sampled files fall in the time frame of the sample (moved within the time period of one month if the sampling period is one month).
- Make sure we version any changes to the Bayesian network structure (variables, dependencies, distribution values, etc.). Such versioning helps us to determine if changes to the network cause an impact on the efficiency of the tiering algorithm.
- Analyze the sampling results over time to see if the trend leads to more or less efficiency. Such analysis can be made using simple visual trend inspection, or more sophisticated machine learning[5] time series analysis and anomalies detection [9].

---

[5] Many cloud providers (such as Microsoft Azure ML), offer anomaly detection algorithms as part of their machine learning packages.

To illustrate with an example say we have decided upon sampling once a month, Fig. 4, in this example, we have a noticeable dip at the 9/1/18 data point, this can be an indicator that the algorithm (or the underlying Bayesian network) may have changed and negatively impacted the efficiency.

SampleDateTime	Average saving (cents)	Sample size
1/1/2018	8	400
2/1/2018	7	600
3/1/2018	8	700
4/1/2018	8	800
5/1/2018	10	800
6/1/2018	12	800
7/2/2018	5	900
8/3/2018	4	950
9/4/2018	3	950
10/5/2018	13	1000
11/6/2018	15	1000
12/7/2018	17	1000

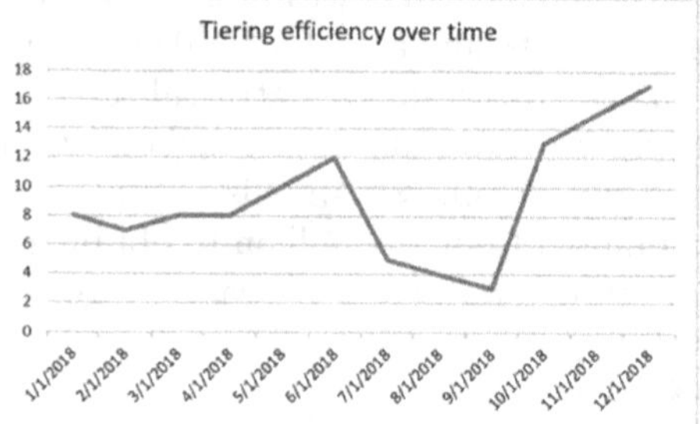

Fig. 4. Tiering efficiency evaluation example

4   Conclusion

In a world where data is the new gold, and the amount of information is increasing at an exponential rate, data and document storage efficiency becomes paramount. In this we paper we explored a method for cost optimization of document storage over different cloud tiers. We also explored a case study applied to the insurance space. Our methodology is probabilistic and emphasizes continuous assessment of the actions undertaken by the method, which is a novel approach in the insurance document storage to the best of our knowledge. Ideally, in the future, tiered cloud storage may include intelligent tiering right out of the box, with available customizable templates per type of business or sector (i.e. Industry, Health care, energy...etc.), such a feature may reduce the burden of tier management for cloud customers and add revenue to the purse of cloud providers.

References

1. Bellandi, A.: Extending ontology queries with Bayesian network reasoning. IMT Institute for Advanced Studies, Lucca, Italy (2008)
2. Bellhouse, D.: The reverend Thomas Bayes FRS: a biography to celebrate the tercentenary of his birth. University of Western Ontario (2001)
3. Cai, H., Xu, B., Jiang, L., Vasilakos, A.: IoT-based big data storage systems in cloud computing. IEEE Internet Things J. **4** (2017)
4. Darwiche, A.: Modeling and Reasoning with Bayesian Networks. Cambridge University Press, Cambridge (2009)
5. Ding, Z., Peng, Y., Pan, R.: BayesOWL: Uncertainty modeling in semantic web ontologies. University of Maryland (2006)
6. Dutta, A.K., Hasan, R.: How much does storage really cost? Towards a full cost accounting model for data storage. In: Altmann, J., Vanmechelen, K., Rana, O.F. (eds.) GECON 2013. LNCS, vol. 8193, pp. 29–43. Springer, Cham (2013). https://doi.org/10.1007/978-3-319-02414-1_3
7. Guerra, J., Pucha, H., Glider, J., Belluomini, W., Rangaswami, R.: Cost effective storage using extent based dynamic tiering. In: Proceedings of the 9th USENIX Conference (2011)
8. Harris, J., Hirst, J.L., Mossinghoff, M.: Combinatorics and Graph Theory. Springer, Heidelberg (2008). https://doi.org/10.1007/978-0-387-79711-3
9. Hodge, V., Austin, J.: A survey of outlier detection methodologies. Artif. Intell. Rev. **22**, 85–126 (2004)
10. Koller, D., Friedman, N.: Probabilistic Graphical Models: Principles and Techniques. MIT Press, Cambridge (2009)
11. Pearl, J.: Probabilistic Reasoning in Intelligent Systems. Morgan Kaufmann, Burlington (1988)
12. Qin, Y., Sheng, Q.Z., Falkner, N.J.: When things matter: a data-centric view of the internet of things. ACM J. (2014)

Some Discoveries from a Concurrency Benchmark Study of Major Cloud Storage Systems

Weiwei Cai[✉], Agustina Ng, and Chengzheng Sun

School of Computer Science and Engineering,
Nanyang Technological University, Singapore, Singapore
{caiweiwei,Agustina,CZSun}@ntu.edu.sg

Abstract. One common functionality in cloud storage systems is file sharing and collaboration, which allows multiple users to share and concurrently manipulate files in common folders or workspaces. Concurrent updates of common files may, however, result in inconsistent results. In this paper, we report some discoveries from applying a comprehensive suite of concurrency benchmark (test cases) to major cloud storage systems, including Microsoft OneDrive, Google Drive, and Dropbox. These discoveries contribute to the general knowledge about consistency issues in existing cloud storage systems.

Keywords: Cloud storage systems · Concurrent operations · Consistency

1 Introduction

Cloud storage systems, such as Microsoft OneDrive, Google Drive, and Dropbox, are commonly used for file sharing and collaboration [1]. They allow users not only to store and share files on the service provider's data centers, but also to replicate files on users' personal computing devices. Users can access and modify replicated files in the same way as accessing native file systems on their personal devices; the underlying cloud storage system takes the responsibility of synchronizing replicated files among user devices and with cloud storage centers as well.

It is well known that concurrent updates of replicated common data objects, such as shared documents in collaborative editing, and shared files in cloud storage systems, may cause conflicts and result in inconsistent results [2]. Indeed, it is not uncommon to hear cloud storage users complaining that their valuable work lost or data files mixed up in the shared workspace for unknown reasons, or they got different or nondeterministic results under the same or similar concurrency scenarios from the same or different cloud storage systems. For example, as shown in Fig. 1, an initial empty workspace is replicated on two users' personal computers, and two users independently create two files (with different contents) with the same name under the same folder. After the two concurrent updates are synchronized by the underlying cloud storage system, the eventual combined results could be divergent or inconsistent on the two users' devices (more elaboration on this example late).

© Springer Nature Switzerland AG 2018
Y. Luo (Ed.): CDVE 2018, LNCS 11151, pp. 44–48, 2018.
https://doi.org/10.1007/978-3-030-00560-3_6

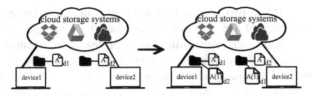

Fig. 1. The workspaces on users' personal computers, 🗀 represents a folder, 🗋 represents a file, d1 and d2 represent the file contents.

The goal of our research is to investigate consistency requirements and maintenance techniques for replicated workspaces in cloud storage systems [3]. To inspire and validate our work, we have devised a comprehensive suite of concurrency benchmark (a set of testing cases) to explore what consistency guarantee real-world cloud storage systems actually deliver (but never explicitly specified) to users. In this paper, we report some of our discoveries from applying this concurrency benchmark to real world cloud storage systems.

2   Sketch of Concurrency Benchmark Design and Execution

The concurrency benchmark suite consists of a comprehensive set of pair-wise file update operations, which could be concurrently generated by users from the same shared workspace but replicated on two computers. A file update operation may be one of the four basic ones: (1) a *CR* (for *Create*) operation that creates a file, folder, or even a subtree in an existing workspace, referred by a pathname; (2) A *DL* (for *Delete*) operation that removes a file or folder referred by a pathname; (3) A *RN* (for *Rename*) operation that changes the name of a file or folder to a new name; and (4) An *UP* (for *Update*) operation that changes the content of a file. These four basic operations are adequate to simulate the functionalities of more complex operations.

To achieve comprehensive coverage of testing cases in the benchmark, we have considered all possible combinations of a pair of concurrent operations along multiple dimensions of variation: *operation type* (i.e. *CR, DL, RN,* or *UP*), *target pathname relation* (i.e. whether the pair of targets are *dependent*, meaning they are the same or on the path of each other, or *independent*, meaning they are different and not on the path of each other), and *target type* (i.e. whether the target is a file or folder), which could have impacts on the combined results of two concurrent operations. By combining all possible variations in these dimensions and eliminating redundant cases, we have derived a total of 61 distinctive testing cases for pair-wise concurrent operations [2], which form the basis for creating concrete testing cases.

For each testing case from the concurrency benchmark suite, four steps can be carried out one by one (either manually or by using a software tool):

1. Create the same initial workspace (suitable for the specific testing case) of a cloud storage system, which is replicated at two different computers;

2. Generate and execute two operations concurrently in the replicated folders. To ensure concurrency of the two operations, the cloud storage synchronization functionality should be disabled during individual operation execution;
3. Combine the effects of concurrent operations. This is achieved by, after step 2, re-enabling the cloud storage synchronization functionality, which will automatically synchronize the two replicas, via a central server or other means, and integrate their results in whatever ways determined by the underlying cloud storage system. This method ensures the final results will reflect what will actually be produced by a cloud storage system under real usage scenarios;
4. Record the final combined effects achieved in this testing case for further analysis.

3 Benchmark Discoveries

3.1 Results for Operations Targeting Independent Files/Folders

When concurrent operations are targeting at independent files/folders in the shared workspace, three cloud storage systems uniformly produce convergent final results on different computers and ensure effects of concurrent operations are fully preserved in the final result. It is good but not surprising to see such results because when targeting independent files/folders, individual operation effects are naturally confined to different sub-folders and would not interfere with each other, automatically resulting in the same union effects no matter in which order these operations are executed.

3.2 Results for Operations Targeting Dependent Files/Folders

When concurrent operations are targeting at dependent files/folders, different cloud storage systems often produce different results, some of which are non-deterministic, confusing to end-users, or even inconsistent, which are summarized below.

Nondeterministic Results. For the same test case, when executed multiple times in the same system, different results, though convergent at two replicas, may be produced. For example, given the initial state T_1 in Fig. 2, O_1 to rename folder A to D, and O_2 to delete folder A. OneDrive may produce two possible final results, each of which contains effects of only O_1 or O_2, as illustrated in Fig. 2. In this example, folder A is renamed or deleted non-deterministically, which is confusing to users. Similar non-deterministic results were also found in OneDrive in the other test cases, including (1) O_1 deletes a folder and O_2 renames a folder under O_1's target folder; (2) O_1 renames a folder and O_2 deletes a folder under O_1's target folder, etc.

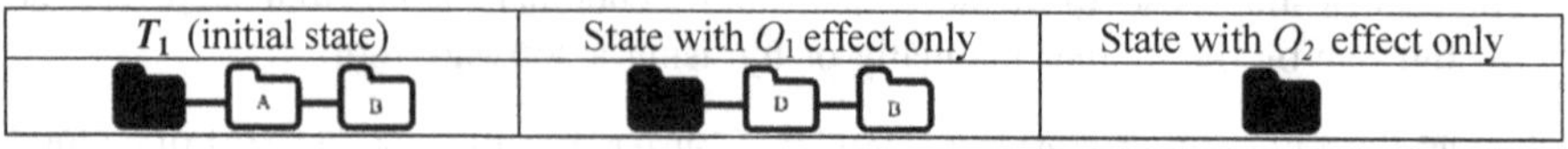

T_1 (initial state)	State with O_1 effect only	State with O_2 effect only

Fig. 2. Different results produced by the same system for the same test.

Undesirable Results. Cloud storage systems may produce undesirable and confusing results to end-users. For example, under the same initial empty root node of the file system T_2, O_1 creates a subtree named A and O_2 creates a subtree also named A; the two independently created subtrees contain different subfolders and files. Dropbox and OneDrive could produce one merged subtree, which mixes up the folders and files under the user-generated subtrees, as shown in Fig. 3.

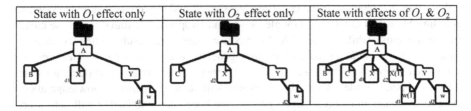

State with O_1 effect only	State with O_2 effect only	State with effects of O_1 & O_2

Fig. 3. Undesirable results delivered to end-users.

This merged result is undesirable and confusing to users, because the content under the mixed subtree is not the same as any user-generated subtree; files and folders under user-generated subtrees may have conflicting names (e.g. two files named X, and two folders named Y), which require recursive resolutions, but recursive resolution outcomes could cause more confusion to users, e.g. a new file X(1) is created to resolve conflicting file creations, but a single folder Y is used to merge conflicting folders and the two files (named W) under Y are further resolved by creating a new file W(1). It would create a heavy burden to users who need to unmerge the merged results (imagine hundreds of different photos under user-generated subtrees). Similar undesirable results are also found in Dropbox under other cases, including: (1) O_1 and O_2 rename two subfolders to the same name; (2) O_1 renames a folder to name q and O_2 creates a folder named q; etc.

Inconsistent Results. The previous example in the introduction section (Fig. 1) revealed an inconsistency problem, which could occur in Google Drive. Under other cases, Google Drive also may produce divergent results but in different forms. For example, under the same initial empty workspace, O_1 creates a subtree named A and O_2 creates a subtree also named A, the final divergent results are illustrated in Fig. 4:

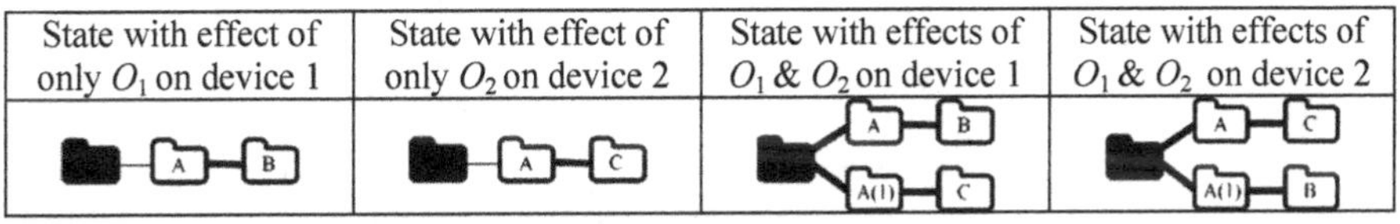

State with effect of only O_1 on device 1	State with effect of only O_2 on device 2	State with effects of O_1 & O_2 on device 1	State with effects of O_1 & O_2 on device 2

Fig. 4. Divergent results on different devices.

Such inconsistent results are undoubtedly problematic to users. Similar inconsistent results were also found in Google Drive under: (1) O_1 and O_2 rename different files/folders to the same name, under the same parent folder; (2) O_1 renames a folder/file to name q and O_2 create a folder/file with name q, under the same parent folder.

4 Conclusions

In this paper, we reported some consistency issues in real world cloud storage systems, including Microsoft OneDrive, Google Drive, and Dropbox. We found that these cloud storage systems, while being able to produce consistent results when concurrent updates are targeting *independent* files, may generate results that are *non-deterministic*, *unexpected* or *confusing* to users, or even *divergent*, when concurrent operations are targeting *dependent* files. These discoveries contribute to the general knowledge about consistency issues in cloud storage systems. We hope such knowledge will help users to better understand and use cloud storage for protecting their data in collaborative work, and cloud storage service providers to improve their services to achieve better consistency.

Acknowledgment. This research is partially supported by an Academic Research Grant (MOE2015-T2-1-087) from Ministry of Education Singapore. The authors wish to thank anonymous reviewers for their insightful and constructive feedback.

References

1. Tang, J.C., Brubaker, J.R., Marshall, C.C.: What do you see in the cloud? Understanding the cloud-based user experience through practices. In: Kotzé, P., Marsden, G., Lindgaard, G., Wesson, J., Winckler, M. (eds.) INTERACT 2013. LNCS, vol. 8118, pp. 678–695. Springer, Heidelberg (2013). https://doi.org/10.1007/978-3-642-40480-1_47
2. Sun, C., Ellis, C.: Operational transformation in real-time group editors: issues, algorithms, and achievements. In: Proceedings of ACM CSCW, pp. 59 – 68. ACM (1998)
3. Ng, A., Sun, C.: Operational transformation for real-time synchronization of shared workspace in cloud storage. In: Proceedings of ACM Group, pp. 61–70. ACM (2016)

A Cloud Architecture for Service Robots

Zuozhong Yin[1,2], Jihong Liu[1(✉)], Chao Zhao[2], and Xin Ge[2]

[1] Beihang University, Beijing, China
13810190327@163.com, ryukeiko@163.com
[2] Beijing Research Institute of Automation for Machinery Industry Co., Ltd,
Beijing, China
zhaochaobzs@163.com, gexin@riamb.ac.cn

Abstract. Service robots face many complicated scenarios. They are required to be smarter and more efficient than industrial robots. We believe that cloud computing technology can help to satisfy such requirements. However, there are still not mature cloud architectures that aim particularly at service robots. In this paper, we propose a cloud architecture for service robots. We present the implementation of the architecture and a demonstrator for concept proof.

Keywords: Cloud · Service robots · Architecture

1 Introduction

Cloud robotics is about applying cloud computing on robots to help them share information and perform the offload computing. Industrial robots are in relatively static application scenarios, while service robots face many complicated scenarios. Service robots involve many techniques, such as Simultaneous Localization and Mapping (SLAM), grasping, language understanding and so on. Most of these technologies require massive data and intensive computing. In this paper, we mainly focus on the cloud for service robots.

From 2011 to 2014, several universities in Europe implemented the RoboEarth project, which aimed to establish a world wide web for robots and developed a cloud engine called Rapyuta, which has been used in practice [1, 2]. The problems of cloud-based multi-robot operation were studied in [3]. Software framework for cloud robots with three systems was designed [4], which includes the intermediate system, background task coordination and the control system. Under this framework, computational, storage and network communication tasks are performed while consolidating Hadoop-MapReduce clusters to provide robots with a stable, scalable, distributed computing system for service sharing among robots.

Service robots have great potential applications in the old-aged and aging societies. In [5], they studied the service robot's promotion for active and healthy aging people. They designed a cloud robot system to coordinate the service robots in two different locations. By accessing to the cloud platform the service robots can locate and cooperate with each other to provide services to users. In [6], a cloud robot platform is designed to implement a cloud-based face recognition. KnowRob in [7] is a knowledge

© Springer Nature Switzerland AG 2018
Y. Luo (Ed.): CDVE 2018, LNCS 11151, pp. 49–56, 2018.
https://doi.org/10.1007/978-3-030-00560-3_7

processing system designed specifically for autonomous robots. The paper [8] applied cloud robot system in the smart city research.

This paper is followed by the following three parts: 1. Architecture: a general cloud architecture is proposed. 2. The implementation: the implementation of the cloud for service robots and describes a demonstrator to prove the feasibility of the architecture. 3. Conclusion and future work.

2   Architecture

Similar to the general cloud robot systems, our proposed service robot cloud overall architecture is divided into three layers: the cloud layer, the middle layer and the service robot layer. The cloud layer here refers to the cloud computing platform. For distinction, this paper defines this layer as a remote cloud, that is, the common cloud computing platform including computation and storage. It is based on the existing mature cloud computing architecture, such as IBM, Amazon, Aliyun and other commercial cloud computing services. They are based on their IaaS or PaaS cloud platform.

The robot layer is consisted of heterogeneous service robots that perform a variety of service tasks. All the service robots have the basic robotics skills such as speech recognition, semantic understanding, item capturing, and SLAM. Robots' communication includes the interaction with other robots (M2M, machine to machine) and the interaction with the cloud (M2C, machine to cloud) described in [9].

The middle layer can be achieved in many ways. Its main functions include: real-time computing and storage, real-time communication, service transfer and resource calls. Between the middle layer and the remote cloud the communication is mainly through existing networks. The main requirements of the robots to the remote cloud are the storage of large amounts of data, large-scale data processing and computation that will take a great deal of computation time. It is difficult for the cloud to meet the real-time requirements of the robots, but the cloud can provide almost unlimited hardware resources. The robot's interaction with the remote cloud can be realized while the robot is not working. This is also a clear distinction between the service and the industrial robots, which are usually working continuously. The learning and evaluation processes can be realized when the robot falls asleep. The "RoboDREAM" project in Europe has performed a study on this topic [10].

Figure 1 shows the proposed cloud architecture. In the figure, the solid line represents the information and control exchange, while the dash line shows the weak connection between the cloud and the robots. A weak connection is used because it is not the best solution for robots to reach cloud immediately.

Compared with the industrial robot cloud, the most important feature for service-oriented robot cloud is that it has to support highly real-time performance. To reduce the latency and disruption of remote networks, we adopt the hybrid and multi-cloud architectures in our proposal. A recent concept of fog computing has been proposed to distribute data, data processing, and applications across devices at the edge of the network rather than all within the cloud.

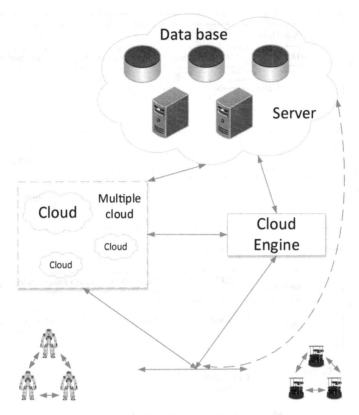

Fig. 1. The cloud architecture for service robots

To improve the performance of service robots, the fog computing and distributed computing techniques are adopted here to deploy, distribute the calculation reasonably to the cloud and the robots.

3 The Implementation

We designed a cloud platform as an experimental system for service robots to prove the feasibility of our proposal. This cloud platform can realize data storage and computing offload. We also implemented a demonstrator to test and verify the system.

3.1 The Experiment System

We divide the cloud into three layers using the general structure: the cloud, the cloud engine, and the robot application layer.

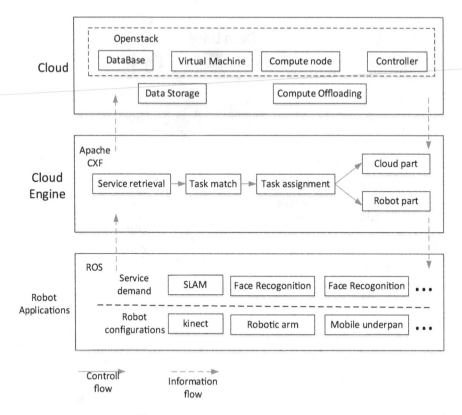

Fig. 2. The service robot cloud platform

Figure 2 shows the architecture of our cloud platform. As the first step the robots send service requests to cloud and upload their configurations to the cloud engine. The cloud engine retrieves the required services according to the requests and the robot configurations. It then assigns the tasks to the cloud part and the robot part and realizes the computing task offload.

The physical resource layer of the cloud (we just call this layer as the cloud) is based on the open source cloud platform OpenStack [11]. The platform provides physical and virtual resources to set up the database, the virtual machine, the computing node, and the controller. See Fig. 3 for more details. The database and virtual machine are used to store the massive amount of data and perform offload computation. The computing node and the controller are used to manage the cloud. Through the OpenStack API, the cloud provides the interface with the cloud engine.

The cloud engine is based on Apache CXF, which provides web services for robots to obtain the cloud service. CXF allows the use of frontend programming API to build and develop services such as JAX-WS. Robots can request service from the cloud by the Web Services Description Language (WSDL). The cloud engine processes requests and matches services from the cloud to the requested robots. An important function for the cloud engine is to assign the tasks requested by the robots to the cloud to realize the

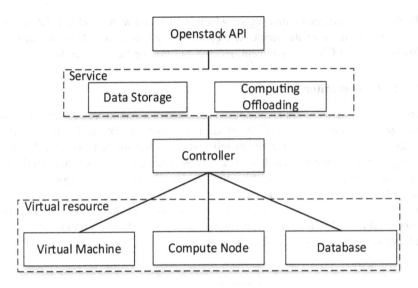

Fig. 3. The cloud architecture based on OpenStack

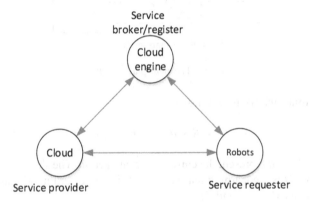

Fig. 4. Service based on the Service-Oriented Architecture SOA

offload computation. Figure 4 shows the Service-Oriented Architecture (SOA) where the cloud engine serves as a service broker; the cloud serves as service provider; and the robots are the service client which request and use the service.

The robot application layer is based on the ROS (robot operation system) installed in the robots to deploy the robot programs. ROS is mainly used to set up a communication environment based on TCP/IP for robots and the cloud platform.

ROS is a distributed process framework that allows the execution of programs which are designed independently, loosely coupled and with real time execution capability. These processes can be grouped by feature packs, so that they can be easily shared and published. ROS also supports system federation of the code base. ROS has now been applied to many projects, such as various types of home service robots.

Each robot is equipped with a laptop which can interact with the cloud platform and control the movement of the robot. The operating system ubuntu is used which can deploy the Apache CXF environment, receive and invoke the web services.

3.2　The Demonstrator

To provide proof of our cloud architecture, we designed a demonstrator with two robots in a maze. The main function of the cloud is to store the data and perform offload computing. In this demonstrator, we mainly test the offloading function and the global planning for robots. We use Turtlebot [12] and Handsfree [13] with Kinect on them to get the maze image. In the cloud platform, we use the Q-learning algorithm [14] to calculate the optimal path offload for the robots - the Turtlebots in our case.

In the demonstrator, the two robots collaboratively explore the maze to reduce iterations and time. The robots get the maze information and upload it to the cloud. The cloud calculates the most optimal path for the robots to go through the maze (Fig. 5).

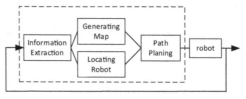

Actual path and maze image

Fig. 5. The path planning flow

The Q-learning matrix is as follows:

$$Q(s,a) = R(s,a) + r \cdot max\{Q(s',a')\} \tag{1}$$

In Eq. (1), the s, a represent the current state and action. The s', a' represent the next state and action. Q is the learning matrix, while R is the reward matrix, and the r is the learning parameter (Figs. 6 and 7).

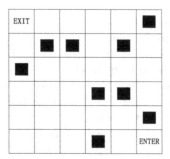

Fig. 6. The 6 × 6 matrix maze with a side length of 4.8 m

Fig. 7. The robots

Here, we do not focus on the communication latency between robots and the cloud. The result is that the robots can quickly find the most optimal path based on the cloud's calculation. More important, it does not cost the robots' CPU time while they are working. The feasibility of the system is well proved by our demonstrator.

4   Conclusion and Future Research

In this paper, we proposed an architecture for the service robots. We successfully demonstrate that the offloading path computing and collaborative working for robots can be achieved based on the cloud technology. In the future, we will enhance the system robustness, improve the communication speed, and improve the system concurrency.

Acknowledgement. This work was supported by the Project funding of the National Key R&D Plan No. 2016YFF0202003.

References

1. Waibel, M., Beetz, M., Civera, J., et al.: Roboearth: a world wide web for robots. IEEE Robot. Autom. Mag. June 2011
2. Hunziker, D., Gajamohan, M., Waibel, M., D'Andrea, R.: Rapyuta: the RoboEarth cloud engine. In: IEEE International Conference on Robotics and Automation (ICRA) (2013)
3. Janssen, R., van de Molengraft, R., Bruyninckx, H.: Cloud based centralized task control for human domain multi-robot operations. Intell. Serv. Robot. **9**, 63–77 (2016)
4. Miratabzadeh, S.A., Gallardo, N., Gamez, N.: Cloud robotics: a software architecture for heterogeneous large-scale autonomous robots. In: WAC 2016, 1570259520 (2016)
5. Bonaccorsi, M., Fiorini, L., Cavallo, F., Saffiotti, A.: A cloud robotics solution to improve social assistive robots for active and healthy aging. Int. J. Soc. Robot. **8**, 393–408 (2016)
6. Lei, Y., Fengyu, Z., Yugang, W.: Design of a cloud robotics visual platform. In: Sixth International Conference on Instrumentation & Measurement, Computer, Communication and Control (2016)

7. Tenorth, M., Beetz, M., KnowRob—Knowledge Processing for Autonomous Personal Robots (2009)
8. Rahman, A., Jin, J., Cricenti, A.: Cloud-enhanced robotic system for smart city crowd control. J. Sens. Actuator Netw. **5**, 20 (2016). https://doi.org/10.3390/jsan5040020
9. Benavidez, P., Muppidi, M., Rad, P.: Cloud-based realtime robotic visual SLAM. In: Annual IEEE Systems Conference (2015)
10. Riazuelo, L., Civera, J., Montiel, J.M.M.: C2TAM: a first approach to a cloud framework for cooperative tracking and mapping (2014)
11. https://www.openstack.org/
12. https://www.turtlebot.com/
13. http://wiki.exbot.net/HandsFree
14. Sutton, R.S., Barto, A.G.: Reinforcement Learning: An Introduction, (Adaptive Computation and Machine Learning). MIT Press, Cambridge (1998)

Improving FBS Representation Model Based on Living Systems Theory for Cooperative Design

Haiyan Xi[✉], Guoxin Wang, Xiaofeng Duan, Ru Wang, and Jun Yu

Beijing Institute of Technology, No. 5 S. Zhongguancun Street, Haidian District,
Beijing 100081, China
xiheye@163.com

Abstract. In traditional FBS framework, the innovative design thinking of cooperative design is given, but there is a lack of standardized description of design elements (function, behavior, and structure). This paper proposes an expression model combining Living systems theory (LST) and FBS framework. This method expresses design elements of the FBS model which are function, behavior, and structure based on LST. A logical and standardized functional expression method is presented by combined with functional vocabularies and the 20 key subsystems in LST. The structural behavior sets are given by quoting the process parameters of LST and the structural expression consistent with the functional expression clearly define the design output. The LST-FBS model shows a standardized expression and mapping method between function, behavior, and structure, which facilitates computerization of conceptual design. Finally, we demonstrate the LST-FBS model by applying it to the variant design of a diesel engine design.

Keywords: Cooperative design · Function-Behavior-Structure
Design representation · Living systems theory

1 Introduction

The FBS (Function-Behavior-Structure) design model formally proposed by Gero [1] has been widely used in cooperative design fields [2]. The FBS model transforms the functional requirements into design description by behavior and structure [3]. It conforms to the habits of design thinking, is easy to implement innovation, and can effectively support cooperative design.

The FBS model developed by Gero et al. proposes the concept of expected behavior and structural behavior, and can better support innovative design. However, the model does not consider reuse of existing examples and does not give expressions of design elements, and cannot effectively use existing cases. Although the model modified by Vermaas and Dorst [4] can use existing examples, it directly derives the structure directly from the function, ignoring the analysis of behavioral elements, but the analysis of behavior in the design process can effectively stimulate the creation of innovative design solutions. This model lacks the process guidance for the design thinking and cannot guarantee the innovative requirements of the conceptual design. At

© Springer Nature Switzerland AG 2018
Y. Luo (Ed.): CDVE 2018, LNCS 11151, pp. 57–63, 2018.
https://doi.org/10.1007/978-3-030-00560-3_8

the same time, the traditional FBS models applied to conceptual design [2] provide the conceptual design framework, but the lack of design element expression and mapping methods lead to low reuse of design knowledge and poor reasoning between design elements. There are some problems in the conceptual design method based on FBS: (1) The FBS framework does not consider the difference between innovative design and variant design, and cannot guarantee innovation and reuse at the same time. (2) The standardized representation of design elements (functions, structures, and behaviors) in the FBS framework is not given, making the mapping between design elements ineffective and unfavorable for design reuse.

The purpose of this paper is to construct the design element expression model of FBS framework and FBS framework based on the expression model which can ensure the innovativeness of cooperative design while improving the reuse rate of design knowledge.

2   Expression of Elements in FBS Framework Based on LST

The basic elements of FBS framework are function, behavior and structure. The function is the goal that the behavior and the structure need to achieve. The structure is the vector of the function and behavior. The behavior is the attribute of the function and structure. The normative expression of design elements is conducive to the mutual mapping between them and the realization of systematic conceptual design. This paper proposes a method of normative expression of FBS design elements based on LST. As a conceptual framework, living system theory is not limited to the description of living systems and has been widely used by many scholars to model non-living systems [5, 6].

2.1   Expression of Function

Function is the purpose of design. LST describes the operation of various living systems by 20 key systems. This paper expresses the functions of the mechanical product design used the key subsystems of the living system and forms a standardized functional expression model.

Functional expression in the FBS framework includes two aspects: functional formal expression and functional relationship expression. The formal expression of the function gives the functional description of the product in conceptual design. The expression of functional relationship obtains the relationship between the functions in the FBS framework and guarantees the comprehensiveness and rationality of the design function. Furthermore, it is convenient to use the living system theory to express the behavior and structure.

Expression of Functional Form Based LST
Expression of functional form based LST uses the function-defined six-tuple form. In conceptual design, the description of the function should include all contents of the six-tuple.

$$LST - F = (DF, NF, TF, VF, FF, BF) \tag{1}$$

Functional definition (DF): refers to key systems' symbolic representation of LST; Functional name (NF): refers to key subsystems' standard name of LST. In particular, the product does not have the ability to reproduce itself but has the function of feedback, the Reproducer is modified to "Feedback"; Functional type (TF): refers to the type of design object, including material, energy, and information; Functional verb (VF): refers to the action description in the process of function implementation. This paper constructs functional verb table by combining the reconciled functional basis [7] and LST. Considering of generality and non-repeatability of concepts, the secondary categories of the functional set is complete, so the functional verb table is generated by reclassifying the secondary categories of the functional set combining with the LST, as shown in Table 1. Functional flow set (FF): refers to the object implemented by the functional verb, which is described by the vocabularies of flow sets. Functional description (BF): refers to expected behavior derived from the function.

Table 1. Functional verb based LST

TF	DF	NF	VF	DF	NF	VF
	⬤	Ingestor	Import	▶	Producer	Couple/Mix
	⋈	Distributor	Distribute/Separate/Transfer/Guide	⊞	Storage	Store/Supply
Key subsystems for material/energy processing	▰	Converter	Convert/Regulate/Change	◉	Motor	Actuate
	◯	Extruder	Export	⊓	Supporter	Stabilize/Secure/Position
	◺	Feedback	Sense/Indicate	▢	Boundary	Stop/Regulate
	⊡	Input transducer	Import	⋈	Associator	Couple/Mix
	☰	Internal transducer	Convert/Regulate/Change	⏚	Memory	Store/Supply
Key subsystems for information processing	⧻	Channel and net	Distribute/Separate/Transfer/Guide	⊠	Decider	Process
	◔	Timer	Time	⋀⋁	Encoder	Encode
	⋙	Decoder	Decode	⌐⌐	Output transducer	Export
	◺	Feedback	Sense/Indicate	▢	Boundary	Stop/Regulate

Expression of Functional Relationship

The realization of complex product functions requires sub-functions about the input, output, and internal transformations. The sub-functions about internal transformation are divided into the type of physical change and the type of chemical change based on the concepts in physics. Sub-functions that do not directly affect the material/energy transition are called physical-change functions, including supporter, storage, and distributor. Sub-functions that directly affect material/energy transition are called chemical-change functions, including producer, motor, and converter. In conceptual design, chemical-change functions should be emphatically analyzed. Such functions will directly reflect the effect of the design.

The construction of the design function logic facilitates the systematic construction of product conceptual design and reduces design iterations. Firstly, the black box theory is used to determine the design boundary. According to the relationship between key subsystems of LST, this paper constructs the functional flow of matter/energy and functional flow of information, as shown in Fig. 1.

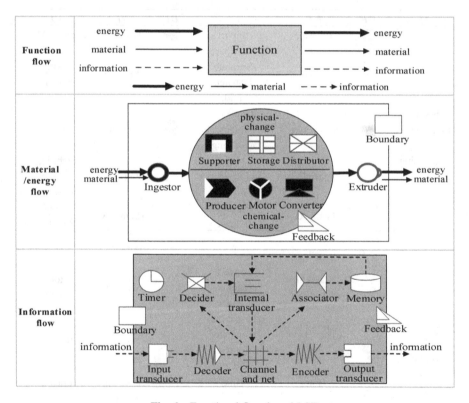

Fig. 1. Functional flow based LST

2.2 Expression of Behavior

In order to realize the mapping of function and structure, Gero et al. define the behavior includes expected behavior and structural behavior. The expected behavior(B_e) refers to the behavior derived from the function, consistent with BF in functional expression; the structural behavior(B_s) refers to the behavior derived from existing structure, described by structural attributes and consistent with BS in structural expression.

Although the behaviors between living system and conceptual design are different, the attributes describing the behavior are universal. Expressing structural behavior B_s of this paper quotes the parameter system table of key subsystems in LST [8]. The attributes in the structural behavior table can be appropriately modified according to different design objects. Obtaining the relevant attribute values in the structural behavior table according to the existing design information as much as possible is favorable for the selection of the optimal structure, the feasibility check, and the provision of more design information for the subsequent design.

2.3 Expression of Structure

The structure is the physical carrier to achieve the function. In order to better achieve the transformation between function and structure, expression of the structure also uses the method of six-tuple. The structural expression is the design output of the conceptual design. The standardized structure expression facilitates the reuse of design knowledge and guarantees the eligibility of design results.

$$S = (DS, NS, TS, CS, GS, BS) \tag{2}$$

DS refers to product structure's sketch; NS refers to structural name; TS refers to the type of structure, and is the same with TF in expression of function; CS refers to the constraints of the structure, which is other constraints required to meet the design requirements except for structural behavior such as the spatial location, environmental requirements, etc.GS refers to goals which the structure can achieve, and is the same with NF in expression of function; BS refers to structural attribute description called structural behavior B_s.

3 Application Case

The design of a diesel engine for heavy truck with a rated power of more than 400 kW is an example applied in variant design. The concept design is performed through LST-FBS model. By analyzing the functional flow of the diesel engine, the case structure that can satisfy the function is searched and the functional flow of the diesel engine is constructed (Fig. 2). Because the diesel engine design does not involve information, the information flow is not constructed.

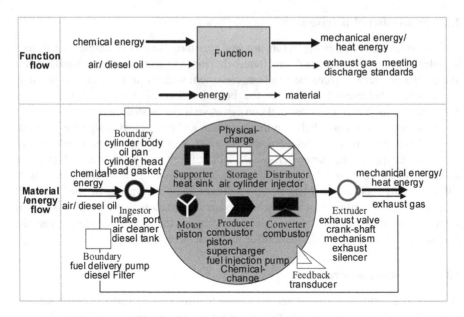

Fig. 2. Function flow of a diesel engine

4   Conclusion and Future Work

It is a difficult problem to ensure the conceptual design innovation in conceptual design and increase the reuse rate of design knowledge. This paper proposes the conceptual design method combining with LST and FBS framework, to solve the problem of the traditional FBS framework that lacks the design element expression and mapping method. This method expresses the design elements of FBS model which are function, behavior, and structure based on living systems theory. In addition, this paper reconstructs the traditional FBS framework considering variant design and innovative design. The LST-FBS model gives a standardized expression mapping method of function, behavior, and structure, which facilitates computerization of conceptual design. However, there are still some problems in this paper that need to be improved in the subsequent research.

(1) Although this paper gives structural behavior sets based on LST, it does not study the internal mechanism of the expected behavioral generation.
(2) The computerization degree of conceptual design can be improved by computerized representation and development based on this paper.

Acknowledgements. The author(s) disclosed receipt of the following financial support for the research, authorship, and/or publication of this article: This research was supported by the National Defense Basic Scientific Research Project of China (no. JCKY2016209B001).

References

1. Gero, J.S.: Design prototypes: a knowledge representation schema for design. AI Mag. **11**(4), 26–36 (1990). http://people.arch.usyd.edu.au/wjohn/publications/1990.html. Accessed 14 May 2007
2. Li, W., Li, Y., Wang, J., et al.: The process model to aid innovation of products conceptual design. Expert Syst. Appl. **37**(5), 3574–3587 (2010)
3. Clark, D.D., Mistree, F., Rosen, D.W., et al.: Function-behavior-structure: a model for decision-based product realization (1997)
4. Vermaas, P.E., Dorst, K.: On the conceptual framework of John Gero's FBS-model and the prescriptive aims of design methodology. Des. Stud. **28**(2), 133–157 (2007)
5. Ham, D.H.: Modelling work domain knowledge with the combined use of abstraction hierarchy and living systems theory. Cogn. Technol. Work **17**(4), 575–591 (2015)
6. Louderback, W.T., Merker, S.L.: Integrating living system process analysis and concrete process analysis with balanced scorecard. Syst. Res. Behav. Sci. **23**(3), 409–418 (2010)
7. Hirtz, J., Stone, R.B., Mcadams, D.A., et al.: A functional basis for engineering design: reconciling and evolving previous efforts. Res. Eng. Design **13**(2), 65–82 (2002)
8. Miller, J.G., Miller, J.L.: Introduction: the nature of living systems. Behav. Sci. **35**(3), 157–163 (1990)

CoVim+CoEmacs: A Heterogeneous Co-editing System as a Potential Solution to Editor War

Bryden Cho$^{(\boxtimes)}$ ⬦, Agustina Ng, and Chengzheng Sun

School of Computer Science and Engineering,
Nanyang Technological University, Singapore, Singapore
DCho003@e.ntu.edu.sg, {Agustina,CZSun}@ntu.edu.sg

Abstract. Most past research efforts in co-editing have focused on *homogeneous* co-editing, where users use the *same* editor to collaborate, but little has been done on supporting *heterogeneous* co-editing, where users may use *different* editors to collaborate. In this work, we explore the rationales behind the design of *CoVim+CoEmacs heterogeneous* co-editing system, which allows *rivaling Vim* and *Emacs* users to edit shared documents in the same real-time session. We argue that *heterogeneous* co-editing can provide a platform for rivaling editors to co-exist and allow advocates of different editors to appreciate each other. In this paper, we report our findings on the main benefits of *heterogeneous* co-editing and its potential role in resolving the *"holy war"* between Vim and Emacs.

Keywords: Computer-supported cooperative work
Heterogeneous collaborative editing · Operational Transformation
Transparent Adaptation

1 Introduction

The task of text editing is becoming a part and parcel in this day and age with a large number of text editors available such as *Vim, Emacs*, and *Notepad* ++. The varying complexity of text editing tasks and requirements by various user groups, create a trend whereby a popular editor in one user group may not be as widely used in another user group. This can be seen in a recent survey by Stack Overflow[1] where Vim editor is widely used by system administrators but loses its popularity in the domain of web and mobile development. Moreover, the vast investment in both time and effort to perfecting the art of operating those editors creates a strong emotional bond between the users and their favorite editors. These factors play an important role in the ignition of *"Holy Editor War"* between Vim and Emacs.

Text editors have evolved over the years, incorporating new features that are deemed important by their users. This creates a trend where certain tasks that can be easily accomplished using one editor are hard/complex to perform using another editor. We believe that *heterogeneous* co-editing, where each editor brings to the table its own

---

[1] Stack Overflow 2018 Developer Survey at https://insights.stackoverflow.com/survey/2018.

© Springer Nature Switzerland AG 2018
Y. Luo (Ed.): CDVE 2018, LNCS 11151, pp. 64–68, 2018.
https://doi.org/10.1007/978-3-030-00560-3_9

unique advantage, can allow complex tasks to be easily performed and those advantages can be used to complement the shortcoming of another editor. This can allow advocates of different factions to better understand and appreciate each other while providing a platform for different editors to co-exist harmoniously. However, there are very few research studying *heterogeneous* co-editing [2, 3], and no prior studies have identified the benefits of *heterogeneous* co-editing and its potential use-cases. In this paper, we report some initial results in our research towards supporting *heterogeneous* co-editing, with focus on identifying the main benefits and advantages of *heterogeneous* co-editing systems, using the goal of resolving editor war as our main motivation.

2   COVIM+COEMACS as Research Vehicle

This work is based on a real-time heterogeneous text co-editing system, *CoVim +CoEmacs*, which provides real-time collaboration capabilities between single-user text editors, Vim and Emacs. *CoVim+CoEmacs* is based on *Transparent Adaptation (TA)* approach to adapt Vim and Emacs into CoVim and CoEmacs respectively, without modifying any underlying source code of Vim and Emacs [1, 4]. Heterogeneities between CoVim and CoEmacs are then resolved to allow seamless collaboration among CoVim and CoEmacs. This *TA*-based *heterogeneous* co-editing approach is achievable through its cornerstone technology – *Operational Transformation (OT)*, which provides the core technique of *consistency maintenance* [4].

CoVim+CoEmacs has been used as a research vehicle for studying a range of issues pertaining to real-time *heterogeneous* collaboration, including the potential benefits of such collaboration, technical issues in bridging different editors, as well as heterogeneous workspace awareness. Our *TA*-based approach in *CoVim+CoEmacs* allows us to retain the rich functionalities and interface features of the original single-user application (Vim and Emacs) while incorporating advance collaboration capabilities [1, 4]. By preserving all the interactions and features of Vim and Emacs, users are able to use their learned knowledge of those editors in a single co-editing session. In turn, this also provides us with the unique opportunity to investigate the benefits of *heterogeneous* co-editing from the viewpoint of users of both Vim and Emacs.

3   Benefits of Heterogeneous Co-editing

3.1   Supporting Favourite Editors and Styles in Co-editing

With the vast amount of single-user editors widely used by people in their daily lives, it would be natural for them to demand to use their preferred editor in co-editing sessions. Conversely, without the support for *heterogeneous* co-editing, users may have to give up their favorite editor during co-editing sessions, which may discourage users from collaboration and cause more discontent between different factions.

To put this into context, with a *homogeneous* co-editing system (CoVim or CoEmacs), supporters of certain editor (Vim or Emacs) are able to use their favorite editor to collaborate within their own user groups. However, if there is a need for users using rivaling editors to work together on shared documents, some users may have to compromise and give up their favorite editor. This can escalate the editor war from debating which individual editor (Vim vs Emacs) is better to which (*homogeneous*) co-editor (CoVim vs CoEmacs) is better. We feel that a *TA*-based *heterogeneous* co-editing system, *CoVim+CoEmacs*, which not only allows users to use their favorite editors, but more importantly, preserves the rich functionalities, interface features and editing styles during co-editing, is a way to appease these rivaling factions of users.

3.2   Promoting Productivity and Mutual Appreciation with Co-editing

Users of any editors would have spent a great deal of time and effort in learning and operating their favorite editor until they are proficient in using them in their daily activities. This is more apparent for seasonal users of Vim and Emacs that have honed their skills to a high level of proficiency which enables them to be very productive in their work. Through *heterogeneous* co-editing, users of *CoVim+CoEmacs* are able to use their accustomed editors to accomplish tasks in a highly productive manner.

This not only can increase the productivity and morale among different users, but also enable users to learn from each other, understand the rationale behind why their favourite editor may not be as widely used in another user group, and recognize some advantages of other editors, which can potentially help to change some of the negative viewpoints about their rivaling editors, thus promoting mutual appreciation.

3.3   Supporting Interdisciplinary Collaboration

Complex and challenging tasks often require the collaboration of people from various domains with diverse skill sets and expertise. As different users may favor certain editors due to their needs and requirements in specific domains, *heterogeneous* co-editing can aid in supporting interdisciplinary collaboration.

For example, with *CoVim+CoEmacs*, a CoVim user (e.g. a backend developer) can use Vim comprehensive editing features to quickly generate multiple SQL statements; while a CoEmacs user (e.g. a Database Analyst) can immediately execute those statements using the *SQL-Mode* in Emacs. Once executed, the CoEmacs user can feedback to the CoVim user with results, such as incorrect results or errors, and they can work together to make necessary changes. This highlight an important benefit of supporting different editors in the same co-editing session: users can use the editors that they feel are most suitable for the tasks in their particular domains without any restrictions.

3.4   Achieving Complementary Collaboration

Features and functionalities of editors are rapidly evolving based on the feedbacks by their user groups. This results in each editors having unique features that can be hard to replicate on other editors. For instance, Vim is able to perform complex plain-text editing tasks such as duplication of text, and increment of numeric values quickly and efficiently; while, Emacs is able to perform tasks like ASCII drawing, and spreadsheet operations with relative ease. It is our belief that different editors will co-exist as long as they are needed or liked by some people. We aim to use those unique features to complement rivaling editors and provide opportunities for rivaling factions to appreciate and understand each other.

An example of such complementary collaboration in *CoVim + CoEmacs* is shown in Fig. 1. In this example, we attempt to utilize the strong suits of CoVim (e.g. generation of multiple lines in Fig. 1(a)) and CoEmacs (e.g. performing spreadsheet tasks in Fig. 1(b)) to complement each other and complete complex task that is not doable on either one of the single-user applications. The underlying core technology in *CoVim +CoEmacs*, *OT*, is used to achieve both *intention preservation* and *convergence* [4]. In other words, *OT* enables *CoVim+CoEmacs* to preserve all CoVim and CoEmacs operations while ensuring that the shared document is identical on both editors during a co-editing session as shown in Fig. 1(c) and (d). Finally, CoEmacs was used to apply those spreadsheet formulas and prettify the table as seen in Fig. 1(e) and (f).

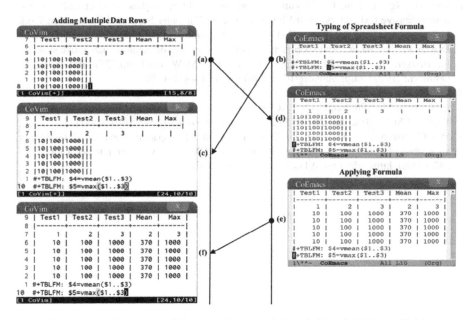

Fig. 1. Complementary collaboration between *CoVim* (left) and *CoEmacs* (right)

This motivating example highlights how *complementary collaboration* can allow *CoVim+CoEmacs* to perform tasks that were previously unimaginable on their single-user application counterparts. We hope that *heterogeneous* co-editing is able to provide the unique stage for rivaling editors to co-exist and make peace with one another, potentially bring an end to the editor war.

4 Conclusion

In this paper, we have presented some novel ideas of using *CoVim+CoEmacs heterogeneous* co-editing system as a means to resolve or alleviate the ongoing editor war. Benefits of *heterogeneous* co-editing systems are multi-fold: (1) Allowing users to use their familiar editors and styles in co-editing; (2) Promoting productivity and mutual appreciation; (3) Supporting interdisciplinary collaboration; and (4) Achieving complementary collaboration. Our project on *heterogeneous* co-editing is still ongoing; comprehensive and in-depth discussions of our work will be reported in future papers.

Acknowledgments. This research is partially supported by an Academic Research Grant (MOE2015-T2-1-087) from Ministry of Education, Singapore. The authors wish to thank anonymous reviewers for their insightful and constructive feedback.

References

1. Cho, B., Ng, A., Sun, C.: CoVim: incorporating real-time collaboration capabilities into comprehensive text editors. In: IEEE Conference on Computer Supported Cooperative Work in Design – CSCWD 2017, pp. 192–197 (2017). https://doi.org/10.1109/cscwd.2017.8066693
2. Dewan, P., Sharma, A.: An experiment in interoperating heterogeneous collaborative systems. In: Bødker, S., Kyng, M., Schmidt, K. (eds.) ECSCW 1999, pp. 371–389. Springer, Dordrecht (1999). https://doi.org/10.1007/978-94-011-4441-4_20
3. Li, D., Li, R.: Transparent sharing and interoperation of heterogeneous single-user applications. In: Proceedings of ACM Conference on Computer Supported Cooperative Work – CSCW 2002, pp. 246–255 (2002). https://doi.org/10.1145/587078.587113
4. Sun, C., Xia, S., Sun, D., Chen, D., Shen, H., Cai, W.: Transparent adaptation of single-user applications for multi-user real-time collaboration. ACM Trans. Comput. Interact. **13**(4), 531–582 (2006). https://doi.org/10.1145/1188816.1188821

Managing Multi-synchronous Sessions for Collaborative Editing

Weihai Yu[✉]

UiT - The Arctic University of Norway, Tromsø, Norway
weihai.yu@uit.no

Abstract. A multi-synchronous collaborative editor allows for both synchronous and asynchronous editing. People can either edit a shared document from different sites simultaneously and see the concurrent updates immediately. Or they can edit the document independently and merge the changes at a later time. This paper presents our initial support for multi-synchronous sessions in the collaborative editing system we have implemented, as well as our experience with the system and open issues for future work.

Keywords: Data replication · Concurrency control · CRDT
Session join · Awareness

1 Introduction

When collaboratively editing a shared document, people may edit the document asynchronously. They first edit their own copies of the document and later manually merge each other's updates. This process typically repeats in several rounds. The merges must be carefully coordinated and may involve tedious work. There might be substantial duplicated or conflicting editing efforts, since the authors are not aware of the concurrent updates until the merges.

Alternatively, people may edit a document synchronously. They see immediately all updates currently made by other people, as the collaborative editing system automatically integrates the concurrent updates. This typically requires the authors to be constantly connected to a central server that hosts the document. The authors might feel distracted by the concurrent updates.

Multi-synchronous editing may help ameliorate the aforementioned inconveniences. At different time, the authors are able to choose the most appropriate synchronous or asynchronous mode to edit the document. We have implemented some multi-synchronous features in a collaborative editing subsystem, Wyde, in the open-source editor GNU Emacs (https://www.gnu.org/software/emacs/). The features include:

- Peer-to-peer real-time collaborative editing. Groups of people can edit the same document synchronously without connecting to a central server.

© Springer Nature Switzerland AG 2018
Y. Luo (Ed.): CDVE 2018, LNCS 11151, pp. 69–77, 2018.
https://doi.org/10.1007/978-3-030-00560-3_10

– Independent off-line editing. An author can edit the document without network connectivity and without distraction by the concurrent updates of the other people. The author may even occasionally use a different editor of her choice, for example due to particular supported features (formatting, debugging etc.) or availability on special devices (mobile phone, remote server etc.), at the cost of loss of Wyde specific functionality like selective undo.
– Joining efforts at convenience. An author may merge her updates with other people's updates at her time of convenience. The system automatically integrates asynchronous concurrent updates. It also provides awareness support so that people can review the updates that have been automatically integrated.

We present session management in Wyde, with an emphasis on starting and resuming collaboration between peers. We also share our initial experience with the system.

2   System Overview

Users carry out synchronous collaborative editing through Wyde *peers*. A peer may be connected with other collaborating peers in a *synchronous group*.

2.1   Peer Structure

A Wyde peer is an instance of the Wyde editor where a user is working on an instance of a document. Figure 1 shows some key elements of a Wyde peer.

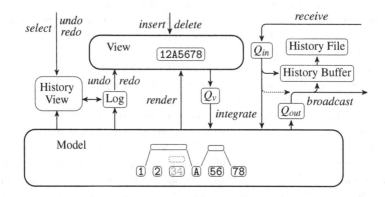

Fig. 1. Structure of a peer

A user edits a document in the *view*. The editing operations take immediate effect in the view. Concurrently, the peer receives remote updates sent from other peers. The peer stores executed view operations in queue Q_v and received remote updates in queue Q_{in}. During a synchronization cycle, it integrates the operations stored in Q_v and Q_{in} into the *model* and shows the effects of integrated remote updates in the view through a *render* operation. The peer stores the integrated local operations in queue Q_{out}. It also records the integrated local and remote operations in the *log*. Later, it broadcasts the operations in Q_{out} to other peers.

A view is mainly a string of characters. A user can insert or delete sub-strings in the view. The insertions and deletions may be in groups. For example, a string substitution is a group consisting of a deletion and an insertion. The user may undo or redo earlier integrated local or remote operations (or groups) selected from the log, such as through the *history view.*

A model implements a CRDT (conflict-free replicated data type) that materializes editing operations and relations among them. It consists of layers of linked nodes that encapsulate characters. An important property of the CRDT is that when two peers have integrated the same set of operations, albeit in different order, they have the same models and views. We refer the interested reader to [9] for more details of the CRDT.

The updates in Q_{in} and Q_{out} are stored with a linearized representation (JSON in our implementation). When a peer integrates remote updates in Q_{in} or broadcasts local updates in Q_{out}, it also records the corresponding updates in a *history buffer*. When the user saves the document, the peer runs a synchronization cycle and flushes the history buffer to a *history file*, so the saved history is in sync with the saved document instance.

2.2 Synchronous Groups

When involved in synchronous collaboration, a peer can be a host, a guest or both. To start a synchronous group, a peer first becomes a *host* by starting a server, to listen and accept new group members as guests. The user of the host informs the collaborating partners of the host address, for example, using email or messaging. Other peers become guests by joining the host with the host address.

While a host may have multiple guests, a guest is only associated with a single host. The host maintains the membership of the group.

A host can also join another host as a guest. Then the two groups merge into one.

When a host disconnects, its associated guests are also disconnected. Groups are thus not robust. Group management is a known distributed system problem that is orthogonal to the issues of our focus.

In a synchronous group, messages are propagated via hosts. When broadcasting messages, a guest simply sends its local updates in Q_{out} (Fig. 1) to its host. A host sends its local updates in Q_{out} to all its guests. In addition, when the host receives a new message from a guest, it forwards the message to the rest of its guests.

3   Session Management

A user performs updates on a document instance in a Wyde session. A session is specific to a peer. In this section, we first discuss the key design issues and then describe how Wyde session management addresses these issues.

3.1   Issues

The Wyde CRDT model assures that if two peers have integrated the same set of operations, their models and document states converge [9]. The order in which operations are integrated is not an issue. The main concern here is that peers should collaborate based on certain common set of integrated operations. However, because a user may edit the document asynchronously, collaborating with one group in a period and with another group in another period, the set of operations integrated in different peers may diverge significantly. Therefore, when a new peer joins a synchronous group for collaboration, the histories of the new peer and the other peers of the group should merge to a certain point. We choose to merge the histories of the new peer and a host of the group and let the host propagate the merge to the rest of the group.

Even though the document states at different peers converge, there might still be conflicts against the intentional efforts of the authors. This is particularly true when the divergence between the operation histories is large. Resolving the conflicts requires the user to be aware of the divergence. Furthermore, concurrent conflict resolution by different people may lead to new conflicts. It is therefore helpful to avoid concurrent and circular conflict resolution and support for awareness of history divergence.

Another challenging issue is that merge of operation histories can be costly. Our general solution requires a peer to send its entire operation history to a remote peer, even though the two histories may have a lot in common. Section 3.5 presents an enhancement for a special (and quite common) case.

3.2   Session Start

When a user uses Wyde to edit an instance of a document, Wyde first starts a session. Because the user may occasionally update the document instance without using Wyde, Wyde session management must take such updates into account.

At the start of a session, Wyde walks through the update history stored in the history file (Fig. 1) to restore the state of the document as at the end of the latest session. If the instance has been modified outside of Wyde since the last session, the restored state is different from the stored state, which is newer. When this is the case, Wyde applies a `diff` [2] of the stored instance to the restored state. The updates performed on the instance since the last session are now integrated in the model. These updates are however at a high (line) granularity, which may make some Wyde-specific features like selective undo and redo less useful.

3.3 Session Join

A peer joins a synchronous collaboration group in terms of a session join. Figure 2 shows how a session at Peer A, as guest, joins a session at Peer B, as host. In the figure, a_0, a_1, b_0, b_1 etc. are sequences of operations.

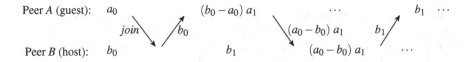

Peer A (guest): a_0 $\qquad$ $(b_0 - a_0)\, a_1$ $\qquad$ $\cdots$ $\qquad$ b_1 $\cdots$

$\qquad$ $join$ $\qquad$ b_0 $\qquad\qquad$ $(a_0 - b_0)\, a_1$ $\qquad$ b_1

Peer B (host): b_0 $\qquad\qquad$ b_1 $\qquad\qquad$ $(a_0 - b_0)\, a_1$ $\qquad$ $\cdots$

Fig. 2. Join of two sessions

Peer A sends a *join* request to Peer B. Peer B verifies the credential of A and replies with a message that includes its operation history b_0. When A receives b_0, it computes the differences between the received history b_0 and its own history a_0, resulting in sub-histories $(b_0 - a_0)$ and $(a_0 - b_0)$. Peer A then integrates $(b_0 - a_0)$.

It is likely that a_0 and b_0 include conflicting or duplicated editing efforts, especially after long asynchronous editing sessions. To avoid spreading the conflicts and duplicates, the user of Peer A, who is joining the remote session, might want to take the opportunity to perform a number of operations a_1 to resolve the conflicts and duplicates.

After integrating a_1 Peer A sends $(a_0 - b_0)a_1$ to B. Peer B then integrates the received operations $(a_0 - b_0)a_1$ and replies with a message that includes the operations b_1 that it has integrated after message b_0. After Peer A has received and integrated b_1, both Peer A and Peer B have integrated all operations in a_0, a_1, b_0 and b_1.

3.4 Awareness Support

In Fig. 2, the user of Peer A may perform operations a_1 to resolve conflicting and duplicated updates involved in asynchronous editing efforts in b_0. In order to do this, the user should be able to know the updates in $(b_0 - a_0)$. The Wyde history view (Fig. 3) allows the user to inspect the updates in the document.

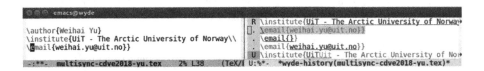

Fig. 3. Document view and history view

Since Wyde maintains the complete operation history of a document persistently across editing sessions, the number of operations can be overwhelmingly large for the user to navigate through. Wyde provides a number ways to display relevant subsets of operations: operations in a given region, operations whose text matches a regular expression, operations generated by a particular user, etc. To support awareness for the user of Peer A, the history view only displays operations in $(b_0 - a_0)$.

The history view helps the user identify the operations. It displays the character strings of the operations as underlined and in different colors according to the types of the operations (insertion or deletion) and whether characters are currently visible in the document. It also displays the surrounding text of the operations. In addition, the history view shows the operation state with a preceding character ("U" for undone and "R." redone). The different background colors of the proceeding characters tell which users performed the operations.

The user can navigate up and down through the history view to perform selective undo or redo. During the navigation, the cursor in the document view moves to the operation boundary accordingly. This not only provides a nice way of navigating through the document, but also presents a rich context of the operation.

3.5   An Enhancement for Session Re-join

The individual editing operations in Wyde are very responsive, both in the view and in the model, independently of document sizes and history lengths, as reported in [9]. However, when the editing history is long, session start and join may take some time.

Suppose Peer A in Fig. 2, after some collaboration, leaves the synchronous group, works asynchronously on the document for some time, and then joins back again. The two peers have to go through the same join process as described in Sect. 3.3. Notice that both peers have already integrated operations in a_0, a_1, b_0 and b_1.

Figure 4 shows a join algorithm enhanced for the re-join of two peers. When Peer A receives operations b_1 from Peer B, it integrates b_1 and records a *join* event that contains the identifiers of the last operations in a_1 and b_1. Eventually, the *join* event will reach Peer B and be recorded in both A and B's histories.

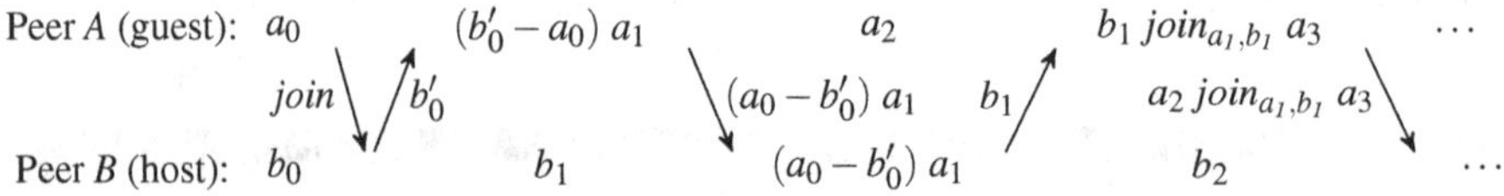

Peer A (guest): a_0 $(b_0' - a_0)\, a_1$ a_2 $b_1\, join_{a_1,b_1}\, a_3$ $\cdots$

$join$ b_0' $(a_0 - b_0')\, a_1$ b_1 $a_2\, join_{a_1,b_1}\, a_3$

Peer B (host): b_0 b_1 $(a_0 - b_0')\, a_1$ b_2 $\cdots$

Fig. 4. Join of two sessions: enhanced for subsequent re-join

At a re-join, when Peer B receives a *join* request from Peer A, it first looks for the last *join* event between itself and Peer A. Let the sub-history of B after the recorded operation (i.e. the last operation of a_1) of the last such join be b_0'. In the new join algorithm, Peer B sends b_0', instead of b_0, to Peer A.

Notice that this enhancement works also when Peer B joins Peer A, i.e., when Peer A is the host at the re-join. There is a difference though. When Peer A is the host, it sends the sub-history starting at a_3. When Peer B is the host, it sends the sub-history starting at b_2, which will include a_2, although a_2 is already part of Peer A's history.

The correctness of the algorithm is straightforward. Due to space limit, we do not present a proof here.

However, this enhancement does not apply generally to two peers that have not directly involved in a join, even though they both have the same *join* event in their histories (e.g. both have the same *join* event between peers C and D).

4 Experience and Open Issues

We have now over two year's experience of practically using Wyde. Through this experience, we have been learning desirable features and making improvements.

Our experience is still very limited in scale. The primary use case is actually not collaborative editing. However, even for single-user editing, the existence of a persistent history and a history view for selective undo and redo proved to be very useful.

As for collaborative editing, the scenario that we have experienced most is with a single long-lasting host session. In fact, informing collaboration partners of new host addresses is often inconvenient, particularly to people who are not constantly connected to a common messaging system. With a long-lasting host session as a server, people can join and leave from different sites at will.

In our cases, with only up to three people collaboratively working on a shared document, concurrent conflicting updates are rare with synchronous sessions. Conflicting updates do become an issue after long asynchronous sessions. The awareness support presented in Sect. 3.4 indeed helps the user identify conflicting and duplicated editing efforts. In an early version of our join algorithm, Peer A replies immediately after the integration of $(b_0 - a_0)$ in Fig. 2. Peer A and Peer B then concurrently resolve conflicts and duplicates, and introduce new ones. Allowing Peer A to resolve the problem first avoids cyclic resolutions and greatly improves the collaboration experience.

In synchronous sessions, we hardly experience any delay for individual editing operations, even when the editing history is long. However, the latency at session start and join becomes noticeable when the editing history is long. For example, for a LATEX document of 50 kbytes and a history of 12K operations, it takes close to a second to start and even longer to join. The join algorithm described in Sect. 3.5 is a response to this issue. For peers that collaborate regularly, the enhanced join is significantly faster for documents with long editing histories. Unfortunately, start of a new session or a join with an unknown peer still experience long delays.

In our experience, allowing (or tolerating) modifications of a document outside of a specific collaborative editor is a necessary requirement. First of all, Emacs, in which Wyde is implemented, is not popular among non-programmers. Even for Emacs users, installing Wyde just for occasional collaboration is not very convincing. Furthermore, people may run scripts to make project-wise updates or accidentally edit the document with whatever editor at hand. Finally, Wyde may crash, forcing people to edit the document with other alternatives.

We first introduced session start as described in Sect. 3.2 because of the instability of Wyde in the early development stages. Applying `diff`, we can (almost) be sure that we are able to continue editing the document according to the last saved state, even when the restored state is somehow different.

Our current solution does have a number of issues. `diff` is line based. After applying `diff` to integrate updates made outside of Wyde, the previous editing operations on the updated lines are buried in the deleted lines rather than in the new inserted ones. Undoing or redoing them will not bring them back to the right places.

Furthermore, if two sessions independently integrate the same updates made outside of Wyde, these updates are duplicated as different Wyde operations. This happens when, for example, somebody updated a document outside of Wyde and committed the updates in a Git repository. Later, people at different sites pull the commit and then edit their document instance with Wyde.

5   Related Work

The vast majority of current real-time collaborative editing systems are based on OT (operational transformation) for concurrency and consistency management [1,3,7]. The collaborating peers are connected to a central server and collaborate in a synchronous fashion. Getting connected is easy because there is only a single network address to deal with. People get instantly updated of the concurrent changes made by the other people, so conflicting or duplicated editing efforts typically do not have long-lasting effect. On the flip side, people are dependent on constant network connectivity and may get distracted by frequent concurrent updates.

CRDT paves the way for peer-to-peer and multi-synchronous collaboration [3–9]. Currently, little is reported on the experience of multi-synchronous collaborative editing. We hope that our work reported in this paper could shed some light on the research issues in this area.

Regarding performance, the collaborative editing community has primarily focused on the complexity of integration of individual operations [4–6,8,9]. As far as our system is concerned, we believe this performance issue has already been addressed [9]. The main performance issue, as we have experienced, is when a large number of operations have to be integrated such as during session start and join. To our surprise, no published work has ever mentioned this issue.

The history view as presented in Sect. 3.4 was earlier presented in [10] as part of the support for awareness of concurrent updates during synchronous sessions.

6   Conclusion

CRDT approaches allow for peer-to-peer and multi-synchronous collaborative editing. In this paper, we report our initial support for multi-synchronous sessions in a collaborative editing sub-system implemented in GNU Emacs. We also share our initial experience with the sub-system as a basis for future research work.

References

1. Ellis, C.A., Gibbs, S.J.: Concurrency control in groupware systems. In: SIGMOD, pp. 399–407. ACM (1989)
2. Hunt, J.W., McIlroy, M.D.: An algorithm for differential file comparison. Computing Science Technical Report 41, June 1976
3. Li, D., Li, R.: An admissibility-based operational transformation framework for collaborative editing systems. Comput. Support. Coop. Work. **19**(1), 1–43 (2010)
4. Oster, G., Urso, P., Molli, P., Imine, A.: Data consistency for P2P collaborative editing. In: CSCW, pp. 259–268. ACM (2006)
5. Preguiça, N.M., Marquès, J.M., Shapiro, M., Letia, M.: A commutative replicated data type for cooperative editing. In: ICDCS, pp. 395–403. IEEE Computer Society (2009)
6. Roh, H.-G., Jeon, M., Kim, J., Lee, J.: Replicated abstract data types: building blocks for collaborative applications. J. Parallel Distrib. Comput. **71**(3), 354–368 (2011)
7. Sun, C., Jia, X., Zhang, Y., Yang, Y., Chen, D.: Achieving convergence, causality preservation, and intention preservation in real-time cooperative editing systems. ACM Trans. Comput. Hum. Interact. **5**(1), 63–108 (1998)
8. Weiss, S., Urso, P., Molli, P.: Logoot-undo: distributed collaborative editing system on P2P networks. IEEE Trans. Parallel Distrib. Syst. **21**(8), 1162–1174 (2010)
9. Yu, W., André, L., Ignat, C.-L.: A CRDT supporting selective undo for collaborative text editing. In: Bessani, A., Bouchenak, S. (eds.) DAIS 2015. LNCS, vol. 9038, pp. 193–206. Springer, Cham (2015). https://doi.org/10.1007/978-3-319-19129-4_16
10. Yu, W., Oster, G., Ignat, C.-L.: Handling disturbance and awareness of concurrent updates in a collaborative editor. In: Luo, Y. (ed.) CDVE 2017. LNCS, vol. 10451, pp. 39–47. Springer, Cham (2017). https://doi.org/10.1007/978-3-319-66805-5_5

Lean-Led, Evidence-Based and Integrated Design: Toward a Collaborative Briefing Process

Daniel Forgues[1(✉)], Maude Brunet[2], and Hafsa Chbaly[1]

[1] École de technologie supérieure, Montréal, QC, Canada
daniel.forgues@etsmtl.ca
[2] HEC Montréal, Montréal, QC, Canada

Abstract. Project Definition is the project phase during which the needs and values of project stakeholders are identified, and appropriate design solutions are developed to satisfy them. However, traditional briefing practices have proved to be inadequate in complex projects involving a great number of stakeholders with, in many cases, conflicting needs and requirements. Moreover, these stakeholders often do not have the skillsets to understand and challenge the brief content or the design solutions proposed by the design professionals.

Different approaches have been proposed to improve the Project Definition process in order to deliver buildings with a better fit for use or purpose. This paper explores three of these approaches: Lean-led Design, Evidence-Based Design and Integrated Design. 3D Modeling is also considered for facilitating users understanding of the design solutions. Using a Canadian case study, for which these approaches were adopted and leveraged using BIM, this research highlights opportunities to derive core principles and methods from these approaches into a unified process to break the barrier between the client and the supply chain regarding the identification and management of users' requirements.

Keywords: Collaborative design · Briefing process · Lean · BIM

1 Introduction

Hospital projects are good examples of the challenges to define and formalize clients' requirements into a design solution. Hospitals represent a complex interaction of various activity systems in constant evolution in both practices and technologies. The problem is the lack of consideration in the briefing process of this rapidly changing clinical dimension. The main issue with hospital design is that poor briefing process can kill. Hospital-acquired infections and medical errors are among the leading cause of death in the United States [1]. Research shows that well-designed physical settings play an important role in making hospitals safer and more healing for patients, and better places to work [2]. There is a need to rethink project management practices in construction to better identify and manage stakeholders' requirements in complex projects. Hospital stakeholders' requirements evolve throughout the project. Core to project

© Springer Nature Switzerland AG 2018
Y. Luo (Ed.): CDVE 2018, LNCS 11151, pp. 78–85, 2018.
https://doi.org/10.1007/978-3-030-00560-3_11

management theory is that changing requirements are major budget and schedule risks so they have to be set at the project outset.

New design approaches have been proposed in recent years to partly address this issue or to improve the project definition process: Lean-led Design, Evidence-based Design and Integrated Design. However, no research has explored how these approaches could be used or integrated to improve the interactions of users and project teams for delivering facilities that are better fit for their purpose or use. This paper presents the case of a mega-hospital for which these approaches and Building Information Modeling (BIM) have been used for the Project Definition Phase to address the clinical and technical complexity of the project. The objective is to shed some light on how these could lead to better building design, and to highlight challenges in rethinking project management practices to provide a stakeholders-centered design and delivery approach.

2 Managing Clients' Needs: The Case of Hospitals

While the population is aging and growing, maintaining and improving the health of a collectivity is a major concern for governments all over the world. There is a trend to build larger and larger hospital facilities in order to meet the rapid expansion of technologies and treatments, while coping with an aging population. These facilities are complex and expensive projects, and have a quite long lifespan. Therefore, the pressure is high to find the right balance between the need to control the explosion of costs while realizing facilities that offer the best fit with their use and purpose.

BIM is now widely adopted for the design, and the management of hospital projects. The adoption of BIM has pushed the development of new project procurement approaches such as Integrated Project Delivery – the replacement of traditional construction management methods by production systems such as Lean Construction are reducing considerably cost and schedule risks. However, the clinical aspect for better-fit physical environment to business needs is not addressed from a design and delivery perspective.

The concept of patient-centered hospital environment is not new. Evidence-based design, which demands for design solutions grounded in solid research findings, is probably what brought this concept back. Research on Evidence-based healthcare design has demonstrated that design strategies such as access to daylight, view of nature, noise-reducing finishes, nursing floor layout, and decentralized supplies have a direct impact on patient healing, or staff effectiveness and satisfaction [2]. However, this approach does not provide design strategies to instantiate these findings.

One of the main issues regarding managing stakeholders' needs in construction is the fragmented and sequential nature of the project delivery in construction. As indicated by Winch [3], construction is essentially a service industry not offering a product but a capacity to produce. Delivering "all and only what the client needs" is core to project quality management. However, in this context, needs are intangible, heterogeneous and inseparable. According to Winch, traditional construction management services suffer from five gaps in the briefing process: (1) the user expectations and management perception of these expectations, (2) the management perception of these expectations and their translation in a brief, (3) the brief and its interpretation by the design professionals, (4) the facility delivered and the information to manage it (handover), and (5) the facility delivered and the users perception of the facility.

Proposed solutions that may contribute to reduce these gaps are to move from fragmented to integrated design and delivery modes. Among them are the concepts of Integrated Design, and Integrated Project Delivery. Both share the same principles of having all the actors of the project coalition being working together iteratively for the entire project lifecycle. However, these are supply chain solutions, focused on achieving the best technical performance of the facility within the cost/schedule constraints, and not on better fulfilling the business needs.

Lean-Led Design has gained popularity in the US and UK for delivering hospitals that offer much better efficiency and quality of service while reducing the costs for their construction and operation. It revolves around the application of the Lean 3P (product, process, preparation) in a participative design process. A team is defining a workspace configuration, analyzing process and determining how to best meet the patient needs. The team develops options for the design, tests them via 2D models or mock-ups, and evaluates the design options against determined criteria. Research [4] has demonstrated that 3P is an effective tool to develop designs that meet the requirements of multiple stakeholders.

Even if these three approaches are promising to address the briefing problem, each one cover only a specific aspect of the problem. Lean-Led Design is user focused. It is not integrated in the briefing or design processes. Evidence-based Design and Integrated Design improve the supply side capabilities to address needs and requirements by a better-grounded definition of the brief through research and a more integrated and collaborative approach in the design process. However, client stakeholders' participation remains limited and the relationship between space configuration and business processes ignored.

2.1   A Lean Thinking Approach to Address the Briefing Process Gaps

An underlying issue with the management of construction projects is the lack of appropriate project management theory to help resolve the briefing problem. Koskela and Howell [5] argue that project management theory is obsolete and propose a new theory of production in construction that integrates three dimensions: Transformation, Flow and Value generation (TFV). This theory provided the foundations for the Lean Construction movement. However, even if Project Definition is part of the Lean Project Delivery System, in practice, there are major inconsistencies between the concepts and application of Lean Design (supply chain perspective) and Lean-Led Design (user perspective). It is proposed in this paper first to develop the Project Definition perspective of the TFV theory, concentrating on the Flow and Value Generation dimensions – which are directly linked to stakeholders' management; and second to explore how these approaches could be better integrated to provide a better interaction between the client and the supply chain systems.

Flow is about waste reduction. It is applied both in Lean-led Design to improve work efficiency and in Lean Construction to remove waste in the construction process. Value Generation is a much less well-managed dimension, an aspect that could be improved by giving the users a proactive role in the briefing process. BIM related technologies such as virtual or augmented reality and 3D models provide new means for them to participate in the development of design solutions. Evidence-based design could become a collaborative design framework in the Integrated Design Process (IDP).

The paper aims at an exploration of this proposition using a mega-hospital project as a case study. This project offers a fertile research ground to understand challenges and issues in defining solutions for the briefing problem: Lean-Led Design, Evidence-based Design, IDP and BIM are integral part of the design process.

Data gathering is built around the triangulation of review of documents, observation, and interviews. The 3P approach has been thoroughly documented and all the information regarding the process was shared with the researchers [6]. Two two-days working sessions were observed. Semi-structured interviews were conducted with Deputy Director, clinical direction of the new hospital complex, the clinician project architect, and the construction project director. The IDP was also well documented, the process being formalized in a guideline and embedded in the design professionals contract.

2.2   A Stakeholder-Driven Requirements Management?

The case is one of the largest hospital project in Canada. It includes the amalgamation of two existing hospitals in a new physical environment, each one having its own vision, culture and operational approach to deliver health services, which was the motive to adopt these approaches. A transition team was put in place to manage this process. The responsibilities to deliver the project on time and within the budget is under the responsibility of a government agency responsible to deliver construction projects for the province government clients. The project was announced in 2013 to be delivered in 2025.

This agency has developed over the year a systematic project planning and control process. It is promoting IDP as means to deliver more sustainable buildings that are also better fit for their use. It is requiring the use of BIM technologies for the design and construction of building facilities. The choice for this project was to use a two phases approach, using a Construction Management delivery mode. This context is similar to an Integrated Project Delivery approach, the construction manager being part of the project team, and the construction project team sharing the project office space with the transition team.

Co-locating design professionals, builders and the project team in a single space, the Project Office, is a common practice for major projects. In this case, the voice of the users was added in this structure through the addition in the Project Office of the transition team, who is responsible for the clinical dimension of this amalgamation of two hospitals. This team faced major challenges: bringing together different cultures, and professional practices to deliver health services; maintaining the operating of the two hospitals within existing facilities, some in which major renovation will be undertaken during construction; and defining the functional requirements that are aligned to the project vision to have services centered around the patient. The transition

team innovated in adapting 3P initiatives used to make clinical operations more efficient into a Lean-led Design process.

The traditional approach used by the government agency responsible for this
project consists of hiring design professionals to help the client identify their needs and
translate them into a set of requirements within what is qualified as the Functional and
Technical Program (FTP), so that the space requirements are broken down in functions
and rooms. Then a hierarchy of interdependencies is defined to identify how these
rooms should be organized. This approach had to be adapted to integrate the transition
team initiative into what was qualified as a Lean FTP. What 3P adds to this process is
the concept of flow, central to Lean Construction TFV theory. The Lean FTP process
addresses the two first gaps in the Briefing Process: the user expectations and management perception of these expectations, the management perception of these
expectations and their translation in a brief. There are usually seven types of flow that
are analyzed, using techniques such as Value Stream Mapping approach: patients,
providers, medications, supplies, information, equipment, and instruments/processes.
The first aim is to remove waste or non-value-added activities in the process (Table 1);
the second aim is to provide a better service at a lesser cost.

Table 1. Traditional waste in healthcare

Type of waste	Example
Motion	Staff travel
Time	Waiting
Inventory	Unit stockpiling
Over-Production	Food, medication, sterile instruments
Transportation	Transfers
Defects	Medical errors, charting
Processing	Collecting the same information

Mapping the flows offers other advantages. First, it helps to instantiate findings for
evidence-based design. Second, in this specific case, it permitted to compare the modus
operandi of the two hospitals and to define a common ground for organizing the work,
material and information flows. Third, it made the users more knowledgeable of their
needs to ensure that the design meets their requirements – improving Value generation.
The Transition Team conducted seven Kaizen exercises (Table 2).

The preparation of the clinical plan was realized in the two first Kaizen workshops.
In the first one were defined the values driving the process: (1) focus on the patients'
interests and well-being, (2) a continuum of complementary, accessible and efficient
care and services that integrate teaching, research and evaluation activities, (3) a Lean
culture of continuous improvement through optimization, innovation and sustainable
development practices, (4) to build a hospital that meets high standards of quality and
promotes the use of the latest technology and equipment, (5) to become an inspiring
reference model by creating a stimulating work and training environment that enables
skills development, and (6) an harmonious urban integration that generates positive
spin-offs on the surrounding community and the region.

Table 2. Overview of Kaizen activities

Date	Phase	Themes
May 2014	Clinical plan	**Building a patient-centered hospital:** To define a common vision along with common principles
October–November 2014		**Knowing and recognizing each other:** To understand the reality of the two hospitals and their patients
January 2015	FTP	**Combining our strengths:** To position the sectors while thinking about the organization effectiveness
May 2015		**Envisioning the future together:** To illustrate different opportunities on the site and to retain the best hypothesis
September–November 2015		**Defining our operating modes:** To transform practices and to prepare for the transition
March, April 2016	Design	**Testing reality with full-size mock-ups:** To validate the optimal configuration of several rooms
November 2017		**Transforming our practices:** To determine how to harmonize practices of the two hospitals

The second Kaizen included two main activities: looking at the flow, tracing the trajectories of five fictitious patients, including one belonging to a specialty specific to each hospital; and defining the essential proximity links for creating a unified vision of what would be the ideal care and service trajectories. After these workshops, the clinical plan was adjusted against the budget constraints.

The next three Kaizen were focused on the development of the Lean-FTP. For Kaizen 3 the objective was to explore the proximity links between spaces (considering the functional, operational and physical constraints), and to rank them according to their importance. At this stage, the architects team hired to prepare the FTP were invited to participate in the process. Evidences from dozen studies conducted by external firms were considered regarding environmental factors, integration in the neighborhood, soil composition, traffic circulation, etc. Building from this workshop, the design professionals prepared five schemes that were discussed and iterated during Kaizen 4 up to one final proposition. It is during Kaizen 5 that a 3P (patient, process, preparation) workshop was conducted – an approach that aims at simultaneously integrating the design of an arrangement, the new process and the new organization of work. The aim was to explore operating modes of about twenty key sectors. It brought together nearly four hundred fieldworkers and took place in five parts for each of the main areas of activity of the future complex: most notably in critical activity, hospital and ambulatory areas. The patient flow was analyzed from five trajectories: the patient for outpatient visits; the patient having scheduled surgery; the patient consulting for an urgent problem of medicine; the oncology patient; the clinical and logistical support circuit. The Lean FTP was then devised stemming from the various activities of Kaizen 5.

The last two Kaizen were the Lean-Led Design part of the project. Consultations began with a large majority of clinical areas, to review the list of premises and equipment, to validate the different flows (logistics, patients, drugs, material, etc.), vertical and horizontal circulation and the adequacy of the functional links identified in the previous steps. Out of 7000 rooms, 80 types of rooms have been selected because of their repetitive nature (for example operation rooms), since they represented about 20% of the space layout. Staff used full-size mock-ups to define the optimal configuration and equipment setting for these rooms.

3 Connecting Lean-Led and Integrated Design

The concept behind Integrated Design Process or IDP is to stimulate innovative solutions to complex design problems through workshops involving all the key stakeholders. The core principles of IDP are: to assemble all the team at the beginning and for the entire project; and design iterations through charrettes (a form of intensive design workshop) starting at the front-end of planning. In theory, IDP should address the gap between the brief and its interpretation by the design professionals since the users are part of this process.

There are, however sociocognitive issues observed in IDP that have a negative impact on the ability of the users to have a valuable contribution in the design, namely the in-groups behavior, the structure of power and influence [7] and the syntactic/semantic issues. The design professionals tend to act as in-groups in IDP, being "us" (the design specialists) against "them" (the users). The architects, traditionally being the ones making the design decisions, resist the idea of sharing this role with the other participants, especially the users. The Lean-led design process changes the balance of power between the users and the design professionals, the former having acquired the spatial understanding of their work scenario. For example, during Kaizen 5, the representatives of the clinician team rejected all the scenarios proposed by the architects, a quite unusual situation in a traditional design process. The conversation that followed to find an acceptable scenario, while not qualified by the project management team as a formal IDP, was directly in line with its core principles.

4 Discussion and Conclusion

Around 85% of the decisions that will affect the quality of the result are taken during the Project Definition [9]. Therefore, close interactions between the decision makers, the users (in this case the clinicians) and the design professionals are required in order to make the best decisions. However, as asserted by various authors [3, 8], the traditional linear design and delivery process creates information gaps in this process, that are creating bias in the decision process. The results for complex projects are building that are sub-optimal regarding their fit for use and fit for purpose. However, while the problems related to the management of this phase are well documented, and their consequence being dramatic to the project success, little has been done to propose solutions. Lean-Led design is a user-driven process, IDP a supply chain led approach, both aiming at solving this same issue. We argue that both should be integrated as a single Project Definition approach.

This paper contributes to a better understanding on how to solve the Briefing Problems regarding the definition and management of users' requirements. Lean-Led design empowers users to master the concept of PEOPLE-PROCESS-SPACE by helping them to understand how better space configuration can improve their work satisfaction and the patients' experience while making their process more efficient. However, more importantly, they change the balance of power between users and design specialists, giving the former more ownership of the design process.

The combination of Lean-Led Design and IDP could provide the means for breaking the barrier between the client and the supply chain system, opening the conversation between the users and the project team. This breakthrough opens the door to adopt practices from system engineering such as configuration or requirement management to formalize a systematic process. Moreover, BIM related technologies, could offer improved visualization capabilities for a better understanding and participation of staff and patients to define the physical environment in which they will work or will be treated. It could also facilitate the understanding of design decisions using visualization through 3D models and virtual reality (VR), and simulations (natural light, energy). This aspect will be explored in future research, the hospital project office acquiring VR technology to improve interactions between users and designers.

References

1. Klevens, R.M., et al.: Estimating health care-associated infections and deaths in US hospitals. Public Health Rep. **122**(2), 160–166 (2007)
2. Ulrich, R.S., et al.: A review of the research literature on evidence-based healthcare design. HERD Health Environ. Res. Des. J. **1**(3), 61–125 (2008)
3. Winch, G.M.: Managing Construction Projects. Blackwell, Oxford (2010)
4. Hicks, C., et al.: Applying lean principles to the design of healthcare facilities. Int. J. Prod. Econ. **170**, 677–686 (2015)
5. Koskela, L., Howell, G.: The underlying theory of project management is obsolete. IEEE Eng. Manage. Rev. **36**(2), 22–34 (2008)
6. Brunet, M., Daneau, E., Blouin-Delisle, C.H., Forgues, D.: Inclusive project definition of a new hospital using the lean approach. Int. J. Proj. Manag. (Forthcoming)
7. Kamara, J.M., et al.: Capturing Client Requirements in Construction Projects. Thomas Telford Publishing, Cornwal Great Britain (2002)
8. Carlile, P.R.: Transferring, translating, and transforming: an integrative framework for managing knowledge across boundaries. Organ. Sci. **15**(5), 555–568 (2004)
9. Prasad, B.: Concurrent Engineering Fundamentals-Integrated Product and Process Organization. Prentice Hall, Upper Saddle River (1996)

Integrating Construction Specifications
and Building Information Modeling

Juliette Bédard and Conrad Boton[(✉)]

École de technologie supérieure, 1100, rue Notre-Dame Ouest, Montréal, Canada
juliette.berard.1@ens.etsmtl.ca, conrad.boton@etsmtl.ca

Abstract. This paper explores how to effectively integrate building specifications into a BIM process. This research found that all the software that claims to include specifications in a BIM process are actually specification drafting software and are not very useful for contractors and subcontractor who needs to use specifications in mobile contexts such as production or construction sites. A new approach to integrating specifications into a BIM-based collaboration process has been proposed. A collaborative process has been formalized, with three levels of integration. One of these levels is prototyped and shows how it is possible to give access to construction specification from mobile devices on a construction site. Both the process and the prototype are evaluated with practitioners.

Keywords: Construction specifications · Building information modeling
BIM · Rapid prototyping · Construction site · Collaborative process

1 Introduction

The introduction of BIM is a paradigm shift in the construction industry. It is presented in many articles as an effective solution to the problems of collaboration, cost overruns, delays and lack of quality of current construction projects [1, 2]. The use of BIM generates profound changes in processes and methods that are still used today in construction [3]. One of the central documents for defining a construction project is the construction specification, which defines all the requirements regarding the project. Errors in its drafting and understanding can quickly lead to inconsistencies and often to errors on the construction site. However, very few research works have been dedicated to the integration of this important document in the BIM process. Thus, even during a project using BIM, the drafting and the use of construction specifications is done in a traditional way, independent of the 3D model. There are still no effective solutions to link the specifications and the model [4]. Of course, some specifications-specialized software vendors have developed programs to associate BIM and specifications. However, these are not yet adapted enough to be adopted by the practitioners. In addition, the existing solutions are only dedicated to the drafting of specifications, which does not correspond to the needs of general contractors or subcontractors. A misunderstanding of current practices and needs by software vendors could be the reason for the lack of effectiveness of these solutions.

© Springer Nature Switzerland AG 2018
Y. Luo (Ed.): CDVE 2018, LNCS 11151, pp. 86–93, 2018.
https://doi.org/10.1007/978-3-030-00560-3_12

The main objective of this ongoing research project is to explore avenues for efficient integration of construction specifications into a BIM approach, in order to cover the needs of the contractors. It is based on a design science approach to provide a good understanding of business needs and possible solutions for better integration. The article is organized in three main parts. As a first step, a literature review is proposed in order to understand the current state of the issue. Then the methodology is presented, so as to understand the proposals formulated in the following part. The results include a formalization of current practices, the proposed collaborative process integrating BIM and specifications, and rapid prototyping of some proposed solutions. The research is double-evaluated through ex-ante and ex-post evaluations.

2 Literature Review

2.1 Construction Specifications

The construction specification plays a vital role throughout a construction project. It is a document part of the "project manual", which provides specific information on products, materials, methods, processes and expected quality [5]. It has a contractual value, that is to say that the stakeholders are obliged to achieve what has been written in the construction specifications. Specifications and drawings are complementary documents that must be interpreted together. Thus, specifications can complete the information provided by the drawings without overloading annotations.

There are two types of specifications: the descriptive specifications and the performance specifications. The descriptive specifications describe the type of materials and the methods and processes to be used to achieve the objective [6]. In contrast, the performance specification sets out the expected results without giving details of the process to get there [6]. Three methods are often used to write descriptive specifications: the normative method that refers to a standard, the descriptive method which gives details of the properties of the products or materials, and the nominative method or method of brands that names the product to use by name. The normative method reduces writing time because it is based on widely recognized practices. The descriptive method may also include requirements for manufacturing, packaging, assembly, installation and protection. In the nominative method, several acceptable products are left to choose. The use of a type of specifications or method is not exclusive. Many specifications mix the types and methods according to the need expressed by the client.

Several classification systems exist and can be used to organize the content of the specifications. Among these systems, Masterformat, Uniformat II, Omniclass and Uniclass are well-known in the North American context [2]. In Canada, a National Master Construction Specification (NMS) provides the framework for construction specification writing. A master specification is an already complete document written by either owners when they have to do regular work, or by organizations offering access to the document to companies wishing to use it. The Canadian National Master Construction Specification (NMS), administered by the National Research Council Canada (NRC), has more than 770 technical sections for a total of more than 8000 pages. The NMS consists of files in *.doc* format offering several choices to the user or text holes to fill according to the needs of the project. It follows the methodology and classification of MasterFormat and helps the drafter prepare construction specifications [7].

2.2   The Current Software Solutions

The Traditional Specification Drafting Solutions. Many software has been proposed to facilitate the drafting of specifications. These programs work in two different ways. The first possibility is to create specifications by deleting information. A complete specification is sold in MS Word format and the editor selects the parts to be deleted in order to adapt his specifications to his specific project. The second method is based on the addition of information. The writer buys access to a database containing all the elements that may be present in specifications. He then selects only those relevant for his project. This methodology allows access to regularly updated databases.

One very known solution is MasterSpec, jointly edited by Avitru, formerly known as Arcom, and the American Institute of Architects. MasterSpec includes more than 900 sections according to the MasterFormat classification. It allows to buy only useful sections for users and to edit the specifications according to the preferred method: addition or subtraction. Another solution is NBS Building, published by the National Building Specification and managed by the Royal Institute of British Architects. NBS Building comes in the form of a software with a complete database to write any type of specifications. The user selects the desired sections and then customizes them with white spaces with multiple choices. Speclink-e, published by BSD, is a software using the addition method for the drafting of specifications. Their database contains more than 780 sections. Speclink-e can be customized in order to encompass sections specific to each company. This software also offers smart links, which when information is selected automatically include or exclude other paragraphs depending on their incompatibility. NMS Edit, published by Innovative Technology Inc., is based on a master specification and the deleting method. It allows the import and export of Word file, and links to the standards used can be activated.

The BIM-Based Solutions. These software packages most often offer plug-ins to install on BIM software to extract from the model the information that will be used in their own software for writing specifications. This methodology is based on the concept of decentralized repository. For example, E-Specs for Revit, edited by Avitru, promises to integrate Revit software and construction specifications. Indeed, it filters the sections to put in the specifications thanks to a checklist automatically filled out from the components of the BIM model. This software is based on the MasterFormat and the Uniformat. Similarly, NBS Create offers the possibility to install a plug-in on modeling software such as Revit. This plug-in makes it possible to synchronize the model and the specifications being written. Using the objects of the library developed by NBS, the software can automatically create the various sections associated with the objects. With their online viewer, different actors can access the specifications while viewing the model. Linkman-e, developed by BSD, synchronizes their Speclink specification software with Revit. In the same way as NBS Create, it is possible to automate part of the specifications writing if the objects of the BSD library are used for modeling. The modification of the specifications is unidirectional, i.e. changes made from the software will not affect the model. Nevertheless, Linkman-e offers a tool to identify the differences between a specification and the corresponding model elements, for example when an object present in the model is not listed in the specifications and conversely when a product on the specifications is not in the model. SPECedit connects to a 3D model via the Model Probe interface, developed by Innovative Technology Inc., to add sections to the specifications from the selected objects in the model. The synchronization between the model and the software can be automated once the link between them has been done manually. BIMdrive is a software published by Spex, recently bought by NBS. For the moment, BIMdrive only works with the use of the national master construction specifications. So, it is necessary to have access to the NMS before being able to use BIMdrive. BIMdrive is based on check boxes to select the sections of the NMS to activate for a particular project. In the same way, it is possible to select the desired characteristics in each section. BIMoffice, edited by Abvent, is actually a complete BIM project management software including a solution to extract specification elements. Thanks to a plug-in, BIMoffice can extract data from different components. The sections created upstream can then be filled automatically with the different characteristics coming from the objects of the model.

Augmented BIM Objects' Properties. The above-cited solutions do not seem to meet the needs of professionals dealing with specifications as they do not give added value to the work of practitioners. "I found it does not add enough value to continue", said a specification specialist cited by Canadian Design and Construction Report [4]. Moreover, another problem can be put forward: all those solutions are addressed only to the writers of specifications. They highlight the specificity of creating a specification in line with a 3D model. But once written, specifications are exported as a simple PDF or Word document. So, the many other stakeholders (contractors, sub-contractors) must use conventional PDF specifications that can be up to several hundred pages. The concept of centralized repository is deepened by Utiome [8] as part of his thesis. The main hypothesis was that the main problems in the construction industry - costs, time and rework - are caused by erroneous or incomplete specifications. The strategy of integrating the specifications directly into a BIM model would then limit some errors. The proposal uses a simulated case study to develop the concept of Specified Augmented BIM Object (SABO). The use of objects in a BIM software is possible thanks to the different libraries. The case study shows a library accessible on Revit via a visible interface in the form of an add-in. The results of this thesis show that it is possible to create augmented BIM objects including specifications. However, all the specification information could not be included in the BIM objects' properties as the data contained in the construction specifications have been divided into three different categories: data to be included in a model (category A), data accessible through a link of the parameters to an external resource (category B) and data to be kept in their traditional form (category C). While the research conducted by Utiome [8] is an important milestone towards a good integration between specifications and BIM models, it is necessary to go beyond. This means that specifications should be integrated not only to the models but also to the whole BIM process, so all the stakeholders can take advantage of such integration in their daily work.

3 Research Methodology

The methodological approach of this project was constructed according to the four steps generally used in design science research [9]. The first step, the identification of the problem, understands the practices related to the use of specifications in the construction industry in Quebec and thus determine the lack of integration of the specifications into a BIM process. This stage includes several activities: the literature review, the technological review and a training on specification, offered by the *Ordre des Architectes du Québec* (OAQ). The second part, an ex-ante evaluation, validates the knowledge acquired during the first stage. This evaluation was done through interviews with professionals. The knowledge acquired from the problem identification and interviews phase formalized how specifications are used in a conventional project. The step of creating the artifact is based on the answers given during the second part of the interviews. The process of using standard specifications is modified at this stage to propose a new bidding process where the specifications are integrated into the BIM model. The processes are schematized according to the BPMN formalisms. Different levels of integration are proposed and the most adapted one is prototyped. The last step, the ex-post evaluation, evaluates both the processes and the prototype through a discussion group and interviews with the professionals.

4 A New Approach for Specifications and BIM Integration

4.1 Three Levels of Specifications and BIM Integration

The idea is to integrate all the technical divisions of the specifications directly into the BIM model. Figure 1, validated with practitioners, shows the exchange of information that would take place during centralized tendering procedures around a numerical model. It is possible to see how the information exchange is simplified by collecting or linking all the data around the BIM model.

Three levels of integration have been identified. The first level can be seen as a link between the model and the specification. That is, when a user studies the 3D model and looks for information about a particular object, it is possible to click on that object and obtain from the properties a link that will take him directly to that object's information in the specifications. A key question for this first level of integration is how to create the link. The specifications in Quebec generally respects the formatting and layout of MasterFormat, which can also be used to classify BIM objects from many BIM software. It would then be possible to make a link via the 6-digit section numbers of MasterFormat. This link should be automatic because there is little point in having someone manually link the corresponding specifications to the object families for each new project. This level of integration is rather weak and would not significantly reduce the number of documents and information exchanged during the bidding process. The

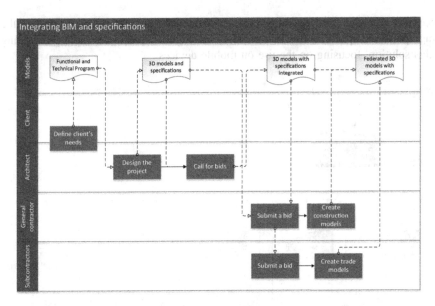

Fig. 1. A simplified collaborative workflow integrating BIM and specifications.

second level of integration consists in information available directly from the model. The idea here is to make the specifications accessible to all the actors of a construction project directly from the 3D model, in different use context, especially on a construction site. This level of integration then proposes to make easily accessible the technical specifications, as well in the office on a computer as on mobile devices at construction sites. The third level of integration proposed in this project is also based on information directly available in the model. The idea of this 3rd level of integration is to improve the data model behind the properties of BIM objects by integrating the technical characteristics of the specification. This level of integration is based on the idea developed by Utiome [8]. Typically, these can be family templates in Revit or go further using IFCs to ensure interoperability between different BIM software. This type of integration would reduce or even eliminate the text that the user must read before finding the information he needs. But its implementation requires to redefine the way specifications are currently presented.

4.2   Proof of Concept

Adapted visualization is important in BIM software adoption [10, 11]. Since it provides visualization capabilities adapted to mobile devices and production site use, the second level of integration is the most adapted to the needs of the industrial partner, a general contractor, associated to this research project. The underlying principle of the proposed solution is simple: from an object of the model, it would be possible, via a new window, to directly access the table of contents of the divisions of the corresponding specifications. Once this table of contents is displayed, the user can select the appropriate division to access a second table of contents, that of the subdivisions. And this process is repeated until reaching the last levels of titles, so the user reaches the paragraph of the specifications that interest him. Figure 2 propose a rapid prototyping of this solution, focusing on the use on mobile devices.

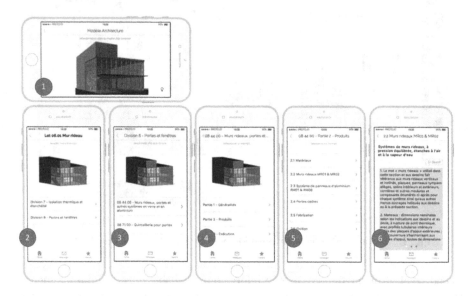

Fig. 2. Menu subdivisions to access the curtain wall specifications from a BIM model.

The first step is to access the 3D model on a mobile phone or tablet. By selecting the curtain wall in the model, it is then possible to access a first menu concerning the specifications of the selected BIM object, as shown in Fig. 2. It was decided that this solution does not include the divisions 00 and 01 related to the contracts and the general conditions. Thus, only the technical parts of the specifications (divisions 07 and 08) are shown in the menu. After having selected the division 08, doors and windows division, the user has access to a second menu allowing him to choose which subdivision he needs. He then accesses the specifications as such. This text is exactly the part of the specifications used as an example, the size has just been adapted to a phone screen format. The main advantage of this method is that it does not modify the current methodology for drafting the specifications. Indeed, the structure of MasterFormat is preserved and this integration is even based on its hierarchy.

5   Conclusion and Future Work

This project made it possible to understand the practices of professionals using the construction specifications. It was thus possible to propose innovative solutions adapted to their needs. Subsequently, it would be interesting to take into account certain limits in order to develop these solutions. The main remark coming from the professionals during the evaluation process of the proposals is to make available the products' data sheets and shop drawings. Since these documents contain very precise and helpful information, it would be interesting to have easy access to them on the construction site. It will also be necessary to take into consideration a possible change of presentation of the specifications. Indeed, a document written in a plain text format does not allow an optimal display on mobile terminals used on construction sites.

References

1. Eastman, C., Teicholz, P., Sacks, R., Liston, K.: BIM Handbook: A Guide to Building Information Modeling for Owners, Managers, Designers, Engineers and Contractors. Wiley, Hoboken (2011)
2. Boton, C., Rivest, L., Forgues, D., Jupp, J.: Comparison of shipbuilding and construction industries from the product structure standpoint. Int. J. Prod. Lifecycle Manag. 11 (2018)
3. Boton, C., Kubicki, S., Halin, G.: The challenge of level of development in 4D/BIM simulation across AEC project lifecyle: a case study. Procedia Eng. 123, 59–67 (2015)
4. Canadian Design and Construction Report: BIM and specification writing: the great disconnect (2017)
5. The Royal Architectural Institute of Canada: Chap. 2.3.8: Construction Documents - Specifications. In: Canadian Handbook of Practice, 2nd edn., pp. 1–14 (2009)
6. Brière, M.: Devis descriptifs ou de performance pour vos projets de construction? Montreal (2014)
7. National Research Council Canada: NMS user's guide. https://www.nrc-cnrc.gc.ca/eng/publications/nrc_pubs/nms/users_guide.html
8. Utiome, E.A.E.: Extending building information models to construction specifications (2010)
9. Baskerville, R., Pries-Heje, J., Venable, J.: Soft design science methodology. In: Proceedings of the 4th International Conference on Design Science Research in Information Systems and Technology - DESRIST 2009, pp. 1–11 (2009)
10. Boton, C., Kubicki, S., Halin, G.: Designing adapted visualization for collaborative 4D applications. Autom. Constr. 36, 152–167 (2013)
11. Boton, C., Kubicki, S., Halin, G.: Understanding pre-construction simulation activities to adapt visualization in 4D CAD collaborative tools. In: Leclercq, P., Heylighen, A., Martin, G. (eds.) CAAD Futures 2011, Designing Together: Proceedings of the International Conference on Computer Aided Architectural Design, pp. 477–492. PUL, Liège (2011)

The Process of Collective Architectural Conception: Characterizing Cognitive Operations of Conception Specific to an Agency

Amira Bejaoui[1,2(✉)], Najla Allani Bouhoula[1], François Guéna[2], and Caroline Lecourtois[2]

[1] 2MRCA, Ecole Nationale d'architecture et d'urbanisme, Tunis, Tunisie
bejaoui.amira.archi@gmail.com, najla.allani@gmail.com
[2] MAP-MAACC, Ecole Nationale Supérieure d'Architecture Paris La Villette, Paris, France
{fguena,Clecourt}@paris-lavillette.archi.fr

Abstract. This paper aims to study the process of the collective architectural conception. We propose to analyze the collective practices in architecture through the exploration of various situations of collective design. Otherwise, we carried out an architecturological study of the architectural design process of some artifacts observed within three architectural agencies. In order to describe the model that characterizes the agency, we question the recurrent cognitive operations from an architecturological analysis grid that allows to identify the repetitions between the processes. Recurrent methodical and representational operations have been also identified; together they characterize the "*architecturological style*" of the agency. In the same way, organizational and graphical recurrences have been decrypted from the analysis of the empirical charters set up in architecture agencies.

All of these recurrences constitute signs of the existence of a designer's collective signature that we suggest to name "*collective style*".

Keywords: Recurrent operations · Architecturological style · Collective style

1 Introduction

With the development of information and communication technologies, collective work took on a new dimension thanks to the sharing of tools that facilitate collective design whether it is about collaboration or a cooperation being held remotely or in co-presence. Many researchers have focused on collective design [5, 11] and distinguished between collaboration and cooperation. Collaboration consists in working together to reach common objectives set at the beginning; it is the result that counts at the end. In the framework of cooperation, it is about cooperating to achieve a single objective with tasks and sub-tasks distributed among the actors. As a result, individual contributions are well identified and the responsibility is individual. However, collaborative work does not require the partition of tasks, all the actors work for the same goal. Together,

© Springer Nature Switzerland AG 2018
Y. Luo (Ed.): CDVE 2018, LNCS 11151, pp. 94–101, 2018.
https://doi.org/10.1007/978-3-030-00560-3_13

they try to find solutions to the constraints and the responsibility is shared. At the level of the organization of work, collaboration is ensured by a mutual commitment of the participants to carry out the same task, it is about an interdependent organization while the organization is joint for the cooperation [8].

1.1 The Cognitive Activity of Collective Architectural Conception

Our research focuses on the process of collective architectural conception specific to an agency. Several researches have already approached the cognitive activity of architectural conception; they questioned it along two criteria: individual or collective conception [11]. Indeed, the comprehension of the design process interested several fields relating to the activities of the conception. Some have focused on individual processes and others on collective processes. We quote the empirical studies that were carried out in cognitive psychology [4], and the theoretical studies developed by [5] that aim to produce a new knowledge on the cognitive processes of collective conception.

Furthermore, the individual conception of architecture refers to the notion of *"starchitects"* (the architects whose celebrity and criticism have given them some notoriety among the general public) which has developed an intense activity around their names [7, 9]. They were able to benefit from a brand effect thanks to their signatures. In parallel, there are architectural agencies that gather designers who have chosen to come together to create an agency. These groups of designers have taken the name of *"collegial"* (refers to collectively which directed in common). They are increasingly widespread in the professional world and they produce many artifacts on behalf of an agency. This artifacts production constitutes an interesting field of research to understand and characterize the activity of the collective architectural conception. Although they have a diversity of professional experiences, they gather for the same interests and the same objectives. These *"collegial"* establish within their agency a group culture based on methods and tools favoring the community. Nevertheless, the longevity of this type of agency leads us to question the secrets of the collective know-how of designers' team. It seems that each agency has a particular way to approach an architectural project. It is characterized by its method of approach, its philosophy and by the experience acquired over time. This method develops through the principles and the concepts gradually established over time to write a specific history of an agency. The main hypothesis of our research was that there are cognitive operations of conceptions that ensure and structure this conceptual conformity among the conceivers. These operations generate, over time, a *"collective style"* characterized by a particular working method and know-how. Therefore, the concept of *"collective style"* is at the heart of our work, which examines the cognitive mechanisms implemented in the collective architectural process and focuses on the modalities of collective conception.

2 Methodology

Our research investigates collective cognitive work in architectural conception in order to characterize its process. Among the disciplines that can be referred to conduct this research, we mention the cognitive ergonomics that have focused on the cognitive and operative aspects of collective conception activities. There are authors who make a distinction between two forms of collective conception, the *"CoDesign"* and the *"Distributed Design"* [5]. We adopted these two concepts to question the collective cognitive process specific to an agency: *"CoDesign"* where designers work *jointly* and *"Distributed Design"* where designers work *simultaneously*. Thus, we distinguished between the tasks which were carried out individually or collectively, simultaneously or jointly.

To query our corpus, we used Architecturology. This is a field of research that focuses on the cognitive activity of architectural conception and questions it in terms of operations of conception. *"The design space"* is the scientific object that emerged from a question for which this research area set up architecturological concepts:

"How does the architect give measurements to his/her space?" [2]. From an architecturological point of view, our study visits the *"design space"* of each project, to identify the cognitive operations implemented individually or collectively and to determine the architecturological scales that proceed through the graphical or oral representations. Thus, architecturology is a tool to explore the designed space through an architecturological analysis of graphics representations accompanied with speeches by architects. Therefore, we opted for an analytical approach resulting from the *"applied architecturology"* [10] in order to determine how designers attribute measures to their artifacts. Subsequently, for each agency, we decoded the repetitions between the phases of the processes in terms of elementary operations of conception. Then, we distinguished between the repetitions of the object from the repetitions of the process [3]. Thus, we identified the recurrent cognitive operations between processes resulting from cooperative or collaborative situations work. In order to characterize the activity of the collective conception specific to an agency, we proceeded with deciphering the phases of the architectural process. Initially, we defined the project activities for each phase in order to distinguish between the actions developed individually by each architect and the actions carried out collectively. Then, we translated them in terms of elementary operation of conceptions: *referencing, segmenting, dimensioning* [2], *orientating* and *positioning* [10] or pragmatic operation of collaboration *(interpretation, pooling, autonomisation, evaluation, and segmentation)* [1].

3 Corpus

The choice of the corpus concerned three cases of *"collegial"* agencies. We studied the case of the associated designers and also the case of agencies which composed by junior designers led by a responsible architect. For each firm, we studied the process design of four projects dealing with different themes.

To collect the necessary data, we started by conducting semi-structured interviews with one senior designer from each agency, then we reconstituted the design process based on the graphical elements collected and architects' discourses. The interviews focused on the process progress and the method of approach adopted by each group. The first objective was to identify the tools and means of cooperation or collaboration that were set up throughout the architectural process. Secondly, we identified the actors involved and tasks developed in each phase of the process for the four projects.

The chosen corpus has been divided into two parts. The first part concerns the agency where one of us worked as an architect and where she participated in the conception of various projects. As researchers, we distance ourselves from these artifacts, which she has reflected upon with the other conceivers in the agency.

In the second part of the corpus, our interest turned towards the cases of agencies that we have explored as external architects and researchers who observed and analyzed the different methods of collective work. We analyzed architects' projects in order to decipher the cognitive recurrences between processes and to characterize the "*architecturological style*" of the architectural firm.

4 Results and Discussion

4.1 The Architecurological Style Specific to an Agency

For the first agency, the designer confirmed that she always followed guidelines and recurrent methods to think up projects without actually identifying them. It seems that they are automatisms and reflexes which the architect develops over time where dealing with different design situations. To assimilate and characterize these methods, we analyzed the design process of these architectural objects by identifying the recurrent tasks and actions that are repeated throughout the project process. We defined three phases whose tasks are identified in (Table 1) whether they are carried out individually or collectively. Based on the recurrent graphical elements, we identified the recurrent cognitive operations of conception implemented in each task and the architecturological scales from which they proceed. Thus, recurrent cognitive operations, methodical and representational operations are observed in this agency.

Table 1. Recurrent methodical operations specific to the agency: recurrent tasks (Agency 1)

	Research phase	Preliminary study	Project sketch phase
Tasks	1-Searching for references 2-Study the program 3-Analysis of the site in context	1-Prepare a preliminary study file (cost of works) 2-Meeting with the client and validate the proposal	1-Disturb tasks among the members of the collective 2-Set the conceptual choices and the project idea 3-Study of functional plans 4-Modeling the digital model

To study this case, we have adopted the methodology of reflective practice developed in ergonomics, which consists in holding the posture of the researcher and the speaker at the same time. This posture requires objectivity from the practitioner architect towards the designed artifacts. Therefore, it is essential to make a total abstraction of all social and relational data that may impact the analysis of the different projects.

For the second agency, based on interviews and descriptive graphical elements of the various projects, we deciphered recurrent cognitive operations of conception that always initialize the design process (Table 2). By examining these processes, there are architecturological scales which are interrelated with a dominance of a type of relationship that connects them. Consequently, these recurrent operations are defined through a specific and recurrent structuration of architecturological scales.

Table 2. Recurrent cognitive operations that initialize the process of conception (Agency 2)

Project 1	Project 2	Project 3	Project 4
Operation 1 Operation of Positioning	**Operation 1** Operation of Positioning	**Operation 1** Operation of Positioning	**Operation 1** Operation of Positioning
–Integration scale –Neighborhood scale –Parcel scale	–Integration scale –Neighborhood scale –Optical scale	–Integration scale –Neighborhood scale –Optical scale	–Integration scale –Neighborhood scale –Parcel scale

The data collected, within the third case of agency, constituted a field of investigation to explore the architectural sketch. Recurrent representational operations have been detected through the architecturological analysis of the '*space of representations*' [10] composed of different graphic elements of the studied projects. Thus, we note recurrent references being reproduced on most of the sketches that inspire the architect. In the same way, the designer has specific ways to represent his ideas, his details, which he explains through cuts, axonometric and perspectives. Through these sketches, he communicates with other collaborators who also have their own personalized representation and often computer-assisted.

In summary, through the *architecturological* analysis of the first agency's collective work in which we had access for all types of information, we identified three types of recurrences between artifacts' processes studied. In order to confirm these results, it was necessary to verify the existence of these three recurrences between the design processes for the other selected agencies. Therefore, we proceeded with interviews for a second time with designers to checking the recurrences which we could not detected from the collected data at the beginning. Thus, the cross-case study was necessary to generalize the definition proposed for the "*architecturological style*" of team designers. This style is determined by the recurrent cognitive operations that initialize the process, the structuration of the architecturological scales and the dominance of relationship that links them through "over-*determination*" or "*juxtaposition*" [2]. These recurrent operations are accompanied by recurrent methodical and representational operation decrypted between the different processes studied. Together, they define the "*architecturological style*" of an agency.

4.2   The Collective Style Specific to an Agency

Based on observations carried out within the studied agencies, it seems that the majority of architectural firms implement an empirical charter that organize and structure the collective work. We divided this charter into two parts; the first part focuses on agency's work organization while the second part deals with the graphical part. To set it up, the team members meet to determine the objectives that evolve over time. They set collectively the plans and the methods of action in the various situations to achieve these goals. In this charter, the rules and laws have been set by the architects according to the objectives and the stakes of the agency, as they develop or readjust other rules. Therefore, the establishment of these organizational and graphical charters personalizes agency's collective work. Thus, over time, the organizational and graphical recurrences become automatisms that affect the work performance and the efficiency of the collaborators.

According to the recurrences resulting from the analysis of the content of the empirical charter and the *architecturological* analysis of the various design processes, we was able to define and specify the collective signature of an agency that we proposed to name *"the collective style"*. To identify it, it is necessary to assimilate agency's work organization and characterize the *"architecturological style"* through the three recurrences identified above. We summarized this definition through this schema (Fig. 1):

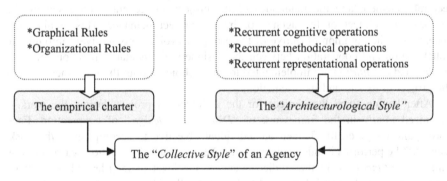

Fig. 1. The recurrences that define the collective style of an agency

4.3   Collaboration or Cooperation

According to the observations of the case studied, the collective architectural conception alternated between the collaborative and cooperative mode. Indeed, there are actions and decisions that were taken collectively and others required the division of tasks between the cooperants. We noted that the division of labor was essential to produce the final work, at the same time, validation and collective bargaining of some choices was necessary to lead to a final result that satisfies all participants.

The first phase of the architectural process is the research phase; it is necessary to analyze the program suggested by the customer and to meet his expectations.

The analysis of the program is a collaborative task; each designer interpreted the data in his/her own way in order to build the first components of the "*common operational reference*" [6]. It is needed for cognitive *synchronization* of the designers to become aware about the complexity of the situation to be treated. However, the collection of data on the site is a cooperative task where each architect tries to gather information on the site. Then, they move on to the reference research phase, which we identify as a cooperative task because each member is responsible for finding metonymic references by referring to similar projects that have dealt with the same theme or metaphorical references resulting from the memorized mental images. It is a *referencing* operation that proceeds from a *model scale* [2]. This *scale* was implemented individually in order to feed the "*common operational reference*" required to carry out the collective activity. In this phase, each designer was autonomous, he/she interpreted and analyzed the data in his/her own way, [1] has defined it as a *pragmatic operation of autonomisation* necessary for cognitive *synchronization*. Once these data are grouped together, the designers collaborated to interpret all this information, *pragmatic operation of interpretation* was derived from the various interpretations of the site and of the program which proceeded from different *architecturological scales* of *neighborhood*, *parcel* and *functional* [2]. The *pragmatic operation of pooling* was involved to make the collective synthesis of all these shared and indispensable data to lead the collective reflection on the architectural object to conceive. The choice of the architectural statement and the main idea of the project are generally proposed by the responsible architect of the agency or by the project manager. This architectural statement is the common objective of the group; it evolves progressively through the collaboration and cooperation between the designers. Elementary operations of *positioning* and *orientation* are implemented to make choices about the implementation of the project in its site and its orientation.

After having fixed the choices for the architectural project design, the work is organized *jointly* in the framework of "*Distributed Design*" of cooperation. Each participant has given him/herself an individual objective to accomplish his/her task. Thus, he/she performs it independently while being aware of the actions carried out by others *simultaneously*. In the studied agencies, the level of interdependence is high since there are linked and dependent tasks, especially when they are assigned to different participants, for example in some cases, 3d modeling can only be done after having dimensioned the template of the 2D project in the plot. Each individual task was evaluated by the group in the form of criticisms and alternative proposals; a *pragmatic operation of evaluation* [1] was involved and ended with a collective decision resulting from a *Co-design*.

The *pragmatic operations of collaboration* identified by [1] were all perceived in the cooperative tasks analyzed. What was moreover decrypted, it is the high level of interdependence set up between the participants and the *coordination* needed to lead to the final result. The *pragmatic operation of coordination* is a cognitive operation that has appeared in the cooperative work situations analyzed. The cooperative approach was structured by coordinating actions between cooperants who interacted and exchanged their experiences. They coordinated and managed the interdependencies in order to adjust contributions to achieve a common goal.

Finally, it is a necessary operation to lead the collective reflection of the group. The consistency of all the actions carried out requires coordination which ensures the progress and the best arrangement of the tasks. Consequently, the success of cooperation is determined by the performance of the group to achieve its objective.

5 Conclusion

In order to identify the *"collective style"* within a team of designers, signs were identified from the analyzed cases to characterize it. These signs come in the form of cognitive, representational, methodical, organizational and graphical recurrences. On the one hand, these signs determine the existence of a *"collective style"* of designers who cooperate or collaborate together. Therefore, we distinguished between cognitive operations specific to collaboration and those are specific to cooperation.

On the other hand, they can serve as prescriptions for organizing collective work in the agency. From these signs, we deduce that the *"collective style"* appears in a group of architects as soon as these signs are all present.

References

1. Ben Rajeb, S.: Modélisation de la collaboration distante dans les pratiques de conception architecturale: caractérisation des opérations cognitives en conception collaborative instrumentée. Ph.D. thesis, Ecole Nationale Supérieure d'Architecture Paris La Villette (2012)
2. Boudon, P., Deshayes, P., Pousin, P., Schatz, F.: Enseigner la conception architecturale, cours d'architecturologie. Editions de La Villette, Paris (1994,2000)
3. Boudon, P., Decq, O., Deshayes, P., Gandillac, A., Schatz, F.: Architecture et Architecturologie. Vol.III: Analyse et Eléments de Théorie. Editions de La Villette, Paris (1975)
4. Chevalier, A., Anceaux, F., Tijus, C.: Les activités de conception: créativité, coopération, assistance. Le Trav. Hum. **72**(1), 1–4 (2009). https://doi.org/10.3917/th.721.0001
5. Darses, F., Falzon, P.: La conception collective: une approche de l'ergonomie cognitive. In: de Terssac, G., Friedberg, E. (eds) Coopération et Conception. Toulouse Octarès (1996)
6. De Terssac, G., Chabaud, C.: Référentiel opératif commun et fiabilité. In: Les facteurs humains de la fiabilité dans les systèmes complexes, Toulouse (1990)
7. Ethier, G.: Architecture iconique: les leçons de Toronto. Presses de l'université de Québec, Québec (2015)
8. Gangloff-Ziegler, C.: Les freins au travail collaboratif, Marché et organisations, (N° 10), pp. 95–112 (2009)
9. Gravari-Barbas, M., Renard-Delautre, C.: Starchitecture(s): Figures d'architectes et espace urbain. Celebrity architects and Urban Space, L'Harmattan, coll. «Gestion de la culture», Paris, 270 p
10. Lecourtois, C.: De la communication sur l'espace: espace conçu et espace perçu de l'architecture et de l'urbanisme Ph.D. thesis, Ecole d'Architecture de Paris La Villette, Paris (2004)
11. Visser, W.: Conception individuelle et collective. Approche de l'ergonomie cognitive. Rapport de recherche RR-4257 INRIA (2001)

PSO-Based Cooperative Strategy Simulation for Climate Game Problem

Zheng Wang[1], Fei Wu[2], and Wanliang Wang[2(✉)]

[1] Department of Computer Engineering,
Zhejiang Institute of Mechanical and Electrical Engineering,
Hangzhou 310053, People's Republic of China
937049626@qq.com
[2] College of Computer Science and Technology,
Zhejiang University of Technology, Hangzhou 310014,
People's Republic of China
1963998924@qq.com, wwl@zjut.edu.cn

Abstract. The climate policy of game theory-based understanding could be used to find some insights about how players might implement different policies. To address this issue, the cooperative climate decision-making model by using agent-based simulation and optimization is established, and the solution of the non-cooperative climate game through particle swarm optimization (PSO) is developed in this paper. Firstly, learning agents are introduced to represent several players in climate game, evolutionary strategy using the decision-making and evaluation model based on individual interests and collective interests of Nash equilibrium is proposed. Then, the nonlinear fitness function of the PSO is designed, as well as the parameter selection and analysis. Finally, the Simulation experiments are performed by the nonlinear function and compared with Genetic Algorithm (GA). Experiment results showed that the proposed algorithm in this paper achieves the expected effect with fast response ability and the model can guide all agents to make a choice rationally in the process of non-cooperative game, so that the individual benefits and collective benefits reach the Nash equilibrium.

Keywords: Climate game problem · Decision-making model
Cooperative climate strategy · Particle swarm optimization · Genetic algorithm

1 Introduction

Global cooperation is proved to be very necessary to control climate change in the climate game [1]. Using game theory to do research on global climate change is an effective way for climate cooperation. Each agent must balance the relationship between economic development and environmental protection and try to find the Nash equilibrium between these two interests [2, 3].

The most famous mathematical metaphor for a social dilemma is the prisoner dilemma [4, 5]. Other well studied models include public goods games [6, 7], which essentially represents a generalization of the pairwise prisoner dilemma to inter-actions in groups of arbitrary size [8, 9], the snowdrift game [2], and world induced

© Springer Nature Switzerland AG 2018
Y. Luo (Ed.): CDVE 2018, LNCS 11151, pp. 102–109, 2018.
https://doi.org/10.1007/978-3-030-00560-3_14

technological change hybrid (WITCH) model which is a dynamic optimal growth general equilibrium model [10]. WITCH model can produce two different solutions: a cooperative one that is global optimal (global central planner) and a decentralized, non-cooperative one that is strategical optimal for each given region (Nash equilibrium) [11]. All of them exemplify situations which are characterized by different degrees of conflicting interests between the individuals and the community [12, 13]. Climate protection programs that appeal to a human sense of fairness, that is, all players contribute a "fair share" to the collective goal, are more likely to avoid irrational self-detrimental behavior [14]. Milinski concluded that one possible strategy to relieve the collective risk dilemma in high risk situations is to convince people that failure to invest enough is very likely to cause grave financial loss to the individual and describes the social window humankind has to prevent dangerous climate change [15]. We expect the strategies adopted in the climate game to be risk averse.

In this paper, the game process will be presented as an optimal model in which the fitness function is a nonlinear function. As particle swarm optimization has better efficiency to optimize the nonlinear function, it will be introduced into the model to find the optimal decision-making program in the next round decision-making set of each agent. The model structure, operation process, and the integration of particle swarm optimization will be described later.

2   Cooperative Climate Decision-Making Model

2.1   Investment Strategy Description

According to [15], thirty groups (six students in each) took part in a climate game to simulate the collective risk via an interactive computer program. In each round, every single student had a chance to contribute a small amount, a generous amount, or nothing at all. If they succeeded, they got to keep some leftover cash. If they failed, however, the climate almost certainly went to hell, in which case they lost everything both the collective fund and their individual stash.

In the experiment, students will be given £40 to their "climate account". They will invest 10 rounds anonymously. In each round, the amount of investment can be £0, £2, or £4. It is known to all students that if the final contributions achieve or exceed £120. For instance, if everyone donates £2 in each round, then after 10 rounds, everyone only remains £20. Otherwise, the team does not attain the target (≥ 120) and the computer will run the dice program, leading to all the students in the team losing their remaining money with the probability of 90%, 50%, or 10%. At all points, the static noncooperative game issue is that both individual interests and collective benefits are maximized for each group. Therefore, each student must balance the relationship between economic development and environmental protection, which is the Nash equilibrium [16]. Agents are powerful and successful approach to build systems operating in complex and dynamic environments. It requires agent values being specified rather than ignored, in order to specify norms that may vary according to circumstances. Multi-agents system is a system composed of multiple interacting intelligent agents [17, 18].

This paper uses agents to represent players or common wealth of players for climate game and regard the climate game problem as an optimization problem and try to obtain the optimal investment scheme for each agent.

2.2 Decision-Making Model

The assumption of cooperation strategy model in this paper is as follows: each agent represents a student or a common wealth of students. If all the agents are rational investment, a game model can be designed to make the agent game process equivalent to optimal decision process. In this case, individual and overall interests will achieve Nash equilibrium.

The method in [15] shows that decision-making is made after completing 10 rounds of investment. It is assumed that each agent is rational and one decision-making is made after every 10 rounds of investment. After the ith decision-making, according to 10 rounds of total investment and other agents' total investment, agent will select the $i + 1$ optimal individual based on genetic algorithm. Thus, the next round decision-making is decided. Therefore, the decision-making model is shown in Fig. 1.

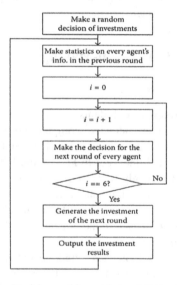

Fig. 1. Decision-making and simulation scheme.

3 PSO Algorithm for Climate Game Problem

3.1 Design of Fitness Function of PSO

Denote the total investments of the kth agent as V_k in the jth round, hence, in the jth round, the set of all six agents' investment is $S_j = \{V_1, V_2, V_3, V_4, V_5, V_6\}$. The average investment of the kth round sum is $S_j = \sum V_k/6$. In order to optimize rational agent's decision-making, an effective and reasonable fitness function is designed in this paper. The nonlinear fitness function in this section is expressed as follows:

$$f(g) = \frac{(1 - |120 - \sum_k v_k| / 120)^a}{\sum_k (|\frac{120}{k} - v_k|^b - 20)},$$

(1)

where a and b are the weights of overall interests and individual interests respectively. If a is larger than b, the particle selection process prefers to choose the overall interests of better particles. otherwise, the particle selection process will prefer to choose the individual interests of better particles. By adjusting the values of a and b, different characteristics will be presented in the whole simulation process and make it consistent with variable reality.

3.2   Individual Representation

Establish a database for each agent to preserve its investment quota and its remaining money in each round. In this case the cumulative investment sum among k agents can be obtained. For instance, if the investment record of the kth agent during 10 rounds is 2220044220, which means the agent invests £2 in the first three rounds, £0 in the fourth and fifth round. Then we can get the total amount of money invested by the kth agent through 10 rounds which is £18. If the cumulative investment sum among k agents during 10 rounds is £110 and the kth agent is chosen to be punished since the target sum (£120) has not been achieved, the kth agent will lose its remaining £22. Put data 2220044220, 22 and 110 in the database for the kth agent.

3.3   PSO Algorithm for Decision-Making

The decision-making process based on PSO is shown in Fig. 2. The initialized PSO produce a group of random particles through iterations to find the optimal solution. In each iteration, the particles are updated by following two "extremes". The first one is the particles to find the optimal solution which is called the individual extremum. The other one is the optimal solution found between the all population and the extreme value and is called the global extremum. Following the current search for the optimal value to find the global optimal is the core of PSO, which is mainly used in this paper. In addition, the single-point mutation strategy is also used in this paper, a random point of chromo some string is selected, and it has the probability to change its value.

4   Simulation Results Analysis

4.1   The Fitness Function Coefficients $a = 1$ and $B = 1$

In the PSO, if the fitness function coefficients $a = 1$ and $b = 1$, the optimization process is shown in Fig. 3(a). The target sum 120 is the default value of the total investment. The sum of investment is the total amount of investment after each decision. Others are the investment of each agent in each round. From this simulation, it can be observed

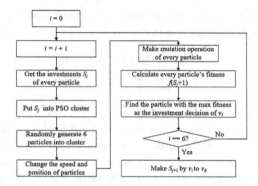

Fig. 2. The flow chart of PSO.

that although the first round of investment is generated randomly, the total amount of investment becomes gradually close to the default value of the total investment after nearly 21 generations of searching, and the total amount of investment is fluctuating but finally matches it. In addition, each investment of each agent is stabile on the investment value of 20 in the end. The PSO algorithm is stochastic, therefore, in this section, thousands of experiments are done based on the same coefficient condition. Statistical result shows that steady generation is after 21. Some representative initial random state simulation results are depicted in Fig. 3(b) and (c).

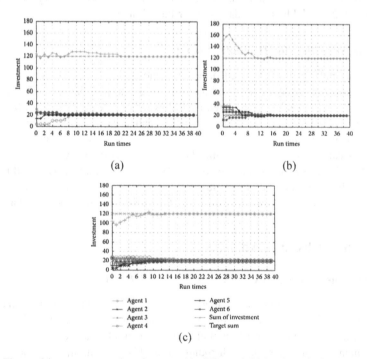

Fig. 3. The total investment results of agent with different initial value of PSO ($a = 1, b = 1$).

4.2   Compared with Genetic Algorithm

Single point crossover strategy and single point mutation strategy are used in this genetic algorithm. In single point crossover method, a random point of chromosome string is selected, and the adjacent points of two chromosomes strings are exchanged to generate two new chromosomes strings. In single point mutation, a random point of chromo some string is selected, and it has probability to change its value. In Fig. 4(a)–(c), the crossover rate and mutation rate are 0.5 and 0.01, respectively. ($pc = 0.5$, $pm = 0.01$). In the case of GA, the optimization process is shown in Fig. 4(a). From this simulation, it can be found that although the first round of investment is generated randomly, the total amount of investment becomes gradually close to the default value of the total investment after nearly 30 generations of searching.

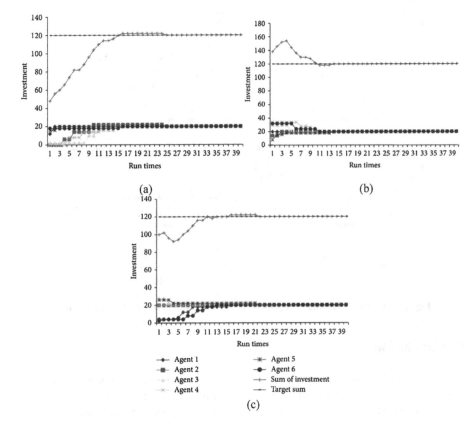

Fig. 4. The total investment results of agent with different initial value of GA ($a = 1$, $b = 1$).

Some representative initial random state simulation results are shown in Fig. 4(b) and (c). From Fig. 3(a)–(c) and Fig. 4(a)–(c), we can see that the statistical result of PSO shows that steady generation is after 21. Thousands of experiments are done based on the same coefficient condition of GA. Statistical result shows that steady generation is between 25 and 35. It can be concluded that the optimal search speed of PSO is faster compared to the GA.

Figure 5 shows the agent and it total investment results with different initial value of GA. In Fig. 5(a) and (b), $a = 1$, $b = 1$, $pc = 0.8$, and $pm = 0.01$. In Fig. 5(c), $a = 1$, $b = 1$, $pc = 0.5$, and $pm = 0.05$. In Fig. 5(d), $a = 1$, $b = 1$, $pc = 0.5$, and $pm = 0.001$. From Fig. 5(a) and (d), it can be observed that the cross rate is higher, and the results converge more quickly. Moreover, the smaller the mutation rate would result in the smaller fluctuation range.

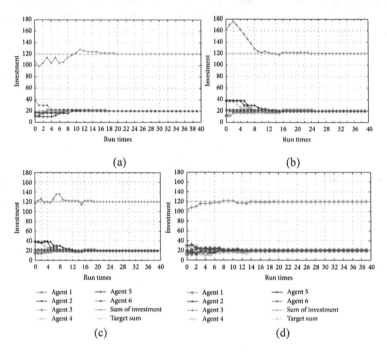

Fig. 5. The total investment results of agent with different initial value of GA.

5   Conclusions

A non-cooperation investment decision-making process based on rational agent was proposed in this paper. An optimal evolution model of individual and overall agents was discussed. By coordinating the balance between overall and individual interests through the iteration of PSO, the unity of the overall and individual interests is completed in the proposed model. In the course of further optimization, the investment sum of each round is decided by each agent. A fitness function coordinating overall interests and individual interests was proposed. Finally, through a large number of experiments and compared with GA, it showed that the proposed algorithm PSO in this paper achieved the expected act with fast response ability.

Acknowledgement. This work was partly supported by the National Natural Science Foundation of China (Grant No. 61572438).

References

1. Rand, D.G., Dreber, A., Ellingsen, T., et al.: Positive interactions promote public cooperation. Science **325**(5945), 1272–1275 (2009)
2. Hauert, C., Doebeli, M.: Spatial structure often inhibits the evolution of cooperation in the snowdrift game. Nature **428**(6983), 643–646 (2004)
3. Wang, Z., Zhang, J.: Agent-based modeling and genetic algorithm simulation for the climate game problem. Math. Probl. Eng. **2012**(8), 1457–1461 (2012)
4. Axelrod, R.: Effective choice in the prisoner's dilemma. J. Conflict Resolut. **24**(1), 3–25 (1980)
5. Axelrod, R., Hamilton, W.D.: The evolution of cooperation. Science **211**(1489), 1390–1396 (1981)
6. Bagnoli, M., McKee, M.: Voluntary contribution games: efficient private provision of public goods. Econ. Inq. **29**(2), 351–366 (1991)
7. Dannenberg, A., Riechmann, T., Stum, B., et al.: Inequity aversion and individual behavior in public good games: an experimental investigation. ZEW-Centre for European Economic Research Discussion Paper No. 07-034 (2007)
8. Hauert, C., Szabó, G.: Prisoner's dilemma and public goods games in different geometries: compulsory versus voluntary interactions. Complexity **8**(4), 31–38 (2003)
9. Doebeli, M., Hauert, C.: Models of cooperation based on the Prisoner's Dilemma and the Snowdrift game. Ecol. Lett. **8**(7), 748–766 (2010)
10. Bosetti, V., Carraro, C., Galeotti, M., et al.: WITCH a world induced technical change hybrid model. Energy J. **27**, 13–37 (2006)
11. Bosetti, V., Carraro, C., Duval, R., et al.: The role of R&D and technology diffusion in climate change mitigation: new perspectives using the witch model. OECD Economics Department Working Papers. FEEM (2009)
12. Hauert, C.: Spatial effects in social dilemmas. J. Theor. Biol. **240**(4), 627–636 (2006)
13. Kagel, J., Roth, A.: The Handbook of Experimental Economic. Handbook of Experimental Economics Results. Princeton University Press, Princeton (1995). 6(3):15
14. Fehr, E., Schmidt, K.: A theory of fairness, competition, and cooperation. J. Econ. **114**(3), 817–868 (1999)
15. Milinski, M., Sommerfeld, R., Krambeck, H., et al.: The collective-risk social dilemma and the prevention of simulated dangerous climate change. Proc. Natl. Acad. Sci. U.S.A. **105**(7), 2291–2294 (2008)
16. Wooldridge, M.: Computationally grounded theories of agency. In: Proceedings of the 4th International Conference on Multiagent Systems, pp. 13–20. IEEE, Boston (2008)
17. Wooldridge, M., Jennings, N.R.: Agent theories, architectures, and languages: a survey. In: Wooldridge, M.J., Jennings, N.R. (eds.) ATAL 1994. LNCS, vol. 890, pp. 1–39. Springer, Heidelberg (1995). https://doi.org/10.1007/3-540-58855-8_1
18. Holt, C.A., Roth, A.: The Nash equilibrium: a perspective. Proc. Natl. Acad. Sci. U.S.A. **101**(12), 3999–4002 (2004)

Use of an Agent-Based Model and Game Theory to Simulate the Behavior of Former Members of the FARC Group in the Reinsertion Process and Peace Agreement in Colombia

Sergio Steven López Martínez[1], Octavio José Salcedo Parra[1,2($\boxtimes$)], and Erika Upegui[3]

[1] Department of Systems and Industrial Engineering, Faculty of Engineering, Universidad Nacional de Colombia, Bogotá D.C., Colombia
{sslopezm, ojsalcedop}@unal.edu.co
[2] Faculty of Engineering, Intelligent Internet Research Group, Universidad Distrital "Francisco José de Caldas", Bogotá D.C., Colombia
osalcedo@udistrital.edu.co
[3] Faculty of Engineering, GRSS-IEEE/UD & GEFEM Research Group, Universidad Distrital "Francisco José de Caldas", Bogotá D.C., Colombia
esupeguic@udistrital.edu.co

Abstract. With the recent signing of the peace agreement in Colombia, we know that a process of reinsertion into the civilian life of the members of the newly dissolved armed group known as FARC will come along with it. Therefore, some doubts remain regarding the success that such reinsertion may have and the effects that it may cause in the Colombian population.

Keywords: Agent · Fuzzy logic · Game theory · Model · NetLogo
Nash balance · Reinsertion

1 Introduction

In this work, different types of reinserted people will be analyzed, through the study of their differential characteristics in order to predict their behavior based on simulations and the effect that the reinsertion process may have in Colombian society. Hence, Colombian citizens can be prepared socially, culturally and economically for the changes that this process may bring to the country. It is important to predict this process in order to set a proper scenario which renders the process less expensive while being more welcoming to the individuals that are introduced into a life as civilians, as well as to other Colombian citizens. The National University of Colombia in its contribution to the peace process has been commissioned to carry out a census [1] over a large group of members of FARC (Revolutionary Armed Forces of Colombia) in order to design reincorporation paths.

© Springer Nature Switzerland AG 2018
Y. Luo (Ed.): CDVE 2018, LNCS 11151, pp. 110–117, 2018.
https://doi.org/10.1007/978-3-030-00560-3_15

2 Background

No records have been found on works discussing models for a reintegration process through agents in NetLogo. However, there are investigations that state the simulation of complex social systems viewed from the humanitarian aspect while others take on the psychological aspect. Some projects are even based on fuzzy logic. A general overview can be found in the book *An Introduction to Agent-Based Modeling: Natural Modeling, Social, and Engineered Complex Systems with NetLogo* written by Ken Khan [2]. The author defines a complex system as a set of elements that interact with each other in order to achieve an objective and in which there is a mutual influence between such elements. This implies that the changes experienced by one element have an impact on the rest of the system. However, what is more striking is that, on one hand, Khan states that in complex social and natural systems new properties emerge that cannot be attributed to the structure (what the system is) nor to its dynamics (what the system does). On the other hand, some of the intrinsic properties of the system are repressed or inhibited. This means that they behave as a whole, in a different way than the individuals that are a part of them. This makes these systems more complex, forcing a thorough research on these individuals not only as individuals but also in terms of their relations with the environment.

The book *Computational Social Psychology* [3] shows formal models presented by multiple psychologists that are implemented in simulations for the research related to the appearance of higher order properties, real-time evolution of the internal states of people and social interactions. Psychologist Robin Vallacher [3] states that agent-based models for the study of social phenomena or problems have great advantages because they have limited knowledge and rationality, enabling a more realistic modeling of the individuals. Despite this fact, it cannot rely entirely on the knowledge of each agent, because even if it is classified thoroughly, human behavior can vary without a clear explanation due to its environment. This could render the description of the model incomplete, which would make the results hard to replicate. In response, Andrzej Nowak suggests in the same article that these unexpected behaviors should also be treated as a model that considers specific situations that may arise. This must take advantage of high-speed machines that shorten the computation processes. Through his e-book, John McCaskill [4] tries to show how important it is to have a vision of the individual characteristics and the risks of a humanitarian intervention. The focus lies on using behavior models and simulations to carry out and evaluate the possible risks and operational strategies to achieve stability and handle counterinsurgency operations in countries with ongoing armed conflicts, including innovative studies on ethical considerations, military participation and non-governmental organizations.

3 Methodology

With data obtained from the census carried out by the National University of Colombia on 10,015 members of the FARC, called the UN-CRN 2017 socioeconomic census delivered on July 6th, a characterization and classification of these members is made based on the occupations in which they are able to work by identifying their skills. The purpose is to capture their future behavior within the system. In addition, cooperative game theory will be used to model the agents' decisions, their interactions and their possible behavior within the system under the NetLogo platform.

The most significant data in the characterization is related to their education, origin, family environment, state of health and job interests during the reinsertion process. In terms of health, it is known that 33% of respondents have some type of physical or mental disability while the remaining 77% have nowhere to live. Additionally, the following information is given (Tables 1, 2 and 3):

Table 1. Data on the education of FARC members - Census UN- CRN 2017

Education level	
Illiteracy	10%
Knows how to read and write	90%
Primary basic education	57%
Secondary education	21%
Vocational secondary education	8%
Higher education	3%

Table 2. Data on the origin of FARC members - Census UN- CRN 2017

Origin zone	
Urban	66%
Rural	19%
Urban Rural	15%

Table 3. Data on job interests of FARC members - Census UN- CRN 2017

Job interests	
Agricultural activities	60%
Housing construction and improvement programs	39%
Road construction and improvement programs	37%
Tourist guide	29%
Illicit crops substitution	28%
Humanitarian demining	27%
Mining	27%

Robert J. Aumann shows evidence in his many works on game theory, specifically in his speech of War and Peace, of the importance of an aspect called the threat of punishment and how it contributes to giving balance in the game as well as in the decision-making process of the players in a long term basis. The players are punished in future stages when there is no cooperation in the current ones, which makes them reconsider their decisions. However, the author also states that the player is dependent on the discount rate, which can be defined as the benefit he would receive if he acted deliberately without seeking cooperation. If the discount rate is low, he will choose to cooperate in order to avoid punishment, but if the discount rate is high, the chances of collaboration decrease considerably. This can be explained by the fact that even if the player has to be punished, the benefit at this point is much higher than the punishment. Finally Aumann concludes with the following theorem: "The results of the nucleus of G coincide with the results of the strong equilibrium of its supergame G∞". This indicates that once all the players achieve a balanced state, none of them think it is convenient to opt for a different strategy because whoever does will not win just by the fact of deviating.

After juggling with the aforementioned aspects and understanding the reinsertion process that is going to be carried out as well as characterizing the agents, it can be stated that the best strategy to handle this situation is to quickly establish a balance between the players, in order to make it easier to maintain it during the entire process. Therefore, a game is proposed which is solely based on the decisions of each individual. This will take place at the time of reinsertion, when the individual is able to choose between behaving correctly while abiding by the law or a delinquent path living as an outlaw. The approach of the game is detailed (Table 4):

Table 4. Design of the cooperative game for reinsertion

	Legal Behavior (LB)	Behavior Outside the law (IB)
Legal	3	2
Behavior (LB)	3	0
Behavior	0	1
Outside the law (IB)	2	1

The game is called Reinsertion Behavior or RB and is based on the studies of Aumann and Nash. It should cause the system to reach a state of balance, because when the players choose to cooperate with good behavior, it makes sure that they receive help from the government in the reinsertion process. With a bad behavior, the player may have a momentary profit, but he would lose the help and be involved in a criminal procedure against him, thus generating the threat of punishment. This will be seen later on with the introduction of a "reputation" system that will generate incentives and punishments based on the player's behavior, who would seek to raise this feature. In this approach, we assume the possible events: when two individuals with legal behavior meet, they will not harm each other in any way. This encounter could lead to a more stable cooperation and development in society. Therefore, in this case, both agents increase their reputation by 3, which is the highest increase in cooperative nature. The following event involves the encounter between an individual with illegal behavior and one with legal behavior. From a logical observation of the Colombian scenery, it is clear that the offender has greater success and increases his reputation by 2, because the well-behaved citizen can be affected in multiple ways. For this reason, it is assumed that illegal behavior in this specific interaction is stronger and leads to more benefits, leaving the legally-behaved individual out of the context. Finally, the encounter between two criminals does not represent a benefit for any of them. It is only a waste of time and becomes a more complex matter, because they think that they can lose benefits if they meet each other. Hence, such encounter is awarded with a value of 1. In addition, we must consider that when working with agents, they not only have an initial behavior based on decisions but they can also change their behavior due to the interaction with the other individuals of the system and the system itself. Therefore, during simulation, each player will be represented with a color, where green indicates legal behavior and red indicates outlaw behavior. When two agents are found, they will be affected by the game, thereby affecting their reputation (Fig. 1).

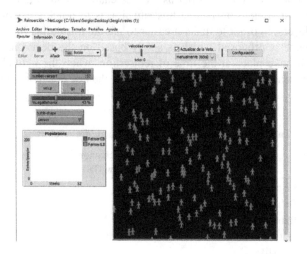

Fig. 1. Initial State of simulation for reinsertion in NetLogo. Source: Authors

The simulation environment is shown in the figure (Fig. 2), where the generation of the reinserted people can be seen with an initial neutral state and an initial probability of their behaviors. From this point forward, multiple simulations will be performed to see the results of the system, which will be evaluated later.

4   Evaluation of Results

After performing multiple simulations, three types of scenarios were determined:

1. *Positive scenario*: In this scenario, a probability of legal behavior on behalf of the agents was detected at 72% and upwards. It is evident that it is the most desired behavior and it indicates that the process was successful, which results in Nash equilibrium. The predominance of positive behavior and how the interactions within the system contribute to cooperation, such behavior is validated as the best strategy for agents. Although it might not indicate a resounding success because some of the agents remain as outlaws, if it can be translated into the real world, then the process can controlled in a better way by quickly eradicating illegal behavior

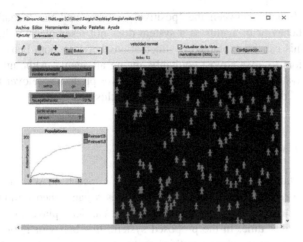

Fig. 2. Simulation for the 'positive' scenario. Source: Authors

2. *Negative scenario:* This is the least favorable scenario where the probability of legal behavior is less than 43% and most of the reinserted guerrillas adopt an outlaw behavior as time passes. As seen in the positive scenario, the reverse behavior is still in place for some agents. However, there is a clear predominance on the number of agents with negative behaviors within the system; this scenario is translated into reality as there is an increase in insecurity and delinquency, as well as a failure of the reintegration process and some aspects of the peace treaty. Interestingly, this scenario also results in Nash equilibrium, because it does not imply that the result was more convenient for the participants as a whole but it only involves the individual results (Fig. 3).

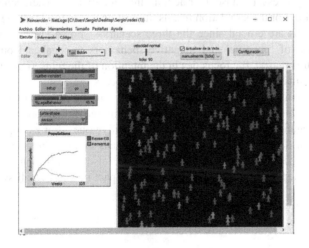

Fig. 3. Simulation for the 'negative' scenario. Source: Authors

3. *Unfinished:* Exactly between the 'positive' scenario and the 'negative' scenario ranges, the behavior of agents as a system does not resemble to either of the two scenarios. This can be explained by fluctuations between both behaviors, causing these behaviors to arise almost equitably among all agents. Although it gives balance to the system, where one behavior will never predominate over the other, the scenario itself does not lead to an accurate conclusion.

5   Discussion of Results

It is really important to mention Robert J. Aumann's speech on War and Peace [5] to understand these results. In his speech, he proposes a game theory model that gives great importance to repetition, and how this aspect can lead players to opt for cooperative behavior over time. In the proposed system, this behavior is present for both main scenarios and it is seen how repetition makes the agents choose the behavior with higher reputation. This makes sense since they interact the most with such behavior and therefore assume is the correct one. Even though the 'positive' and 'negative' scenarios are opposite cases, they share this particular characteristic. However, the 'unfinished' scenario shows no repetition because even if the game is repeated over time, players have different states that affect future decisions and having a wide variety of these individuals with different behaviors, with which they can interact, makes the repetition to not act correctly. They do not assume any of the two behaviors as the correct one, and they make decisions based on individuality, causing the cooperation mentioned by Aumann to not occur.

6   Conclusions

- It is concluded that reinserted people have most of the responsibility for the success of the entire process, because their actions are unpredictable when being introduced to civilian life. For the simulation results, it must be understood that the decisions of the individuals are crucial since the three scenarios shown are built on an initial establishment of 'positive' and 'negative' behaviors as legal and outlaw respectively. For this reason, the focus lies in the intention of the reinserted which can also become the main obstacle of the reinsertion process.
- The government and the organizations that carry out the process must aim all their efforts at organizing, controlling and managing the initial process in order to minimize negative behaviors and encourage positive ones. For example, they could adopt programs that check up on these individuals and can help them to reincorporate into civilian life. In that manner, they can also control their actions and the possible missteps that could have a negative impact on the overall system.

References

1. Rueda de prensa censo Socio-económico UN-CRN (2017). http://www.reintegracion.gov.co/es/sala-de-prensa/SiteAssets/Presentacion%20rueda%20de%20prensa%20Julio%206%202017.pdf
2. Kahn, K.: An introduction to agent-based modeling: modeling natural, social, and engineered complex systems with NetLogo. Phys. Today **8**, 55 (2015)
3. Vallacher, R.R., Read, S.J., Nowak, A.: Computational Social Psychology. Routledge, New York (2017)
4. McCaskill, J.: Agent-Based Modeling in Humanitarian Interventions: Emerging Research and Opportunities. Information Science Reference, Hershey (2017)
5. Guerra y paz Fundación Nobel 2005, versión del discurso pronunciado por el profesor Robert J. Aumann y Thomas C. Schelling (2005)

Joint Digital Simulation Platforms for Safety and Preparedness

Maryna Solesvik[1(✉)], Odd Jarl Borch[1], and Yuriy Kondratenko[2]

[1] Nord University Business School, Nord University, P.O. Box 1490, 8049 Bodø, Norway
mzs@hvl.no, odd.j.borch@nord.no
[2] Petro Mohyla Black Sea National University, Mykolaiv 54000, Ukraine
y_kondrat2002@yahoo.com

Abstract. We present a case study of joint digital simulator in a virtual campus that aims to use cloud-based technology to facilitate management of knowledge from different actors and competence development of personnel that will be engaged in search and rescue operations in the High North.

Keywords: Digital simulation platform · Visualization · Maritime industry Interfirm collaboration · Cloud-based technology

1 Introduction

Digitalization is one of the key priority areas of the Norwegian maritime industry [1]. Modern ICT technologies open unique possibilities for a new era of functional solutions in the maritime sector from remotely operated vessels to autonomous ships. One area of innovation is the interaction between shore and sea-based services, i.e. coordination and control, including planning, testing and training the elements of these services. Simulator technology can be an excellent bridge from pure virtual simulations to real-time remote control over the vessels. Shipping companies operating in remote waters like the Arctic regions face different challenges such as operational planning and continuous training [4]. Long distances to education infrastructure together with extra demands to planning, competences, and renewal of certificates call for flexible planning and training platforms. This study has the objective to illuminate the challenges and opportunities related to joint simulation platforms integrating 3rd party emergency response technology with maritime simulators.

Through the creation of an open, secure and collaborative simulator platform, exploiting advanced digital infrastructure, the vessels may have access to high-end shore-based simulators integrated with vessel technology on board. The added value is related to fast and flexible competence development through training opportunities and simulator opportunities that may facilitate safe navigation and increase operational efficiency. The solutions may also serve as a platform for joint operations in case of emergencies. Crisis and emergency response demand close cooperation between shore, air and sea-based units. The simulator resources may contribute to finding optimal solutions for joint operations in different sea areas. It may also provide training

Y. Luo (Ed.): CDVE 2018, LNCS 11151, pp. 118–125, 2018.
https://doi.org/10.1007/978-3-030-00560-3_16

facilities for both shore and sea-based personnel. Joint digital simulation platforms allow the collaboration between the faculty at universities, training centres and real vessels in operation, and will facilitate shared simulation activities. The solution will be useful for maritime education and training universities and schools, and commercial simulator centres, promoting university-business cooperation [2]. It may also improve the resources available for shipping companies and rescue services, in case of emergencies through integrating computer systems and this may facilitate optimal emergency response solutions. The main research question of this study is: How can safety and emergency preparedness for vessels in remote areas like the Polar Regions be increased through improving the competencies of the vessel crews with the help of cloud-based platforms and simulators?

The paper is organized in the following way. In Sect. 2, we explain theoretical background of the study related to collaboration and digital simulation technology. In Sect. 3, we present the Method used in this study. In Sect. 4, we demonstrate an illustrative case study showing how the collaborative IT simulation technology contributes to the solution of search and rescue operations in Northern Norway. Finally, we present conclusions as well as theoretical and practical implications.

2   Knowledge and Competence Management with the Help of Digital Platforms Technology in the Maritime Industry

2.1   Knowledge Management

The importance of ICT tools in the knowledge economy is recognized by firms and organizations that have made significant investments into the development and implementation of ICT applications [3]. The implementation of ICTs to support collaborative knowledge management in automobile and manufacturing industries has proved to be effective [4]. However, the application of knowledge management ICT in other industries (such as, construction) has not been so successful [5]. Scholars argue that managing knowledge using ICTs is not an easy task and it is difficult to leverage knowledge using an ICT [6].

Knowledge management is a significant interdisciplinary field of research. Knowledge management is defined as a method that facilitates the process of sharing, distributing, creating, obtaining and understanding a firm's knowledge [7]. Knowledge is often divided into explicit and tacit [8]. Explicit knowledge in the maritime preparedness context consists of documents, instructions and plans that are easy to communicate through and share between people. Tacit knowledge is not straightforwardly visible and expressible. It is difficult to communicate and share tacit knowledge [9]. Tacit knowledge, related to maritime preparedness consists of experience and expertise, lessons learned from prior operations, expert suggestions, knowledge and innovations [10]. ICT solutions enable knowledge management. Lindvall *et al.* [11] have identified three groups of ICT-enabled tools that are relevant for knowledge management: tools for collaboration, tools for managing documents and content, and tools for managing competence. However, it is recognized that ICT solutions shall be developed and implemented effectively in order to support knowledge management.

Otherwise, ICT solutions will not be useful for knowledge management and knowledge will not be leveraged by organizations properly [6].

2.2 Competence Management

The competence-based perspective considers a firm as a bundle of competences that may be stretched out across the business. Five ingredients of the competence are recognized, relating to stand-alone assets (i.e. both tangible and intangible assets which can be sold or acquired); cognitive capabilities, which embrace individual and collective knowledge, individual skills, technologies and know-how, patents; processes and routines which coordinate the organization's operations; organizational structure; and the behavioural and cultural dimension, such as shared values and beliefs [12]. This study explores this gap in the knowledge base related to competence management. Prior research into competence-based view suggests that a firm, as an open system, may link firm resources, capabilities and competences in strategic alliance networks in order to respond to quickly changing market opportunities.

The competence-based view distinguishes between competence leveraging and competence building. The competence-based approach recognizes that a firm can leverage firm-specific and firm-addressable resources and competences to achieve goals and competitive advantage. Firm-addressable competences may be obtained through market transactions or through strategic alliances. In a network, members have immediate access to necessary competences without the need to invest in developing these competences internally. Competence building implies qualitative changes in the existing asset stocks and flows as well as abilities to coordinate and deploy new and existing assets in order to achieve firm's goals. Competence building influences on the industry dynamics. Firms identify and seek to change desirable changes in stocks and flows of assets through learning. Organizational learning may be realized through partnerships and collaboration. Furthermore, through the lens of the shipbuilding industry's cyclicality [13], the competence leveraging and competence building alliances might be considered as contra-cyclical activities.

3   Method

The unit of analysis in this study is a strategic alliance in the form of virtual campus. A strategic alliance is formed by maritime educational institutions and an industrial firm and is aimed to create a joint digital simulation platform. The strategic alliance is therefore a suitable unit of analysis when studying the processes of cooperation. This study analyzes how ICT-enabled collaborative management system facilitates (a) interorganizational collaboration and (b) serves training and education purposes for safety preparedness and rescue operations.

The empirical data was obtained in 2017 from observations of the virtual campus activities in Northern Norway. The narratives of the involved managers from universities and a firm were also used. Information available on the Internet was also used to triangulate and supplement basic information from the observations and narratives. Few studies have examined how ICTs may facilitate interfirm collaboration [14–16].

This study will empirically explore the role of ICT systems with regard to collaboration during preparedness and rescue operations. The role of ICTs in reducing coordination costs and improving knowledge management during the collaboration process will be explored in the case study in the next section.

4 Case Study: Join Digital Simulator for Safety and Preparedness

The demand for the highly qualified personnel is growing in the world. The level of technical advancement and sophistication of ship technology is steadily growing. Personnel should thus have advanced engineering and technology knowledge and skills in order to manage modern vessels. Crew on board can also meet different novel threats (like terror attacks or Green Peace actions). On the other hand, technology also offers new possibilities for visualization, virtual reality and simulation. One of such tools is a ship simulator. Ship simulators are used to train young specialists and keep qualified crew up-to-date. There are different types of ship simulators, i.e. a navigation simulator, an engine room simulator, a dynamic positioning simulator, and others. Notably, simulators are expensive. This means that single organizations or universities can afford only one or a limited number of simulators. In this case, several organizations may be interested to combine their simulator facilities using Kongsberg's Kognifai system (Fig. 1). Novel cloud-based technology makes it possible to combine several different simulators located in different places.

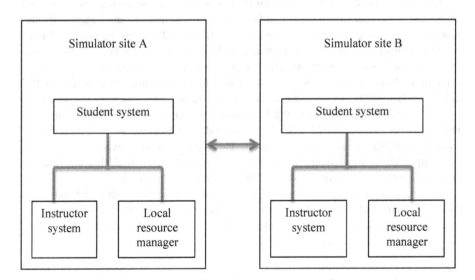

Fig. 1. Kognifai for simulation connectivity

This idea was successfully realized in Northern Norway. The first trials to join three simulators were carried out in 2017. The virtual campus concept has linked simulators situated in one University and two maritime schools. Each of them has a unique simulator. They share navigation and emergency modules. One maritime school owns an oil spill preparedness simulator. The second maritime school acquired a dynamic positioning simulator for operations in emergency situations and the University got a new part-task ship's bridge simulator with visual scenes, command and control systems and log systems, which are essential in crisis management education and training. The second goal of joining simulator facilities is to provide training for joint rescue and safety operations. Linking different actors via cloud-based facilities will allow orchestrate activities of different actors to be involved, that are similar to real rescue operations where different services are involved. The utilization of cloud-based technology will make it possible to collect data and process it, as well as to connect the navigation, safety, security and other decision-support systems of the vessels.

As per April 2018, we have carried out 8 exercises connecting three simulators at three educational institutions using broadband at one region in the North of Norway. The exercises were carried out in three waves. The very first wave was carried out from December 2017 until January 2018 and was devoted to trials to connect. It was the first attempt to connect navigational simulators in the world. There were trials and mistakes. However, the attempt is estimated to be successful. The second wave was devoted to joint exercises in oil recovery in the sea, search and rescue operations, communication, and collaborative decision-making. The third wave included exercises 7 and 8. There were 63 and 43 participants in three campuses respectively in Exercise 7 and 8. The goal for this exercise was to develop collaboration skills. The Universities in Canada and the US expressed interest to carry out joint exercises.

The first conclusions after the initial trials said that the connection via broadband functioned well. There were some conflicts between new and old simulation software. However, the University and maritime schools have made a new contract and have agreed to deliver new simulator parts that would substitute old simulators with the new ones. This will solve the incompatibility problem. Parties expressed very positive impressions from the first trials. They underlined that the learning process was fruitful and the collaboration between the campuses and Kongsberg was very useful for all sides. The collaboration between the University and maritime schools started in 2016 and it was very successful as well. Parties consider joint operations and their collaboration in general as a win-win situation. The joint simulation exercises were also highly appreciated by students from the three campuses. They think that they learned more during the three-campus exercises than from individual exercises.

To allow the enabling of integrated systems, the partnership will collaborate with industrial firms and organizations. Such collaboration would be enabled by cloud technology at all stages from data collection to storage through analytics. The virtual simulator platform will enable:

(1) Safe operation planning through simulations of search and rescue and other emergency response operation patterns, using integrated simulator-navigation planning.
(2) The increase of situational awareness and efficient shore-vessel decision-making in emergency response actions through connecting different subsystems including safety management systems, maintenance systems and administrative systems in the cloud.

(3) SAR and oil spill response mission coordinator tools facilitating simulation of emergency prevention, preparedness and response through integration of command and control systems, log systems and vessel simulator systems.

(4) Flexible training facilities for personnel at sea integrated with university and training center's faculty for both certificate and emergency response training.

The joint digital simulation platform is built upon the digital-twin ship concept. This will be important in integrated operations at sea, for example for search and rescue operations. So far, the actors involved in SAR operations do not have access to each other's data. Notably, this is a threatening situation since during critical situations at sea, when each second counts on the rescue of people's lives, time is used to collect information that is available at other actors and different data streams are coordinated. The creation of a platform that collects and presents the situation image of all relevant actors gives all involved parties instant access to real time data. The implementation of the digital platform will lead to cost reduction during rescue operations.

In the future, we expect to connect simulators to the vessels in the sea and to carry out training, as well as search and rescue operations together with experienced crew members. Next, the information from different actors, at the moment, is not shared. The goal of the joint digital platform would be to serve as a platform for collecting and analyzing the existing data coming from different actors (police, rescue company, shipping companies, coast guard, etc.) (Fig. 2).

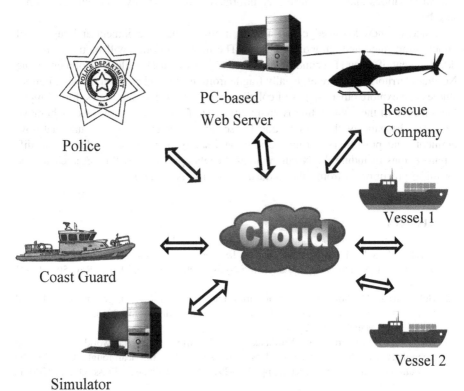

Fig. 2. Functional structure of the joint digital platform for the future.

5 Conclusions

Digitalization has been named one of the strategically important areas of the Norwegian maritime industry. Modern ICT technologies create unique possibilities for many industries, including the maritime sector [17–19]. Green ICT technologies will be very important in a new era in the maritime sector from remotely operated vessels to autonomous ships [20]. Maritime simulators may be excellent bridges from pure virtual simulations to real-time remote control over the vessels. This research focuses on virtual collaboration of Universities, maritime schools, shipping companies, the coast guard, and other stakeholders responsible for safe navigation in the Arctic area. The Norwegian Government pays significant attention to the issues of maritime safety and preparedness. Norway can be named an innovation leader in the safety, preparedness and sustainability areas. The research question that has guided our research was: How can safety and emergency preparedness for vessels in remote areas like the Polar Regions be increased through improving the capabilities of the vessels to interlink through cloud-based platforms with the mainstream shore-based simulators?

In this study, we explained how the connection of virtual simulators would contribute to the development of skills of maritime personnel on board and cooperating organizations onshore necessary in case of critical situations in the sea. The new cloud-based digital simulation technology will allow training personnel to act in possible critical situations and share necessary information possessed by different actors on a safe basis.

Later, the new knowledge will also be useful in the development and support of remotely-operated and autonomous ships. The new knowledge will be useful for the development of green IT technologies, aimed to support sustainable development of the Northern territories that are especially fragile from the ecological point of view. Further studies can explore other aspects of collaboration using ICT technologies, for example, the selection of the right partner is vitally important for the success of the collaborative venture. The paper will be interesting for scientists, representatives of national governments and practitioners from maritime and safety preparedness industries in different regions including the Northern areas. Insights provided by this research will be useful to practitioners from other industries that use simulators.

References

1. Borch, O.J., Solesvik, M.Z.: Innovation on the open sea: examining competence transfer and open innovation in the design of offshore vessels. Technol. Innov. Manag. Rev. 5(9), 17–22 (2015)
2. Gulbrandsen, M., Solesvik, M.: Comparing university-industry linkages in two industrial clusters in Norway. In: Academy of Management Proceedings, vol. 2015, no. 1, p. 18826. Academy of Management (2015)
3. Knox, H., O'Doherty, D., Vurdibakis, T., Westrup, C.: Screenworlds: information technology and the performance of business knowledge. In: Scarbrough, H. (ed.) The Evolution of Business Knowledge, pp. 273–292. Oxford University Press, Oxford (2008)

4. Dave, B., Koskela, L.: Collaborative knowledge management - a construction case study. Autom. Constr. **18**, 894–902 (2009)
5. Al-Ghassani, A.M.: Literature review on km tools. Report, Department of Civil and Building Engineering, Loughborough University, Loughborough, United Kingdom (2002)
6. Solesvik, M.: A collaborative design in shipbuilding: two case studies. In: 2007 5th IEEE International Conference on Industrial Informatics, vol. 1. IEEE (2007)
7. Davenport, T.H., Prusak, L.: Working Knowledge: How Organizations Manage What They Know. Harvard Business School Press, Boston (1998)
8. Amin, A., Cohendet, P.: Architectures of Knowledge: Firms, Capabilities, and Communities. Oxford University Press, Oxford (2004)
9. Polanyi, M.: The Tacit Dimension. Anchor, Garden City (1967)
10. Zhang, X., Mao, X., AbouRizk, S.M.: Developing a knowledge management system for improved value engineering practices in the construction industry. Autom. Constr. **18**(6), 777–789 (2009)
11. Lindvall, M., Rus, I., Jammalamadaka, R., Thakker, R.: Software tools for knowledge management. In: Proceedings of DACS State-of-the-Art Report (2001). https://www.thedacs.com/techs/abstracts/abstract.php?dan=347159
12. Durand, T.: Strategizing for innovation: competence analysis in assessing strategic chance. In: Heene, A., Sanchez, R. (eds.) Competence-Based Strategic Management, pp. 127–150. Wiley, Chichester (1997)
13. Solesvik, M.: Interfirm collaboration in the shipbuilding industry: the shipbuilding cycle perspective. Int. J. Bus. Syst. Res. **5**(4), 388–405 (2011)
14. Solesvik M., Kondratenko Y., Kondratenko G., Sidenko I., Kharchenko V., Boyarchuk A.: Fuzzy decision support systems in marine practice. In: IEEE International Conference on Fuzzy Systems (FUZZ-IEEE), 9 July 2017, pp. 1–6. IEEE (2017)
15. Encheva, S., Kondratenko, Y., Solesvik, M.Z., Tumin, S.: Decision support systems in logistics. In: AIP Conference Proceedings, vol. 1060, no. 1, pp. 254–256. AIP (2008)
16. Borch, O.J., Solesvik, M.Z.: Collaborative design of advanced vessel technology for offshore operations in arctic waters. In: Luo, Y. (ed.) CDVE 2013. LNCS, vol. 8091, pp. 157–160. Springer, Heidelberg (2013). https://doi.org/10.1007/978-3-642-40840-3_23
17. Borch, O.J., Solesvik, M.Z.: Partner selection versus partner attraction in R&D strategic alliances: the case of the Norwegian shipping industry. Int. J. Technol. Mark. **11**(4), 421–439 (2016)
18. Solesvik, M.Z., Encheva, S.: Partner selection for interfirm collaboration in ship design. Ind. Manag. Data Syst. **110**(5), 701–717 (2010)
19. Solesvik, M., Gulbrandsen, M.: Partner selection for open innovation. Technol. Innov. Manag. Rev. **3**(4), 11–16 (2013)
20. Solesvik, M.: Partner selection in green innovation projects. In: Berger-Vachon, C., Gil, L. A., Kacprzyk, J., Kondratenko, Y., Merigó, J., Morabito, C. (eds.) Complex Systems: Solutions and Challenges in Economics, Management and Engineering, vol. 125, pp. 471–480. Springer, Cham (2018). https://doi.org/10.1007/978-3-319-69989-9_28

IIS-MSP: An Intelligent Interactive System of Patrol Robot with Multi-source Perception

Xin-Wei Yao$^{(\boxtimes)}$ ⓘ, Meng-Na Zhang, Hang-Jie Zhang,
Chao-Chao Wang, Qiang Li, and Wei Huang

College of Computer Science and Technology,
Zhejiang University of Technology, Hangzhou 310023, China
{xwyao,mnzhang,zhanghj,ccwang,
qiangli,huangwei}@zjut.edu.cn

Abstract. In recent years, the quality requirement of power supply has been significantly increased in smart grid industry. As most of the current substations are in an unattended or under-represented state, it is difficult for us to detect the defect of power equipment and other potential safety hazards in time. To solve this problem, we propose an intelligent interactive system based on patrol robots which have multi-source perceptions. Our proposed system consists of three main parts: a Backstage Management System that is designed for data analysis, image processing, automatic alarms and scheduling optimization; an automatic Patrol Robot System that is capable of path planning, image recognition and speech signal processing; and finally a Communication System which enables communication between human and robots, as well as the cooperation between different patrol robots.

Keywords: Patrol robots · Multi-source perception · Machine perception
Interactive system

1 Introduction

Typically, in a traditional substation, inspection tasks are often completed by the substation staffs. They detect the transformer equipment and record the relative information of the equipment in a quality standard inspection workbook by using sensors and a number of matching test instruments. However, there are many drawbacks of the traditional manual patrol inspection, such as high labor intensity, low work efficiency, high management cost, human negligence, and so on [1]. With the gradual maturity of robot technology, using robots to complete difficult operations and high precision work are increasingly considered by industry. Japan is among the first batch of countries which successfully implement 500 kV substation robot inspection and realize automatic measurement of equipment temperature with infrared sensors in the 1990s [2, 3]. In China, a number of intelligent patrol robots running along 10 kV to 500 kV overhead conductors/ground lines developed by Wuhan University in the first decade of 21st century, have already been successfully applied in many power supply companies [4]. The integrated automation system of substations will replace or update the traditional substation secondary system, which has become the new development direction and

Y. Luo (Ed.): CDVE 2018, LNCS 11151, pp. 126–133, 2018.
https://doi.org/10.1007/978-3-030-00560-3_17

trend of power system. The objective of this paper is to develop an intelligent interactive system based on patrol robots which have multi-source perception for inspection of substation equipment. The new generation of robots is more efficient in inspection. Especially, our system can achieve the linkage operations with the subsystems, which builds an information contact and sharing platform between machines.

2 System Design

2.1 System Structure

The proposed intelligent interactive system of patrol robots with multi-source perception (IIS-MSP, as shown in Fig. 1) is composed of a Backstage Management System (BMS), a Patrol Robot System (PRS) and a Communication System (CS). The BMS consists of four subsystems, which are designed for data analysis, image processing, automatic alarms and scheduling optimization respectively. The host, server and industrial switch are connected to the wireless network through a wireless AP. The PRS consists of a shape module, a chassis motion module, a main control module, a communication module, a battery management module, and a sensor module. The sensor module consists of a laser radar sensor, an integrated pan, a visible light camera, a thermal infrared imager and so on, all of which are connected to the main control module for integrated control. The main control module is connected to the industrial switch and wireless AP to realize the wireless network connection and data transmission with the monitoring background.

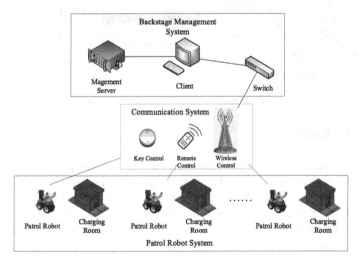

Fig. 1. The structure of the inspection system

Through the CS, which is composed of a key control, a remote control and a wireless control, the substation staffs can control the patrol robots to perform different missions, and the BMS is able to interact with the patrol robots. The computer network of the central control room is mainly equipped with LAN for data transmission and communication control while the patrol robots outside the substation mainly communicate with the control center through the wireless network [5, 6]. AP nodes are deployed outside the substation to achieve wireless network coverage and integrated into the wireless LAN. In addition, the robot itself is equipped with a universal wireless router. In the case of AP wireless network coverage, the self-positioning information and working status of the patrol robots can be smoothly reflected on the control host.

2.2   Design and Implementation

The framework of overall research technology is shown in Fig. 2. Firstly, a basic trackless navigation system, including autonomous charging and obstacle avoidance, constitutes a comprehensive system. On this basis, the mutual cooperation between machines is realized, so is the implementation of the intelligent inspection includes the inspection path planning, intelligent meter reading, foreign object suspension detection, and abnormal sound detection [7]. Secondly, a network communication system is established for data transmission between patrol robots and a monitoring background. Finally, the storage of basic data and patrol data, the human-computer interaction interface, and data analysis functions such as inspection reports and historical data curves are implemented by the development of system software and database.

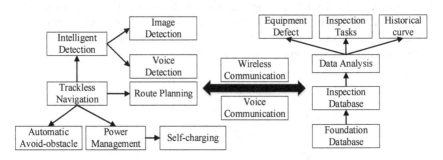

Fig. 2. Framework of overall research technology

3   Key Technology

The patrol robots receive their missions from the CS, and then perform the missions correspondingly. Each patrol robot has to refine its missions, and then plan its routes and paths, coordinate the resulting plans and paths with other robots and execute all these actions (such as image detection, voice detection, etc.), monitor critical situations (such as unknown obstacles), and report unrecoverable action failure (such as automatic alarm, most of which requires operators' assistance) to the BMS [8].

3.1   Path Planning

According to the robot's mastery of the patrol environment information, path planning problems can be divided into two categories: the global path planning and the local path planning [9]. In the global path planning, after the robot obtains the environment information through its laser, a map model is established by using visible image method. In the known map model, the robot uses search algorithms to find a route that meets the planning conditions. Based on the global path planning, the local planning method plans the moving path of the robot in real time and realizes the robot's self-moving without touching in the substation according to the environmental information detected by ultrasonic sensors. Considering the complex patrol environment of sub-stations, the results of global path planning and the local path planning are combined to assist the robot to complete its self-moving without touching.

3.2 Image Recognition

By applying the image recognition technique, our system is capable of automatically collecting, identifying, recording the meter readings and determining whether there is an abnormal operation. Later, the system will process the thermal imaging image, compare and judge the historical records, and make fault diagnosis and early warning. We divide the image recognition method into two categories: namely the meter recognition and the transmission line abnormality recognition.

A. Meter Recognition

In this paper, the Meter recognition includes two parts which are meter scale recognition and digital character recognition.

- **Meter scale recognition:** Typically, image preprocessing is used to obtain a clear binary image, which can then be used to extract characteristic of image and guarantee that follow-up pointer recognition is efficient and precise. The main steps are shown in Fig. 3. After that, Hough transform is utilized to get pointer angle, at last the reading of the pointer will be calculated using the proportional formula of angles and scale value of instruments.

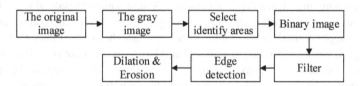

Fig. 3. Procession of image processing

- **Digital character recognition:** According to the prior knowledge of digital characters, a projection algorithm is used to divide the characters, and then the structural features are used to identify single characters. The reading area consists of multiple digits arranged in a regular pattern and the digits are fixed in a LCD screen. Before entering the recognizer, the digits to be recognized in the reading area of the meter must be divided into individual numeric characters.

The proposed image recognition technique has the following advantages: work well in real-time, high precision and low time-consuming, which is quite significant to the practical application in engineering.

B. Transmission Line Abnormality Recognition

- **HD graphics:** The patrol robots will capture high-definition graphics of the relevant equipment. The substation staffs can visually check the operation status of the equipment and observe whether the equipment is defective.
- **Infrared temperature measurement:** The infrared heat map of wall-through sleeve is shown in Fig. 4. The interior of the cable, porcelain insulators, porcelain insulating pillars and diversion elements will generate heat during operation. According to the photograph taken by the infrared camera, the distribution of the temperature field on the surface of the equipment and the temperature rise condition can be grasped. By combining the Infrared temperature information, the substation staffs can diagnose equipment failures.

Fig. 4. Infrared heat map of wall-through sleeve

3.3   Speech Signal Processing

In addition to image recognition, IIS-MSP is also capable of speech signal processing. Figure 5 is a schematic diagram of substation equipment's operation status detected by signal processing and identification techniques. Sound source signals of the substation electrical equipment are collected using a microphone array. The microphone array can effectively suppress ambient noise interference and aim the beam at the target signal to obtain a good device operating sound signal. Owing to the sounds emitted by these interference sources and electrical equipment are statistically independent, an independent component analysis (ICA) is proposed to separate useful electrical equipment sound signals and to extract characteristics of these separated sound signals. By checking working sound characteristics library of the equipment, we could easily identify if the collected equipment working sound is within the normal working range. If the collected sound beyond a certain range, an alarm will ring and the substation staffs will be informed accordingly. Finally, clear voice communication is realized by PRS, which has the advantages of good reliability and low cost.

3.4   Data Analysis

Typically, a patrol robot has to inspect different lines multiple times, and obtain a lot of on-site information during each inspection. The substation staffs will not only have a large workload but also be prone to errors if these large numbers of patrol inspection

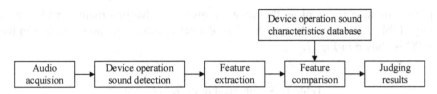

Fig. 5. Signal process flow

data are managed and diagnose manually. Therefore, it is necessary to establish a comprehensive backstage management system for robot inspections.

All the information files are stored in the local memory and named as "line name-detection number-time", which is obtained by the patrol robots. The BMS identifies the file name and automatically imports it into the background to associates it with the inspection database. The acquired information can be divided into instrument pictures, line picture, audio information, etc. Different kinds of files are respectively stored in different databases, and will be analyzed by the system. If an abnormality occurs in the diagnosis, the system will alarm. All the equipment defect reports, the inspection task reports and the temperature history curves are generated automatically by the system. All the data, including diagnostic results, are archived and users can easily access queries and print required reports when needed.

4 Experiment Result

The patrol robots have been successfully applied in 35 kV step-down station in Bei-touzui, China. This station is equipped with two patrol robots and two charging rooms (as shown in Fig. 6). There are 486 inspection points, 51 inspection locations and 13 local turning points. A patrol robot will perform a full mission inspection (approximately 150 min) every morning, afternoon and evening respectively. After the

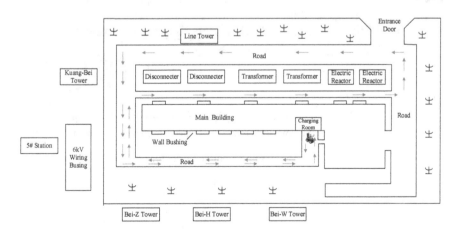

Fig. 6. Schematic diagram of patrolling path of mobile robot

inspection mission is complete, the robot returns to the charging room to recharge its battery. Table 1 illustrates the specification of a patrol robot. The user interface in the host PC is shown in Fig. 7.

Table 1. Specification of the patrol robot

Item	Specification
Dimension	Length: 900 mm Width: 560 mm Height: 1400 mm
Weight	≤ 80 kg
Navigation method	3D trackless navigation
Positioning accuracy	Lateral: ± 10 mm Longitudinal: ± 10 mm
Speed	0–60 m/min, Bidirectional
Gradeability	$15°$
Ingress protection ratings	IP55
Editable inspection point	≥ 4000
Battery life	≥ 8 h

Digital map   Mission calendar

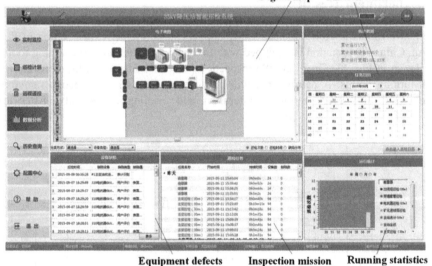

Equipment defects   Inspection mission   Running statistics

Fig. 7. User interface running in the host PC

5 Conclusion

In this paper, an intelligent interaction system of patrol robot with multi-source perception is proposed. Particularly, the success of 35 kV step-down station inspection robot project has accumulated valuable experience for researches and applications of intelligent inspection robots with larger inspection area and complex inspection path environment. At the same time, it also provides guidance and suggestions for the promotion and application of the wireless grid inspection system in the future.

Acknowledgments. This work was supported by the National Natural Science Foundation of China (NSFC) under Grant No. 61772471 and 61771430.

References

1. Cui, H., Zhou, L., Han, G.: Development and application of intelligent patrol system for power substation. Agricult. Sci. Technol. Equip. **5**, 27–29 (2012)
2. Takahashi, H.: Development of patrolling robot for substation. IERE Council, Special Document R-8903. 10:19, Japan (1989)
3. Nakashima, M., Yakabe, H., Maruyama, Y., Yano, K.: Application of semi-automatic robot technology on hot-line maintenance work. In: Proceedings of Distribution 2000, vol. 1, pp. 843–850 (1995)
4. Wu, G., Xiao, H., Xiao, X., Huang, Z., Li, Y. Transmission line inspection robot and deicing robot: key technologies, prototypes and applications. In: International Conference on Applied Robotics for the Power Industry, pp. 1–6. IEEE (2010)
5. Balch, T., Arkin, R.C.: Communication in reactive multiagent robotic systems. Auton. Rob. **1** (1), 27–52 (1994)
6. Alami, R., Fleury, S., Herrb, M., Ingrand, F.: Multi-robot cooperation in the martha project. Robot. Autom. Mag. **5**(1), 36–47 (1988)
7. Floreano, D., Godjevac, J., Martinoli, A., Mondada, F., Nicoud, J.D.: Design, control, and applications of autonomous mobile robots. In: Tzafestas, S.G. (ed.) Advances in Intelligent Autonomous Systems, vol. 18, pp. 159–186. Springer, Dordrecht (1999). https://doi.org/10.1007/978-94-011-4790-3_8
8. Khamis, A., Hussein, A., Elmogy, A.: Multi-robot task allocation: a review of the state-of-the-art. In: Koubâa, A., Martínez-de Dios, J.R. (eds.) Cooperative Robots and Sensor Networks 2015. SCI, vol. 604, pp. 31–51. Springer, Cham (2015). https://doi.org/10.1007/978-3-319-18299-5_2
9. Aki, M., et al.: Road surface recognition using laser radar for automatic platooning. IEEE Trans. Intell. Transp. Syst. **17**(10), 2800–2810 (2016)

Expected Time for Comfort Achievement in Human-Robot Emotion Communications

Sebastià Galmés[✉] [ID]

University of Balearic Islands, 07122 Palma, Spain
sebastia.galmes@uib.es

Abstract. This paper considers a cyber-physical system consisting of a user, a robot and the computing resources in the cloud. Specifically, the robot reads the emotional state of the user and relies on the cloud to determine the most appropriate action on the environment. Since this process generally involves several interactions until user comfort is achieved, its real-timeliness becomes a critical issue. This problem is addressed in this paper by using a Markovian representation of the emotional state sequence.

Keywords: Human-robot interaction · Emotional state
Markov chain · First passage time

1 Introduction

In today's Internet era, sensor network technology constitutes a powerful interface to the physical world. Environmental variables are measured and converted into digital bitstreams by sensor nodes, which cooperatively send these data to one or several remote locations for subsequent processing and interpretation. One of the next steps in this evolving process towards a cyber-physical world is the recognition and communication of subjective variables, like human emotions. In the area of human-machine interaction [1], a lot of research results have been achieved regarding methods and technologies for the machine to be able to identify human emotions. According to [2,3], these methods can be divided into four categories depending on the type of information captured to infer the emotional state: audio-visual information, physiological signals, tactile perception and multi-modal (combined) information.

Additionally, like in the case of sensor and actor networks, where the sensed information can be used to properly act on the environment, in human-machine interaction the perceived emotion can be used to determine the robot's action that drives the user to a more comfortable state. Since emotion identification involves high computational overhead, usually robots rely on the cloud to determine the user's emotional state and hence the action to be performed. However, since this process typically requires several iterations until user's comfort state is

© Springer Nature Switzerland AG 2018
Y. Luo (Ed.): CDVE 2018, LNCS 11151, pp. 134–137, 2018.
https://doi.org/10.1007/978-3-030-00560-3_18

achieved, it may incur high delays that degrade the user's quality of experience (QoE). Hence, this paper focuses on the analysis of the expected response time until user's comfort is achieved after several iterations from a non-desired initial state. Specifically, a Markovian approach is used to characterize user's state transitions, as suggested in [4]. So, the rest of this work-in-progress paper is organized as follows. In Sect. 2, the problem is formulated. In Sect. 3, the expected response time is analyzed via the notion of first passage time of a Markov chain. Finally, Sect. 4 exposes pending research activity.

2   Problem Formulation

Fig. 1 shows the architecture of the cyber-physical system under consideration. As it can be noticed, it consists of three elements: user, robot and cloud platform. This architecture is similar to the so-called Solo-Mode emotion communication mode in [4], though the role of the robot in the present work is merely an intermediary subsystem as it does neither have own emotions nor it incarnates user's emotions. Basically, the robot collects emotion-related data from the user and transfers these data to the cloud platform for analysis and interpretation. The cloud platform processes the data in order to identify user's emotion, and then determines the most appropriate action to enhance user's experience. The action identifier is send back to the robot for subsequent execution. This may consist of a direct action on the user or, indirectly, on the environment that surrounds the user.

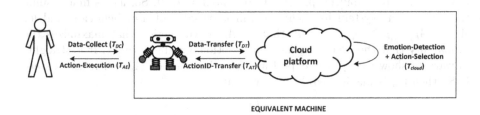

Fig. 1. Architecture of the cyber-physical system under analysis.

Let us assume that the emotional state of the user falls within a discrete set $E = \{E_1, E_2 \ldots E_n\}$, with E_n denoting the maximum comfort state. Let us also characterize a feedback action as setting a group of variables to specific levels. For instance, one of these variables could be room temperature, and its levels could be categorized as low, moderate, high or very high. More formally, let $V = \{v_1, v_2 \ldots v_m\}$ be the set of variables controlled by the robot, and $L_i = \{l_{i1}, l_{i2} \ldots l_{iq}\}$ the set of levels for variable v_i, with $i = 1 \ldots m$. Note that, for simplicity, without compromising generality, it has been assumed that all variables have the same number of levels (q). Accordingly, an action A_k is defined as follows: $A_k = (v_1 : l_{1f(1,k)}, v_2 : l_{2f(2,k)} \ldots v_m : l_{mf(m,k)})$, where $f(i,k)$

is a function that signals the specific level of variable v_i in action A_k. Note that $k = 1 \ldots q^m$, with q^m the total number of actions.

As stated above, a Markovian approach is adopted for the characterization of the evolution of the user's emotional state. Specifically, user behavior is represented by a transition matrix for every action, thus resulting in a total of q^m transition matrices per user. Let $M_k = (p_{ij,k})$ be the transition matrix that characterizes user reaction when action A_k takes place. Obviously, $i, j = 1 \ldots n$ and $\sum_{j=1}^{j=n} p_{ij,k} = 1, \forall i, k$. At this point, it is interesting to distinguish between three types of users:

- *Deterministic user.* A deterministic user always reacts in the same way under the same stimulus (action). Thus, a deterministic user obeys the following statement: $\forall i, k \, \exists j^* \, | \, p_{ij^*,k} = 1$ and $p_{ij,k} = 0 \, \forall j \neq j^*$.
- *Homogeneous user.* A homogeneous user does not always react in the same way, but its behavior is statistically stable and predictable. It corresponds to the general case of $0 < p_{ij,k} < 1, \forall i, j, k$.
- *Erratic user.* In this case, the probabilities $p_{ij,k}$ depend on time and thus user behavior is very difficult to predict.

This work focuses on homegeneous users (from which deterministic users constitute particular cases). Note that all transition matrices characterizing a user can be grouped into a single one, namely $M = (p_{ij})$, where $p_{ij} = \sum_{k=1}^{k=q^m} p_{ij,k} prob(A_k/S_i)$ and $prob(A_k/S_i)$ is the probability that the expert system running in the cloud platform decides action A_k given that user's state is S_i. Note also that, in order to speed up the transition process towards the comfort state S_n, probabilities p_{in} should be maximized $\forall i$. So, let us first assume that the expert system has achieved full knowledge of user behavior, and let $A_{i^*} = A_k | p_{in,k} \geq p_{in,s} \forall s \neq k$, that is, A_{i^*} is the action that maximizes the probability that the user switches from emotional state S_i to S_n. It is straightforward to show that, if the expert system selects action A_{i^*} when user's state is S_i, then p_{in} is maximized. In fact, we have:

$$p_{in} = p_{in,i^*} prob(A_{i^*}/S_i) + \sum_{k=1, k \neq i^*}^{k=q^m} p_{in,k} prob(A_k/S_i) = p_{in,i^*} \tag{1}$$

Here, it has been taken into account that $prob(A_{i^*}/S_i) = 1$ and $prob(A_k/S_i) = 0 \, \forall k \neq i^*$ according to the expert system decision rule.

3   Expected System Response Time

Let R be the time elapsed between an initial perception of user state (suposedly S_i, with $i \neq n$) and the achievement of the comfort state (S_n). According to Fig. 1, this time can be formulated as $R = N(T_{DC} + T_{DT} + T_{cloud} + T_{AT} + T_{AE})$, where N is the number of Markov chain transitions until comfort state. Accordingly, the expected response time, namely $\mathcal{E}[R]$, can be formulated as:

$$\mathcal{E}[R] = \mathcal{E}[N](T_{DC} + T_{DT} + T_{cloud} + T_{AT} + T_{AE}) \tag{2}$$

Current work has focused on analyzing the impact of the number of transitions (N) on the response time, and thus the rest of parameters, all of them "technological times", have assumed to be constant for now. $\mathcal{E}[N]$ can be analyzed by relying on the notion of first passage time (FPT) of a Markov chain [5]. This is the time until a given state is first reached from an initial different state. In particular, the mean number of transitions from state S_i, with $i \neq n$, to state S_n, namely m_i, obeys the following expression:

$$m_i = 1 + \sum_{j=1, j \neq i}^{n-1} p_{ij} m_j, \forall i \neq n \tag{3}$$

This is a linear system of $n-1$ equations with $n-1$ unknowns ($m_i, i = 1 \ldots n-1$), which can be solved straightforwardly. Then, if p_i denotes the steady-state probability of state S_i, the average number of transitions can be formulated in this way:

$$\mathcal{E}[N] = \sum_{i=1}^{n-1} p_i m_i \tag{4}$$

4   Further Research

The expected response time formulated in the previous section is valid under the assumption that the expert system has full knowledge of user behavior; thus, it represents an optimistic time. Hence, further research should focus on the design of a machine learning algorithm that approaches such an ideal situation, and on the recalculation and optimization of a more realistic response time.

References

1. Goodrich, M.A., Schultz, A.C.: Human-robot interaction: a survey. Found. Trends Hum.-Comput. Interact. **1**(3), 203–275 (2007)
2. Yan, H., Ang Jr., M.H., Poo, A.N.: A survey on perception methods for human-robot interaction in social robots. Int. J. Soc. Robot. **6**(1), 85–119 (2014)
3. Mccoll, D., Hong, A., Hatakeyama, N., Nejat, G., Benhabib, B.: A survey of autonomous human affect detection methods for social robots engaged in natural HRI. J. Intell. Robot. Syst. **82**(1), 101–133 (2016)
4. Chen, M., Zhou, P., Fortino, G.: Emotion communication system. IEEE Access **5**, 326–337 (2017)
5. Cox, D.R., Miller, H.D.: The Theory of Stochastic Processes. Chapman & Hall, London (1965)

Wi-Fi Based Teleoperation System of a Robot with Four Degrees of Freedom Using a Computer and a Smartphone

Julián Arturo Hoyos Rodríguez[1], Octavio José Salcedo Parra[1,2](✉),
and Javier Medina[3]

[1] Department of Systems and Industrial Engineering, Faculty of Engineering,
Universidad Nacional de Colombia, Bogotá D.C., Colombia
{jahoyosr,ojsalcedop}@unal.edu.co
[2] Faculty of Engineering, Intelligent Internet Research Group, Universidad
Distrital "Francisco José de Caldas", Bogotá D.C., Colombia
osaceldo@udistrital.edu.co
[3] Faculty of Engineering, GEFEM Research Group, Universidad Distrital
"Francisco José de Caldas", Bogotá D.C., Colombia
rmedina@udistrital.edu.co

Abstract. This article details the development of a project that involves robotics and network communications. It consists on controlling a PhantomX Pincher AX-12 robot from Dynamixel through an app. The app was developed on the Android system and it has an intuitive and easy-to-use GUI (Graphic User Interface). The project requires an additional entity serving as an intermediary between the robot and the smartphone, which in this case is a PC. It will be in charge of communication, information processing and saving the trajectories during the teleoperation. The PC and the smartphone communicate via the UDP protocol, through an easy and simple transmission. Successful teleoperation of a simple robot was achieved, using a smartphone and a personal computer thus avoiding the costs of control acquisition and communication devices.

Keywords: Communications protocols · Teleoperation · Smartphone

1 Introduction

The teleoperation of a robot involves knowledge on both robotics and computer networks. This operation mode is used in service robots or industrial robots, since it provides an important tool for their control without being in the same place. One of the problems of teleoperation is that it often requires very costly devices such as a robot (of course) and high-range computers which allow control over long distances.

With a less costly solution, teleoperation would sacrifice its performance using a common smartphone as the controlling device. Taking advantage of the fact that smartphones are omnipresent in our current society, since almost everybody has one of them and carries them everywhere, said devices have useful characteristics such as computational power and processing speed.

Y. Luo (Ed.): CDVE 2018, LNCS 11151, pp. 138–144, 2018.
https://doi.org/10.1007/978-3-030-00560-3_19

The development of a mobile application is very fitting for the project because a number of them are used every day mainly for entertainment, communication and learning purposes.

2 Background

An autonomous robot that works with stereo vision provided by a smartphone is basically a low-cost solution resembling a car with two motors which will serve as the actuators being under control. The software for control is managed from a computer, which communicates to the smartphone via Wi-Fi [1].

Networks have been implemented for aerial robots by using several smartphones which receive information from sensors like accelerometers, gyroscopes and other electronic components that can be inserted in a last-gen smartphone. These types of robot can communicate between each other to avoid collisions and efficiently explore a workspace. It is possible to assign a predefined path in real time through another smartphone. Software modeling has been used to capture the environment with a telephone based on tridimensional points generated by rigid bodies [2].

Controlling a robot with gesture recognition involves a motor-type robot that includes a gripper for lifting and moving objects. It is a low-cost project with some limitations regarding its movement in rough surfaces or lifting very heavy objects. Through an app, the smartphone's sensors (such as accelerometers and gyroscopes) are used to detect the device's current position and send a Bluetooth signal to the robot. In addition, the application relies on an interface in the shape of a steering wheel that allows driving the car remotely. Some gestures control the degrees of inclination related to the speed and some control the action of closing and opening the gripper [3].

The 6lowPAN protocol is a modified version of the IPv6 protocol that compresses or encrypts some data packets rendering the transmission much easier. The purpose of this protocol is to combine the robust power from networks with the flexibility of lower processing and consumption devices. The internal structure and viability of this strategy are studied in depth over electronic devices, seeing the 6lowPAN protocol as a part of an IoT application [4].

A service robot can be controlled with an application from a smartphone or a tablet. The operating principle is that the control function is shared by several remote devices. In this case, the chosen robot is capable of moving in environments with obstacles and performing simple tasks. This project is crucial for people who need constant support to accomplish daily tasks, in particular the elderly. The robot is highly sophisticated since it relies on multiple sensors to monitor and facilitate the control task because information is being provided from the environment allowing a constant feedback control. This contributes to avoiding accidents and increasing robustness and safety [5].

A police car that combines image processing technology, fuzzy logic, wireless communications and smartphones to achieve real time movement was proposed. It can perform object recognition, follow-up and remote monitoring. A robot that includes a camera is used to monitor the car's surroundings from anywhere; such robot is capable of calculating the relative position of a specific target and giving the order to go there as fast as possible [6].

A service robot combined with a smartphone is used to establish a special wireless network, making it possible to remotely control the robot from an application developed for Android. The communication system consists in a two-way transport layer: the Transmission Control Protocol (TCP) and the User Datagram Protocol (UDP) [7].

3 Design

3.1 App

A friendly and easy-to-use interface is designed to allow the client to control a robot with four degrees of freedom. The application has two main panels: the **start panel** and the **control panel**.

Start Panel: This menu screen welcomes the user and includes the *start*, *settings* and *exit* options (See Fig. 1). When the *start* button is clicked, the user can access the second panel of the application.

Fig. 1. Start panel of the application. Source: Authors

Control Panel: Since the robot has four degrees of freedom, its movement can be controlled through four sliders, one for each joint's independent movement. The fifth slider can open or close the robot's gripper (See Fig. 2).

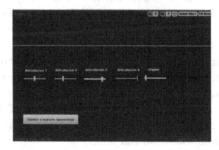

Fig. 2. First section of the control panel. Source: Authors

Within the control panel, it is possible to change the environment. The second section of the control panel makes it possible to control the robot in a more intuitive way. This environment has three text blocks, which correspond to the tridimensional coordinates (x, y and z) that are inside the workspace's boundaries. The last parameter defines the desired orientation of the gripper (See Fig. 3).

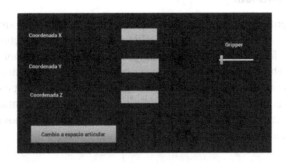

Fig. 3. Second section of the control panel. Source: Authors

3.2 Matlab Code

The development of the program in Matlab has two essential parts. The first part corresponds to the routine that allows the acquisition of the information being sent from the smartphone. This routine runs in an infinite cycle that will be constantly asking if there is any information waiting to be processed. If there is, it will be directly sent to the function in charge of moving the robot.

3.3 UDP Protocol

For the implementation of the UDP protocol, it needs to be installed in both devices that will be connected. This means that the specific parameters have to be set correctly in the computer and smartphone in order to use this protocol. Matlab has functions that can read ports with UDP, serial and other protocols. This will ease the implementation of the protocol in the PC. Furthermore, the UDP protocol has to be implemented in the app so that the smartphone is capable of sending data. In this case, only one-way communication is required so one UDP entity is declared to send data from the smartphone and one UDP entity is declared to receive it in the PC.

4 Implementation

4.1 Matlab Code

Dynamixel libraries have to be previously installed in order to use specific functions for controlling the robot through Matlab. Afterwards, the computer's COM ports need to be set properly to avoid connection problems between the computer and the Pincher robot. For the latter, an *USB2Dynamixel* converter is used which requires the installation of a driver for its use. The first development stage of the routine in Matlab R2016b consists on calling the Dynamixel libraries and initializing the main parameters of the robot such as joint speed, joint limits and torque limits. Several functions are in charge of the robot's configuration.

4.2   Forward Kinematics

Once the aforementioned functions have been implemented, there is sufficient code to control the robot's movement by simply calling the *setPosition* function and entering the desired values for the joints. Unfortunately, these parameters are not intuitive for an inexpert person, who does not have previous knowledge of manipulators or robots, for this reason the second environment is implemented. This environment receives the final effector's positions depending on the coordinated axes and the orientation, since it is the easiest way to move the robot into a specific position instead of moving one joint at a time. This is illustrated in Fig. 4.

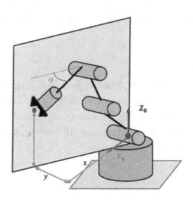

Fig. 4. Input parameters for the forward kinematics. Source: Authors

4.3   App

Matlab offers a support package for the development of Android-based applications. This app includes functions to establish Wi-Fi communication between the computer and the smartphone. This solution was chosen because the received data is kept in the Matlab console which facilitates their use in controlling the robot's movement. The only inconvenient of this support package is that the interface cannot be customized since the package generates a widget by default. As a consequence, the interface designed in the design section will not be implemented.

Moving on to the Simulink platform, there is a block diagram in charge of generating the C code that will be later installed in the smartphone. This code includes both the graphical interface and the functional core of the application (See Fig. 5).

The block has to be programmed block by block through the definition of the type of variable to be used, the limits of the sliders, the sample time, the resolution of each slider and the multiplexer (See Fig. 6).

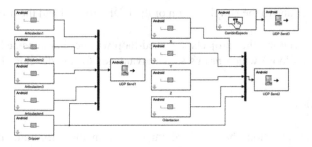

Fig. 5. Block diagram of the UDP Send function in Simulink. Source: Authors

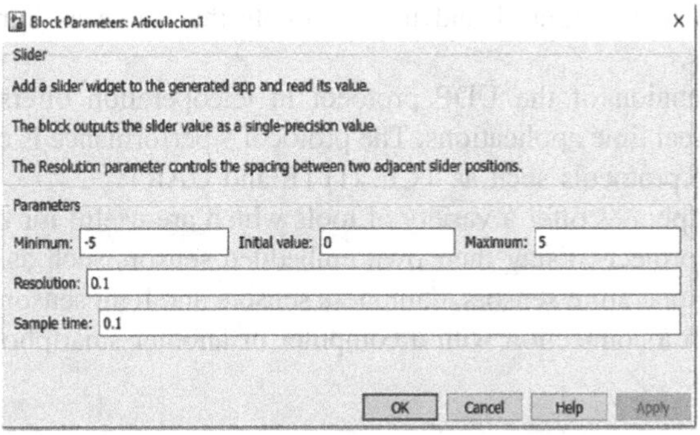

Fig. 6. Configuration of blocks for the app. Source: Authors

Once all the blocks have been correctly declared, the app is installed in the smartphone thanks to the *Deploy to hardware* function in Simulink, which takes charge of building the app, installing it and then executing it in the target device. The application has two main panels.

The first one allows the interaction with the user, while the second one gives information about the application. The latter helps to know about the network and the connection's IP, so that the UDP protocol can be configured later on.

5 Analysis of Results

The objective was to create a teleoperation system with accessible technology with a simple but efficient protocol. On one hand, a last generation cellphone's multiple functionalities were used while, on the other hand, the interconnectivity feature of a common computer was harnessed.

The application's performance is comparable to the benchmarked prototypes' performance. To begin with, an approximate delay of 200 ms was perceived between changes in the sliders and the robot's movement. However, this delay can be useful for some applications. In comparison with the project developed in references [2, 7], which have response times of 15 and 5 ms respectively, the communications in this project were a bit slower due to the simplification of the UDP protocol and the use of common devices.

Unlike it is seen in other projects, a closed-loop was not implemented (the system works in an open loop) which brings some advantages for the developed application.

6 Conclusions

- Nowadays, applications have gained importance in the telecommunications and teleoperation fields, as robots are slowly becoming a part of modern households. The remote control of a robot represents a huge advance in multiple research areas.
- An app-based teleoperation system is the simplest method to establish a first approximation to the control and use of robots that serve as home assistants in everyday tasks.
- The implementation of the UDP protocol in teleoperation offers reliability and efficiency for real time applications. The protocol's performance is comparable with other common protocols such as TCP, HTTP and UART.
- Last-gen smartphones offer a variety of tools which are useful for the development of interesting projects, using their own embedded sensors such as accelerometers, gyroscopes, temperature sensors, dampness sensors and light sensors. They can also easily establish a connection with a computer or another smartphone.

References

1. Bodenstein, C., Tremer, M., Overhoff, J., Würtz, R.P.: A Smartphone-Controlled Autonomous Robot. Ruhr-University Bochum, Germany (2015)
2. Loianno, G., Mulgaonkar, Y., Brunner, C., Kumar, V.: A Swarm of Flying Smartphones, Daejeon, Korea, 9 October 2014
3. Singh, R.K., Sarkar, A., Chakravarty, D., Goyal, P., Sharma, A.: Bluetooth communication controlled robot based on gesture recognition
4. García, D.C.: Estudio de 6lowPAN para su aplicación en internet de las cosas, pp. 2–44. Universidad La Laguna, España, 9 June 2015
5. Song, K.-T., Jiang, S.-Y., Lin, M.-H.: Interactive teleoperation of a mobile manipulator using a shared-control approach. IEEE Trans. Hum.-Mach. Syst. **46**, 834–845 (2016)
6. Juang, S.-Y., Juang, J.-G.: Remote Control of a Mobile Robot for Indoor Patrol. Taiwan National University, 15 March 2016
7. Lu, X., Liu, W., Wang, H., Sun, Q.: Robot Control Design Based on Smartphone. Shandong University of Science and Technology, Qingdao

Urban Transdisciplinary Co-study in a Cooperative Multicultural Working Project

Ursula Kirschner[(✉)]

Faculty of Humanities and Social Sciences,
Institute of Urban and Cultural Area Research, Leuphana University Lüneburg,
Universitätsallee 1, 21335 Lüneburg, Germany
kirschner@uni.leuphana.de

Abstract. "Today's frontiers are not at the edge of the known world, but at the heart of global cities" [1].

Two International Summer Schools entitled "Frontier Zones," carried out as collaborative projects by one Brazilian and three German universities, highlight the value of experience-based learning approaches and the method of documentary filmmaking with the focus on the audiovisual without explanatory words. To find out what frontier zones in modern urban areas are, we explored the urbanism applying the method of documentary filmmaking as a medium to reveal new insights and readings of the contemporary city. These case studies emphasize new forms of transdisciplinary research on the urbanism of global cities.

In analyzing and comparing the conceptual framework of the two Summer Schools with different schedules and different ways in which the participants were asked to work, the author demonstrates the potential benefits of the binational and transdisciplinary working environment when seeking answers to urban "frontier zones" challenges.

Keywords: Cooperative urban exploration · Transdisciplinary co-study
Documentary film as an interface for urban analysis

1 Introduction

In this paper two concepts of International Summer Schools on the topic "Frontier Zones" are compared and assessed based on two online evaluations each year and on the interpretation of the final products, including the opinions of viewers in Brazil and Germany.

Discovering frontier zones in urban areas and examining them from a variety of perspectives applying the language of documentary filmmaking as a way to explore urban areas is based on the thesis posed by the media scientists Horwitz et al. [2]. They propose that, through the use of images, film allows one to get "closer" to social realities than would be possible with text-based empirical social research.

Film has always been an ideal way to obtain an overview of the transformational forces of urban development. If one thinks of space as motion in time – "In space we read the time" [3] - this correlation becomes tangible. After all, film is also founded on motion in time.

© Springer Nature Switzerland AG 2018
Y. Luo (Ed.): CDVE 2018, LNCS 11151, pp. 145–152, 2018.
https://doi.org/10.1007/978-3-030-00560-3_20

Use of the camera as the "retina" of the observer, and the "selfie" as a new form of reporting (the so-called autobiographical approach) were explained as media to get inside the reality of the people of São Paulo. The subsequent reflection of the experienced is deepened in common discourse. The result is greater interest in the (digital) perception and consideration of urban life in a global city, which could reveal a correlation between population and habitation.

2   The Framework of the Summer Schools

We explored São Paulo with interdisciplinary groups of Master and Ph.D. students (journalists, sociologists, architects, artists, musicians, social scientists, city planners) from all over Brazil. Our approach was strongly collaborative between students, the German and Brazilian researchers of architecture, documentary filmmaking, city planning and auditive culture, and the people we filmed on the streets. There is no neutral observer, only authors with different cultural and personal backgrounds. Our host university was in São Carlos, three hours by bus from São Paulo. This is where we did the editing and some of the preparation.

For advertising and the communication before, during and afterwards we used facebook©. Two online evaluations were done by EvaSys©[1], the results of which are assessed here. We provided four HD video cameras (Sony EX3) and sound recorders (Sennheiser MK46), but we also allowed the use of personal cameras. The editing was done with the software Premiere©.

At the end of both Summer School sessions, we presented the final films to the public and discussed the frontier zones insights at a culture center.

The ultimate objective is to produce short films in different cities worldwide, to superimpose them, and to analyze the interference. For that we created a platform[2] where everyone can upload and download clips.

3   The Theoretical Input

The theoretical interdisciplinary input on frontier zones was given in both Summer Schools with the greater intention of making clear that the issue is a transdisciplinary challenge. In the first one we gave lectures every morning during the five-day preparation phase, and in the second we organized a public two-day conference (see Table 1). We also invited two Brazilian keynote speakers (Beiguelman[3], Anelli[4]) from São Paulo to the second Summer School.

---

[1] EvaSys© is a software for the creation of surveys and their evaluation. It automatically generates SPSS records that can be used to perform statistical analysis.

[2] Link to the platform: http://www.nomads.usp.br/resourcespace, last access 2018/04/12.

[3] Prof. Dr. Giselle Beiguelman is an artist and professor at the Faculty of Architecture and Urbanism of the University of São Paulo (FAU-USP).

[4] Prof. Dr. Renato Anelli is a full professor for architecture history at the Institute of Architecture and Urbanism at USP in São Carlos (IAU-USP).

Table 1. Schedules of the summer schools in 2015 and 2017

2015: 14 days, 18 participants, 8 instructors	2017: 13 days, 20 participants, 8 instructors
4 days São Carlos 3 days: introduction, lectures, documentary film evenings, practical work (in varying groups), 1 day finding a group and finding a topic. **Working in groups**	6 days São Paulo 2 days: introduction, public lectures starting with two Brazilian keynote speakers and a public movie screening. 4 days: shooting area in the old center of São Paulo
1. **Online evaluation**	1. **Online evaluation**
5 days São Paulo: shooting area along the metro "Linea 1"	7 days São Carlos 2 days: viewing the material, first individual skit **Working in groups using the complete material**
5 days São Carlos: editing, using the material from own group	5 days: editing
2. **Online evaluation**	2. **Online evaluation**

The German and the Brazilian chairs of the Summer Schools are architects and urban researchers. The Brazilian architect gave his introduction on frontier zones focusing on the shooting area in São Paulo. For him a frontier zone is a territory, a place of consensus and conflict. So more than just registering physical spaces, reading the city means identifying the loci where the coexistence of differences happen. He proposed a brief reading of the chosen areas along the oldest metro Linea 1 in 2015 and for the Summer School 2017 in downtown São Paulo.

The German architect analyzed the special atmosphere of frontier zones and how to perceive them. Her intention was to discover frontier zones and to analyze them with the language of the documentary as an exploratory medium. She presented the solutions of one study, where the Films from 2015 were used for a hermeneutic sequence analysis by applying what is seen to a different urban context, thus obtaining insights into the initial place and the new place – or into frontier zones in different large cities [4].

One German photographer and urban researcher showed documentary approaches to the city. He presented the long photography and film history of debates discussing the indexicality and representation of the picture and the depicted. It boils down to the question of what we see while viewing pictures; what is the relation between the image and reality?

The group of instructors in filmmaking changed from 2015 to 2017. In 2015 we had a very powerful film critic who was able to talk about pictures and to imagine pictures and scenes. For him documentary filmmaking is a kind of adventure, like entering the unutterable and the non-displayable [5]. He presented several documentary films with explanations of what the aim was and how the director transports it. He sees this medium as a valuable tool for sociologists to make city life visible and, in addition to statistics, to receive material for research.

In 2017 we were able to gain a so-called non-linear filmmaker. She introduced the students to film montage as a method of thinking. Editing focuses on the idea of combining, connecting or interrelating individual parts from varied sources. One of the most fascinating aspects of montage is the intense process of analyzing. Editing is the construction of a film experience.

So it starts before even turning on the camera and continues when the setting for the presentation is designed. With respect to editing, the notion of reading the city involves gathering material guided by curiosity and a feel for correlation. Thus inventing the urbanism would mean exploring the vast connectivity of this material.

Her counterpart focused on creating a story with images. A film – whether a documentary or a fictional film – tells its story with a sequence of images. Each image stands for certain information or a statement. This leads to the question faced by filmmakers: Which images and sequences of images support the intention of the film?

In both Summer Schools an urban sound researcher sensitized the students to sound as a core resource for gaining a more profound knowledge of the urban space. He gave an introduction to some key concepts of sound research applied by the "Frontier Zones" project. He supported students in capturing sound and composing images, and he demonstrated how sound relates to a topic.

Each Summer School also received support from three German instructors: a visual researcher, a filmmaker and a sound producer.

4   Implementation and Schedule

The essential difference between the two schedules was the beginning. In 2015 we had four days of preparation, with lectures and experimental sessions. On the fifth day the participants were asked to form groups and find a topic. They subsequently worked together as an interdisciplinary group and produced one linear documentary.

In 2017 we started in São Paulo and after two days of introductions and lectures, we asked the students to go into the city and to capture images and sound clips individually or in varying groups. The editing took place in São Carlos each time. The intention of the final clips was to convey impressions from frontier zones without offering explanations. There were two reasons for changing the process: one was to reduce travel time and money, and the other was to inspire the students to just go into the city perceiving, seeing and capturing. The idea is based on Jane Jacobs [6][5], a recognized American urban researcher: Trust your eyes and instincts by walking through the city. Her deductive research approach aims to assess neighborhoods in terms of their quality of living by collecting and evaluating phenomena.

5 The Student Evaluation

Two online evaluations were conducted. The first was in 2015, conducted before traveling to São Paulo. In the questionnaire we asked about the reasons for participating, preparation of the summer school and what kind of special support they would like in São Paulo. In 2017 the first one took place when we arrived in São Carlos after the shooting days. The second ones were about 4 days after the end of the Summer Schools. The assessment of the students' evaluation results are focused on four aspects: collaboration skills; skills in documentary filmmaking, skills in urban exploration of frontier zones and creative skills on how the main important topics are translated into a film. In 2015 the first evaluation was completed by 13 students and the second by 14 of 19 students. Some had technical problems. In 2017, the first 19 of 20 and the second 18 of 19[6] participants completed the questionnaires. The questionnaires were designed with about 30% open questions and 70% with multiple choice answers.

The automated evaluation report of the software EvaSys[©] is not part of this paper.

5.1 Collaboration Skills

In both Summer Schools the collaboration skills received high ratings. The students made a lot of new friends in both - nearly 100% mentioned this. And the instructors received 4.8 and 4.9 out of 5 points. Comments on working in an interdisciplinary team were mentioned in 2015 nine times and in 2017 14 times. In 2015 there were a few negative comments, e.g. "Maybe the agenda and even some activities could be discussed more with the group, with more space for the argumentation, even participation of the students. Maybe there could be less of a distinction between "instructors" and "students," but in a more "horizontal way," a more professional way of work. If everyone could participate to a greater degree, everyone could get to know each other better and work better together in the group!" In 2017, there were only positive comments on this aspect, e.g. "The interaction between participants and the body of professors was really good. It was a very good environment to work in and we, the students, didn't feel there was a gap between participants and professors/assistants."

In conclusion, it was clear that changing groups several times and having professors act as participants foster a better atmosphere among all participants. In 2017 we taught more like Socrates, who did not want to lecture; instead, he gave the impression that he wanted to learn from his interlocutor, the students [7].

---

[5] In the sixties Jacobs was well known for organizing grassroots efforts to protect existing neighborhoods from "slum clearance." Today a global community is continuing walks in the tradition of Jacobs (janeswalk.org).

[6] One student had to cancel because of illness.

5.2   Documentary Filmmaking Skills

In regard to the benefit of the documentary filmmaking skills gained, the number of references was the same in both years: in 2015 14 times by 14 collected questionnaires and in 2017 19 times by 19. In 2015 some students would have liked more theoretical input on how to transport contents into a documentary (perspective, light, movement). One student in 2017 was somewhat disappointed, "I wish I could use the Summer School to learn and use this knowledge in my future work, but it was less than I expected." But most of the comments describe the outcome as strong and valuable, like "I've had the opportunity to learn about architectural elements, sound recording techniques and filmmaking approaches" or "Acquired new points of views and perspectives on how to record urban spaces." From a maximum of 5 points, students gave 4.4 (2015) and 4.6 (2017) for the use of the technical know-how in my subsequent study, and according to the individual learning success 4.3 (2015) and 4.4 (2017).

5.3   Urban Exploration Skills

The urban exploration skills are the most important ones, because the others are media tools to explore the urbanism. In both Summer Schools students were impressed by the "[New] perception of space - (camera filming) what we see with the naked eye is not the same as with a camera lens. How sound is important to define the space, a frontier" (2015). Or the summer school "[H]elps me improve my knowledge and also understand more deeply other aspects of the city as well as make contact and get to know other people from different cultures and [with] different thoughts." The topic "Frontier Zones" was in both cases highly rated with 4.7 (2015) and 4.9 (2017), and the applied method of documentary film for making frontier zones visible was rated 4.4 (2015) and 4.6 (2017). In both cases nobody was unhappy with the topic, but some would have liked to have more time to discuss the day's results as well as the final results and the insights into frontier zones. The results are elements of the so-called "code of the street" or they describe what is missing for the street to be considered a cosmopolitan canopy." Both sociological terms are defined and described as narratives of the interaction in public space by Elijah Anderson[7]. "The cosmopolitan canopy is peculiar in that people of diverse backgrounds feel they have an equal right to be there" [8].

5.4   Creative Skills

The results were quite different. In 2015 we had four socially critical issues: the segregation of ethnic groups; the sunrise and the sunset over the city; the informal meets the formal business and the revitalization of a place with a history like a massacre. These films were composed as a story out of stories and the viewer is encouraged to think about the different perspectives of the topics. The viewers commented that it was sometimes difficult to figure the main focus. In 2017 the products were

---

[7] Elijah Anderson holds the William K. Lanman, Jr. Professorship in Sociology at Yale University, he is well-known for his urban ethnography projects, which include the award-winning books "Code of the Street" and "Streetwise."

experimental films like artwork.[8] Here each frame is a collage of pictures that transfer content which can be interpreted in different ways. The titles are also more poetic, like "Do skyscraper have eyes?" or "Unvoiced Conflicts." The viewers thought that access is easier because the ideas are more open and everybody feels free to provide their own interpretation (Fig. 1).

Fig. 1. Screenshot from the clip "Do skyscraper have eyes?" [9]

6 Conclusion

This kind of International Summer School as a creative interdisciplinary teaching/ research project fosters a trusting relationship between all participants. At the beginning the two chairs need a high level of communication skills to prevent misunderstandings. In this special program the partner from abroad has to invite students from the whole country. Therefore it is necessary to have a strong network and functional ways to spread information. To build a team of instructors is the next very important step. The experience and the evaluation of the two Summer Schools ensure that it is conducive to creating a warm and labor-intensive community to work in the beginning in small groups and to change the groups very often. Instructors should integrate themselves in the groups and try to communicate at eye-level with the students. To work for 13 or 14 days together, starting at 9:00 a.m. and ending with dinner together 10:00 p.m., is an intense experience for everyone involved. A positive environment and good technical staff are essential to reducing stress.

---

[8] All clips can be viewed under https://www.leuphana.de/universitaet/personen/ursula-kirschner/ forschung-projekte.html, last access 2018/04/18.

The most important skills that the students learned were collaboration and the urban exploration skills. The collaboration value and the interest in the urban topic were later evident on facebook©. There is still a community sharing information on "Frontier Zones."

Acknowledgements. The two International Summer Schools are sponsored by the German Academic Exchange Service (DAAD), with funding from the Federal Ministry of Education and Research (BMBF). Thanks to all participants of the two Summer Schools "Frontier Zones."

References

1. Sassen, S.: Saskia Sassen 1/6 - Global Cities as Today's Frontiers - Leuphana Digital School. https://www.youtube.com/watch?v=Iu-p31RkCXI. Accessed 12 Apr 2018
2. Horwitz, M., Joerges, B., Potthast, J. (Hrsg.): Stadt und Film. Versuch zu einer „Visuellen Soziologie", 1996, discussion paper FS-II 96–503. Berlin Wissenschaftszentrum. http://bibliothek.wz-berlin.de/pdf/1996/ii96-503.pdf. Accessed 12 Apr 2018
3. Schlögel, K.: Im Raum lesen wir die Zeit, Carl Hanser Verlag (2009)
4. Kirschner, U.: A Hermeneutic Interpretation of Concepts in a Cooperative Multicultural Working Project, pp. 610–615. Blucher, São Paulo (2017). https://doi.org/10.5151/sigradi2017-094
5. Rudziker, W.: Making-of 4:42 Minutes (2015). https://www.leuphana.de/universitaet/personen/ursula-kirschner/forschung-projekte.html. Accessed 12 Apr 2018
6. Jacobs, J.: The Death and Life of Great American Cities. Vintage Books, New York (1961)
7. Gaarder, J.: Sophies Welt, München, p. 82 (1993)
8. Anderson, E.: The Cosmopolitan Canopy, New York, p. 278f (2011)
9. de Oliveira, F.A., Trujillo, J.C., dos Reis, M.B.: Frontier Zones. Summer School (2017)

Cooperative Design in a Visual Interactive Environment

Ewa Grabska, Barbara Strug, and Grażyna Ślusarczyk(✉)

The Faculty of Physics, Astronomy and Applied Computer Science,
Jagiellonian University, ul. Lojasiewicza 11, 30-348 Kraków, Poland
{ewa.grabska,gslusarc}@uj.edu.pl

Abstract. This paper deals with a CAD-like tool supporting the conceptual phase of a visual design process. A new design system supporting collaboration among different domain designers is proposed. The system is based on visual languages of icons, graph patterns and graph rewriting. It offers a simple graphical interface, where various sets of icons representing design structural components can be specified by different designers. Graph nodes labelled by icons are arranged by users to create graphs representing spatial and structural relationships between components of design drawings. The system provides schemes of rules, which are most often applied to develop graphs. Cooperating designers can extend existing or add new rule schemes in order to modify graphs being generated according to their needs. Moreover, the system supports attributed graphs which allow for propagating semantic information and capturing parametric modeling knowledge. The approach is illustrated on examples of designing bridges, gardens and different forms of buildings.

Keywords: Cooperative design · Visual language · Composition
graph · Graph pattern · Graph rewriting

1 Introduction

This paper deals with a CAD-like tool supporting the conceptual phase of design process. Conceptual design is based on individual skills but in its essence design is collaborative. We concentrate our attention on the conceptual aspect of collaborative design which depends on appropriate general attitude to the design itself.

In this paper a new design system supporting collaboration for conceptual design is proposed. The system is based on visual languages of icons, the graph patterns and graph rewriting. It extends the existing design system VIZMOGR (Visual MOdelling with GRaphs) [1] for collaborative work. VIZMOGR offers a simple graphical interface, where various sets of icons representing the design structural components can be specified by different designers. When using this system the users begin designing with the specification of icons representing object components the design drawings are to be generated of. Then a set of

© Springer Nature Switzerland AG 2018
Y. Luo (Ed.): CDVE 2018, LNCS 11151, pp. 153–162, 2018.
https://doi.org/10.1007/978-3-030-00560-3_21

graph nodes labelled by icons is created. Nodes with icons force the users to think about the interplay between structural components. Two nodes connected by edges represent related components. A graph is created by adding selected nodes connected by edges representing relations between components corresponding to nodes. Such a graph represents a conceivable solution of a given design task.

On the other hand a design drawing can be seen as composed of parts corresponding to visual design patterns [2], which are generated with basic elements of the visual language. In this concept a visual pattern reflects a characteristic feature or/and frequently appearing part of the drawing. VIZMOGR gives the possibility of arranging nodes with icons into graphs representing visual design patterns.

In the design process graphs representing design solutions are modified according to changes introduced in designs. Therefore the system provides schemes of rules, which are most often applied to develop graphs and can contain previously defined graphs corresponding to visual patterns. It is shown that the specification of graph rewriting rules can be facilitated by presenting them on the visual level. The cooperating designers can extend existing or add new rule schemes in order to modify graphs being generated according to their needs. Moreover the system supports attributed graphs which allow for propagating semantic information and capturing parametric modeling knowledge.

In this paper the system VIZMOGR is extended to enable the cooperation of different domain designers. In Fig. 1 a model of the workflow in VIZMOGR collaborative design system is presented. For each domain a specific set of icons is used and a common set of schemes. These schemes are adapted with the use of domain icons to generate domain specific rules, which allow the designer to generate graphs representing designs belonging to a particular domain (for example gardens, buildings, bridges etc.). The system makes it possible to create a multi-domain design environment by importing the general schemes as well as icons from domains involved. Moreover, it allows for adding local schemes that may be needed in a multi-domain design. The collaborative dimension of the conceptual design phase is supported by the graph-based representation of designs. It ensures the proper connections between design elements by maintaining the admissible structures. The design knowledge is encoded in schemes of rules which are often used in graph development steps and can be applied to automatically generate repeating fragments of designs.

The proposed approach is illustrated on examples of designing bridges, gardens and different forms of buildings. An example of a design drawing representing a building surrounded by trees depicts the introduced possibility of collaborative work between different domain designers.

2   Graph Representation of Designs

In the proposed VIZMOGR system design objects are internally represented by means of CP-graphs. A CP-graph is a labelled and attributed graph, where nodes represent components of artefacts and are labelled by names of these components. Moreover, attributes specifying properties of components are assigned

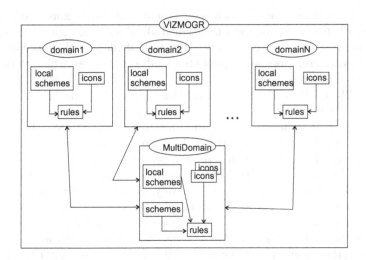

Fig. 1. The workflow in VIZMOGR collaborative design system

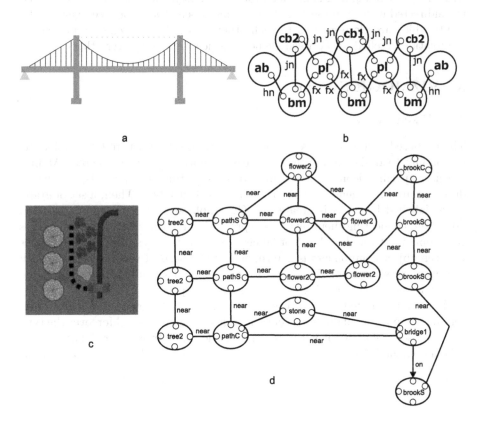

Fig. 2. (a, c) A bridge and a garden layout, (b, d) CP-graphs representing them

to nodes representing them. To each node a number of bonds expressing potential connections between components is assigned [3]. Bonds are connected by edges representing relations between components and labelled by the relation names. Non-symmetrical relations are represented by directed edges, while symmetrical relations by undirected ones.

In Fig. 2b a CP-graph representing the structure of the bridge shown in Fig. 2a is presented. All its edges are undirected as they represent symmetrical relations. This structure is a solution internal representation obtained as a result of the modeling process controlled by the user and described in the next section. Nodes of this CP-graph represent abutments, pylons, beams and two types of cables, which constitute structural components of the bridge, and are labeled as *ab*, *bm*, *pl*, *cb1* and *cb2*, respectively. Bonds assigned to nodes are connected by undirected edges representing relations between bridge components. The edge labels *fx* and *hn* denote fixed and hinged connections between components of the bridge. The edge label *jn* denotes the join relation. A CP-graph representing the layout of a garden presented in Fig. 2c is shown in Fig. 2d. Nodes of this CP-graph represent one type of flowers and trees, a stone, a bridge, and straight and winding fragments of a brook and a path. Node bonds are connected by undirected edges representing the relation labelled *near* between garden elements which are close enough to each other, or by directed edges representing the relation labelled *on* between elements which are placed over others.

3   VIZMOGR System

3.1   Visual Icons

The proposed system offers a simple graphical interface, where CP-graphs corresponding to design drawings being early solutions, can be created. At first the user specifies icons representing object structural components the design drawings are to be generated of together with their labels. Then, a set of graph nodes labelled by icons is created. A CP-graph is created by adding selected nodes and connecting them by edges representing relations between components corresponding to nodes. A set of labels representing types of possible relations between object components is determined on the basis of visual relations which can occur between icons. Moreover, for each node a set of attributes specifying properties of a corresponding component can be specified.

It should be noted that each designer can specify his own set of icons representing components of objects occurring in his design domain. Moreover the type of icons used is consistent with the design style characteristic for the considered design domain. Thus the icons can be in the form of 3D objects, top projections or side views.

Exemplary icons, which are used in case of designing bridges to represent structural components of models, together with their labels are presented in Fig. 3a. Labels *ab*, *pl*, *bm*, *ar1*, *cb1*, *cb2* and *cb3* denote abutments, pylons, beams, one type of arches, and three types of cables. Exemplary icons representing three types of trees, two types of flowers, and winding fragments of brooks and paths are shown in Fig. 3b. Exemplary icons representing elementary shapes called geons in Biederman's Recognition-By-Components theory [4], which are used to design different forms of buildings are presented in Fig. 3c.

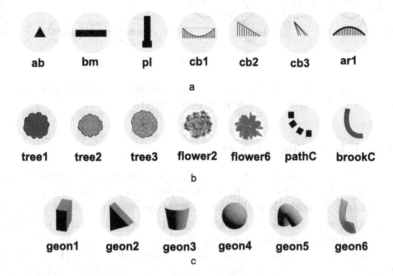

Fig. 3. (a, b, c) Icons representing components of bridges, garden elements and 3D components of buildings

3.2 Design Patterns

A design drawing can be seen as composed of parts corresponding to visual design patterns, which are generated with basic elements of the visual language. VIZMOGR gives the possibility of arranging nodes with icons into graphs representing visual design patterns. Such patterns are convenient in design when the same structure is to be repeated a number of times [5]. They can also reflect characteristic features of designs.

Two visual design patterns, which represent parts of bridges, are shown on the left-hand side of Fig. 4a, while CP-graphs corresponding to them are shown in Fig. 4b. On the right-hand side of Fig. 4b two CP-graphs representing design patterns from the right-hand side of Fig. 4a corresponding to requirements for a Japanese-style garden [6] are presented. On the right-hand side of Fig. 4a garden patterns related to a winding path and the existence of a footbridge over a brook are shown.

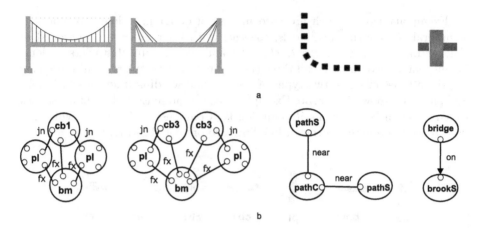

Fig. 4. (a) Visual design patterns representing two parts of bridges and two garden style features, (b) CP-graphs representing these patterns

3.3   Graph Rewriting Schemes

In the design process graphs representing design solutions are modified according to changes introduced in designs. In the conceptual stage of the design process the designer visually explore his preliminary ideas, discovers important features in a design drawing and repeatedly changes it using physical actions, which consist of such operations as drawing, copying, dividing and erasing elements. Each of these actions can be transformed into a CP-graph rule, where the CP-graph of the left-hand side represents the element or elements which are changed and the right-hand side CP-graph represents a new configuration of shapes. CP-graphs representing design drawings can be further modified by automatically applying sequences of CP-graph transformation rules selected by the user.

Therefore the system provides schemes of rules, which are most often applied to develop or change graphs. These rules can contain previously defined graphs corresponding to visual patterns and allow to replace them by graphs representing other patterns. It is shown that the specification of graph rewriting rules can be facilitated by presenting them on the visual level.

A CP-graph rewrite rule consists of two CP-graphs L and R. The former (L) describes a subgraph of a derived CP-graph that after application of the rewriting operation is replaced by the latter (R), which is embedded in the rest CP-graph. Graphs L and R with the same number of free bonds, i.e. the ones which are not connected, can easily replace each other with the constant embedding in the rest part of the CP-graph. In Fig. 5 the rhombuses connecting red solid edges with blue dotted ones are used to indicate bonds of R which replace bonds of L in the derived CP-graph. VIZMOGR system allows users to define rewriting rules with other embeddings by drawing red solid edges with rhombuses for all free bonds of the CP-graph L and drawing blue dotted edges connecting free bonds of the CP-graph R with appropriate rhombuses.

VIZMOGR system offers five schemes of rules, which are presented in Fig. 5. These schemes correspond to rules which are most often applied in order to develop graphs. The rule presented in Fig. 5a allows for adding a new node and connecting its bond by an edge with a bond of the existing node. The rule from Fig. 5b allows for adding a new node and connecting its bonds by edges with bonds of the two already existing nodes. The rules shown in Figs. 5c–e allow for adding two new nodes with bonds connected by an edge and connecting bonds of them with bonds of the existing node. The difference in rules from Figs. 5c– e lies in location of free bonds in the nodes of the rule right-hand sides. The embedding of the scheme rules is indicated using rhombuses. The cooperating designers can extend existing or add new rule schemes in order to modify graphs being generated according to their needs. After selecting a given rule scheme the user gives labels to nodes and edges, specifies numbers of bonds for nodes, and direction of edges. Schemes can be adapted for modelling all types of objects for which sets of icons have been specified.

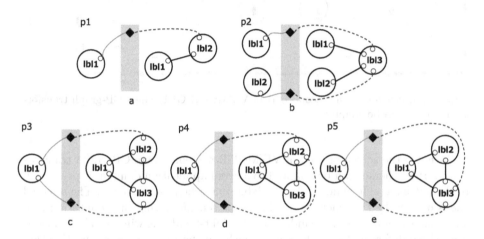

Fig. 5. Five CP-graph transformation rule schemes (Color figure online)

The system supports attributed graphs which allow for propagating seman- tic information throughout the modelling process. Applying CP-graph trans- formation rules leads to generation of different CP-graphs representing possi- ble design object structures with geometry and material properties specified by graph attributes. Each rewriting rule is also equipped with a predicate of appli- cability specifying conditions under which the rule can be used.

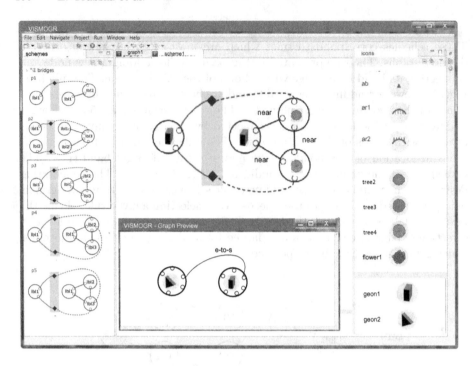

Fig. 6. A screenshot of the second part of VIZMOGR GUI, where CP-graph transformation rules can be adapted

In Fig. 6 the screen of GUI of VIZMOGR system, where CP-graph transformation rule schemes can be adapted to a given application domain, is presented. In the left-hand side window the available rule schemes are shown. The selected one is marked by the black frame. The same scheme during the adaptation process is shown in the central window. In the right-hand side window labelled icons from three different design domains, which can be used in the adaptation, are presented. A preview window with a current state of the graph to which adapted rules can be applied is also shown.

A CP-graph presented in Fig. 7a is obtained as the result of collaboration of a garden designer and an architect. It represents a fragment of a building in the Neoclassical style to which a winding path with six trees at the back adjoints (see Fig. 7c). In Fig. 7b a visual pattern representing a characteristic feature of the Neoclassical style is illustrated.

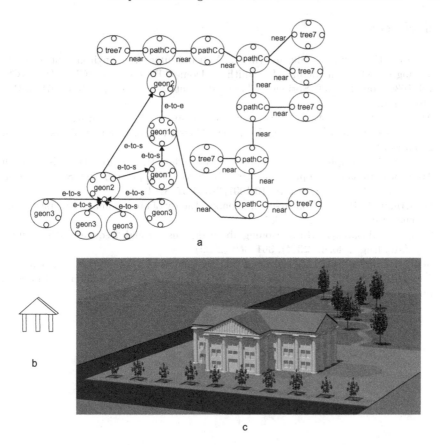

Fig. 7. (a) A CP-graph representing a fragment of the bottom design, (b) a visual pattern representing a characteristic feature of the Neoclassical style, (c) a building in the Neoclassical style with an adjoining path and trees.

4   Conclusions

In this paper the prototype interactive system which supports collaboration of different domain designers has been described. It enables encoding fragmentary knowledge as the users can specify various sets of icons representing components of objects related to different fields. The graph nodes with icons are arranged in the form of CP-graphs representing preliminary designs. The conceptual phase of the object design process is also supported by providing schemes of CP-graph transformation rules in a visual editor. The presented examples show the way in which the system supports encoding knowledge needed to design bridges, gardens and different forms of buildings.

In the next steps of our research the memory of graph rules will be used to ensure the presence of a predefined number of selected components within a designed object and to preserve some required characteristics of the design.

References

1. Grabska, E., Strug, B., Ślusarczyk, G.: A visual interactive environment for engineering knowledge modelling. In: Smith, I., Domer, B. (eds.) EG-ICE 2018. LNCS, vol. 10863, pp. 219–230. Springer, Cham (2018). https://doi.org/10.1007/978-3-319-91635-4_12
2. Alexander, C., Ishikawa, S., Silverstein, M., Jacobson, M., Fiksdahl-King, I., Angel, S.: A Pattern Language: Towns, Buildings, Construction. Oxford University Press, Oxford (1977)
3. Grabska, E.: Graphs and designing. In: Schneider, H.J., Ehrig, H. (eds.) Graph Transformations in Computer Science. LNCS, vol. 776, pp. 188–202. Springer, Heidelberg (1994). https://doi.org/10.1007/3-540-57787-4_12
4. Biederman, I.: Recognition-by-components: a theory of human image understanding. Psychol. Rev. **94**, 115–147 (1987)
5. Strug, B., Ślusarczyk, G.: Reasoning about designs through frequent patterns mining. Adv. Eng. Inform. **23**(4), 361–369 (2009)
6. Strug, B., Ślusarczyk, G., Grabska, E.: Design patterns in generation of artefacts in required styles. In: Proceedings of the 19th Generative Art Conference, Florence, pp. 71–78 (2016)

Automatic Generation of Architecture in Context

Agnieszka Mars[✉]

Jagiellonian University, Kraków, Poland
agnieszka.mars@uj.edu.pl

Abstract. Fitting a new architectural object into existing context requires thorough investigation of local environment, including its cultural and historical background. This paper summarizes problems connected with designing architecture in context and raises an idea of a system able to automatically generate architectural forms with regard to the surroundings. On the basis of reference buildings' models, graph grammars are created and used for constructing new prototypes which possess a character of the place they belong to. Methods of adaptation of an automatically created grammar to the designer's needs are proposed.

Keywords: Collaborative design of architecture · Architecture in context Automatic generation of architecture

1 Introduction

Fitting a new architectural object into existing context requires thorough investigation of local environment, including its cultural and historical background [2]. This paper summarizes problems connected with designing architecture in context and raises an idea of a system able to automatically generate architectural forms with regard to the surroundings. On the basis of reference buildings' models, graph grammars are created and used for constructing new prototypes which possess a character of the place they belong to. Methods of adaptation of an automatically created grammar to the designer's needs are proposed. The paper is organized as follows: The next section raises main issues associated with fitting a new design into architectural context. The third section presents a method of automatic creation of a graph grammar that can be used for generation of new buildings prototypes. Finally, some conclusion is made.

2 Fitting into Context

This section raises main issues associated with fitting a new design into architectural context. Creating architecture is a complex task which requires wide knowledge about design rules and broadly defined context of the proposed object. The Royal Australian Institute of Architects NSW Chapter and the Heritage Office have published a guide for design infill architecture in the historic environment [3]. According to the guidelines, new development in a conservation area must be appropriate under the following

© Springer Nature Switzerland AG 2018
Y. Luo (Ed.): CDVE 2018, LNCS 11151, pp. 163–166, 2018.
https://doi.org/10.1007/978-3-030-00560-3_22

criteria: scale, form, siting, materials and color, detailing. All of them define the character of an individual building or group of buildings. New designs are expected to introduce novel ideas, but also to keep the character of the place. Although the fitness criteria are often vague and contradictory, it seems possible to construct a tool for automatic generation of architectural prototypes on the basis of the character of reference buildings. The method of evaluation of architecture in context was proposed in [1]. It uses composite graphs for structural representation of architectural objects. The graphs are constructed on the basis of Biederman's Recognition-By-Components theory (RBC), a model of visual perception which assumes that human brain divides objects into primitives and investigates relations between them in order to perform identification. Therefore, each graph consists of attributed nodes representing RBC primitives – geons, and attributed edges representing relations: RBC edge-to-edge (ee) and edge-to-side (es), and relation of immersion (i). Each node contains bonds that represent geon's surfaces and each graph edge connects two bonds. Once the graphs of the proposed building and its architectural context are constructed, it is possible to automatically generate graph grammars that define languages of both new building and its context. The comparison of the obtained grammars enables to assess to what degree the new building uses the language of the surrounding architecture. Figure 1a presents a buildings characteristic for Kraków district Bronowice. 1b. contains the model of the building composed of geons, and 1c. contains a subgraph of its graph representation. The nodes represent the inner part of the roof and the building's main solid in edge-to-edge relation. The bonds are numbered and represent components' surfaces. Simplified production rules of a graph grammar which defines the architectural language of the discussed building are shown if 1d. Each new building can now be examined in terms of belonging to the defined language. The same method can be used for generation of new objects that fit into the context, however it is necessary to define the graph grammar more precisely in order to avoid incompatible projects.

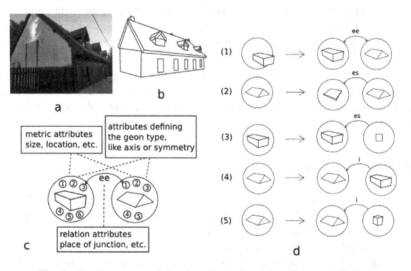

Fig. 1. Graph grammar defined on the basis of the reference building

3   Constructing a Grammar of Architectural Context

This section presents a method of automatic creation of a graph grammar that can be used for generation of new buildings prototypes with regard to the architectural context. The first step of this process requires the designer to provide models of the exemplary buildings whose character we want to imitate. The models should be composed of geons, which enables the generative tool to prepare their internal representation in the form of graph. On the basis of the obtained graph, a graph grammar is constructed. This process requires to determine an axiom graph, which consists of one node representing one of the biggest geons located on the ground. Then, for each related geon a production rule is created unless it does not already exist. If the new geons on the production right hand side are related to any other primitives in the graph structure, another rule is created, and so on. For example, the third rule in Fig. 1d adds a window to the building's main solid. It is defined only once, as multiple windows can be added with the use of this production. However, the grammar presented in Fig. 1d has some limitations. For example, it is possible to obtain a building which lacks components necessary for a given character, like a sloping roof over an oriel. Because exact location of each new geon is random for the purpose of diversity, it is also possible to generate a prototype with windows placed chaotically on the wall, which in case of the discussed type of buildings is contrary to the expected result. In order to define the context language more adequately, some system-designer interaction seems necessary. The user should be able to indicate groups of geons composing integral parts of a building. Figure 2 presents a groups of geons marked as s roof (a) and an oriel (b) The graph grammar is then constructed as presented in Fig. 2d. A building part is represented by a node labelled with its name, and there exists a production of replacing this node with a graph containing required geon nodes. In order to embed the new graph correctly, each of its node is indexed. The bonds of the ROOF node refer to all the surfaces of the geons from the derived graph. Each bond is labelled with an index of a node and a number of a surface bond. After replacing the ROOF node with the graph it is easy to determine the embedding edges. Production rules 1, 2, 6 and 7 refer to the building parts determined by the designer. Another example of the user's interaction with the system can be indicating a set of components that should be somehow related to each other, for instance aligned to the same line or plane (Fig. 2c). This results in a special production rule containing a group node, like WINDOWS in rules 4 and 5 of the discussed grammar. The node is attributed by location-y equal to p, which means that each derived node will have the same p value of the location-y attribute. The p value is then randomly assigned only once for the whole row of windows. It seems also necessary to provide the user interface with possibility to determine a number of buildings components. For example, one can need buildings that contain only one row of windows and no more than three chimneys. This can be achieved by adding a control diagram to the graph grammar to determine how many times each production rule should be used.

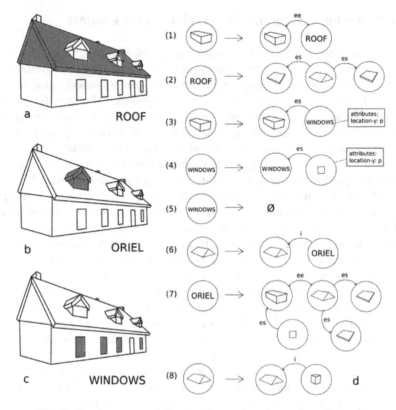

Fig. 2. Graph grammar defined with regard to the user's preferences

4   Conclusion

The presented method enables automatic recognition of the buildings character and generation of similar prototypes fitting into the context. This approach may be used in computer aided design of architecture, but also in automatic generation of scenery for computer games.

References

1. Mars, A., Grabska, E.: Aesthetics evaluation of architecture in context. In: Luo, Y. (ed.) CDVE 2017. LNCS, vol. 10451, pp. 193–201. Springer, Cham (2017). https://doi.org/10. 1007/978-3-319-66805-5_24
2. Unwin, S.: Analysing Architecture. Routledge, London (2003)
3. New South Wales. Heritage Office. & Royal Australian Institute of Architects. New South Wales Chapter: Infill Guidelines Working Party. Design in Context: Guidelines for Infill Development in the Historic Environment. Parramatta, NSW (2005)

Designing Cooperative User Experience for Smart Locks

Rui Zhang[1](✉), Yunfei Tian[2], and Hao Zhang[1]

[1] Hubei University of Arts and Science, Xiangyang 441053, China
xyrui1983@163.com, 358020431@qq.com
[2] Zhejiang University of Technology, Hangzhou 310014, China
25815556@qq.com

Abstract. As an emerging intelligent product, smart locks have not been widely used, with a late start. Users are facing with some problems of personal information input and output, and interaction with smart locks. This paper engages with this concern by presenting a double-funnel user research model of smart lock design. By surveying the current smart lock market, we devised a distributed system framework of cooperative user experience design. We also analyzed the relationship between the double-funnel user research and the cooperative user experience. Finally, we explored an application of the theoretical model of cooperative user experience on the smart lock design practice.

Keywords: Cooperative user experience · Smart lock
Double-funnel user research

1 Introduction

With the latest development of information technology and the Internet of Things, smart home systems and smart appliances become more popular. For security reasons, people prefer to install smart door locks as the traditional locks are considered less safe. Smart door lock is a smart authentication access control device replying on authorized person to lock/unlock the door in a smart home. One of the advantages of smart door lock is to control door open/close by an authorized person, other advantage is the access via smart phone where the user's regular key might have been lost or stolen [1].

In the process of smart locks research, development and innovation, the role of users should not go underestimated. There are quite a few research papers on the user experience and its application on the product design. In general, the aim of user experience research is to understand users' lifestyle: to explore users' consumption patterns, to understand users' experience with products, to identify users' motivation and expectations of products, to find out existing problems, and to collect users' opinions and requirements regarding product services.

In the life cycle of smart locks, users' requirements are always changing. For improving the market competitiveness of products, the smart lock innovation

Y. Luo (Ed.): CDVE 2018, LNCS 11151, pp. 167–175, 2018.
https://doi.org/10.1007/978-3-030-00560-3_23

requires collaboration with customers. It is important to understand users' needs and to incorporate the users' feedback into the product development. Therefore, this paper presents a collaborative approach to designing a solution by taking the user experience regarding smart locks into account. Based on the market analysis of smart locks, we extend the traditional user research, which focuses on the users' psychological experience, to a new double-funnel approach which combines user research with the design optimization.

The contributions of this paper are as follows: (i) we introduce and illustrate an approach to collaborative user experience design and the need for users' involvement, and (ii) we present shortly the best practices of smart lock design case as well as we draw a conclusion.

2   User Research for Smart Locks Design

2.1   Different Features of Smart Locks Design

A smart door lock, by and large, provides the safety and security of a traditional door lock by the use of smart technology and without physical keys. From the perspective of design, although different smart lock brands are all somewhat different in what they offer, some features of smart locks might include: appearance, operation, security, and service life. Table 1 summarizes selected features of designing smart locks and suggests design principles to meet users' expectations. It also highlights the benefits of owing a smart lock and challenges that can be used to analyze users' expectations.

Table 1. Smart lock design features, principles, benefits and challenges.

Design Features	Design Principles	Benefits	Challenges
- Demand: Solve the existing design issue and pull the innovation to make sure the smart lock design can directly take advantage of an opportunity in the market. - Invention: Push the innovation through research within the advanced technology.	- Respect the users preferences. - Design feasible function to meet the consumers requirements. - Avoid severe malfunctions. - Balance the usability and beauty. - Simplify the design for easier producing, less costs and more reliable product. - Good quality. - The interaction should be easier and more natural.	- Smart: Connecting to other devices (e.g. mobile phones, digital clocks, and televisions) for better management. - Convenience: providing simple and keyless entry. - Customization: Programing various codes to provide unique access to each person. - Making life easier and safer with the advanced technology.	- Smart technology can fail, e.g. suddenly stop working or cannot read users fingerprint. - Smart locks can be hacked. - Costs: smart locks cost much more than traditional locks. - After-sale service needs to be improved. - Good appearance design can be copied. - Artificial intelligence improves users experience.

2.2   User Study

In November 2017, we randomly interviewed 100 users of age from 25 to 55, with stable incomes, for learning about their consumer experience, opinions, attitudes and perceptions of smart locks. Each interview was sound recorded in a session lasting 45 min. A questionnaire with questions about gender, age, occupation, marital status, family structure and expectations for the smart locks was prepared. All interviewees were citizens of Wuhan, representing urban dwellers in the biggest metropolis in central China. Table 2 summarizes consumers' information and their expectations for smart locks.

The findings are grouped into two parts. The first part illustrates the necessity of owing a smart lock. Figure 1 (left) shows that, for 32% of interviewees, smart locks are helpful but not required, while 50% of them would like to purchase cost-effective smart locks at some point in the future. The number of customers who were ready to purchase smart locks of good quality straight away accounts for 18%.

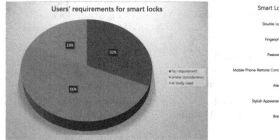 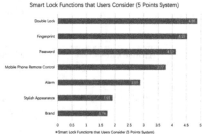

Fig. 1. (*left*) The users' requirements for smart locks. (*right*) Traits of different smart locks that users considered important.

The second part presents users' preference of features. Most interviewees appear to value the smart Double-Lock function while the fingerprint locking, password locking and mobile phone remote control functions seem also highly valued. In contrast, the proportions of other features such as the style, alarm, and brand are relatively low (see Fig. 1 (right)).

We have also found that the user demand for smart locks varies according to different age groups, incomes and values. For example, users of age from 35 to 50 are the main force of the customer market. Most of them are well educated and expect high life quality. For these customers, smart locks should be fully-functional with a long life cycle. These users desire a good quality and experience from smart locks. However, users who are over 50 years old, with traditional views, prefer more convenient products with a simple functionality.

Product designers often take their personal experience for the user experience. As the product design plan often does not match users' requirements, we suggest that users should participate in the process of product design to help

Table 2. Interviewees' information and their expectations for smart locks.

Users	Sex	Occupation	Age	Status	Expectations for smart locks
1	F	Officer	28	- Single - Lives alone	- Double-lock - Password - Alarm - Fingerprint lock
2	M	Primary school teacher	36	- Married - Lives with wife, son and old father	- Easy operation (His father has Alzheimer) - Password - Alarm - Low-cost
3	M	Student	26	- Single - Lives in uni apartment with roommates	- Fashion - Fingerprint lock - Facial recognition
4	M	Gymnast	30	- Married - Lives with wife and daughter	- Double-lock - Customized password - Fingerprint lock
5	F	Student	25	- Single - Lives alone	- Customized password - Fingerprint lock - Mobile remote control - Low-cost
6	F	Housewife	45	- Married - Lives with husband and daughter	- Password - Fingerprint lock - Low-cost
7	M	Professor	52	- Married - Lives with wife	- Easy operation - Double-lock - Fingerprint lock - Mobile remote control
8	F	Project manager	36	- Single - Lives alone	- Fashion - Fingerprint lock - Mobile remote control - Alarm
9	M	Hotel manager	37	- Married - Lives with wife - No child	- Customized password - Fingerprint lock - Mobile remote control
10	F	Communication designer	28	- Married - Lives with husband - No child	- Easy operation - Double-lock - Fingerprint lock - Mobile remote control
11	F	Housewife	54	- Married - Lives with husband	- Easy operation - Customized Password - Low-cost
12	M	Chef	33	- Single - Lives alone	- Fingerprint lock - Mobile remote control - Low-cost
...	...	...	...	...	...
100	M	Accountant	32	- Married - Lives with wife and son	- Fingerprint lock - Mobile remote control - Alarm

user requirements to be met, and their experiences to be stored and reused. The user study above helped us to define the product concept and understand the target user group. The smart lock design should focus on the users' requirement and expectations, while designers should share professional knowledge with users and cooperate with them.

2.3 The Double-Funnel User Research Model

The collection of data and questionnaire survey are carried out to find out characteristics of the target group. After a qualitative research on the chosen target group, we get user data by optimizing and integrating it followed by defining users' roles and situations. Then, designers can simulate the target environment and the ways the product is used to propose more feasible design. Particularly, the user observation and interview are the direct resource for qualitative research, which helps researchers understand users' motivations.

During the smart locks development, the user research is continuously expanding and opportunity seeking process which goes from the single stage before progressing to multiple stages. It can be considered as a funnel by starting from a single point, while the design decision focuses on details in top-bottom manner. Thereby, a double-funnel user research model with non-linear features can be devised.

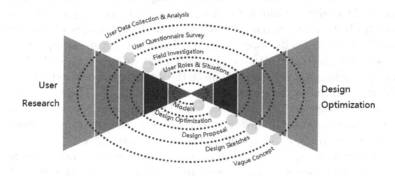

Fig. 2. Double-funnel user research model.

As shown in Fig. 2, designers propose some fuzzy concepts based on understanding the user background information, and then propose schematic design according to results of the questionnaire survey. In the stage of user interview, designers can acquire direct and effective suggestions from users by presenting design sketches. Next, design sketches can be modified to fit various user roles and situations. Meanwhile, designers can improve design concepts by making product models. Specifically, in this double-funnel model, we combine the user research with the design optimization in order to stimulate users by suggesting to them detailed design concepts continuously. This approach promotes innovation in the product design stage. More importantly, even if the user research process is interrupted by any unforeseen circumstances, the outcomes of the user research will not be lost and can be still used in the design stage.

Due to the double-funnel user research, smart lock design should be an interactive process which is based on the users' experience and developed between researchers and designers. Knowledge of smart locks is generated by users and will be used as the design information. On one hand, researchers collect useful information that benefits smart lock innovation and share the information with designers so that designers can explore new approaches. On the other, smart lock design should not only be focused on the users' needs or knowledge, but it also should consider the users' opinions and activities.

3   Cooperative User Experience Design for Smart Locks Based on Double-Funnel User Research

3.1   Double-Funnel User Research as a Main Motivation

Based on the double-funnel user research, the most valued features of smart locks can be identified. Moreover, the innovative design can be pushed through the research on users' expectations of smart locks and differences in the expectations between different user types. The double-funnel user research focuses on users' participation and interactivity which helps designers to filter useless user data and take right design decisions. In this process, as users compare experiences, they are likely to find various advantages and disadvantages of the product and classify them in specific usage contexts. The users' entire experience process cannot be easily abstracted. However, we can re-design this process. In designing for user experience, it is necessary to make the designs concrete so that they can be easily experienced by designers and future users alike [2]. Therefore, we would like to design a new cooperative user experience to help solving the existing design issue and promote innovation to make sure the smart lock design can directly take advantage of an opportunity in the market.

The cooperative experience is about user experiences in social interaction. It happens when experiences are created together or shared with others [2]. For smart locks design, the cooperative user experience design means that designers and users cooperate to achieve the product innovation based on the user experience research. Guided by the double-funnel user research model, we propose two approaches for designers to cooperate with users to improve the user experience.

User-Oriented Cooperation. Firstly, target user groups are formed. Designers invite users to share their personal knowledge and experiences with each other by collecting user data and treating user roles and situations as the outcome. Meanwhile, the original initial concept of a smart lock will be verified by the users' experience. Accordingly, designers can make smart lock models with low fidelity and develop diversified prototypes in order to transform the research outcome into effective products.

Product-Oriented Cooperation. The cooperation also can be initiated with the smart lock at focus. Firstly, one can define the smart lock features and create a few of initial concepts in brainstorming sessions. By analyzing the relationship between smart locks and users, designers translate initial concepts into design sketches. Next, designers can improve and verify design sketches according to the user observations, user interviews or expert interviews. Moreover, they can deduce the user roles and situations by the use of low fidelity smart lock models and conclude the users' knowledge and experiences.

However, during the product innovation process, important information is easily overlooked. The designers and users should maintain good communication by phone calls, video conferences, on-line file transfers, and remote information sharing. Thus, users will be able to cooperate with designers effectively even if they operate from different locations.

3.2 Cooperative User Experience Framework

According to the user study, we devised a cooperative user experience framework which provides an opportunity for users to participate in the process of smart lock design. In this process, they can contribute their design ideas and make design decisions.

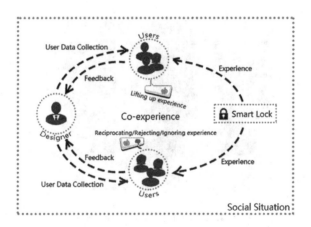

Fig. 3. Cooperative user experience framework.

Figure 3 shows how a user shares a significant experience while other users say that their experiences in choosing smart lock have been similar. All their shared experiences are communicated to the designer so that the designer can improve the smart lock designs. In this process, participants may use technology to share meaningful experiences and suggest what functions need to be improved, or even to reject any unnecessary features of smart locks.

3.3 Cooperative User Experience in Smart Lock Conceptual Design

In this smart lock design case, we address the user-oriented cooperation.

Due to the user study, the security, technology and convenience are the primary factors that users expected. We chose plenty of modern design elements during the brainstorming sessions to simplify the design concepts and finally determined two keywords: security and technology (see Fig. 4). A security system is defined as a device which detects intrusion, unauthorized entry into a building or a protected area and denies such unauthorized access to protect personnel and property from damage or harm [3]. The technology means the intelligent upgrade of door locks and the enhancement of human-product interaction. The design principles are as follows:

1. Consistency: Product concepts should be consistent with the user cognition. Smart lock commands should be consistent with user needs.
2. Comfortability: Smart lock dimensions should conform to the ergonomics.
3. Conciseness: The smart lock operation should be simple and easy to understand. Commands should be clear. The transmission of data should be fast.
4. Aesthetics: The design style conforms to the current aesthetic and fashion trends.

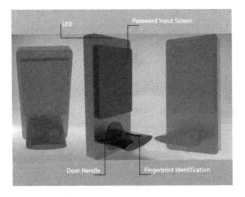

Fig. 4. Smart lock design sketches.

4 Conclusion

In the product design process, a cooperative user experience is created by interaction between designers and users. Observations from designers and feedback from users help product design in a cooperative social environment. The cooperative user experience leads to an advanced understanding of user experience and design possibilities. It is important to see what the design content is, what users do, how they share experiences, and how they put information into the design context. The cooperative user experience provides new opportunities for product design by focusing on the role of human-product interaction while providing inspiration for both designers and users.

This is a pilot study of the cooperative user experience in the product design. We have characterized current approaches to experience from a number of disciplines and presented a framework for designing the cooperative user experience for the smart lock design. In the future, we will present how this framework can be applied by a product design team to understand and generate all kinds of interactions and experiences that new product and system designs may require.

References

1. Abdullah, S.M.: Design secured smart door lock based on jaro winkler algorithm. Tikrit J. Pure Sci. **21**(6), 154–158 (2016)
2. Forlizzi, J., Battarbee, K.: Understanding experience in interactive systems. In: Proceedings of the 5th Conference on Designing Interactive Systems: Processes, Practices, Methods, and Techniques, Cambridge, MA, USA, pp. 261–268 (2014). https://doi.org/10.1145/1013115.1013152
3. Hossain, M.K., Biswas, P., Mynuddin, M., Morsalin, S.: Design and implementation of smart home security system. Int. J. Mod. Embed. Syst. **2**(6), 7–10 (2014)

3D CyberCOP: A Collaborative Platform for Cybersecurity Data Analysis and Training

Alexandre Kabil[1]([✉]), Thierry Duval[1], Nora Cuppens[1], Gérard Le Comte[2], Yoran Halgand[3], and Christophe Ponchel[4]

[1] IMT Atlantique, UBL, Lab-STICC, UMR CNRS 6285, Brest, France
{alexandre.kabil,thierry.duval,nora.cuppens}@imt-atlantique.fr
[2] Societe Generale, Paris, France
Gerard.Le-Comte@socgen.com
[3] EDF, Paris, France
yoran.halgand@edf.fr
[4] AIRBUS Defence and Space, Elancourt, France
christophe.ponchel@airbus.com

Abstract. Although Immersive Analytics solutions are now developed in order to ease data analysis, cyber security systems are still using classical graphical representations and are not harnessing yet the potential of virtual reality systems and collaborative virtual environments. 3D Collaborative Virtual Environments (3DCVE) can be used in order to merge learning and data analysis approaches, as they can allow users to have a better understanding of a cyber situation by mediating interactions towards them and also by providing different points of view of the same data, on different scales. So we propose a 3D Cyber Common Operational Picture (3D CyberCOP) that will allow operators to face together a situation by using immersive and non immersive visualizations and by collaborating through user-defined roles. After visiting French Security Operations Centers (SOCs), we have defined a collaborative interaction model and some use-cases, to assess of the effectiveness of our solution.

Keywords: Cybersecurity · Collaborative interaction · Virtual reality

1 Introduction

Cybersecurity is a cross-domain activity that requires ground skills on several fields such as data analysis, scripting, compilation, risk assessment etc. This is why modern trend is to put the emphasis on user's education and data analysis, as everything that occurs on a network is logged and data breaches are very often due to mistakes made by negligent employees. Far from pop culture stereotypes, cyber operators use classical Command Line Interfaces (CLI) and Graphical User Interfaces (GUI) to detect incidents and cyber threats whereas other domains look at Natural User Interfaces (NUI) to increase user's situational awareness,

Y. Luo (Ed.): CDVE 2018, LNCS 11151, pp. 176–183, 2018.
https://doi.org/10.1007/978-3-030-00560-3_24

which is one of the main objectives of data visualization solutions. Likewise, expert cyber training tools lack visual information, even though several serious games for cybersecurity are available. Although the actual trend is to regroup cyber operators into specific structures, few collaborative systems are used in cybersecurity.

We firstly show that 3D Collaborative Virtual Environments (3DCVE) can be used in cybersecurity as a mix between Immersive Analytics approaches and serious games for training to put users into cyber-physical environments where realistic scenarios and real-time data can be provided and we will propose a 3D Cyber Common Operational Picture (3D CyberCOP) to deal with these issues. Then we present the model we built after visiting French SOCs and analysing operators collaborative and visualization needs. Several roles and collaboration types, cyber-physical views and mutual awareness cues should be used in order to provide a relevant cyber COP both for experts and novice users.

Finally, we present a specific use case we are developing based on a ransomware attack scenario where analysts, coordinator and client roles will have to cooperate in order to determine Wannacry's Indicators Of Compromise (IOCs).

2   Collaborative Virtual Environments for Cybersecurity

As more and more data are generated and collected on networks, analysts face a 'needle in a haystack' problem when they want to detect attacks. Thus, cybersecurity visualizations face a paradox: they need to be simple enough in order to help analysts to understand what is going on the network and they need to be precise enough to help them investigating incidents. 3D collaborative data visualizations and Immersive Analytics solutions can help solving these problems by either separate views towards different analysts but letting them having a common ground, or proposing aggregated 3D interactive data representations that can give more information [2,5]. Even if 3D representations are useful in some cases highlighted by Cliquet et al. [3], we have not seen much 3D visualizations for cybersecurity, apart from the 2012 Daedalus-viz project developed by Inoue et al. [6]. Moreover, even if operator training is an important topic in cybersecurity, only few systems propose virtual environment for training, serious game-based scenarios and expert data analytics tools [1,10].

This is why we are currently working on an immersive collaborative system for cybersecurity called 3D CyberCOP: we propose a 3DCVE that can be fitted for collaborative cybersecurity investigations and reporting practices [7] (Fig. 1). Collaborative approaches can take advantage of metaphoric representations as each user can have her/his proper way of interacting and visualizing data according to her/his practices, and in order to analyze these practices and contexts of use, we have developed a collaborative activity model for cybersecurity.

3   Modeling Cybersecurity Collaborative Activities

Actual national trend is to regroup cybersecurity employees into collaborative structures as Security Operations Centers (SOCs) or Computer Emergency

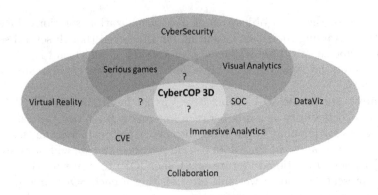

Fig. 1. Venn diagram of 3D CyberCOP, which is at the crossroads of CVE, DataViz and cyber security.

Response Teams (CERTs). SOCs for example are well-defined structures[1] where networks are constantly monitored in real-time by analysts, who are separated in three technical levels and who investigate incidents either for client companies or for internal security. There exists studies about SOCs practices [11,12] but as cybersecurity is by definition a confidential field it is still difficult to record data for making activity analysis.

3.1 SOC Activity Analysis

Thanks to our industrial partners from the CyberCNI chair[2], we have had the opportunity to visit some French SOCs to perform studies by asking questions and sending questionnaires inspired from [4]. Day to day SOC's operators work relies on getting aware of alerts from cybersecurity sensors, suppressing false positive alerts, analyzing network meta-data and application logs, creating incident reports and exchanging information and requests with customer teams (network, security, decision). They need to work quickly, so if they consider that an incident is out of their technical scope, they forward it to an expert (escalation process). We found out that operators work usually alone by taking tickets from the Security Information and Event Management (SIEM) tool, backbone of SOCs, which collects different kind of data, correlate them and raise alerts (with a quite high rate of false positives).

Collaboration is not so much mediated as operators exchange directly between them or during meetings with managers and decision-makers. As a consequence, some of them have expressed the needs for user-adapted visualization tools that will allow them to share information and even to interact simultaneously on datasets. We found out too that SOCs cannot act against malicious activities if decision-makers or clients does not give them proper authorizations.

---

[1] https://www.mitre.org/capabilities/cybersecurity/overview/cybersecurity-blog/ten-strategies-for-becoming-a-world-class.

[2] https://www.chairecyber-cni.org/en/home/.

These findings have allowed us to define a collaborative activity model that will complete our 3D CyberCOP proposal.

3.2   3D CyberCOP Collaborative Activity Model

As shown in Fig. 2, 3D CyberCOP aims at proposing SOC operators adapted visualizations according to their individual (black arrows) and collaborative (red arrows) practices and interactions: with 3D CyberCOP, first we propose to enhance the individuals interactive systems to make them collaborative and/or more immersive, with collaborative interactions mediated by the systems (green arrows), and second we adapt the level of immersion (Virtual Reality, Windows, Icons, Menu and Pointers (WIMP), post-WIMP interfaces) to user's roles. After taking into accounts SOC operators' information, we have decided to build our model regarding these points:

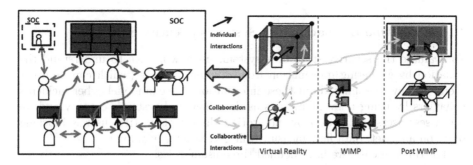

Fig. 2. Classical SOC activities (Left) and the role adaptation we want to do in 3D CyberCOP (Right).

- Inspired from [9], user-defined roles as analyst (who dig into data), coordinator (who have a high-level view of the situation) and decision-maker (who can authorize remediation actions) will be proposed. These roles will be complementary as they give access to different kind of data.
- 2D, 3D and immersive views will be provided in order to give high and low level information. Egocentric and exocentric point of views and the abilities to filter data and to switch between views will facilitate data correlation. For example, network topology information could be displayed on a classical 2D dashboard or within a 3D cyber-physical environment where the physical position of its assets into company's offices will help operator to make direct links between IP Addresses, geographic positions and last known users.
- Horizontal (between user that have the same interaction and visualization capabilities) and vertical collaboration (between users that have not the same capabilities) will be supported with respect to hierarchical links and roles. Asymmetric interaction will be defined as well in order to provide mutual

awareness by using annotations or orders, as in [8]. For example, analysts will be able to share their investigations traces with each other by letting visual cues on assets and Coordinator will be able to give them orders even if they are not sharing the same space by highlighting zones of interests.

– We will consider using aggregated SIEM-like data instead of raw information to build cyber incidents scenarios developed by experts in order to provide relevant situations, like in a serious-game approach.

In order to implement and evaluate our model, we have selected with our industrial partners a real-time attack analysis use-case.

4   3D Cyber COP Real-Time Analysis Use Case

We have decided to work on a real-time system's security state evaluation use case and we are currently developing a scenario based on a ransomware attack.

4.1   Real-Time Evaluation of a System's Security State

To evaluate the security state of a system, users will have to understand the situation by gathering information from different sources (which can be other users) and by reasoning about these information. We can model cyber incidents behaviors by using relevant metrics as data flow and system's entropy and we can assess users interaction by monitoring these metrics (if a user is blocking ports on an asset, data flow measure will decrease for example).

For this use case, we have defined three users' roles:

– The analyst will be able to investigate data and report incidents or anomalous behaviors to coordinator. S/He will take advantage of immersive technologies in order to better apprehend the situation by switching between cyber and physical representations of the environment.
– The coordinator will dispose of an holistic view of system's security state. S/He will take analysts' reports and give them instructions according to what they are dealing with. He/She will give reports to client.
– The client will have access to specific visualizations (e.g. running applications and processes of his/her computers) and s/he will be able to ask for remediation actions from the analyst or a status report from the coordinator.

Each operator will have to deal with partial system's information. They will have to switch between exocentric or egocentric point of views or to collaborate in order to correlate information and to understand a situation. Figure 3 shows different operators' interfaces ((a) and (b) are coordinator views and (c) and (d) are analyst's ones)): (a) contains a God's Eye View of the 3DCVE (red square) where red dot is an analyst and greed dot a selected asset and information about metrics and alerts (black square); (b) have a graph view of the network (red square) and information about assets and graph filters (black square); (c) and (d) are cyber-physical views of the environment that display different information.

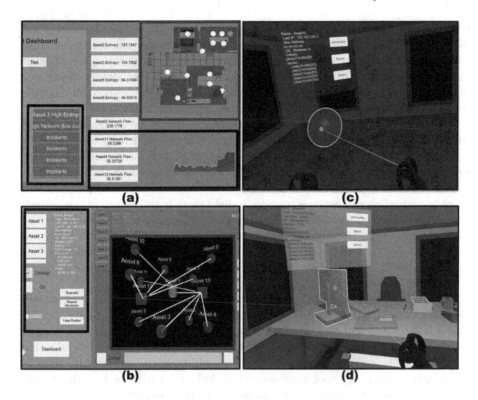

Fig. 3. Several views of our 3D CyberCOP Prototype. (Color figure online)

As we want 3D CyberCOP to be used both for data analysis and training, we will rely on experts specifications to provide deterministic situations:
data investigation will be simplified to allow novice and experts to perform system's security state evaluation. Novices will be able to deal with the situation
by making simple actions (as an example getting network or operating system
information from assets by selecting them and clicking an interface button),
monitoring simple metrics (network data, as in Fig. 3) (a)) and having visual or
audio feedbacks of incidents (specific sound or particle effects) whereas experts
will have the opportunity to dig into specific piece of evidence by creating data
filters (by highlighting assets that shares common aspects) or exchanging precise
information (by selecting a specific UI button while selecting an asset).

We are currently using an attack scenario based on Wannacry ransomware
to develop a use case as an example of a possible use of our system.

4.2 3D CyberCOP Wannacry Attack Scenario

Wannacry is a ransomware that caused a lot of damages last year by encrypting
computer's files and propagating itself through networks using operating systems
exploits (DoublePulsar and EternalBlue). It only have attacked computers on
Windows 7, not updated and without a direct link to internet. These behavior

cues are called Wannacry Indicators Of Compromise (IOC). We have modeled Wannacry by using only two metrics, the asset's entropy and data flow: if an asset is infected, its entropy rises and when the ransomware propagates to other assets the data flow increases. These metrics can represent simply Wannacry malicious activities but they can measure false positive activities too (for example if someone is doing a file backup on an extern server, both metrics will increase).

Scenario objective is to determine Wannacry IOCs by correlating partial information taken from cyber-physical representations and from classical data dashboards. Analysts will be able to use virtual reality interfaces to find evidences. Coordinator and client will have access to classical or tactile displays, with respect to SOC practices. Asymmetric interactions between operators will provide mutual awareness cues in order to help users to understand their respective actions such as providing a visualization of operators' actions history or assets highlighting. Data filtering and cyber-physical visualizations will be provided in order to ease correlation. Visual or audio cues will be available for novices in order to help them in the incidents detection. Collaboration will be co-localized and users will have roughly 15 min to find IOCs.

We are still working on 3D prototypes and scenarios (Fig. 3) but soon we will be able to drive our first alpha experiments that will compare our solution to 2D classical ones, and will give us information on which parts of prototypes we need to improve and which parts work well. Cyber situational awareness evaluation methods will be employed too. Moreover, we will have the opportunity soon to use a real cyber-range tool provided by an industrial partner in order to use realistic cybersecurity data and scenarios rather than modeled ones.

5   Conclusion

Cybersecurity domain relies heavily on data analysis and people education in order to face a growing number of cyber attacks that exploit now employees mistakes more than security flaws to compromise systems. Struggling against cyber threats is a more and more demanding task but we have shown that practices are still underestimating the capabilities of 3D CVEs and virtual reality technologies. In order to tackle these issues, we propose a 3D CyberCOP platform that aims at coupling data visualization and serious gaming approaches. After visiting French SOCs where we have seen that the expected collaboration between users is not well mediated, we have proposed a collaborative activity model and we are developing a scenario based on a real-time cyber attack analysis in order to evaluate the platform. The objective of our 3D CyberCOP will be to merge immersive data visualizations with learning approaches by adapting existing cybersecurity collaborative practices in order to increase users cyber situational awareness.

Acknowledgments. This work was supported by the Cyber CNI Chair of Institute Mines Télécom, which is held by IMT Atlantique and supported by Airbus Defence and Space, Amossys, EDF, Orange, La Poste, Nokia, Société Générale and the Regional Council of Brittany. It has been acknowledged by the Center of excellence in Cyber Security.

References

1. Alotaibi, F., Furnell, S., Stengel, I., Papadaki, M.: A review of using gaming technology for cyber-security awareness. Int. J. Inf. Secur. Res. (IJISR) **6**(2), 660–666 (2016)
2. Chandler, T., et al.: Immersive analytics. In: Big Data Visual Analytics (BDVA), pp. 1–8. IEEE (2015)
3. Cliquet, G., Perreira, M., Picarougne, F., Prié, Y., Vigier, T.: Towards hmd-based immersive analytics. In: Immersive analytics Workshop, IEEE VIS 2017, Phoenix, United States, October 2017. https://hal.archives-ouvertes.fr/hal-01631306
4. D'Amico, A., Buchanan, L., Kirkpatrick, D., Walczak, P.: Cyber operator perspectives on security visualization. In: Nicholson, D. (ed.) Advances in Human Factors in Cybersecurity, pp. 69–81. Springer, Cham (2016). https://doi.org/10.1007/978-3-319-41932-9_7
5. Hackathorn, R., Margolis, T.: Immersive analytics: Building virtual data worlds for collaborative decision support. In: 2016 Workshop on Immersive Analytics (IA), pp. 44–47, March 2016. https://doi.org/10.1109/IMMERSIVE.2016.7932382
6. Inoue, D., Eto, M., Suzuki, K., Suzuki, M., Nakao, K.: Daedalus-viz: Novel real-time 3D visualization for darknet monitoring-based alert system. In: Proceedings of the Ninth International Symposium on Visualization for Cyber Security, VizSec 12, pp. 72–79. ACM, New York (2012). https://doi.org/10.1145/2379690.2379700
7. Kabil, A., Thierry, D., Nora, C., Gerard, L., Yoran, H., Christophe, P.: Why should we use 3D collaborative virtual environments (3dcve) for cyber security? In: 2018 IEEE Third VR International Workshop on Collaborative Virtual Environments (3DCVE), March 2018
8. Le Chénéchal, M., Chalmé, S., Duval, T., Royan, J., Gouranton, V., Arnaldi, B.: Toward an enhanced mutual awareness in asymmetric CVE. In: Proceedings of International Conference on Collaboration Technologies and Systems (CTS 2015) (2015)
9. McKenna, S., Staheli, D., Meyer, M.: Unlocking user-centered design methods for building cyber security visualizations. In: 2015 IEEE Symposium on Visualization for Cyber Security (VizSec), pp. 1–8. IEEE (2015)
10. Richards, D., Taylor, M.: A comparison of learning gains when using a 2D simulation tool versus a 3D virtual world. Comput. Educ. **86**(C), 157–171 (2015). https://doi.org/10.1016/j.compedu.2015.03.009
11. Sundaramurthy, S.C., McHugh, J., Ou, X., Wesch, M., Bardas, A.G., Rajagopalan, S.R.: Turning contradictions into innovations or: How we learned to stop whining and improve security operations. In: Twelfth Symposium on Usable Privacy and Security (SOUPS 2016), pp. 237–251. USENIX Association, Denver (2016). https://www.usenix.org/conference/soups2016/technical-sessions/presentation/sundaramurthy
12. Takahashi, T., Kadobayashi, Y., Nakao, K.: Toward global cybersecurity collaboration: cybersecurity operation activity model. In: Proceedings of ITU Kaleidoscope 2011: The Fully Networked Human? - Innovations for Future Networks and Services (K-2011), pp. 1–8, December 2011

Conflict Coordination and Its Implementation Probability of Product Low-Carbon Design

Fangzhi Gui[1], Jianqiang Zhou[2], Yanwei Zhao[1(✉)], Linan Zhu[3], and Fen Zhu[1]

[1] School of Mechanical Engineering, Zhejiang University of Technology, Hangzhou 310014, People's Republic of China
guifangzhi@qq.com, zyw@zjut.edu.cn, 870524683@qq.com, 1206952448@qq.com
[2] School of Mechanical Engineering, Quzhou University, Quzhou 324000, People's Republic of China
zjqaydf@163.com
[3] School of Computer Science and Technology, Zhejiang University of Technology, Hangzhou 310014, People's Republic of China
zln@zjut.edu.cn

Abstract. To solve the demand-attribute conflict problem of product low carbon design, a conflict coordination method, which integrates TRIZ (Theory of Inventive Problem Solving) and Extenics, is put forward. The low-carbon attributes are mapped to the product structures that is related to the core conflict problem. And then, the complex conflict problems are transformed to simple and independent ones relatively. The conflict problems with single or multi structure are coordinated by a formal conflict model and we can calculate the coordination probabilities to get a design scheme guide. At the end, a carbon footprint requirement for a screw compressor is taken as an example to verify the effectiveness and feasibility of the coordination method.

Keywords: Low carbon design · Conflict coordination · TRIZ
Extenics

1 Introduction

Low-carbon design, which aims to reduce the carbon emission, is a hot topic in product design [1, 2]. It is beneficial to product, economics, and society when the carbon footprint is optimized [3]. However, there are many design conflicts in the low-carbon design of the product, which increase the design cost, prolong the design cycle, and lead to a significant reduction in design efficiency [4, 5]. Therefore, the coordination of design conflicts is of great significance to application.

Low-carbon design conflict coordination, which is based on integration of Extenics and TRIZ, is a common method [6]. In this method, the core conflicts, which is described as incompatible problems and antithetical problems [7], of low-carbon innovative design are converted into physical contradictions and technical

© Springer Nature Switzerland AG 2018
Y. Luo (Ed.): CDVE 2018, LNCS 11151, pp. 184–191, 2018.
https://doi.org/10.1007/978-3-030-00560-3_25

contradictions. After that, the engineering parameters and contradictory matrices are determined, and the principle solutions of TRIZ are obtained by analysis of the separation principles and inventive principles. On the basis of the function principle innovation, structural innovation, optimization of structural parameters, etc., these principle solutions are classified to identify the transformable objects and incentive features of conflict coordination. Finally, the implementation probability is calculated under different variation strategies in different kinds of problems and constraints, and the feasible scheme will be output as well.

2 Variation Analysis of Related Structure of Core Conflict

With regard to the low-carbon attribute conflict, it is important to decompose a complex problem into simple problems, and the relatively innovation problems can be coordinated with a systematic design method. As shown in the following 5 steps:

Step 1: Model and classify complex system problems.
Step 2: Decompose the complex low-carbon attributes conflict problem into relatively simple and independent low-carbon technology innovation problems.
Step 3: Solve the problem of low-carbon technology innovations.
Step 4: Coordinate the decomposition of low-carbon technology innovation results.
Step 5: Evaluate the coordination result and decide to output or feedback.

If it is highly modularized, the relationship between low-carbon attributes of the product and the mapping of modules and structures would be clear. At the same time, it is easy to establish a single mapping relationship among low-carbon attribute, module and structure. Therefore, if there are many integrated modules, a low-carbon attribute-module-structure map can be established with integrated one (see Fig. 1., where $n \le m \le 1$, and ① indicates a one-to-one mapping; ② indicates a one-to-two mapping,

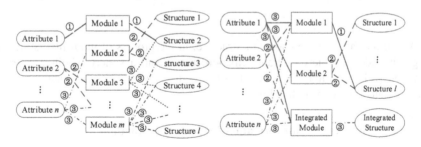

Fig. 1. Modular and integrated low-carbon attribute structured mapping

and ③ indicates a one-to-three or more mapping).

3   Multi-type Structure Innovation Conflict Coordination

3.1   Structural Analysis of Low Carbon Attribute Problems

Low-carbon design problems are classified into the incompatible and antithetical problems, and the core conflict problem of low-carbon attributes can be modeled as Eq. (1).

$$Q = IM * FS * DR = \{im_1, im_2, \ldots\} * \{str_1, str_2, \ldots\} * \{dr_{per}, dr_{cost}, dr_{env}\} \quad (1)$$

Where Q represents the conflict problem of low-carbon attributes; IM is the innovative principle solution (im is detailed principle solution); FS is the function structure (str is the detailed structure), and DR is the design constraints, such as the performance, cost and environment.

The extension transformation T, which is origin from the innovative principle solution IM, is used to transform structure str_i, which is shown in Eq. (2):

$$T str_i = str_i', str_i' \in \{str_{i,1}, str_{i,2}, \cdots\} \quad (2)$$

The analytic hierarchy process is applied to weight the all principle solutions, as shown in Eq. (3).

$$AHP(im_1, im_2, im_3, \ldots) = (\lambda_{im_1}, \lambda_{im_2}, \lambda_{im_3}, \ldots) \quad (3)$$

If Q_i and Q_j have a same solution, that is $IM_i \cap IM_j = imk$, and the result can be get as Eq. (4).

$$\begin{cases} \lambda_{im\_k}|_{im_k \in IM_i} \neq \lambda_{im\_k}|_{im_k \in IM_j}, & IM_i \cap IM_j = im_k \\ st_i' \neq str_j', & IM_i \cap IM_j = im_k, (str_i \neq str_j \text{ or } str_i = str_j, Q_i \neq Q_j) \\ str_i' = str_j', & IM_i \cap IM_j = im_k, str_i = str_j, Q_i \approx Q_j \end{cases}$$
$$(4)$$

Due to the fact that the choice of structure, in the process of innovative structural design, includes a variety of transformation factors and a variety of different transformation paths, resulting in a variety of structural innovation combinations under different transformation probabilities.

3.2   Single-Structure Transformation Conflict Coordination

The single-structure transformation refers that the single structure is implemented as the active transformation. It means that the other structures (including the transmission, position and supporting structures) will be changed conductively when the feature of incentive structure is changed. And there are 3 types:

Incompatible Problems or Physics Contradictions. When the interface F_{str_i} of structure str_i is active transformed, that is $\varphi F_{\text{str}_i} = F'_{\text{str}_i}$, and the linked interface $F_{\text{str}_{i-1}}$ and $F_{\text{str}_{i+1}}$ will be changed conductively, like Eq. (5).

$$\varphi F_{\text{str}_i} = F'_{\text{str}_i} \Rightarrow \begin{cases} T_{i-1} F_{\text{str}_{i-1}} = F'_{\text{str}_{i-1}}, & F_{\text{str}_{i-1}} \in \text{str}_{i-1}, F'_{\text{str}_{i-1}} \in \{F'_{\text{str}_{i-1,1}}, F'_{\text{str}_{i-1,2}}, \cdots\} \\ T_{i+1} F_{\text{str}_{i+1}} = F'_{\text{str}_{i+1}}, & F_{\text{str}_{i+1}} \in \text{str}_{i+1}, F'_{\text{str}_{i+1}} \in \{F'_{\text{str}_{i+1,1}}, F'_{\text{str}_{i+1,2}}, \cdots\} \end{cases}$$
$$\Rightarrow \begin{cases} T'_{i-1} \text{str}_{i-1} = \text{str}'_{i-1}, & \text{str}'_{i-1} \in \{\text{str}_{i-1,1}, \text{str}_{i-1,2}, \cdots\} \\ T'_{i+1} \text{str}_{i+1} = \text{str}'_{i+1}, & \text{str}'_{i+1} \in \{\text{str}_{i+1,1}, \text{str}_{i+1,2}, \cdots\} \end{cases}$$

$$(5)$$

The implementation probability of this solution will be calculated as Eq. (6).

$$p_1 = \lambda_{\text{im}_k} \bullet \lambda_{\text{str}_i} \bullet (\lambda_{\text{str}_{i-1}} + \lambda_{\text{str}_{i+1}}) \tag{6}$$

Where λ_{im_k} is the probability of active transformation, λ_{str_i} is the probability of conduction, $\lambda_{\text{str}_{i-1}}$ and $\lambda_{\text{str}_{i+1}}$ are conduction probabilities of previous and next level structure.

Technical Contradictions, and There Is a Common Structure Contained. That is $FS_i \cap FS_j = \text{str}_r$, and the method is same as above.

$$p_2 = \lambda_{\text{im}_k} \bullet \lambda_{\text{str}_r} \bullet (\lambda_{\text{str}_{r-1}} + \lambda_{\text{str}_{r+1}}) \tag{7}$$

Any Contradictory Problem, and There Is a High-Integrated Structure. For the highly integrated structure STR, there is no conduction, and the probability is:

$$p_3 = \lambda_{\text{im}_k} \bullet \lambda_{\text{STR}} \tag{8}$$

3.3 Multi-structure Transformation Conflict Coordination

The multi-structure transformation refers to: (1) for design conflicts of incompatible problems or physical contradictions, there are 2 or more structures related to each other; (2) for antithetical problems or technical contradictions, there are 2 or more interconnected structures.

Multi-structure Transformations in Incompatible Problems or Physical Contradictions.

Step 1: Simultaneous transformation the structures.

$$\Phi\{\text{str}_1, \text{str}_2, \cdots\} = \{\varphi_1 \text{str}_1, \varphi_2 \text{str}_2, \cdots\} \tag{9}$$

Step 2: Conduction transformation of internal structures:

$$\varphi_i \text{str}_i \Rightarrow T_{\varphi_i} \text{str}_i = \text{str}_i', \quad \text{str}_i' \in \{\text{str}_{i,1}, \text{str}_{i,2}, \cdots\} \tag{10}$$

Step 3: Determine the relevance of the structures and calculate the conduction transformation of external structures:

- When some structures are spatially independent, there is no direct external conduction transformation:

$$\varphi_i \text{str}_i \Rightarrow \begin{cases} T_{\varphi_i} \text{str}_i = \text{str}_i', & \text{str}_i' \in \{\text{str}_{i,1}, \text{str}_{i,2}, \cdots\} \\ T_{\varphi_i} \text{str}_j = \varnothing, & i \neq j \end{cases} \tag{11}$$

And the probability can be calculated as Eq. (12).

$$p_4 = \lambda_{\text{im}_k} \bullet \sum \left(\lambda_{\text{str}\_j} \left(\sum \lambda_{\text{str}_i'} \right) \right) \tag{12}$$

- When structures are spatially related, there is a direct external conduction transformation on the interface:

$$\varphi_i \text{str}_i \Rightarrow T_{\varphi_i} \text{str}_i = \text{str}_i' \Rightarrow T_{\varphi_i}' F_{\text{str}_i} = F_{\text{str}_i}' \Rightarrow T_{\varphi_i}'' \text{str}_j = \text{str}_j', \\ \text{str}_j' \in \{\text{str}_{j,1}, \text{str}_{j,2}, \cdots\}, i \neq j \tag{13}$$

And the probability is:

$$p_5 = \lambda_{\text{im}_k} \bullet \prod \left(\lambda_{\text{str}_i} \left(\prod \lambda_{\text{str}_j} \right) \right) \tag{14}$$

Multi-structure Transformations in Incompatible Problems or Physical Contradictions. The steps are same as above except the step 3.

- If the structures are matched after transformations, the probability is:

$$p_6 = \lambda_{\text{im}_k} \bullet \prod \left(\lambda_{\text{str}_i} \left(\prod \lambda_{\text{str}_j} \right) \right) \tag{15}$$

- If the structures are not matched after transformations, the conductive transformation will be implemented:

$$\varphi F_{\text{str}_i} = F_{\text{str}_i}', F_{\text{str}_i}' \in \{F_{\text{str}_i,1}, F_{\text{str}_i,2}, \cdots\} \Rightarrow \begin{cases} \text{matched} \\ T_{\varphi} \text{str}_i = \text{str}_i', \text{str}' \in \{\text{str}_{i,1}, \text{str}_{i,2}, \cdots\} \end{cases} \tag{16}$$

And the probability will be:

$$p_7 = \lambda_{im_k} \bullet \prod \left(\lambda_{str_i} \left(\prod \lambda_{str_j} \right) \right) \bullet \lambda_{F'_{str_i}} \bullet \lambda_{str'_i} \tag{17}$$

4 Case Study

In this section, a screw air compressor is taken as an example to verify the proposed method. The screw air compressor is composed of drive motor, gear box, screw engine, oil-gas separation barrel, cooling system, control system and so on. It is highly modular and has characteristics like: (1) stable and high-integrated modules. (2) clear boundaries. (3) strong correlation of structures. (4) clear mapping between modules and low-carbon attributes.

In Table 1, the main information of the case library for low carbon design is shown. From that, the carbon footprint, which is taken as an example, is mainly reflected the emission in the usage stage of the life cycle as well as obtained through indirect conversion of fuel and electricity [8].

Table 1. Case data of screw air compressor

No	Type	Low-carbon parameters	Value	Unit
1	JN37-8	Listed carbon footprint	20005.3	$kgCO_2e$
		Usage carbon footprint	161262.4	$kgCO_2e$
		Purchase cost	42800	yuan
		Usage cost	1655150	yuan
		Recovery cost	18550	yuan
		Motor power	37	kW
		Mass	500	kg
		Exhaust rate	10	m^3/min
		Exhaust pressure	0.8	MPa
		Noise	69	dB
2	...	...	...	...

The mapping function can be constructed: $CF_{use} = f(M_1, M_2, M_3, M_4)$.

The low-carbon attribute requirements CF_{use} can be converted into TRIZ engineering parameters: (1) Improving features is 19 (use of energy by moving object), and worsening features is 9 (speed), and the principles are: 8 (anti-weight), 15 (dynamics), 35 (changing state, parameters, properties of materials); (2) Improving features is 30 (Object-affected harmful factors), and worsening features is 39(productivity), and the principles are 22 (convert harm into benefit), 35 (changing state, parameters, properties of materials), 13 (inversion) and 24(intermedia means).

According to the analysis above, the principles can be set: $IM = \{im_{13,2}, im_{15,1}, im_{15,2}, im_{22,2}\}$. The weights can be given according to AHP: $\lambda_{im_{13,2}} = 0.15$, $\lambda_{im_{15,1}} = 0.35$, $\lambda_{im_{15,2}} = 0.4$, $\lambda_{im_{22,2}} = 0.1$. $FS = \{M_1, M_2, M_3, M_4\}$, and the core problem model: $Q = IM * FS * DR$ can be obtained:

$$Q = \begin{cases} \{im_{13,2}, im_{15,2}, im_{22,2}\} * M_3 * DR & ① \\ im_{15,1} * \{M_1, M_2, M_3\} * DR & ② \\ im_{15,1} * M_4 * DR & ③ \\ im_{13,2} * M_4 * DR & ④ \end{cases}$$

Seen that ①③④ are single-structure transformation and ② is multi-structure transformation for each module, the transformations are mainly listed as follows:

- Vibration module:
    - $str_{3,1}$: increase vibration reduction module
    - $str_{3,2}$: fix the structure to ground;
    - $str_{3,3}$: change the way of air compression;
    - $str_{3,4}$: replace the high-flux noise elimination module;
    - ...
- Control system:
    - $str_{4,1}$: replace the components;
    - $str_{4,2}$: upgrade control program;
    - ...
- Cooling system:
    - $str_{2,1}$: replace the mute fan;
    - $str_{2,2}$: add water cooling module;
    - $str_{2,3}$: turn the closed hood into a non-closed;
    - ...
- Gas compression system:
    - $str_{1,1}$: replace the new rotor;
    - $str_{1,2}$: separate oil and gas;
    - $str_{1,3}$: replace the compressor with the piston structure;
    - $str_{1,4}$: motor driven;
    - ...

For example, to improve the gas compression system, and $str_{1,2}$ is taken as a case.

In Fig. 2, the structure of oil-gas separator is shown. According to the above, the implementation probability of single-structure variation is $p_2 = 0.35*0.5*(1 + 1) = 0.35$.

Since $str_{1,2}$ is internal structure change and parameter optimization, there is no conduction transformation. Thus, according to the parameters of screw air compressor: rated exhaust rate: 10 m^3/min; Output rate: 76L/min; rated exhaust pressure: 0.8 MPa; exhaust temperature: $82 \sim 102$ °C, the gas flow is calculated $Q = 580.56$ m^3/h, and the liquid-state flow is 4.56 m^3/h. A structure scheme can be obtained after optimization, it can reduce the carbon footprint in the usage phase by 23180 $kgCO_2e$ (about 15%).

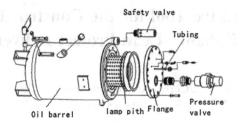

Fig. 2. Oil-gas separator

5 Conclusion

For antithetical and incompatible problems of low-carbon design conflict, the principle set of TRIZ is obtained by contradiction matrix and separation principles. The extension transformation object and the low carbon design conflict coordination are further determined through the analysis of the variation of the low carbon instance structure. Then, the solution strategy of different types of problems is given and the implementation probability under each condition is calculated. The integrated method of TRIZ and extension to coordinate the low carbon conflicts generates a variety of feasible solution.

Acknowledgments. This work was supported by the National Natural Science Foundation of China (Grant No. 61572438, 61701443) and the Planning Project of Application Research for public Service Technology of Zhejiang Province (grant No. 2017C1331072).

References

1. Zhang, C., Huang, H.H., Zhang, L., et al.: Low-carbon design of structural components by integrating material and structural optimization. Int. J. Adv. Manuf. Technol. **95**, 1–14 (2018)
2. Zhao, Y.-W., et al.: Overview and prospects of product low carbon design. Comput. Integr. Manuf. Syst. CIMS **19**(5), 897–908 (2013)
3. Xu, X., Li, F., Zhou, L., et al.: Status and future trends research on low carbon design. Comput. Integr. Manuf. Syst. **22**(7), 1609–1618 (2016)
4. Zhao, Y.-W., Hong, H.-H., Zhou, J.-Q., et al.: Overview and prospects of product low carbon design. Comput. Integr. Manuf. Syst. **19**(5), 897–908 (2013)
5. ElMaraghy, W., et al.: Complexity in engineering design and manufacturing. CIRP Ann. **61**(2), 793–814 (2012)
6. Ren, S., Gui, F., Zhao, Y., et al.: Accelerating preliminary low-carbon design for products by integrating TRIZ and Extenics methods. Adv. Mech. Eng. **9**(9), 1–18 (2018)
7. Yanwei, Z., Nan, S.: Extension Design. Science Press, Beijing (2010)
8. He, B., Tang, W., Wang, J.: Product model integrated with carbon footprint for low-carbon design. Int. J. Precis. Eng. Manuf. **16**(11), 2383–2388 (2015)

Collaborative Tool for the Construction Site to Enhance Lean Project Delivery

Julia Ratajczak[1,2(✉)], Christoph Paul Schimanski[3], Carmen Marcher[3],
Michael Riedl[3], and Dominik T. Matt[1,3]

[1] Free University of Bozen-Bolzano, Piazza Università 1, Bolzano, Italy
Julia.Ratajczak@natec.unibz.it
[2] Budimex S.a, ul. Stawki 40, Warsaw, Poland
julia.ratajczak@budimex.pl
[3] Fraunhofer Italia Research, via Volta 13a, Bolzano, Italy

Abstract. Efficient construction management is highly depending on respective persons in charge and their ability to steer the inherent complex flow of information. A lack of standardized short-term task scheduling and monitoring routines as well as not fully reached potentials of digital aids have been identified by authors. Both short-comings are tackled in this paper introducing a location-based scheduling and monitoring concept, which has been implemented in an interactive Dashboard application for the construction site. A tiered Location-based Management System (LBMS) methodology, which incorporates process monitoring on the lowest measureable level have been introduced. The Dashboard application can be used by different stakeholders of a construction project to monitor the work performance, progress and productivity on a daily basis. In Dashboard, KPIs like PAR, PPC, RNC as well as generic parameters describing progress, delays and economic losses have been included. This application aims to improve productivity, collaboration between project participants as well provide tailored information to the user. To reach this goal the following methods and technologies have been adopted: LBMS, Tiered Structure methodology and BIM.

Keywords: Lean Construction · Dashboard · Project delivery
BIM · Construction KPIs

1 Introduction

1.1 Research Background

The construction industry (CI) is a project-based industry characterized by heterogeneity, extreme complexity, fragmented supply chain and variability of trade performance. It is widely recognized that the CI is one of the less efficient sectors, if compared to other industries like manufacturing. According to [1] only 16% of construction projects are brought to the conclusion on time, within the budget, meeting all required quality standards. This is due to the inadequate and inaccurate monitoring and control processes [2]. Construction managers are not able to focus on important task because they spend 30–50% of their time to collect and analyze site data due to the manual methods for

© Springer Nature Switzerland AG 2018
Y. Luo (Ed.): CDVE 2018, LNCS 11151, pp. 192–199, 2018.
https://doi.org/10.1007/978-3-030-00560-3_26

monitoring and controlling of construction works [3]. Insufficient management and poor quality controls affect also delays, project profitability, cost increase. During the construction, not enough time (only 12%) is dedicated for the evaluation of construction progress [4]. Site managers use also inadequate tools to visualize and represent the information [5]. Real-time control of construction works based on high-quality data is still needed to identify discrepancies between desired and actual performance. If successful progress monitoring is applied, it is possible to reduce execution schedule deviations up to 15% [6], project cost up to 10% [7] as well as cost of reworks, claims and disputes [8]. In recent years, the adoption of Information and Communication Technologies (ICT) in the CI has had a significant impact on both productivity and economic growth of construction companies [9]. However, to support construction management efficiently, ICT systems, which consider Lean Construction (LC) methods and provide automatically real-time information on construction process are still required.

2   Project Goal

The goal of this paper is to describe a concept and functionalities of the interactive web-based Dashboard application that integrates Lean Construction methods like Location-based Management System (LBMS) [10] in order to support the construction management system on site. This application is an easy tool that allows different stakeholders to have tailored view on construction works, to make conscious and fast decision if any deviations occur and to control the work performance, progress and productivity on a daily basis. The prototype of this application has been developed in the European project – ACCEPT, funded within the Horizon 2020 Framework Program. The Dashboard is a part of the ACCEPT system for the management of construction works. The description of the whole system can be found in [11, 12] or on the web page: www.accept-project.com.

Fraunhofer Italia Research has elaborated the methodology applied into Dashboard, which is a topic of the Ph.D. research project carried out at the Free University of Bozen-Bolzano together with the polish general contractor – Budimex S.A.

3   Methodology

3.1   Tiered Structure Methodology

The Tiered Structure (TS) methodology has been implemented in Dashboard to deliver tailored Key Performance Indicators (KPIs) regarding the construction process in a simple and understandable way. Each level of the TS methodology corresponds to the construction project structure and its respective KPIs (Fig. 1). This methodology is comprised of four tiers (Tier 0–3):

- **Tier 0** represents high-level of project information - building level (e.g. building A), where tailored information are delivered to a client and general contractor by means of KPIs like project progress and percentage planned completed (PPC), project delay, expected end date.

- **Tier 1** refers to construction work package level (e.g. structures). Relevant information are provided to the owner (e.g. project manager), who can control the work packages progress, performance ability ratio (PAR), reason for non-completion (RNC), PPC and extra effort, which can filtered by locations.
- **Tier 2** is related to construction task level (e.g. concrete slab). The owner of this level is a site manager. The site manager can manage information at the task level by location using KPIs like task progress, PAR, RNC, PPC and extra effort.
- **Tier 3** represents the lowest level of the project information – workflow, which defines a sequence of construction activities (e.g. formworks) that should be performed by a crew to complete a task on tier 2. This tier creates a foundation for the monitoring of the entire construction process. The monitored KPIs refer to activities and they are the same as in tier 2.

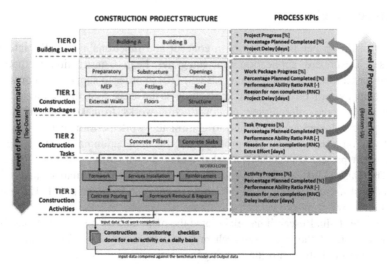

Fig. 1. Tiered structure methodology

3.2 Construction Production Planning and Controlling

The concept of "pitching" [13] is used to apply LBMS and thus entails the opportunity to schedule and monitor location-based tasks on a daily basis. One "Pitch" is defined as the maximum daily job content that can be done by a composed crew of workers within a certain location. The LBMS consists of planning and scheduling of construction works. It considers that the project is broken down to physical location, to which different activities can be assigned. Each activity is defined according to location hierarchy level, so-called Location Breakdown Structure (LBS). Construction activities and their controlling should refer always to those locations. Organizing activities by locations allows the user to get information that is more comprehensive, avoid interruption between different trades, and enhance constancy of the workflow. The construction production is defined according to TS methodology, which offers a possibility for scaling information and measuring construction process at different levels (tiers). To plan and schedule the construction production according to LBMS and TS, site manager uses the SiMaApp (another application of the ACCEPT system) to create workflows with activities (tier 3) for a specific location and assign crews/workers to these activities. The workflow is attached to a task (tier 2) within the given time frame. In SiMaApp, a construction process checklist is used by foreman to report the percentage or absolute value of completed activities (input data) on a daily basis. If a daily goal has not been met, the remained work content will be considered during the following days. Through the daily monitoring of activities, the collected input data are used for calculations of construction process KPIs, which are afterwards displayed on Dashboard. The monitoring at the lowest measureable level (activities) is applied, because it allows the projection and aggregation of information in order to deliver the overall process status on superior tiers.

3.3   Construction Process KPIs

In the Dashboard, user can access data related to construction process KPIs following the TS methodology. The data are presented at different levels of abstraction such as: project level (tier 0), work package level (tier 1), task level (tier 2) and workflow (tier 3). KPIs are visualized by means of charts, widgets and 3D viewer. KPIs calculated by the Dashboard are reported in Table 1. The definition of each KPIs refers to the activity level (tier 3). The most of these KPIs are reported to superior tiers by doing data aggregation from lower tiers.

Based on Delay Indicator it is possible to calculate accumulated delay of the entire project, work package or task, which allows one to predict end dates based on actual on-site data. Accumulated extra effort can be used to provide information also regarding economic losses by taking into account known and set-up cost rates for men-hours in terms of labor costs.

4   Dashboard

4.1   Functionalities

The Dashboard is the interactive web based-platform, which provides users with KPIs referred to a specific location of the construction project. The Dashboard home page is divided into 3 sections (Fig. 2): 1) **3D BIM Viewer** of the current project; 2) **panel for displaying the information** relevant to the selected level (tier) of the project and 3) **graphs** to illustrate certain KPIs trends. Functionalities of the Dashboard illustrated in Fig. 2 are described referring to the workflow (tier 3).

In Sect. 1, the user can interact with 3D model of the project by zooming in/out, rotating the model and selecting each element. The 3D BIM Viewer is used also to point out elements, which are linked to a specific task and location. This is done automatically, once the user selects a work package name or task name and location. On the model, basic information like actual progress and delay indicator are displayed.

Table 1. Construction process KPIs

KPIs	Definition
Current Progress – CP	**CP** [%] is the relation of the pitch content of a single activity to the overall pitch content of the whole workflow
Performance Ability Ratio – PAR	**PAR**-value [-] is the ratio of the defined content of 1 pitch to the actual measured progress on-site. Value > 1 indicates a lack of performance with respect to the expected performance. Value = 1 means that the foreseen goal has been met. Value < 1 refers to a more powerful performance than expected. Ranking activities regarding this criterion provides perception towards improvement potentials of a single activity
Reason for non-completion – RNC	**RNC** [-] states the root cause for non-completed activities on time. It allows the analysis of poorly running task.
Percent Plan Completed – PPC	**PPC** [%] is the ratio of fulfilled assignments (achieved goals) to the total number of assignments scheduled for a particular day. If the goal is achieved, PPC value is 100%, if not it is 0%. The PPC-value provides information regarding the reliability of the scheduling and the smoothness of the workflow
Delay Indicator – DI	**DI** [days] is the difference between planned working days and remaining days (calculated only for tier 3)
Extra Effort – EE	**EE** [days] is the sum of Delay Indicator of each activity in a task or tasks of a work package (calculated only for tier 0–2)

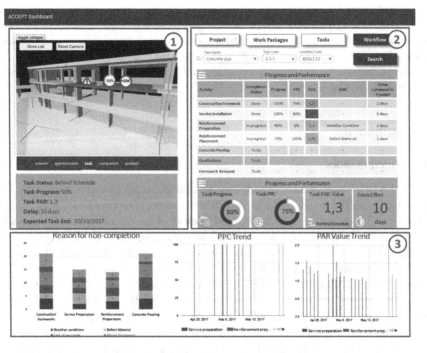

Fig. 2. Dashboard layout – workflow

The selected element attributes also a color based on the task status (red = behind schedule, green = on schedule, blue = ahead schedule). The BIM model is imported to the 3D Viewer with location-based scheduling metadata. For each component/material in the BIM model, task codes - WBS code (WBS – Work breakdown Structure) and location codes - LBS code (LBS – Location Breakdown Structure) have been embedded beforehand. These data can be read by the Dashboard to provide a graphical representation of where construction works should be executed and how they are progressing. The combination of both codes – WBS and LBS allows the identification of components/materials that have been assigned to a task in a specific location. In Sect. 2, the user can choose "Workflow" tab and select a task defined by name and its WBS code and a location in the construction project defined by LBS code. The main user of the workflow monitoring is a foreman. Based on the initial configuration, a table with workflow activities attached to this task is displayed. The table contains data for each activity such as: (a) **completion status** [done, in progress, to do]; (b) **current activity progress** [%]; (c) **PPC** [%], (d) **PAR-value** [-]; (e) **RNC**; (f) **cumulative delay** [days]. Below the table, widgets with data related to the whole workflow are reported as well. Actual information about the workflow progress, PPC, PAR-value and delay indicator is visualized. Values of these KPIs are calculated based on input data, collected by the Construction progress checklist in the SiMaApp.

In the Sect. 3, graphs are included to illustrate: (a) **number of detected RNC** for each activity; (b) **PPC trend** with the weekly distribution of PPC for each activity; (c) **PAR-value trend** with the weekly distribution of PAR-values for each activity.

4.2 Monitoring of Tasks (Tier 2)

The user of tier 2 (e.g. site manager) chooses "Tasks" tab and selects a task and a location or all available locations. The layout of the web page dedicated to tier 2 is composed of 3D BIM Viewer, widgets and graphs. Widgets include KPIs, which are relevant to evaluate the current task progress and performance like: **(a) task progress** [%], which is calculated as the sum of cumulative contribution progress of all activities multiplied by their scheduled working days and divided by scheduled working days of the task; **(b) task PPC** [%], which is calculated as the sum of cumulative goals achieved of each activity divided by the number of monitored days and multiplied by 100%; **(c) task PAR-value** [-], which is calculated as the sum of PAR-value of each activity multiplied by their scheduled working days and divided by scheduled working days of the task; **(d) task Extra effort** [days], which is calculated as the sum of Delay Indicator of each activity of the task - if the number of days is negative, it means that works have been completed ahead schedule. The **RNC graph** shows the number of detected RNC in the task by summing RNC in all activities related to this task. The **PPC trend** illustrates a weekly PPC distribution of activities for this task. The **PAR trend** shows a weekly PAR-values distribution of activities for the task.

4.3 Monitoring of Work Packages and Project (Tier 1, Tier 0)

The user of tier 1 (e.g. project manager) chooses "Work package" tab and selects a work package name and a specific location or all available locations. In that case, the

Dashboard returns the same type of data for the selected work package as in tier 2. The user of tier 0 (e.g. client, company manager) chooses "Project" tab and gets access to the following data: **(a) project progress** [%], which is calculated as the sum of cumulative contribution progress of all activities in all work packages multiplied by their scheduled working days and divided by scheduled working days of the project; **(b) project PPC** [%], which is calculated as the sum of cumulative goals achieved of each activity in all work packages divided by the number of monitored days and multiplied by 100%; **(c) project delay** [days], which is calculated as planned progress minus actual progress divided by planned progress and multiplied by total scheduled working days in the project; **(d) expected end data**, which is calculated as scheduled end date of the project plus project delay.

5   Conclusion

This paper describes a concept and functionalities of the interactive web-based Dashboard application that integrates Lean Construction methods like Location-based Management System in order to support the construction management on site. The Tiered Structure methodology has been created for this application to provide users with tailored KPIs regarding the construction process. The Dashboard application allows user to monitor construction process (progress, productivity and performance) by locations of the construction project. Data are visualized by means of tables, widgets, graphs and 3D BIM Viewer. This application empowers users to reduce waste and cost, smoothen processes, improve productivity as well enhance collaboration among different stakeholders. The first prototype of the Dashboard have been done within the ACCEPT project by LUCID Lab at the University of Liege. The user partner of this project – Epitessera Architects has tested it during the construction of the English School in Nicosia (Cyprus) and has achieved promising results: compared to conventional procedures, the time needed for the workflow monitoring was reduced by more than 50% using the Dashboard. In addition, automatically extraction of intuitively comprehensible project KPIs and their BIM-related visualization in the Dashboard application have been appreciated as a very powerful tool. The monitoring methodology is the topic of the Ph.D. research project. Therefore, Dashboard functionalities will be improved and tested further. It is planned to test the monitoring methodology with the polish general contractor – Budimex S.A. A specific use case will be selected and several construction tasks will be monitored to evaluate the effectiveness of this methodology. The special focus will be put on KPIs to measure process improvement due to the use of the application and to introduce additional indicators that can be relevant for different tier users.

Acknowledgments. The authors would like to thank the European Commission for their funding of the ACCEPT project within the Horizon 2020 Framework Program. The authors gratefully acknowledge the contributions of other partners from the consortium, especially of Peter Leo Merz from TIE Germany responsible for the implementation of lean construction methods in Profile Nexus, Vincent Delfosse, Hatem Bejar, Anabelle Rahhal, Pierre Leclercq from LUCID Lab for the development of the Dashboard, Jason Page and Edward Gooden from Ingleton Wood for the co-development of Tiered Structure.

References

1. Frame, J.D.: Establishing project risk assessment teams. In: Kahkonen, K., Artto, K.A. (eds.) Managing Risks in Projects. E & FN Spon, London (1997)
2. Memon, A.H., Rahman, I.A., Aziz, A.A.A.: The cause factors of large project's cost overrun: a survey in the southern part of peninsular Malaysia. Int. J. Real Estate Stud. 7(2) (2012)
3. McCulloch, B.: Automating field data collection in construction organizations. In: Construction Congress V: Managing Engineered Construction in Expanding Global Markets, pp. 957–963 (1997)
4. Golparvar Fard, M.: Assessment of collaborative decision-making in design development and coordination meetings. Master thesis dissertation, University of British Columbia Library, Vancouver, Canada (2006)
5. Lee, S., Pena-Mora, F.: Visualization of construction progress monitoring. In: Joint International Conference on Computing and Decision Making in Civil and Building Engineering, pp. 2527–2533 (2006)
6. IBC: Industry Benchmarking Consortium: Project Control Best Practice Study by IPA – Independent Project Analysis (2000)
7. IBC: Industry Benchmarking Consortium: Cost Engineering Committee (CEC) (1999)
8. Yates, J.K., Epstein, A.: Avoiding and minimizing construction delay claim disputes in relational contracting (2005). (In: Yeomans, S. (ed.): ICT Enabled Collaborative Working Methodologies in Construction. EngD thesis, Loughborough University, UK (2006))
9. Sendra, S., Lloret, A.T., Lloret, J., Rodrigues, J.J.P.C.: A wireless sensor networks deployment to detect the degeneration of cement used in construction. Int. J. Ad Hoc Ubiquitous Comput. 15(1–3), 147–160 (2014)
10. Seppänen, O., Ballard, G., Pesonen, S.: The combination of last planner system and location-based management system. Lean Constr. J. 43–54 (2010)
11. Ratajczak, J., et al.: Digital Tools for the construction site. a case study: ACCEPT project. In: LC32017: Volume I – Proceedings of the Joint Conference on Computing in Construction (JC3), Heraklion, Greece, pp. 981–988 (2017)
12. Ratajczak, J., Schimanski, C.P., Marcher, C., Riedl, M., Matt, D.T.: Mobile application for collaborative scheduling and monitoring of construction works according to lean construction methods. In: Luo, Y. (ed.) CDVE 2017. LNCS, vol. 10451, pp. 207–214. Springer, Cham (2017). https://doi.org/10.1007/978-3-319-66805-5_26
13. Dallasega, P., Matt, D.T., Krause, D.: Design of the building execution process in SME construction networks. In: Thompson, K. (ed.) Proceedings of the 2nd International Workshop on Design in Civil and Environmental Engineering, Worcester, UK, pp. 7–15 (2013)

Integrated Simulation Modeling Method for Complex Products Collaborative Design Using Engineering-APP

Jun Yu[⊠], Zhenjun Ming, Guoxin Wang, Yan Yan, and Haiyan Xi

Beijing Institute of Technology, No. 5 S. Zhongguancun Street, Haidian District,
Beijing 100081, China
15652661558@163.com

Abstract. The design and development process of complex products is a multi-disciplinary collaborative process, which requires the cooperation of distributed teams. However, traditional simulation methods are usually discipline-oriented and there is a lack of efficiency in terms of share and reuse of the existing simulation models in a distributed and collaborative environment. In order to address this problem, we propose a multi-level knowledge framework for simulation model knowledge representation, retrieval and reasoning. Specifically, a simulation knowledge model by the name of "Engineering-APP" is developed to enable simulation knowledge sharing by using Web Service technology. The Engineering-APP model represents an integrated simulation knowledge wrapper, which includes information about the geometric model, design algorithm or analysis codes. Based on the Engineering-APP model, an intelligent collaborative prototype system is developed to support the design process with different stakeholders. Through an engineering case study, it is demonstrated that the proposed framework and Engineering-APP are effective and efficient for the representation and reuse of existing simulation models knowledge.

Keywords: Simulation model · Multi-level knowledge framework
Engineering-APP · Collaborative environment

1 Introduction

The development of complex products is characterized by its large-scale, multi-variable and high-complexity. Specifically, it involves the coordination of a variety of resources, integration of multi-disciplinary models, and the consideration of issues at all stages of the whole product lifecycle [1]. To support collaborative design of complex products, simulation is becoming an essential method for rapidly improving the efficiency of design and optimizing its behavior. Simulation-Based product design has gained importance in past few years in many complex product design fields, particularly in aerospace and Vehicle. As simulation models become the main corner stones for the virtual commissioning, the purpose of this paper is to support interoperation of the simulation models within automated design systems.

© Springer Nature Switzerland AG 2018
Y. Luo (Ed.): CDVE 2018, LNCS 11151, pp. 200–208, 2018.
https://doi.org/10.1007/978-3-030-00560-3_27

Although the application of simulations brings a lot of benefits, there are still a few barriers of effectively applying those simulation tools to collaborative design. First, a recent study has revealed difficulties to design and control simulation execution due to the characteristics of heterogeneous and hierarchical structure of simulation. Second, current approaches are to some extent insufficient to satisfy designers' knowledge requirement due to the fact that multi-disciplinary knowledge is involved in the complicated design phase.

These deficiencies are to some extent ascribed to the separation of the personalization and simulation views in the current study on complex product design. The main motivation of this paper is to address this gap by developing a unified knowledge simulation model to arrange designers in the very center of the simulation models created and reused process. The capture of explicit knowledge and tacit knowledge of simulation model created and shared during collaborative design can provide important simulation design context [2]. Additionally, specific attention is given to exploring the potential of the collaborative simulation technologies towards the development of Industry Internet.

2   Literature Review

The extraction and reuse of simulation knowledge for supporting complex product design and their automation are vital assignment in the emerging area of knowledge-based engineering (KBE). The most relevant works are summarized below.

2.1   Integration of Simulation Models

The existing integration methods are mainly focused on reusing simulation code in the simulation area. On account of providing simulation results to all user groups, a complex general integration environment is desperately required, but not yet [3].

The multi-domain modeling simulation method based on interface is the most widely used in simulation domain. The key factor of the method is the interface, which has no open ability and turns into a bloated system as the integrated software is increasing. A widely cited method of the simulation models integration is the High Level Architecture (HLA) [4]. However, it doesn't figure out the data source problem. In addition to the lack of data source management, the downside of this framework is lack of semantics.

2.2   Semantic and Technical Integration

The automated integration approach of simulation model design usually relies on repetitive manual work, which is not satisfactory in future flexible systems. A promising integration approach is semantic integration. Effective communication and consistent understanding based on semantic integration between design engineers can support the creation of high-efficiency knowledge sharing and dissemination.

With the development of artificial intelligence, computer technology and web services, a new approach based on Semantic Web has been developed [5]. Semantic

Web is aimed at realizing knowledge reusing and reasoning throughout the semantic expression in a formal and machine-understandable structure through ontologies [6]. Therefore, ontologies are applied to the simulation models in order to ensure understanding and semantic interoperability among the different partners. There are three categories for the ontological models: (i) Representation of models supplied by language expressively; (ii) Embedded intelligence on account of their reasoning capability and (iii) Collaboration afforded by their queries and Web services [7].

In summary, the multi-disciplinary, multi-level and high-collaborative nature of complex product design has evoked the requirement of designers' communication and collaboration in capturing and reusing simulation knowledge. Thus, the paper aims to address the gap by exploiting simultaneously the different potentialities of simulation model and semantic integration in order to support the development process of complex product. It can greatly improve the simulation models' availability and effectiveness, and then help enhance design quality and reduce design cost. Finally, a Web-based virtual ICDS environment has been developed to validate the effectiveness of the method.

3 Representation of Integrated Simulation Model for Collaborative Design

3.1 A Multi-level Modeling Framework for Integrated and Collaborative Simulation Management

Nowadays, personal customers and users' requirements of complex product market are transformed to specific information taken up with manufacturing complex product during the design process. The design and development of complex product generally requires a synergy of multi-disciplinary development team [8]. To give an overview of Integrated and Collaborative Design System (ICDS) scheme as well as its key components, a framework is shown in Fig. 1(a). In the outsides of the figure, Collaborative design team can participate in the collaborative design environment, meanwhile in the center of the figure, product design lifecycle stages of knowledge management are in connection with specific design activities. As for every activities, explicit knowledge of simulation models and tacit knowledge of decision-making process is connected with an integrated simulation model.

Before developing the integrated simulation models, collaborative design process and activities of complex product should be taken into special consideration. According to the top-down design principle, the multi-level Modeling framework of complex product design process based on the product topological function and simulation structure is illustrated in Fig. 1(b). As described in Fig. 1(b), it should be determined first the function set according to the customers' design demands. Then each function can be further divided into a set of sub-functions and sub-flows. When the overall functions of complex product are decomposed zigzag, simulation modules are also designed or selected form an available module base. The simulation module could be further decomposed into a set of sub-modules and parameters whose values should to be determined.

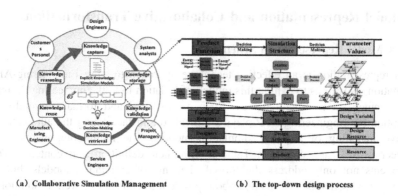

(a) Collaborative Simulation Management   (b) The top-down design process

Fig. 1. The design framework of complex product development

3.2   Formulation of Collaborative Simulation for Engineering-APP

Simulation models for complex product are software representations of mathematical models of the physical prototype. Converting mathematical models to executable simulation models usually depend on manual effort of simulation experts. As shown in the Fig. 2(a), each simulation model has inputs and outputs, which are states of design variables in the mathematical sense, and parameters are constants specifying model dynamics. For specific complex design problem, a simulation using a constraint-based representation, as shown in equation I. Based on this, the paper proposes the collaborative simulation model of Engineering-APP synthesizing simulation models and knowledge models as shown in Fig. 2(b). The Engineering-APP can be divided into four parts, they are the constituent elements, the running engine, the database, and the solver library. The significant difference of Engineering-APP is the operating engine providing the power and support conditions for combination of Simulation models and knowledge extracted from experts.

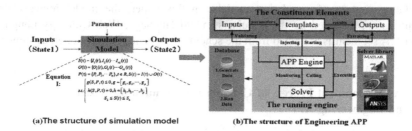

(a)The structure of simulation model   (b)The structure of Engineering APP

Fig. 2. Difference structure of simulation and Engineering-APP

4 Model Representation and Collaborative Transformation

4.1 A Model Representation Schema

Model representation is an effective technique approach to store Engineering-APPs' information, as well as to exhibit this model information to both engineering designers and computers in a structured way. Such a structured and formal comprehensive description for Engineering-APP plays a critical role in facilitating the automatic and effective matching of required simulation models. The main components of the Engineering-APP are shown in Table 1 with their definition and contents. These components not only address the formal elements of simulation models, but also contain formal semantic information about problem to consider as well as solutions to develop. Specifically, "Object" component denotes the targeted design object. "State" component denotes the main variables alongside the main targets. Then the "Problem" component drive the design process to proceed to detailed tasks, while the "Solution" component is used to describe a possible solution of simulation models. Finally, the "Resource" components can be obtained to search the corresponding data or analysis solvers to execute the simulation models.

Table 1. Engineering-APP knowledge representation

Component	Definition	Content
Objects (O)	Targeted object of design	Products, assembly, parts
State (St)	State of design variables	Constants parameter, design variables
Problem (P)	A design problem to consider	e.g. Geometric modeling
Solution (So)	A possible simulation solution	e.g. FEA simulation model
Resource (R)	Corresponding analysis solvers	UG, ADAMS, MATLAB

Referring to the components of Engineering-APP mentioned above, the integrated simulation knowledge model provides a comprehensive and clear description whilst facilitating capture of simulation models. In this paper, the model representation schema is implemented by the popular standard language, Web Ontology Language (OWL). A segment is extracted from the schema of vehicle chassis model, as shown in Fig. 3.

4.2 A Development Process of Collaborative Simulation Based on Engineering-APP

After the Engineering-APP is put forward, it is essential to establish the collaborative simulation mechanism based on Engineering-APP. As shown in Fig. 4, a complex product design can be divided into three sub-models which have interactions among each other at the run-time of simulation. A collaborative design process usually begins with the design objectives and ends with the decision-making for the subsequent simulation model, involving a wide variety of knowledge reuse and reasoning, where some simulation models are integrated.

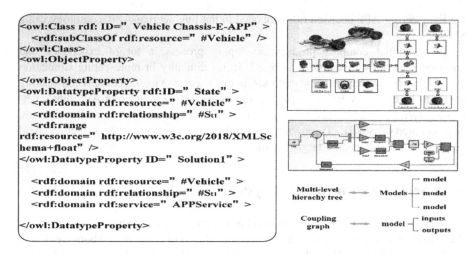

Fig. 3. The vehicle chassis's Engineering-APP based on OWL

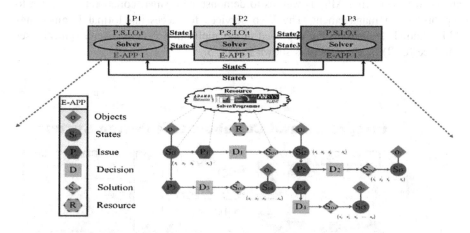

Fig. 4. Complex product development of network graph based on Engineering-APP

Therefore, the paper expand the potentialities of the OWL approach combined with SWRL for the automation of Engineering-APP configuration and design process. SWRL is able to provide restrict rules for the semantic-based decision support platform to assist complex products' automatic design process [9]. Table 2 represents a part of

Table 2. Engineering-APP decision rules based on SWRL

SWRL rules	Explanation
S(?s)∧S_P(?s,?pq)∧S_input(?s, ?r)∧R_quatity(?s,? rq)∧swrlb:lessThanEqual(?pq, ?rq) → WS_hold_at(? s, 1)	Determine the effective collection of Engineering-APPs

the Engineering-APP decision rules encoded in the Engineering-APP's ontology using SWRL.

In traditional complex product developing process, a lot of experience and knowledge of design experts is involved, it has difficulty in representing simulation models through simple semantic methods. In this paper, the intelligent decision-making approach based on SWRL is employed to transform the Engineering-APP into a network graph for states changes as Fig. 4 shows. "Decision" refers to the decision process based on SWRL. Through executing these Engineering-APPs, a solution could be developed until specific target are met.

5   A Service Oriented ICDS System

To demonstrate the supposed effectiveness of the proposed methods and frameworks, a Web-based ICDS prototype system has been developed in a visual collaborative design mode. ASP.NET and ADO technology are adopted in this system to connect and access database. ICDS system is aimed for evaluating the validity and effectiveness of the proposed Engineering-APP as well as to demonstrate a smart collaborative pattern to support design management. The Web services for accessing formal Engineering-APP's knowledge records are deployed in the application system. The Graphical User Interface (GUI) of the system is shown in Fig. 5.

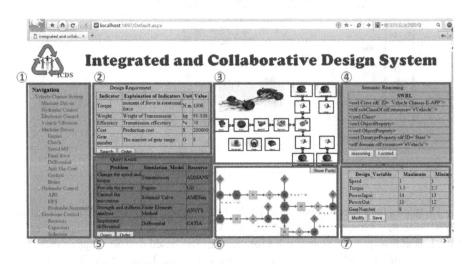

Fig. 5. Web-based ICDS prototype system based on Engineering-APP

In Fig. 5, the window marked "①" is the product structure tree to locate the design position of the product and manage the product design cycle. The window marked "②" is the design requirement and the window marked "⑤" is the candidate cases, which demonstrates the models and resources for collaboration. The window marked "③" is the visual product structure and the window marked "⑥" is the reasoning process of the current states. The windows marked "④" exhibits the OWL description in which Engineering-APP is organized and recorded. The window marked "⑦" shows the design variables with each step.

Using the Engineering-APP design paradigm to design vehicle chassis, it involves making a decision on how the Engineering-APP is to be instantiated, either in a top-down design decomposition manner or in a bottom-up design evolution manner. Engineering-APP are software approximations of real dynamic behavior of chassis, which can capture knowledge required for design and integration of simulation models for design automation. The seamless technical integration of various automation tools is addressed as well. And the ICDS system also considers the process how to grab data in the knowledge base, and retrieve them out in terms of supporting the design of simulation models and their integration within design automation environments.

6   Conclusion and Future Work

The development of large-sized complex products needs a much more digital, integrated and collaborative methods to support efficient and modular design. Nowadays, utilizing design knowledge in the design and development of complex products has already become a common practice. In this paper we propose an integrated design framework for product collaborative simulation which are able to capture, represent, retrieve and assemble simulation models. The presented method will enable geographically distributed complex product designers to work together in a virtual collaborative design environment powered based on Web Services.

This paper puts forward an integrated simulation model for complex product design named Engineering-APP. This model contains several major components for facilitating the representation of simulation model knowledge. A prototype system is developed and the method based on the Engineering-APP is implemented in a vehicle chassis design problem. The structure of the Engineering-APP reduces difficulty in the capture and reuse of simulation models knowledge. More importantly, the model also emphasizes the flexibility integration of explicit and tacit knowledge. This flexibility can be further enhanced by using a service-oriented computing environment for simulation model access and resource integration. However, the work is still in its early stage. In our future work, we will focus on the further advance of the model and the system application version of large design project will be updated.

References

1. Li, Y.L., Zhao, W.: Development of an integrated-collaborative decision making framework for product top-down design process, pp. 497–512. Pergamon Press, Inc. (2009)
2. Peng, G., et al.: A collaborative system for capturing and reusing in-context design knowledge with an integrated representation model. Adv. Eng. Inform. **33**, 314–329 (2017)
3. Mordinyi, R.: Integrating heterogeneous engineering knowledge and tools for efficient industrial simulation model support. Adv. Eng. Inform. **29**(3), 575–590 (2015)

4. Zhang, H., et al.: A model-driven approach to multidisciplinary collaborative simulation for virtual product development. Adv. Eng. Inform. **24**(2), 167–179 (2010)
5. Tateno, T., Tudjarov, B.: Web-based mechatronic simulation environment for open collaborative design. In: Mecatronics (2015)
6. Grolinger, K., Capretz, M.A.M.: Ontology-based representation of simulation models. In: International Conference on Software Engineering & Knowledge Engineering (2012)
7. Peng, G., et al.: BOM-based design knowledge representation and reasoning for collaborative product development. J. Syst. Sci. Syst. Eng. **25**(2), 159–176 (2016)
8. Wang, H., Zhang, H.: Using collaborative computing technologies to enable the sharing and integration of simulation services for product design. Simul. Model. Pract. Theory **27**(3), 47–64 (2012)
9. Abadi, A., Ben-Azza, H., Sekkat, S.: Improving integrated product design using SWRL rules expression and ontology-based reasoning. Procedia Comput. Sci. **127**, 416–425 (2018)

Smart and Cooperative Visualization Framework for a Window Company Production

Luis Antonio Usevicius⬤, John Doucette⬤,
and Yongsheng Ma$^{(\boxtimes)}$⬤

University of Alberta, Edmonton, AB, Canada
{useviciu,john.doucette,yongsheng.ma}@ualberta.ca

Abstract. A framework to develop inputs for production visualization and decision analysis was developed for a manufacturer of windows to renovation market (custom products). The proposed framework creates a pre-planning phase for analysis and production decision taking in a company currently implementing a new ERP system. This planning uses linear programming to model different scenarios for analysis as: (i) minimize the PVC material consumption by modeling the CSP (Cutting Stock Problem), (ii) minimize the assembly time in the line or optimizing the flow based on the window configurations, (iii) minimize the assembly workers solving the ASBL (Assembly Line Balancing) problem. A complete case study is presented for the CSP problem on scenario (i).

Keywords: Production planning cooperative visualization
Cutting stock problem · Cutting pattern generation
Production scenarios for decision analysis

1 Introduction

Usually production input information is the output of ERP system modules as capacity planning, inventory management. At production completion new reports are generated in Excel for production control, back-orders, inventory consumption, production hours and manpower used. Such reports are produced after the fact to evaluate production inefficiencies for planning the next production cycle. Common efficiency metrics are first pass yield (no rework), cost per box (direct labor hours, material) and less work-in-process in the production flow.

Theoretical frameworks to understand the manufacturing systems are available in texts like Factory Physics [13]. Collaborative framework approaches as computer aided process planning (CAPP) or agent technology in process planning systems have been widely researched to develop the manufacturing systems and to increase production efficiency [16]. Such cooperative approaches for solving process planning systems become complex to implement and must be customized to different situations. An example is the proposed research variations of CAPP as CoCAPP (Cooperative CAPP)

© Springer Nature Switzerland AG 2018
Y. Luo (Ed.): CDVE 2018, LNCS 11151, pp. 209–216, 2018.
https://doi.org/10.1007/978-3-030-00560-3_28

or cooperative distributed problem-solving framework (CDPS) for CAPP in rigid hierarchical structure tasks [16].

A suitable framework for a window company must be simple to implement. The product in case has a square or rectangular shape built of PVC material linear segments, so the framework consists of retrieving incoming orders product data configuration (sizes, color, types, and lamination). The data is classified and analyzed, clustering the windows by sizes for planning the assembly lines. Then it is available for modeling using linear programming providing feedback information on cost of materials and labor for incoming orders back to schedule department. The construction of a Smart and Cooperative Solution Visualization Framework to a window company could foster collaboration and a more productive environment.

2 Literature Review

The cutting stock problem was first investigated in 1939 [1]. In 1961 [1] the CSP was described as intractable due to the large number of variables involved or too many cutting patterns or columns. Cutting problems are considered too complicated and not easy to find an optimized response [6] or computationally difficult to solve [5]. They are described as NP-Hard and intractable to find optimal solutions in a reasonable time for medium and large size problem [6]. Generating the cutting patterns prior to solving the linear program provides close to optimal solutions for the small and mid-size problems [7]. The auxiliary problem in generating the cutting patterns can be solved by an algorithm using search tree [14].

This article exemplifies in a business case study the algorithm [14] and proposes a change in its first sorting step of the cutting sizes (lengths or width) according to their size in descending order. It studied variations in the algorithm by sorting step 1 by demand in descending order and demand in ascending order and not by size. The proposed change presented better results with optimal solutions while the descending order by size was not feasible in some cases.

3 Business Case

The window company has processes that can be modeled using linear programming as Fig. 1. The models range from cutting stock problem, machine assignment, assembly line balancing and production sequencing according to truck delivery routes.

In process step 1, cutting profiles for welding, a vendor CSP software is used.

The current production policy is fragmented as material cut sheets and product assembly barcode labels are printed to the factory for production. Assemblers do not have visibility of the product flow (incoming orders configuration) to their stations nor do they understand how to balance the work load at their assembly stations. It also creates waiting time in assembly and shipping delays as production is not synchronized to truck loading and shipping sequence.

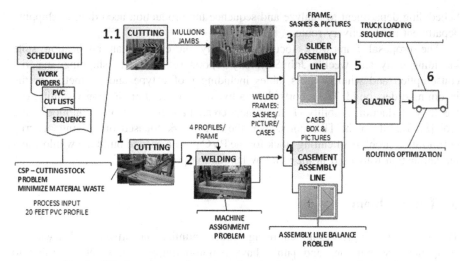

Fig. 1. Window process flow chart. Lamination process not displayed.

The proposal framework on Fig. 2 seeks to display the production information five days in advance as a production roadmap for the scheduling department and production managers to plan the production and job assignment.

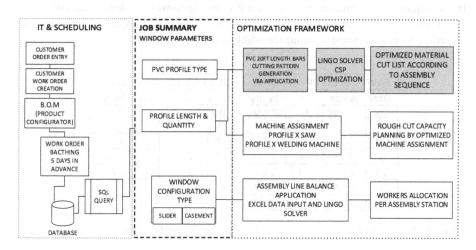

Fig. 2. Framework proposal

4   The Framework

The cooperative visualization process for production includes; IT department which developed a special application suite to retrieve incoming orders from the system five days in advance; Industrial Engineering which creates the optimization reports for

Scheduling department to analyze and sequence the production according to shipping department truck delivery routes.

The proposal framework focused primarily on creating an application suite including daily and weekly Job Summary reports sequenced to shipping, material consumption and window sizes tables including profile type and geometry for the incoming orders build. The reports show a five days forward production visibility. For the daily production visibility IT department created a real time production monitoring tool [8]. Based on the IT reports, then the framework focused on solving material optimization problem of cutting stock for the PVC profile used to build the window and the lamination rolls used in the window lamination process.

5   The Problem

The window frame profiles are cut using vendor optimization software. Other window components as mullions and jambs have a non-optimized cut sheet according to window size. In the lamination process the operator decides which cutting patterns to slit to meet the production demand.

5.1   Cutting Examples

A cutting sheet example is seen in Fig. 3 for PVC bars and lamination rolls. A window frame requires four components cut according to the window ordered size (W × L). The window frame can incorporate a lamination film. The lamination rolls are slit according to consumption demand for width and film color.

SAW PROCESS - PVC PROFILE				SLIT PROCESS - LAMINATION			
Order by size		Order by qty		Order by size		Order by qty	
Qty	Cut length	Qty	Cut length	Qty	slit width	Qty	slit width
8	65.2	13	47.2	4	75	2	25
6	59.2	9	53.2	4	50	2	27
9	53.2	8	65.2	2	27	4	50
13	47.2	6	59.2	2	25	4	75
1	41.2	3	25.2				
3	25.2	1	41.2				

Fig. 3. Examples of saw and slit cutting list showing demand (qty) per length and width.

5.2   Model Formulation

The formulation goal is to minimize trim waste of the 20 feet length PVC profile cuts and for the slitting process of the 660 mm length master coil for lamination.

The main data for the formulation is the set of cutting patterns i according to the set of widths wi; trim waste (waste i) after the master roll or bar is cut according to pattern i; demand per roll or PVC bar type j; maximum stock of rolls or PVC bars allowed.

a_{ij}: amount of rolls or bar type j produced according to cutting pattern i

x_i: main decision variable is the number of cuts according to the cutting pattern i.

The model formulation seeks to minimize waste (1) meeting the demand (2) and the maximum stock allowed (3).

$$Min \sum_{j=1}^{N} waste \ i * x_j \tag{1}$$

Subject to:

$$\sum_{j=1}^{N} a_{ij} \ x_i \tag{2}$$

$$\sum_{j=1}^{N} a_{ij} x_i \leq demand \ j + maxstock \tag{3}$$

The waste is defined by the Eq. (4) where the length of the roll L (or PVC bars) are cut according to widths w_i and the cutting pattern a_{ij} (i = item type i according to width w, and cutting pattern j)

$$waste_i = L - \sum_{i=1}^{N} w_i * a_{ij} \tag{4}$$

5.3 Pattern Generation

Pattern generation presents one of the basic difficulties associated into solving the CSP [2] in an optimal and reasonable time. The activities of cutting in a specific manner and assign a value or the variable xi for the different cutting possibilities [1] can be expanded in its semantics and can be further intelligent defined attaching more information on the activity as part of the product design [3]. Patterns then can be treated as an associative feature for modeling in the product design and manufacture [4]. This also can elevate the patterns generation to the field of Engineering Informatics to be addressed in the company IT system [9].

The business case proposal objective is to simplify the pattern generation turning it simpler and visible to all parties involved in the plant and mainly to solve the optimization problem faster.

5.4 Algorithm Proposed

An algorithm [14] ran in VBA code generated feasible patterns (Fig. 4) for the color FIR for widths as 75, 50, 27 and 25 mm. The algorithm based on a search tree [14] represents the totality of cutting patterns. For the FIR color a total of 658 feasible patterns were generated in 2 s when sorting the widths in descending order by size as in the search tree [14]. The pattern 659 presents a negative column value. When the sorting was changed to ascending order by the demand the code generated 1784 feasible patterns in 256 s. Pattern 1785 presents a negative column value. Although the ascending order by demand table generated more patterns it generated a feasible pattern # 1406 which was not generated in the descending order table by size. When running the Solver, the solution was faster (0.44 s) using the ascending order by demand even with more patterns while the descending order by size was unfeasible. To have a feasible solution it was required to add excess stock, so the problem met the constraints condition.

LAMINATION ROLLS CUTING PATTERNS - 4 WIDTHS - COLOR FIR

SORTED BY SIZE (LARGEST TO SMALLER)

Patterns	1	2	39	79	657	658	659
660 w'_k	a_1	a_2	a_{39}	a_{79}	a_{657}	a_{658}	a_{659}
75 w_1	8	8	6	4	0	0	0
50 w_2	1	0	0	7	0	0	0
27 w_3	0	2	0	0	1	0	-1
25 w_4	0	0	8	0	25	26	27
Waste i	10	6	10	10	8	10	12

SORTED BY DEMAND (SMALLER TO LARGEST)

Patterns	1	2	1406	1784	1785		
660 w'_k	a_1	a_2	a_{1406}	a_{1784}	a_{1785}	w_i	DEMAND
25 w_1	26	25	2	0	0	25	2
27 w_2	0	1	2	0	0	27	2
50 w_3	0	0	4	0	-1	50	4
75 w_4	0	0	4	8	9	75	4
Waste i	10	8	56	60	35		

Fig. 4. Tables showing feasible cutting patterns using a search tree [14] and VBA code

The pattern generation code was run for different parts and widths as sorting them according to demand to generate feasible patterns for the solver. In one example for slitting 14 different widths it took the VBA code 12 s to generate 1000 combinations of cutting patterns and 29 s to generate 5000 cutting patterns in computer AMD Phenom II N870 Triple-Core Processor 2.30 GHz.

5.5   Model Interface in Excel and Results

The generated patterns in Figs. 4 and 5 were uploaded to Excel, and then solved using LINGO interface [12].

PVC PROFILE CUTING PATTERNS FOR 6 WITHS

SORTED BY SIZE (LARGEST TO SMALLER)

Patterns	1	2	3	130	131
236.0 w'_k	a_1	a_2	a_3	a_{130}	a_{131}
65.2 w_1	3	2	2	0	0
59.2 w_2	0	1	1	0	0
53.2 w_3	0	0	0	0	0
47.2 w_4	0	0	0	0	0
41.2 w_5	0	1	0	0	-1
25.2 w_6	1	0	1	9	10
Waste i	15	6	22	9	25

SORTED BY DEMAND (LARGEST TO SMALLER)

Patterns	1	2	190	191	192		
236.0 w'_k	a_1	a_2	a_{190}	a_{191}	a_{192}	w_i	DEMAND
47.2 w_1	4	4	0	0	0	47.2	13
53.2 w_2	0	0	0	0	0	53.2	9
65.2 w_3	0	0	0	0	0	65.2	8
59.2 w_4	0	0	0	0	0	59.2	6
25.2 w_5	1	0	1	0	-1	25.2	3
41.2 w_6	0	1	5	5	6	41.2	1
Waste i	22	6	5	30	14		

Fig. 5. Feasible patterns for PVC linear cuts (6 widths) generated by VBA code

For the case of cutting linear PVC material profile in Fig. 5, the algorithm sorting the order by descending demand generated 191 patterns comparing to 130 patterns when the algorithm was sorted by descending order size. When running LINGO solver, the pattern with 191 combinations presented a faster solution in fractions of a second while for the 131 patterns the solution was reached in 641.95 s. The descending order by demand also resulted in 1.88% waste and the use of 9 bars while the descending order by size used 10 PVC bars and a waste of 11.6% matching the vendor saw optimizer solution although with different patterns. The demand is an important factor in the pattern generation for solving the cut of PVC bars as the quantity of widths must be exact for building the window. This is not the case when slitting the rolls where excess of widths rolls can be generated as the rolls are slitted to restock an inventory of pre-cut rolls.

6 The Programming Results

The proposed LINGO formulation with Excel interface and pattern column generation using the search tree which supplies all feasible pattern combinations provided fast response and useful results in practice.

Before the development of the VBA coding for the automatic generation of patterns, 216 cutting patterns were generated for the color FIR (4 widths) using Excel formulas manually. The LINGO formulation solved by branch and bound algorithm ran for 24 h. Having all possible patterns generated for each case greatly reduces the optimal solution time and currently all cutting patterns are fast to generate using the pattern generation algorithm in VBA code.

7 Recommendations and Conclusions

The business case generated a proven solution for the company cutting stock problem with significant less waste comparing with current vendor software optimizer.

Firstly, this solution was made possible through the collaboration of the IT department that created a data mining tool which retrieves data from the company ERP to be analyzed using the linear programming tools. Secondly the development of the pattern generation using VBA coding allowed to quickly test many scenarios and validating the pattern generation based by demand and not only by size descending order [14]. This is an innovation that is being expanded to create and automatic and smart intelligent optimization which considers the demand of the widths, the sequence of shipping the window and decides how to generate the patterns. The code is being expanded to stop when it starts generating unfeasible patterns or when the pivot algorithm [14] becomes negative.

An important expansion of the CSP problem is to define the patterns as a generic feature to be treated in the field of engineering informatics technology to support product and process development as proposed in Semantic Modeling and Interoperability in Product and Process Engineering [9–11, 15]. This will enhance the framework involving IT, Product Design, Process Engineering, Purchasing and Scheduling in the company.

References

1. Gilmore, P.C., Gomory, R.E.: A linear programming approach to the cutting stock problem. IBM (1961)
2. Gilmore, P.C., Gomory, R.E.: A linear programming approach to the cutting stock problem – Part II. IBM (1963)
3. Liu, J., Cheng, Z., Ma, Y.S.: Product design-optimization integration via associative optimization feature modeling. In: Ma, Y.-S. (ed.) Semantic Modeling and Interoperability in Product and Process Engineering. Springer, London (2013)
4. Ma, Y.-S., Briton, G.A., Tor, S.B., Jin, L.Y.: Associative assembly design features: concept, implementation and application. Int. J. Adv. Manuf. Technol. **32**, 434–444 (2007)
5. Mustakerov, I.C., Borissova, D.I.: Combinatorial optimization modeling approach for one-dimensional cutting stock problems. Int. J. Syst. Appl. Eng. Dev. **9**, 13–18 (2015)
6. Nozarian, S., Jahan, M.V., Jalali, M.: An imperialist competitive algorithm for 1-D cutting stock problem. Int. J. Inf. Sci. **2**(2), 25–36 (2013)
7. Pereira, V., Gomes, H.C.: Integer linear programming for the one-dimensional cutting stock problem with waste reuse. Revista GEINTEC. Sao Cristovao/SE **1**(2), 01–13 (2011). ISSN 2237-0722
8. Ramakrishnan, P.: A conceptual framework for real-time adaptive supply chain systems based on Internet of Things (IoT). Master thesis, University of Alberta (2017)
9. Sajadfar, N., Xie, Y., Liu, H., Ma, Y.S.: Introduction to engineering informatics. In: Ma, Y.-S. (ed.) Semantic Modeling and Interoperability in Product and Process Engineering. Springer, London (2013)
10. Sajadfar, N., Xie, Y., Liu, H., Ma, Y.S.: A review of data representation of product and process models. In: Ma, Y.-S. (ed.) Semantic Modeling and Interoperability in Product and Process Engineering. Springer, London (2013). https://doi.org/10.1007/978-1-4471-5073-2_2
11. Tang, S.-H., Chen, G., Ma, Y.S.: Fundamental concepts of generic feature. In: Ma, Y.-S. (ed.) Semantic Modeling and Interoperability in Product and Process Engineering. Springer, London (2013). https://doi.org/10.1007/978-1-4471-5073-2_4
12. Souza, S.J.: Simulated annealing application in cutting stock problem. Unicamp (2012)
13. Spearman, M.L., Hoop, W.J.: Factory Physics. Waveland Pr. Inc., Long Grove (2011)
14. Suliman, S.M.A.: Pattern generating procedure for the cutting stock problem. Int. J. Prod. Econ. **74**, 293–301 (2001). Elsevier
15. Xie, Y., Ma, Y.: Well-controlled engineering change propagation via dynamic inter-feature association map. Res. Eng. Des. **27**, 311 (2016). Springer, London
16. Zhang, W.J., Xie, S.Q.: Agent technology for collaborative process planning: a review. Int. J. Adv. Manuf. Technol. **32**, 315–325 (2007)

Reduction Methods for Design Rationale Knowledge Model

Jiaji Wang and Jihong Liu[✉]

School of Mechanical Engineering and Automation,
Beihang University, Beijing 100191, China
ryukeiko@buaa.edu.cn

Abstract. Design rationale knowledge is to solve problems based on the thinking of designers. It is an important design process knowledge. Design rationale knowledge model is an effective method to obtain and express design rationale. This paper proposes two reduction methods for design rationale knowledge model to improve the efficiency of designers' reuse of design rationale knowledge model. The structure reduction method introduces quotient space theory to extract design intent - decision structure and building hierarchical structure. The semantic reduction method is based on improved manifolds ranking algorithm. The algorithm ranks the relevance of the design rationale knowledge segments and retains the high-relevance segments to form the core of the design process. The semantic reduction method realizes deletion of redundant information in the design rationale knowledge model, improves collaborative design efficiency. The two methods are verified by developing a prototype system, improving the efficiency of designers' collaborative design.

Keywords: Design rationale knowledge · Structure reduction
Semantic reduction · Collaborative design

1 Introduction

Collaboration and knowledge are very important topics for businesses. The brand new product development model and enterprise collaboration model make the demand for knowledge of the enterprise reach an unprecedented height. Design rationale knowledge records the detailed reasoning process of product design [1]. Design rationale knowledge model is graphical representation of design rationale knowledge [2], and helps designers build a more intuitive, clear, and profound understanding of existing process of product design. Design rationale knowledge model can improve reuse efficiency of design rationale knowledge, and contribute to designers collaboration.

During the past years, several studies on the design rationale knowledge capturing and modeling have been proposed. To facilitate decision-making within collaborative design, Rockwell et al. [3] developed decision support ontology (DSO) which includes decision-related information such as the design issue, alternatives, evaluation, criteria and preferences. Liang et al. [4] put forward an ISAL (issue solution and artifact layer) model for design rationale knowledge capturing, they based on text mining extract issue solution and artifact layer from patent documents. Zhang et al. [5] proposed an

© Springer Nature Switzerland AG 2018
Y. Luo (Ed.): CDVE 2018, LNCS 11151, pp. 217–224, 2018.
https://doi.org/10.1007/978-3-030-00560-3_29

ISAA (issue solution artifact and argument) model which is an ontology-based semantic representation model for design rationale knowledge. Carignano et al. presented a model that allows architects to represent the design rationale knowledge generated during software system architecture design [6]. Babar et al. considered providing an effective mechanism to access design rationale knowledge has great potential to improve software maintenance processes [7]. Based on OWL language, Hu et al. proposed a design rationale knowledge model for knowledge sharing [8].

Although many optimization methods have been proposed in the past to improve the design rationale knowledge capturing and modeling, few research works have been done in the field of the model processing. The design rationale knowledge model is a completely complex and huge design process for a product. Specifically, the designers in different design stages need different design rationale knowledge, but they can only find the knowledge that they need under the same huge model. Therefore, this paper presents two reduction methods for design rationale knowledge model, and the methods include structure reduction method and semantic reduction method.

In previous study, we have proposed Fine-Granularity design rationale knowledge model [8]. The model is connected by five elements (design intent, design option, design decision, design basis, design operation) and six relationships (decompose-into, achieved-by, decided-by, refer-to, realized-by, initiate) as shown in Fig. 1.

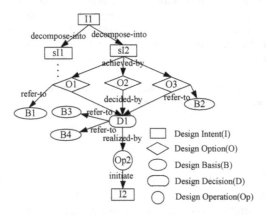

Fig. 1. Fine-granularity design rationale knowledge model

2 Structure Reduction Method

2.1 Design Rationale Knowledge Fragment

Design rationale knowledge fragment is the implementation process of meta intention that cannot be decomposed in the model. On this basis, this paper decomposes the model into design intent fragments, analysis process fragments and design decision fragments, as shown in Fig. 2. This result enables the computer to understand the designer's thinking process more clearly, and take it as the basic operation unit of design rationale knowledge model reduction.

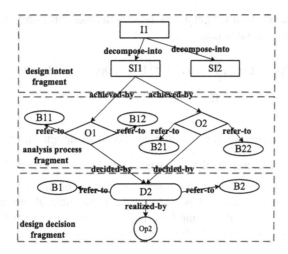

Fig. 2. Design rationale knowledge fragment structure

2.2 Hierarchical Modeling

The quotient space theory expresses the domain, attribute and structure of the problem in terms of three tuple (X, f, T), and granulates according to the given equivalence relationship, thereby obtaining the quotient space of the original question ([X], [f], [T]) [9]. Granularity refers to induce multiple elements with similar properties into a new element. The process of granulation is clustering by giving a similarity criterion.

We map the design rationale knowledge model into the three tuple form of the quotient space. X is fragment of design rationale knowledge, which represents the domain of the design rationale knowledge model; f represents the attributes of each design rationale knowledge fragment, this attribute is defined as the level of design intent in design rationale knowledge fragment. The initial intent triggered by design decisions or design operations is the first level, the indivisible meta-intent obtained by intent decomposition is the last layer. T represents the internal structure of design rationale knowledge fragment.

Design intent and corresponding design decisions drive the design process. Therefore, omitting the analysis process fragments helps designers quickly understand the design process. Extracting the design intent-decision tree from the Fine-Granularity design rationale knowledge model initially reduces the complexity of the model. We apply formula (1) to define the equivalence relation that is granulating any analysis process fragments into decided-by relationships, getting design intent-decision tree.

$$TP \sim decided - by \Leftrightarrow \forall Tp = Tp_1, Tp_2, \ldots, Tp_i = decided - by \qquad (1)$$

The decomposition process of design intent in design rationale knowledge model leads to fragment nesting structure in the model. The purpose of building a hierarchical structure is to simplify these nested structures, the specific method is: granulate the obtained intent-decision structure into the parent-intent node of the intent fragment according to its level; then we get a new intent - decision structure. The equivalence relation is shown in formula (2):.

$$\left(\mathrm{Ip}_{j+1}, \mathrm{Dp}_{j+1}\right) \sim \mathrm{sIk}_j \Leftrightarrow \forall \left(\mathrm{Ip}_{j+1}, \mathrm{Dp}_{j+1}\right) \subseteq \left(\mathrm{Ip}_j, \mathrm{Dp}_j\right)$$
$$\left(\mathrm{Ip}_j, \mathrm{Dp}_j\right) \geq k, j = 1, 2 \ldots n; k = 1, 2, \ldots, n - 1$$

(2)

where $\left(\mathrm{Ip}_j, \mathrm{Dp}_j\right)$ represents the structure composed of design intent fragments and design decision fragments in the j_{th} layer; $f\left(\mathrm{Ip}_j, \mathrm{Dp}_j\right)$ represents the hierarchical attributes of the structure; sIk_j is the parent intent node of the central intent of the extracted design intent fragment; k is the threshold for hierarchical attributes. By taking the value of the hierarchical attribute from large to small, we can get the hierarchical design rationale knowledge model from fine to coarse granularity.

3   Semantic Reduction Method

Manifold ranking mainly solves the ranking problem related to the topic [10]. By giving a query and a set of data points, it ranks the correlation of data points along a potential manifold structure based on the correlation to the query. It contains two basic assumptions: (1) Adjacent nodes tend to have similar ranking scores; (2) Nodes on the same structure tend to have similar ranking scores.

In the design rationale knowledge model, the realization process of the meta-intent that cannot be further decomposed is the smallest complete unit of the model. Therefore, the operation of the smallest complete unit ensures the correctness of the logical relationship after the reduction. We define this minimal complete unit to Minimum-Length design rationale knowledge Segment. The more keywords a fragment contains under the initial condition, the higher its relevance to the topic is. Intuitively, the close segments are highly correlated, and will be given similar scores in the ranking process.

In this paper, the query sample is t, which is covered by the domain ontology of the relevant design object.

Input: Design theme keywords, design segments

Output: Segment rank score

Step1. Define a semantic sentence graph G (D, W) to build sentence relations.

G (D, W) is built with the design rationale knowledge segments in X as nodes. The link weights defined by a matrix W indicate semantic segments similarity, where ω (d_i, d_j) is relevance between segment d_i and d_j, as shown in formula 3.

$$\omega\left(d_i, d_j\right) = r(d_i \cap T) + r(d_j \cap T)$$

(3)

In the formula, r(di ∩ T) represents the sum of the TF-IDF values of each key word contained in design rationale knowledge segments di shown in formulas 4 and 5. According to the characteristics of the model, the TF-IDF value calculation method of each word is defined in formulas 6 and 7. The TF value of the word t_k is determined by the ratio of the number of times that word appears and the number of times all the words appear. The IDF value is determined by the logarithmic value of the total number of fragments and the number of segments in which the word appears.

$$r(d_i \cap T) = \sum_{t_k \in d_i \cap T} I(t_k) \tag{4}$$

$$I(t_k) = TF - IDF(t_k) \tag{5}$$

$$TF(t_k) = \frac{\text{The number of times the keyword } t_k \text{ appeared}}{\text{the number of times all the keyword appear}} \tag{6}$$

$$IDF(t_k) = \log \frac{\text{total number of fragments}}{\text{number of segments in which the word } t_k \text{ appears}} \tag{7}$$

Step2. The similarity matrix W is symmetrically normalized by formula 8.

$$M = Q^{-\frac{1}{2}} W Q^{-\frac{1}{2}} \tag{8}$$

Step3. Sort the segments based on the scores of the segments and the relationships between the segments. We propose new assumptions based on the improved manifold sort algorithm: (1) the nodes include keyword; (2) Segments adjacent to segments containing subject words tend to have similar rank scores.

Define matrix $y = [y_1, y_2, y_3, \ldots, y_n]T$, when di contains words in T set $y_i = 1$; when di doesn't contain words in T set $y_i = 0$. Define matrix $f = [f_1, f_2, f_3, \ldots, f_n]T$, where fi represents the rank score of the segment di, f(r) denotes the value of f in the r_{th} cycle, set initial value $fi(0) = 1/n$, where n is the number of design rationale knowledge fragments contained in the model. Iterating by formula (9):

$$f(r+1) = dMf(r) + (1-d) \tag{9}$$

After parameter initialization, apply iterative functions for iterative processing until the difference of f between adjacent segments is less than the set threshold σ, where d is the attenuation coefficient ($0 \leq d \leq 1$).

Step4. Arrange the fragments according to their final ranking points $f^* = [f_1^*, f_2^*, \ldots, f_n^*]$, then extract pre k% fragments to form design decision context fragment.

4   Instance Verification

Through the development of design rationale knowledge modeling software and the example of model of blanking die, the effectiveness of the model reduction methods are verified in this paper.

(1) Extracting design intent - decision structure: as shown in Fig. 3, the solid line section is the six layout methods proposed by the designer during the layout design of the sheet material. The dashed line part is the two edge value calculations proposed by the designer during the determination of the edge value of the strip. After the design intent-decision tree extraction function is selected, the analysis process fragment is converted to a decided-by logic relationship connection. The process reduces the complexity of the model.

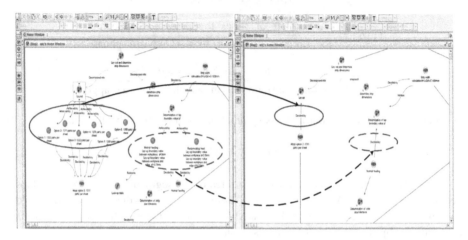

Fig. 3. Extraction of design intent decision structure

(2) Building hierarchical structure: when selecting hierarchical structure construction function, the system will prompt the designer to input the level threshold. As shown in Fig. 4, when setting the level threshold to 3, the system performs a reduction of the design rational knowledge segment formed by the two intents of "determining the edge value a1" node and "determining the value of the gap between the strip material and the guide plate material".

(3) Semantic Reduction: by choosing semantic reduction function of design rationale knowledge model, as shown in Fig. 5, ten keywords are set up: including blanking, mould, terrace die, die, stamp, pressure, machining, layout, shape and structure. The final sort result shown on the right side of Fig. 5, is sorted by the design intent node, with "Calculation of the wall thickness of the die", "Calculation of the wall width of the die", and "Calculation of the wall length of the die" ranked in the last three positions. Select the design intent node and click the "Insert to View" button to locate the corresponding node in the diagram. It can be seen from the figure that the three meta-intention nodes are located close to each other and match the manifold ranking result, reducing the design rational knowledge segment of the three design intent nodes to achieve the deletion of the design process that is less relevant to the design theme.

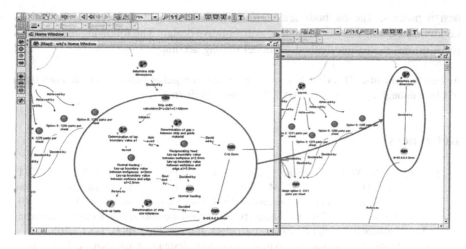

Fig. 4. Reduction of the level threshold of 3

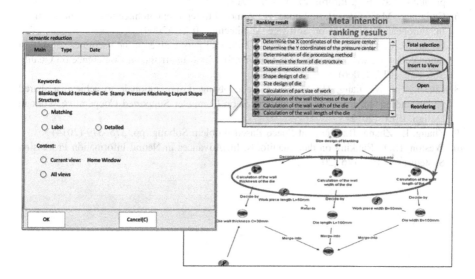

Fig. 5. Design rationale knowledge model semantic reduction

5 Conclusion

This paper proposes two reduction methods for design rationale knowledge model, including structure reduction method and semantic reduction method. Structure reduction method by extracting design intent - decision structure and building hierarchical structure enables designers to analyze design problems from different levels of granularity. Semantic reduction method ranks the relevance of the design rationale knowledge segments, and retains high-relevance segments to form the core of the design process. The methods are verified by developing a prototype system, thus, improving the efficiency of designers' collaborative design. The following research will focus on the evaluation method of model mining accuracy.

Acknowledgements. This work has been supported by Project of National Science Foundation of China through approval No. 51475027 and No. 51575046.

References

1. Lee, J., Lai, K.: What's in design rationale. Hum.-Comput. Interact. **6**(3), 251–280 (2011)
2. Regli, W.C., Hu, X., Atwood, M., Sun, W.: A survey of design rationale systems: approaches, representation, capture and retrieval. Eng. Comput. **16**(3–4), 209–235 (2000)
3. Rockwell, J.A., Grosse, I.R., Krishmanurty, S.: A semantic information model for capturing and communicating design decisions. J. Comput. Inf. Sci. Eng. **10**(3), 1–8 (2010)
4. Liu, Y., Liang, Y.: Learning the "Whys": discovering design rationale using text mining - an algorithm perspective. Comput. Aided Des. **44**(10), 916–930 (2012)
5. Zhang, Y., Luo, X., Li, J., Buis, J.J.: A semantic representation model for design rationale of products. Adv. Eng. Inform. **27**, 13–26 (2013)
6. Carignano, M.C., Gonnet, S., Leone, H.: A model to represent architectural design rationale. In: European Conference on Software Architecture. IEEE (2009)
7. Babar, M.A., Tang, A., Gorton, I., et al.: Industrial perspective on the usefulness of design rationale for software maintenance: a survey. In: Sixth International Conference on Quality Software. IEEE (2006)
8. Liu, J., Hu, X., Jiang, H.: Modeling the evolving design rationale to achieve a shared understanding. In: International Conference on Computer Supported Cooperative Work in Design. IEEE (2012)
9. Zhang, L., Zhang, B.: Quotient Space Based Problem Solving, pp. 375–379 (2014)
10. Weston, H.D.: Ranking on data manifolds. In: Advances in Neural Information Processing Systems, pp. 169–176 (2017)

SysML Extension Method Supporting Design Rationale Knowledge Model

Shu De Wang, Ji Hong Liu$^{(\boxtimes)}$, and Chao Fu

School of Mechanical Engineering and Automation,
Beihang University, Beijing 100191, China
ryukeiko@buaa.edu.cn

Abstract. To solve the problem of some system models with insufficient ability of supporting design process knowledge presentation, we propose an extension method for the systems Modeling Language (SysML) that supports the design rationale model in a collaborative design environment. We introduce the design rationale knowledge model into system modeling. Through this method, the expressiveness of the design context is enhanced. The designers' understanding to the overall scheme can be improved.

Keywords: MBSE · SysML · Design rationale knowledge
Cooperative design

1 Introduction

With the promotion of Model-based System Engineering (MBSE) in collaborative design of complex products, its advantages over Text-based System Engineering (TSE) [1] are constantly emerging: traceability, program verifiability, and consistency. However, there are still some problems in the practical application of MBSE.

The knowledge in product design consists of two categories: design result knowledge and design process knowledge [2]. Although the system model in MBSE contains a complete design scheme with requirement analysis, function decomposition, structure parameters, etc., it lacks the description of the design principle and cannot capture the knowledge during the design process. This causes difficulty of overall understanding during the design process by engineering personnel and poor reusability of the design scheme in the process of collaborative design.

To solve the problem, we introduce Design rationale knowledge (DRK) model into the MBSE process. Design rationale is the description of design process knowledge [3]. It is mainly used to explain why a product is designed in a certain way. In this article, Fine-Granularity DRK model proposed in our previous study [4] is applied because of the need of recording the most detailed and original design process. The model is connected by five elements (design intent, design option, design decision, design basis, design operation) and six relationships (decompose-into, achieved-by, decided-by, refer-to, realized-by, initiate).

© Springer Nature Switzerland AG 2018
Y. Luo (Ed.): CDVE 2018, LNCS 11151, pp. 225–228, 2018.
https://doi.org/10.1007/978-3-030-00560-3_30

2 Related Work

In order to enhance the traceability of MBSE, Jackson presents a relationship visualization method, which shows the traceability through a variety of traceability relationships, but it does not support process knowledge [5]. Julien shows the design process through collaborative diagram, while it lacks a feasible implementation [6].

3 Method

3.1 DRK Model Considering Conceptual Design Process

According to the way of system model expression, it is necessary to refine the DRK model with the characteristics of conceptual design phase. The conceptual design is generally based on the RFBS (Requirement-Function-Behavior-Structure) process [7].

The RFBS method is essentially functional modeling based on functional requirements. The function is taken as the design intent, and the structure is solved based on behavior. By simple analysis, the method can contain two design rationale segments. The system function is designed based on the functional requirement, and determines the system boundary according to the use case. The function can be decomposed to obtain the sub-intent based on the stream type and other design basis.

To achieve sub-intent, different structure options can be chosen based on the behavior. Then the design decision will be made according to the non-functional requirements, the inherent constraints, and the trade of parameters.

3.2 SysML Extension Oriented to DRK Model

To support the construction of design context from system model, the semantics related to design rationale should firstly be extended at the meta-model layer based on the SysML extension mechanisms. In this study, the extension method of defining stereotypes to extend the constructs that already exist in SysML is used because it can be implemented easily with the existing MBSE tools [8].

Combined with the analysis in the second part, the design rationale semantics for each type of element should be extended. The proposed sub-profiles describe the semantics of designing rational elements, and stereotypes of the elements and the meaning of each prototype are shown in Table 1. The relationships included in DRK model are also extended based on the existing relations. Based on the Class diagram in

Table 1. Sub-profile for specifying the DRK model

Stereotype name	Basic stereotype	Semantics
Design intent	Requirement, activity, use case	Goal, plan, and purpose for design thinking
Design option	Activity, block	Options to achieve the intent
Design basis	Requirement, behavior, constraint, rationale	Reason to explain the decisions and operations
Design decision	Activity, block	Final solution to achieve the design intent
Design operation	State machine, interaction	Operation to realize the decision

UML, a design rationale diagram is established in this paper. This diagram can contain design rationale elements which are extended based on requirements, functions, behaviors, and structures to support the design rationale of the design scheme.

3.3   DRK Model Automatic Construction Based on SysML

The method of model construction is shown in Fig. 1:

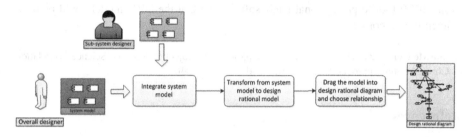

Fig. 1. Fine-granularity DRK model

3.4   Instance Verification

The approach presented in this article is based on the release of No Magic's Cameo Systems Modeler 18.5 plug-in. The design of interior environment control integrated system of a vehicle is selected as application to verify the method in this paper. The design of rationale segment to achieve the requirement of Refrigeration and Heating is shown in Fig. 2. From this case, based on the design principle and product specifications, semiconductor refrigeration can be selected as a design option. Based on non-functional requirements, constraints, and the solution trade-offs, evaporation cycles and centrifugal fans can be selected as the decision options.

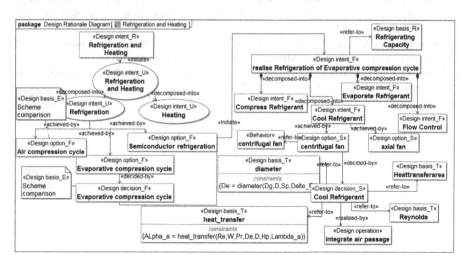

Fig. 2. Design rationale segment

4 Conclusion

To solve the problem of system model with insufficient ability of supporting design process knowledge, we propose a SysML extension method that supports the design rationality model in a collaborative design environment. However, with this method the construction of design rational segment needs to be built manually, and cannot be automatically identified and converted according to the model relationship.

Further research could be expanded towards the transformation of DRK model from MBSE tool to professional DRK software so that the DRK model could be used efficiently and correctly.

Acknowledgements. This work has been supported by Project of National Science Foundation of China through approval No. 51475027 and No. 51575046.

References

1. Rashid, M., Anwar, M.W., Khan, A.M.: Towards the tools selection in model based system engineering for embedded systems - a systematic literature review. J. Syst. Softw. **106**(C), 150–163 (2015)
2. Regli, W.C., Hu, X., Sun, W.: A survey of design rationale systems: approaches, representation, capture and retrieval. Eng. Comput. **16**(3–4), 209–235 (2000)
3. Lee, J., Lai, K.Y.: What's in Design Rationale?, pp. 21–51. L. Erlbaum Associates Inc., Mahwah (1996)
4. Liu, J., Zhan, H.: A reconstruction method of the design rationale model based on design context. In: International Conference on Fuzzy Systems and Knowledge Discovery, pp. 492–497. IEEE (2014)
5. Jackson, M., Wilkerson, M.: MBSE-driven visualization of requirements allocation and traceability. In: Aerospace Conference, Montana, pp. 1–17. IEEE (2016)
6. Gardan, J., Matta, N.: Enhancing knowledge management into systems engineering through new models in SysML. In: The International Academy for Production Engineering, Elsevier, Paris (2017)
7. Christophe, F., Bernard, A., Coatanéa, É.: RFBS: a model for knowledge representation of conceptual design. CIRP Ann.- Manuf. Technol. **59**(1), 155–158 (2010)
8. Yuan, W., Liu, Y., Zhao, J.: Pattern-based integration of system optimization in mechatronic system design. Adv. Eng. Softw. **98**, 23–37 (2016)

A Network Embedding Based Approach for Telecommunications Fraud Detection

Xiao Liu$^{(\boxtimes)}$ and Xiaoguo Wang

College of Electronics and Information Engineering, Tongji University,
Shanghai 201800, China
{0xiaoliu,xiaoguowang}@tongji.edu.cn

Abstract. Over the last few years, telecommunications fraud has caused substantial economic losses. A bank fraud management system is a cooperative system, which needs the data integrated from multiple sources and cooperative work among different departments. In this paper, we design a cooperative workflow for telecommunications fraud control and propose a network embedding based approach for telecommunications fraud detection. We conduct experiments on real-world data to demonstrate the effectiveness of the proposed method.

Keywords: Telecommunications fraud · Data mining
Cooperative application · Fraud detection · Network embedding

1 Introduction

Recently, telecommunications fraud has become a serious problem. Telecommunications fraud is composed of three major steps: (1) obtaining funds from normal accounts by fraud conducted via telecommunications networks, (2) conducting complex transactions among the fraudulent accounts to hide the sources of the funds, i.e., money laundering, and (3) withdrawing the funds from the fraudulent accounts.

To evade detection by bank fraud detection systems, fraudsters need many fraudulent accounts to conduct numerous transactions with small amounts of money through e-bank in the second step. By analyzing the IP address usage of the fraudulent accounts and the normal accounts, we find that many fraudulent accounts are accessed by a common set of IP addresses, which is rare among the normal accounts. Based on this observation, we propose a network embedding based approach for detecting the fraudulent accounts that are accessed by a common set of IP addresses.

The work most closely related to our work is EVILCOHORT [6], which can detect fraudulent accounts in various online services. EVILCOHORT works in three phases. First, it builds an account-IP bipartite graph using online service logs. Then, it performs a weighted one-mode projection to build a projected graph, in which the nodes are the accounts and the weights of edges are the numbers of IP addresses shared by the pairs of accounts. Finally, it uses the

© Springer Nature Switzerland AG 2018
Y. Luo (Ed.): CDVE 2018, LNCS 11151, pp. 229–236, 2018.
https://doi.org/10.1007/978-3-030-00560-3_31

Louvain method [2] to find the communities in the projected graph. However, IP addresses are usually dynamically allocated. EVILCOHORT ignores this fact, which can cause many false positives in practice. Another similar work is SynchroTrap [3]. SynchroTrap detects malicious activity by grouping the accounts that perform similar actions (e.g., using the same IP addresses) in the same period of time. SynchroTrap assumes that fraudulent accounts perform similar actions synchronously, but we find that it is not always true in telecommunications fraud.

2   The Cooperative Workflow for Fraud Control

Although it's important to fight fraud in each silo, the ideal approach shall involve the whole bank [1]. Figure 1 shows a fraud management system integrated from end to end, which includes:

- Data management. This module assimilates data from different and heterogeneous sources. It will perform data clean and data standardization for the data from different sources and create a shared database.
- Fraud detection. This module uses various methods to detect potential fraudulent behaviors.
- Alert management. This module accepts alerts from various fraud detection and distributes them to related departments. Then, the departments can work cooperatively to deal with the alerts.
- Case management. This module records how each fraud is resolved, total losses, prevented losses, and other details.
- Exploratory data analysis. Fraud experts from different departments can use this module to explore data, share discoveries, warn each other, and work cooperatively to improve existing fraud detection rules and models.

Figure 2 summarizes the workflow of our approach for telecommunications fraud control. In this workflow, fraud detection models, counter and analysts from the e-bank department work cooperatively to identify and act against potential fraudulent accounts. A transfer restriction will be set for the accounts in the suspicious account group detected by our method for a period t. During the period t, users cannot withdraw money or transfer money to other accounts through ATMs and e-bank. If a user contacts the bank and complains about this, the bank will suggest that he performs his operations from the counter. The teller will ask him to fill in a questionnaire when he comes to the counter. The account will be frozen if the answers are obviously flawed.

The suspicious account groups will be sent to bank analysts during the period t. The bank analysts will analyze other information related to each suspicious account group. If it is confirmed that the group of accounts is involved in money laundering, all the accounts will be frozen; otherwise, the transfer restriction will be removed, and the accounts will be added to the white list.

The efficiency of the fraud control workflow depends on the performance of the detection method. If the detection method outputs many suspicious account groups every day, it will be very difficult for the bank analysts to complete their analysis in a short period of time.

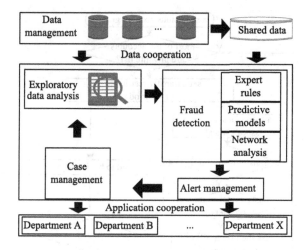

Fig. 1. Fraud management system.

3   Methodology

3.1   Problem Definition

Let $A = \{a_1, \ldots, a_n\}$ be a set of n accounts, and let $B = \{b_1, \ldots, b_m\}$ be a set of m IP addresses. Let $G_t(A \cup B, E_t)$ be a snapshot of the account-IP graph at day t. In G_t, the weight of the edge between account a and IP b is the number of times that a has used b at day t.

In our application, we want to find a set of accounts S that often use a common set of IP addresses. Let $\hat{p}(v|u)$ be the probability that account v uses an IP address used by account u. $\hat{p}(v|u)$ will be high if $u \in S \wedge v \in S$, and it will be low if $u \in S \wedge v \notin S$. Formally, we want $\hat{p}(v|u)$ to approximate the empirical distribution $p(v|u)$:

$$p(v|u) = \begin{cases} 1 & \text{if } v \in Proximities(u) \\ 0 & \text{if } otherwise \end{cases} \tag{1}$$

Proximities(u) in Eq. (1) is a set of nodes that are around u in G_t. The first-order proximity of account node u is a set of IPs used by u. For example, in Fig. 3, the first-order proximity of a_3 are b_3 'and b_5. The second-order proximity of account node u is a set of accounts that have shared IPs with u. For example, in Fig. 3, the second-order proximities of a_3 are a_2 and a_5. Higher order proximities can be defined similarly.

3.2   Network Embedding

Let $\Psi : u \rightarrow \mathbf{R}^d$ and $\Psi' : u \rightarrow \mathbf{R}^d$ be two mapping functions. Each of them maps an account u to a d-dimensional representation vector. The mapping functions can be adjusted toward a certain property that we want. The estimated

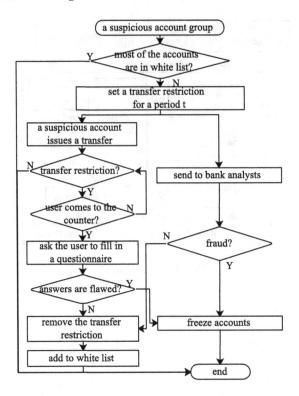

Fig. 2. The cooperative workflow for telecommunications fraud control.

distribution $\hat{p}(v|u)$ can be defined as follows:

$$\hat{p}(v|u) = \frac{\exp(\Psi(u) \cdot \Psi'(v))}{\sum_{t \in A} \exp(\Psi(u) \cdot \Psi'(t))} \tag{2}$$

We can preserve the similarity property in the representation vectors by minimizing the gap between the estimated distribution $\hat{p}(v|u)$ and the empirical distribution $p(v|u)$. We define the loss function for our problem as follows:

$$L = d(\hat{p}(v|u), p(v|u)) \tag{3}$$

where $d(\cdot, \cdot)$ is the distance between two distributions. We adopt the Kullback-Leibler (KL) divergence as the distance function. Using the KL divergence to replace $d(\cdot, \cdot)$ in Eq. (3), we have

$$L = -\sum_{u \in A} \sum_{v \in Proximities(u)} \log \frac{\exp(\Psi(u) \cdot \Psi'(v))}{\sum_{t \in A} \exp(\Psi(u) \cdot \Psi'(t))} \tag{4}$$

However, the cost of computing the softmax in Eq. (4) is proportional to the number of accounts, which makes it computationally intractable on a large

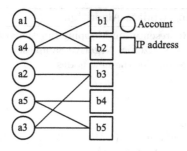

Fig. 3. The structure of the account-IP bipartite graph.

dataset. We adopt the negative sampling method [5] to approximately optimize Eq. (4). Therefore, we attempt to optimize the following loss function in practice:

$$L = -\sum_{u \in A} \sum_{v \in Proximities(u)} \log \sigma(\Psi(u) \cdot \Psi'(v)) + k\mathbf{E}_{t \sim P(t)}[\log(-\sigma(\Psi(u) \cdot \Psi'(t)))]$$

$$= -\sum_{u \in A} \sum_{v \in Proximities(u)} \log \sigma(\Psi(u) \cdot \Psi'(v)) + \sum_{i=1}^{k} \log(-\sigma(\Psi(u) \cdot \Psi'(t_i)))$$

$$(5)$$

where $\sigma(x) = \frac{1}{1+\exp(-x)}$ is the sigmoid function and $P(t)$ is the pre-defined noise distribution. For each pair (u, v), k negative samples will be drawn from $P(t)$. We define $P(t)$ as $P(t) \propto deg(t)$, where $deg(t)$ is the weighted degree of node t.

Algorithm 1 is the pseudocode of how to update the representation mapping functions using a graph snapshot. For each account node u, we first generate a random walk of length $2l$ from u. We only save the account nodes on that random walk (line 5–line 9). Then, for each node u on that random walk, we use a slicing window of size w to encircle the demanded positive sample, i.e., the proximities of u (line 12). For each positive sample, we generate k negative samples from the noise distribution $P(t)$ (line 12–line 18). We update Ψ and Ψ' using stochastic gradient descent according to Eq. (5) using one positive sample and k negative samples (line 19).

In algorithm 1, $ProximitySampling(v)$ function samples a node according to the degree distribution of node v. $NegativeSampling$ function samples an account node according to the total degree distribution of G_t. Both functions can be implemented efficiently using the alias method [7].

Algorithm 1. Embedding Update Algorithm

Require: Snapshot: G_t, Representation Mapping functions: Ψ and Ψ', Walk Times: t
, Walk Length: l , Window Size: w, Negative Samples: k

1: Initialize the representations for the new nodes
2: **for** $i = 1$ to t **do**
3:     **for** $u \in A$ **do**
4:         $walk = [u]$
5:         **for** $i = 1$ to l **do**
6:             $b = ProximitySampling(walk[-1])$
7:             $pos = ProximitySampling(b)$
8:             $walk = Append(walk, pos)$
9:         **end for**
10:        **for** $i = 1$ to l **do**
11:            $u = walk[i]$
12:            **for** $v_{pos} \in walk[i - w : i + w]$ **do**
13:                $P = \{(u, v_{pos})\}$
14:                $N = \{\}$
15:                **for** $j = 1$ to k **do**
16:                    $v_{neg} = NegativeSampling()$
17:                    $N = Add(N, (u, v_{neg}))$
18:                **end for**
19:                Update Ψ and Ψ' using stochastic gradient descent by minimizing
        equation (5)
20:            **end for**
21:        **end for**
22:    **end for**
23: **end for**
24: **return** Ψ , Ψ'

3.3 Clustering

For each pair of accounts (u, v), we can use the cosine similarity between $\Psi(u)$
and $\Psi(v)$ to measure the similarity between u and v. The representation vectors
of a set of accounts that accessed by a common set of IP addresses will form a
high-density cluster in the $\mathbf{R}^d$ vector space. We can use a density-based clustering
algorithm, such as DBSCAN [4], on the representation vectors to find those high-
density clusters.

4 Experiment

In this section, we conduct experiments to demonstrate the effectiveness of our
method on a real-world dataset. We use the following metrics to evaluate the
performance (where TP, FP and FN are true positives, false positives and false
negatives, respectively):

- Precision = $\frac{TP}{TP+FP}$
- Recall = $\frac{TP}{TP+FN}$

- F1-score = 2 * (Precision * Recall)/(Precision + Recall)

The dataset used in the experiment is the real transaction logs provided by a bank institution. The basic information of the dataset is listed in Table 1.

Table 1. Basic information of the dataset.

#transactions	#accounts	#IPs	#fraudulent accounts
17,441,949	3,046,079	2,393,096	195

We use 10,000 normal accounts and 195 fraudulent accounts (provided by the bank) as our labeled data to evaluate the performance of our method. We also evaluate two state-of-the-art methods for comparison. The parameters of the different methods are listed below:

- EVILCOHORT: The degree threshold s is set to 6. We output the communities with a size of greater than 10 as fraud communities.
- SynchroTrap: The action-matching window size is set to 1 hour. The per-constraint similarity and overall similarity are set to 0.15 and 0.1, respectively. We output the clusters with a size of greater than 8 as fraud clusters.
- Our Method: The walk times, walk length, window size, negative samples and vector dimension are set to 40, 100, 2, 5 and 100, respectively. We set min_pts and ϵ of the DBSCAN algorithm to 10 and 0.2.

Table 2. Experimental results

Method	Precision	Recall	F1-score
EvilCohort	0.241	0.415	0.305
SynchroTrap	0.825	0.123	0.214
Our Method	0.732	0.595	0.656

The results are shown in Table 2. Our method performs better than EvilCohort and SynchroTrap when considering the F1-score. Our method can detect more than half of the fraudulent accounts and only produces 43 false positives. Moreover, our method outputs 0.71 suspicious account groups on average each day, and the average size of a suspicious account group is 21.4. Therefore, analysis of the suspicious account groups discovered by our method can be done in a short period of time.

5   Conclusions

In this paper, we propose a network embedding based approach for telecommunications fraud detection. We convert each account in the account-IP bipartite graph to a low-dimensional representation vector and perform a clustering analysis on the representation vectors using the DBSCAN algorithm. The experimental results show that our method has considerable performance advantages and is suitable for the cooperative workflow for fraud control proposed in this paper. In further work, we will attempt to combine our method with other transaction feature based methods to achieve more accurate detection.

References

1. Avivah, L.: Fraud detection and customer authentication market overview. Technical report. Gartner Research (2008)
2. Blondel, V.D., Guillaume, J.L., Lambiotte, R., Lefebvre, E.: Fast unfolding of communities in large networks. J. Stat. Mechan.: Theor. Exp. **2008**(10), P10008 (2008)
3. Cao, Q., Yang, X., Yu, J., Palow, C.: Uncovering large groups of active malicious accounts in online social networks. In: Proceedings of the 2014 ACM SIGSAC Conference on Computer and Communications Security, CCS 2014, pp. 477–488. ACM, New York (2014)
4. Ester, M., Kriegel, H.P., Sander, J., Xu, X.: A density-based algorithm for discovering clusters a density-based algorithm for discovering clusters in large spatial databases with noise. In: Proceedings of the Second International Conference on Knowledge Discovery and Data Mining, KDD 1996, pp. 226–231. AAAI Press (1996)
5. Mikolov, T., Sutskever, I., Chen, K., Corrado, G., Dean, J.: Distributed representations of words and phrases and their compositionality. In: Proceedings of the 26th International Conference on Neural Information Processing Systems, NIPS 2013, vol. 2, pp. 3111–3119. Curran Associates Inc., New York (2013)
6. Stringhini, G., Mourlanne, P., Jacob, G., Egele, M., Kruegel, C., Vigna, G.: EvilCohort: detecting communities of malicious accounts on online services. In: Proceedings of the 24th USENIX Conference on Security Symposium, SEC 2015, pp. 563–578. USENIX Association, Berkeley (2015)
7. Walker, A.J.: An efficient method for generating discrete random variables with general distributions. ACM Trans. Math. Softw. **3**(3), 253–256 (1977)

Internet of Things for Epilepsy Detection in Patients

Karen Vanessa Angulo Sogamoso[1], Octavio José Salcedo Parra[1,2(✉)], and Miguel J. Espitia R.[1]

[1] Faculty of Engineering, Intelligent Internet Research Group,
Universidad Distrital "Francisco José de Caldas", Bogotá, D.C, Colombia
kvangulos@correo.udistrital.edu.co,
{osalcedo,mespitiar}@udistrital.edu.co
[2] Department of Systems and Industrial Engineering, Faculty of Engineering,
Universidad Nacional de Colombia, Bogotá, D.C, Colombia
ojsalcedop@unal.edu.co

Abstract. This article details the design of a web application working alongside a device that uses sensors to capture and transmit data related to the brain's activity (normal or abnormal) from a patient who experiences symptoms of epilepsy. The purpose is to prevent this disease from causing harm and irreversible effects on that specific population. The sensors are powered by a mobile device that connects via Bluetooth when changes are detected. Then, a signal is transmitted which is analyzed using neural networks for the debugging and processing of the information. A decision is then made regarding the state of the patient who could be suffering from an epileptic seizure. In such case, a report is issued in order to save his life. Specific characteristics found in people with critical episodes of epilepsy are combined with a hybrid system consisting of a logical controller based on an Adaptive System of Neural-Diffuse Inference (ANFIS). This study concludes that the model validated with a database including 198 signs in the years 2010, 2011 and 2012 has an accuracy of 95.5% in diagnosing or predicting an epileptic seizure. The performance matches the accuracy found in other techniques.

Keywords: Artificial intelligence · Bluetooth · Cybernetics · Epilepsy
Internet of Things · Internet of Nano-things · Sensors

1 Introduction

Over the past few years, the Internet of Things (IoT) has become an impressive force in human life, where applications can offer many benefits. As a consequence, IoT is often associated with household chores, industrial processes and mechanical automation [1].

Nonetheless, humanity has always dreamt of imitating human behavior through the use of technology and even predicting such behavior (leading to the origin of robotics). Along with that train of thought, computers have become increasingly small serving in medical applications going from the diagnosis and control of diseases to assistance methods in medical centers [2].

© Springer Nature Switzerland AG 2018
Y. Luo (Ed.): CDVE 2018, LNCS 11151, pp. 237–244, 2018.
https://doi.org/10.1007/978-3-030-00560-3_32

2 Background

Sensors have boosted the development of IoT allowing the acquisition of relevant health information in a practical manner. The devices involved in IoT offer constant, wireless and bidirectional data flows in contact with the cloud, thus enabling a precise recollection and its subsequent analysis at vertiginous speeds [2]. This type of dynamic interconnection in health care has helped to promote preventive care, deliver diagnosis and even treatment measures.

At this point, an important question arises: How does an IoT-based medical application work today? According to Carolyn Mathas in the article "The Role of Sensors in IoT Applications for Healthcare and Health Care", this relationship is based on seeing the Internet of Things as a network of devices that connect directly with each other to capture and share vital data through a secure connection layer (SSL) protocol capable of connecting to a cloud server. This is achieved with the combination of sensors, microcontrollers, microprocessors and gates where the data from the sensors is analyzed in detail through complex algorithms and is then wirelessly sent to the cloud allowing patients and health care providers to access the information [3].

In this sense, IoT faces great challenges in health care that need to be overcome and dealt with in terms of the standards required for their correct application. The main problem which also increases complexity is related to having a large number of devices at different levels, because IoT works hand in hand with wireless communications between monitoring devices and sensors [3]. This is where standard-related efforts and activities emerge, such as:

– The Continua Health Alliance is a coalition of technology and healthcare companies created to establish guidelines for interoperability solutions in personal health. It includes specifications that can be applied to interoperability in order to allow Continua-certified devices to operate between each other for IoT applications in a guaranteed manner [3].
– IEEE standards for LAN define Wi-Fi (IEE 802.11) and ZigBee (IEE 802.15.4) networks. The PAN standards include Bluetooth and BLE, IEEE 802.15.4j, IEE 802.15.6 which are associated with Body Area Networks (BAN) [3].
– Some standards for cellphone networks include GSM/UMTS and CDMA [3].

In summary, the US Food and Drug Administration (FDA) has recognized and listed 25 standards that support the interoperability and safety of medical devices [3]. The Embrace smart wearable device can control physiological variables such as stress, sleep or excitement that can lead to an epileptic seizure as well as monitor everyday activity through user notifications.

3 Methodology

After comparing the devices that are currently available on the market, it was determined that the solution to solve this dilemma is to use electronic sensors based on graphene, as they can detect the electrical activity of the brain minute by minute.

Thanks to their accuracy and high resolution, they contribute to the early detection of any abnormalities in the brain's functioning.

Needless to say, the developed device is made of an array of graphene microsensors mounted over substrates of malleable polymers that adapt to the morphology of the brain surface. It is noteworthy that this device is not implanted in the brain, but it is present on the skin's surface. Each sensor in a transistor configuration is able of detecting small changes in the electrical activity of its surroundings and sending a series of signals [4].

Artificial Neural Networks

A neural network is a system that establishes a linear or non-linear relationship between its inputs and its outputs. Its characteristics are inspired by the nervous system which offers several advantages such as adaptive learning, self-organization and parallel operation in real time. Its redundant coding enables fault tolerance [6].

From a problem solving perspective, neural networks are different from conventional computers that use sequential algorithms. While neural networks act as the human brain by processing information in parallel [6], they can also learn and generalize situations which may have not been included in the training process.

Neural networks can process information faster than conventional computers but the drawback is that they cannot follow a step-by-step response as can be done by running a conventional program on a computer. This makes it harder to pinpoint errors [6]. In addition, neural networks are very effective in solving complex classification and pattern recognition problems. The most common strategy is known as the forward propagation call.

Figure 1 shows a forward propagation network with two hidden layers. The number of inputs depends directly on the information available for classification while the number of output neurons is equal to the number of classes that need to be separated. The units of a layer are often interconnected unidirectionally with those in the next layer. Their outputs are then multiplied by a specific weight that is different for each connection.

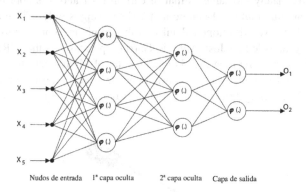

Nudos de entrada   1ª capa oculta   2ª capa oculta   Capa de salida

Fig. 1. Neuronal network forward propagation call

Adaptive Systems of Neuro - Diffuse Inference
An ANFIS [7] is a type of artificial neural network that emulates the inference process in fuzzy systems. From a statistical point of view, it is a non-parametric non-linear regression technique with the ability to approximate any function defined in a compact domain. It can be considered a universal approximation of functions.

The basic concept of ANFIS consists in dividing each input variable (or regressor) into two or more regions. Hence, the domain of the problem is divided into a set of regions that arise from the intersection of the regions where each regressor has been divided [7]. The typical architecture of the ANFIS system is presented in Fig. 2.

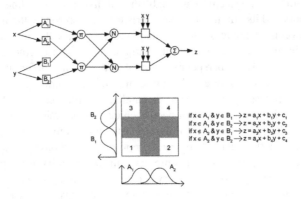

Fig. 2. Typical architecture of ANFIS

4 Design

The sensors used are built from a substance called graphene, which is made of pure carbon, with its atoms arranged in regular hexagonal patterns, similar to graphite but in a sheet which is as thick as an atom. It is considered 100 times stronger than steel, its density is approximately the same as that of carbon fiber and it is approximately five times lighter than aluminum; a 1-square-meter sheet weighs only 0.77 milligrams [4].

This technology was developed thanks to the combined contribution of the scientific research groups led by José Antonio Garrido, professor at the ICREA of ICN2, Rosa Villa, a CSIC researcher at the National Center of Microelectronics (CNM-IMB-CSIC) and CIBER-BBN and Maria Victoria Sánchez Vives, a professor at the ICREA of the Institut d'Investigations Biomédiques August Pi i Sunyer (IDIBAPS) [4] (Fig. 3).

Fig. 3. Graphene-based sensor

It can be argued that graphene has infinite potential to be used in many applications since it is a two-dimensional material that is strong, flexible, transparent and conductive. For these reasons, graphene microsensors were arranged in a matrix form having an approximate size of 10 microns per 10 microns. The material to which they were subjected to was a substrate of flexible polymers [4]. The design of the device placed on a human patient is shown in Fig. 4.

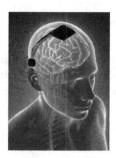

Fig. 4. View of the device placed on a patient suffering from epilepsy.

Each sensor is able to detect small changes in the nearby electrical activity, which generates a series of Bluetooth signals that were captured from a mobile device.

The application was hosted and installed on mobile devices such as smartphones, tablets, phablets and smart watches. Its development can be defined as a compatible hybrid application for operative systems Android 6.0, iOS 9.3 and their earlier versions.

In addition, based on the exhaustive research carried out by skilled staff (neurologists and general physicians) on epileptic patients, it was possible to collect the necessary data to feed the database and the 'expert' system in order to establish a series of parameters in which the system could notify states of normality, alert or risk.

5   Implementation

The sensors, which were present in the device to detect the brain's activity, were made of graphene since it is the thinnest material in the world and it is also very strong (about 150 times more than steel). It is also an excellent conductor (about 250 times more conductive than silicon) [5].

The secret to achieving high speeds is to develop smaller transistors, so that the distance travelled by the electrons is reduced as much as possible. The speed of the electrons is also very important and in fact graphene allows an electron to move up to 200 times faster than it would in silicon [5].

Graphene sensors with a size of 10 microns per 10 microns were subjected to a substrate of flexible polymers and their operation is described in the following Fig. 5.

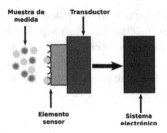

Fig. 5. View of the device placed on a patient suffering from epilepsy.

The array of sensors captures the brain's electrical activity in the form of signals emitted by the neurons. Such signals are then sent through a wire to the device that was responsible for transmitting them via Bluetooth 4.0 technology.

6   Discussion of Results

When performing the simulation of the sensor in Matlab R2013b, it was detected that the Action Potential (AP) emitted by the graphene electrode inside the controller, responded with amplitude of 162 μV (Vpp) during a period of 1.5 ms. In addition, the captured signal's SNR was close to 30.2 ± 2.45 dB. Figure 6 shows this result by including a signal within the simulation.

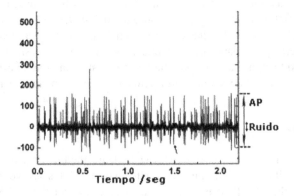

Fig. 6. Record the simulation of a signal on a graphene sensor.

These results demonstrate the great potential of graphene sensors in terms of recording and capturing neural signals. It offers a better performance when the signals are separated and recognized in order to achieve an efficient detection of neuronal symptoms for the prevention of subsequent seizures.

Table 1 refers to the difference between the simulation of artificial neural networks and the initial data.

Table 1. Mean square error for each system

	Mean square error	Accuracy	Prioritization
Neural network 1	3.1100e–04	–10.65%	3
Neural network 2	3.4964e–04	–11.97%	2
Neural network 3	3.8200e–04	–13.08%	4
ANFIS	2.4884e–04	8.52%	1

Such small errors (with an order of 10^{-4}) show the reliability and efficiency of applying the techniques in the diagnosis and prediction of epileptic seizures. The Adaptive System of Neural-Fuzzy Inference showed a better performance, since the model takes into consideration a set of parameters based on learning rules. This leads to less error in the predictions in comparison to the other models. As a conclusion, the difference between the network's output and the desired output from the training pairs is much smaller.

Regarding the accuracy or effectiveness of these techniques, a comparison was made based on what Kulkarni described in his study "Computer Vision and Fuzzy-Neuronal Systems". It was established that the Neuro-Fuzzy Inference System has an accuracy of 2.9237e–04 on other methods.

Furthermore, thanks to the application of hybrid learning (i.e. ANFIS) over several groups of signals, the training periods could establish that some patients have abnormal crises. Epileptic seizures are hard to calculate since the disease itself shows some alterations on what is considered normal. Figure 7 describes this phenomenon.

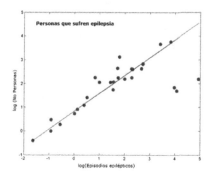

Fig. 7. Standard deviation for people with epilepsy

7 Conclusions

The ANFIS neural network delivered an average quadratic error of 3.4884e-08 which indicates that its performance is lower when compared to the other models: artificial neural network with 17 inputs and one output, artificial neural network with 17 inputs, 3 hidden layers and one output and artificial neural network with 17 inputs, 3 hidden layers and one output. In this case, the ANFIS Network is the best modeling option due to its accuracy and interpretability.

The effectiveness of the algorithm implemented in the ANFIS (neuro-diffuse) neural network surpasses the other 19.17% for the discussed system. It can be concluded that this type of artificial neural network serves as a control method with better performance in both the assessment and the overall accuracy of the results.

References

1. Organización Panamericana de la Salud: "Estrategia y plan de acción sobre epilepsia", Washington, D.C., EUA, CD51/10, Rev. 1 (Esp.)/ORIGINAL: ESPAÑOL (2011)
2. Organización Panamericana de la Salud: "Informe sobre la epilepsia en Latinoamérica" AG Publicidad. Edited in Panamá (2008)
3. Mora, I.: Detección de crisis epilépticas a partir de señales EEG mediante índices basados en el algoritmo de LempelZiv. Elsevier España S.L, España (2013)
4. Manco, O.O., Medina, S.: Design of a Fuzzy Expert System: Credit Risk Assessment of Stock Brokerage Firms in Granting Financial Resources. Elsevier España S.L, España (2007)
5. Bojadziev, G., Bojadziev, M.: Fuzzy Logic for Business, Finance, and Management. World Scientific Publishing Co., Pte. Ltd, U.K. (2002)
6. Magni, C.A., Mastroleo, G., Facchinetti, G.A.: Fuzzy expert system for solving real option decision processes. Fuzzy Econ. Rev. VI 2, 51–73 (2001)
7. Kulkarni, A.: Computer Vision and Fuzzy-Neuronal Systems. Prentice Hall, New York (2001)

Design Rationale Knowledge Management: A Survey

Gaofeng Yue[1], Jihong Liu[2(✉)], and Yongzhu Hou[2]

[1] China National Institute of Standardization,
Beijing, People's Republic of China
[2] Beihang University, Beijing, People's Republic of China
ryukeiko@buaa.edu.cn

Abstract. Design rationale is an explicit expression of the reasons behind decision making when designing an artifact. Despite its potential wide usage recognized by researchers and practitioners, it is still hard to be captured in practice. Most of research considered design rationale as a kind of tool from the scientific and engineering view and ignored humanity factor from the management view. From the perspective of knowledge management, we provide an introduction to the definition, acquisition, representation, integration, application of design rationale in this paper. We conclude with a discussion about the potential causes why the design rationale is hard to capture.

Keywords: Design rationale · Tacit knowledge · Knowledge management

1 Introduction

It is nearly fifty years since the IBIS (Issue-based Information System) [1], the origins of design rationale, was proposed in 1970. After then, it has been introduced into software engineering, civil engineering, manufacturing, human-computer interaction, industrial automation and integration, and even for theory development of human-computer interaction [2] and as a theoretical and empirical tool for design research [3]. As an important tool, design rationale has the potential usage for collaborative design, design verification, design knowledge reuse, design training and teaching, design dependency management. However, there still few useful and usable industrial applications; the research and practitioners encountered a bottleneck.

On the other hand, knowledge management has achieved big success in theories and applications. From the concept of "knowledge worker" [4], to the tacit knowledge [5], to the SCEI model and "Ba" [6, 7], to national and international knowledge management standards [8, 9], this all means that it has been widely accepted by researcher and industries. From the viewpoint of knowledge management, this paper introduces the relevant research literature on the concepts and definitions, acquisition, storage, application, methods and tools of design rationale.

© Springer Nature Switzerland AG 2018
Y. Luo (Ed.): CDVE 2018, LNCS 11151, pp. 245–253, 2018.
https://doi.org/10.1007/978-3-030-00560-3_33

2 Definition of Design Rationale

IBIS model was used to achieve coordination and planning support for the political decision-making process. In the 1980s, it was introduced into the design fields [10]. In 1988, gIBIS [11] brought IBIS into practice through the introduction of graphical management and hypertext technologies. Potts et al. [12] proposed a design rationale method for recording design deliberation and the relation. Conklin et al. [13] proposed a process-based approach and MacLean et al. [14] proposed a structural approach (Question-Option-Criteria, QOC), both are cases for capturing rationale entails the elicitation and formalization of tacit knowledge [15].

From the information view, design rationale is the explicit representation of tacit design knowledge. Design rationale means information that explains why an artifact is structured and why it has such behavior [13]. Gruber et al. [16] define design rationale as an explanation of why an artifact, or some part of it, is designed as it is. MacLean et al. [14] define design rationale as a representation for explicitly documenting the reasoning and argumentation that make sense of a specific artifact; it is necessary to understand why the system so designed. One of the most comprehensive definitions is proposed by Lee [17] that design rationale is an important tool that includes not only the rationale behind design decisions, but also the justification for decision making, other alternatives, trade-offs and the process of demonstrating the decision making. Design rationale is also viewed as a tool for making explicit some valuable tacit knowledge during software development [18].

From the knowledge view, design rationale is the design process knowledge embeded in the information. There are two types of design knowledge, design process knowledge and design object knowledge [19]. Design process knowledge describes how, whereas design object knowledge is largely fact knowledge that describes what. Following the General Design Theory, design is a mapping from the function space to the attribute space and proposed a computable design process model to implement intelligent computer aided design [20]. On this basis, an intention is seen as a key factor in making decisions [21]. Intentions can be modeled as reasons and justifications for decision making during a design process. Liu et al. [22] argued that the design is not just a problem-solving process but also a cognitive activity that is continuously iterative and evolving and further proposed an improved intent-driven design rationale model to represent the evolving design rationale. Kimura et al. [23] argued that there are two types of product information: foreground information and background information. Foreground information represents mainly "what a product is", while background information involves "how" and "why," such as design requirements, design specifications, design intents, design methods, design standards, standard parts, design history, design modification records, engineering analysis and manufacturing process/resource information. The designers can know "design rationales" from the background information so other designers can modify independently according to background information.

3 Acquisition of Design Rationale

The barrier to design rationale acquiring. Almost all researchers reach a consensus that it is not so easy to acquire design rationale. There are two main barriers: The first is that it is a time consuming and would disturb the normal design process to acquire design rationale. Researchers call this interruption as "intrusiveness". Documenting all design decisions can be time consuming and expensive [13, 24, 25]; such formal design rationale document collection during the design process is bound to interrupt the design process. The second barrier why design rationale is difficult to capture lies in that design rationale acquisition is a process of extracting tacit knowledge from designers. Tacit knowledge could not be easily codified or learnt. One of the key limitations of design rationale acquisition is due to tacit knowledge [26]. Designers may not be able or willing to spend the energy to articulate their thoughts into the design rationale system, especially when they reach breakdowns and are focusing on understanding and resolving the problem at hand. Cost-benefit tradeoff of design rationale acquisition is a slippery tightrope to walk, and we could not expect designers altruistically enter quality design rationale solely for the possible benefit of a possibly unknown person at an unknown point in the future for an unknown task [27].

Where does design rationale come from? We could acquire design rationale from the mind of individual designer, communication among design team, negotiation between designer and stakeholders, technical review meetings, thematic analysis meetings. Besides, we could also acquire design rationale from design documentations, such as design requirement specification, technical specification and designer's personal notes.

The past design data or documents as design rationale source. Capturing design rationale from design history is also called design rationale reconstruction. A process-oriented design rationale acquisition method capture design rationale from the design history [13]. An integrated approach addresses the three kind of design rationale based on argumentation, communication, and documentation [28]. The approach try to incorporate e-mail text, word processor documents, video of meetings, voice mail conversations, scanned documents, photographs, and CAD drawings into a single, hypermedia database. Some design rationale are embedded not only in formal documents such as design specifications, meeting abstracts, and interface documents, but also in informal media such as phone conversations, black board sketches, and discussions over lunch [17].

Design rationale is the result of externalization and formalization of tacit knowledge from individual designers or design teams. The approach that acquiring design rationale while design decisions occur are recognized by most researchers. As not all design rationale information are recorded into design documents, and most of design rationale information is typically very incomplete, falling short of the information required to replicate the decisions made [16]. So it has inherently shortage to acquire design rationale from the design document history. The following approach is acquiring design rationale from a designer or design team during design:

- *Win-win* approach [29]. By negotiating and analyzing requirements, using win-win negotiation approach throughout the software development can help key stakeholders prioritize their requirements and capture the decision rationale.
- *Apprentice* approach. The approach have the computer act as an intelligent apprentice to the designer to assist documenting projects and capturing design rationale information [30].
- *Rationale Construction Framework*. It [31] captures design rationale by recording design-related events and data as designers use CAD.
- *DRed* [32, 33]. DRed is an IBIS-based tool that could assist designers to structure their design thinking, to captures the rationale as they gain understanding of and solve design problems, and to reduces the need for written reports.
- *Compendium* [27]. Compendium is a powerful tool for groups and project teams to work together and allows teams to analyze, design, communicate, manage, and collaborate.

Acquiring design rationale knowledge automatically. Because it is time consuming and expensive to capture design rationale, studies were devoted to capturing design rationale automatically, especially in engineering design. An intuitive virtual reality (VR) design system was employed to unobtrusively capture design rationale through real-time logging, capturing and post-processing of design data [34]. Sung et al. [35] presented a prototype automated knowledge capture system for logging individual designer behavior and system interactions within a single-user CAD system. A tool methodology for design rationale capture within the Cax Environment from the employees during design session was used for enterprise knowledge retention [36].

Further, some researchers focused on the design rationale extraction from the design documentation through text mining technology. Rogers et al. [37] tackled the issue of extracting rationale from text by describing a mechanism for using General Architecture for Text Engineering and Waikato Environment for Knowledge Analysis. Liang et al. [38] focused on algorithm design to automatically extract design rationale information from a kind of publicly available design documentation (patent information).

4   Representation of Design Rationale

Representing design rationale for human reading and understanding. Design rationale comes from designers and serves different persons. So it is naturally represented properly for human reading and understanding. The "Record-and-replay" [17], method simply captures rationales synchronously via video conferencing or a shared screen or asynchronously via bulletin board or e-mail based discussion.

In the past ten years, the research paid more attention to ontology method to represent design rationale knowledge in a more formal way suitable for computer processing. Wang et al. [39] proposed an integrated representation scheme based on DRed for effective design rationale retrieval. Peng et al. [40] proposed a knowledge model to describe a design process using a connected graph model. Based on IBIS and the Bayesian approach, the model uses object, state, issue, solution, resource, iteration as components which address the formal elements and less formal contextual information about issues or solutions. Based on IBIS, Zhang et al. [41] proposed an ontology-based semantic representation model for design rationale information, which is defined by OWL and Semantic Web Rule Language.

5 Integration of Design Rationale

Integrating design rationale segments to build a design rationale system. gIBIS is used on large, complex design problems by facilitating building and browsing typed IBIS networks. With hypertext and graphical technologies, gIBIS integrates the design deliberations of team members within the local area network to form an IBIS knowledge network. A typical IBIS node that employ network to organize and manage decision rationale is composed of issue, position and argument. Later, based on gIBIS and QOC, a broader approach, Compendium, which is a concept map based on hypermedia environment is used for collective sense making [42].

Integrate various files into a design document base. Integrating related design rationale documents of different designers, different formats and different uses in the enterprise into a design information space that serves as a knowledge base for communication and discussion of the design collaboration [28, 32]. The scope of design rationale capturing include all the major kinds of digital media, such as e-mail text, word processor documents, video of meetings, voice mail conversations, scanned documents, photographs, and CAD drawings.

Integrating different stages of design rationale. Burge et al. [43] proposed a method for integrating different design rationale with a design process model. The process model could be annotated with design rationale behind the process, such as rationale in the system doing the designing, with rationale generated in the design trace created by the system, and with rationale for the specific design developed for the customer. For mutual understanding and business collaboration of different engineers across product design and tool design process, Poorkiany et al. [44] represent design rationale in a designer commonly used file formats was used for design rationale capturing, structuring, and access across product design and tool design.

6 Application of Design Rationale

IBIS was designed to support coordination and planning of the political decision-making processes. After then, design rationale was introduced into software engineering. Dutoit et al. [15] conclude the application of design rationale in software engineering as supporting design collaboration, knowledge reuse and change, quality improvement, knowledge transfer. In human-computer interaction area, design rationale was used for supporting the design science and methodology that provides a foundation for ecological science, action science and a framework for a synthetic science [2]. In industrial automation system and integration, design rationale has potential utility of facilitating understanding, sharing and integration of product data model during the exchange of industrial data [45]. Design rationale is also used as a tool for knowledge retention. Design rationale is used for capturing knowledge assets, particularly in the context of the global enterprise, with its increased risk of knowledge loss through staff movement and attrition [18].

Most of design rationale capture occur in the early design stages. The WinWin approach was used to captures a system's requirements [29]. Apprentice approach, PHIDIAS [46], DRed and gIBIS were all used for capturing the rationale in the early design stages. Both Agouridas et al. [47] and Tang et al. [48] addressed design rationale model on traceability techniques and root-cause analysis.

7 Discussion and Conclusions

Design rationale capture is the process of explicit expression of tacit design knowledge from designer's mind. As for enterprise, tacit design knowledge is a strategic asset for sustainable development. As for designers, design rationale is the embodiment of their strengths and values. If designers explicitly record their design knowledge, there may have potential impacts on them:

Firstly, after the tacit design knowledge was extracted as design rationale, the designers' advantage over knowledge monopoly will be gradually lost. As the Chinese old saying goes, "The apprentice learned, and then the master starve to death". This illustrates the important value of knowledge in a sense. If designers resist design rationale acquisition deeply, then the design knowledge of individual designers, especially those in detailed design, is hard to obtain.

Secondly, design rationale acquisition may incur additional workload for designers. On the one hand, design rationale capture would increase their workload and may interrupt their normal design thinking processes; on the other hand, after understanding the design intent and alternative solutions, it would also increase designers' concerns on additional criticisms, censure, and comments from colleagues, executives, users and others.

Based on these considerations, it would be very hard to capture design rationale if we only consider design rationale as a design tool. Nevertheless, most of the existing design rationale studies ignored the designers' factor, management of design rationale as the intellectual capital, and the strategic value of tacit knowledge to organization and to individual designers themselves.

Acknowledgements. This work was supported in part by National Natural Science Foundation of China (NSFC) Grant Research on Design Decision Context Knowledge Modeling Methods and Application (NO. 51475027). Additional support was provided by Standardization Administration of China (SAC) Grant Knowledge Management in Consumable Industry.

References

1. Kunz, W., Rittel, H.: Issues as elements of information systems. In: Working Paper 131, Institute for Urban & Regional Development, University of California Berkeley (1970)
2. Carroll, J.M., Rosson, M.B.: Design rationale as theory. In: Carroll, J.M. (ed.) HCI Models, Theories, and Frameworks, pp. 431–461. Morgan Kaufmann, San Francisco (2003). https://doi.org/10.1016/b978-155860808-5/50015-0

3. Haynes, S.R., Bach, P.M., Carroll, J.M.: Scientific design rationale. Artif. Intell. Eng. Des. Anal. Manuf. **22**(4), 359–373 (2008). https://doi.org/10.1017/S0890060408000243
4. Drucker, P.F.: Landmarks of Tomorrow: A Report on the New "Post-Modern" World. Transaction Publishers, New Brunswick (1996)
5. Polanyi, M.: The Tacit Dimension. University of Chicago Press, London (2009)
6. Nonaka, I.: The Knowledge-Creating Company, pp. 96–104. Harvard Business Review, Brighton (1991). 69
7. Nonaka, L., Konno, N.: The concept of "Ba": building a foundation for knowledge creation. Calif. Manag. Rev. **40**(3), 40–54 (1998)
8. GB (China national standard) GB/T 34061.1–2017: Knowledge Management System—Part 1: Guidelines, Standardization Administration of China, Beijing (2017)
9. ISO (International standard) ISO/PRF 30401: Knowledge management systems – Requirements, ISO, Geneva (2018)
10. Noble, D., Rittel, H.: Issue-based information systems for design. In: Computing in Design Education: ACADIA Conference Proceedings, Gainesville, Florida. ACADIA. University of Florida (1988)
11. Conklin, J., Begeman, M.L.: gIBIS: a hypertext tool for exploratory policy discussion. ACM Trans. Inf. Syst. **6**(4), 303–331 (1988). https://doi.org/10.1145/58566.59297
12. Potts, C., Bruns, G.: Recording the reasons for design decisions Proceedings. In: 11th International Conference on Software Engineering, pp. 418–427 (1988). https://doi.org/10.1109/icse.1988.93722
13. Conklin, E.J., Yakemovic, K.C.B.: A Process-oriented approach to design rationale. Hum.-Comput. Interact **6**(3), 357–391 (1991). https://doi.org/10.1207/s15327051hci0603\&4_6
14. MacLean, A., Young, R., Bellotti, V., Moran, T.: Questions, options, and criteria: elements of design space analysis. Hum.-Comput. Interact **6**(3), 201–250 (1991). https://doi.org/10.1207/s15327051hci0603&4_2
15. Dutoit, A.H., McCall, R., Mistrík, I., Paech, B. (eds.): Rationale Management in Software Engineering: Concepts and Techniques, pp. 1–48. Springer, Heidelberg (2006). https://doi.org/10.1007/978-3-540-30998-7_1
16. Gruber, T.R., Russell, D.M.: Design knowledge and design rationale: a framework for representation, capture, and use. Technical report, KSL 90–45. Stanford University, Stanford, California (1991)
17. Lee, J.: Design rationale systems: understanding the issues. IEEE Expert **12**(3), 78–85 (1997). https://doi.org/10.1109/64.592267
18. Nkwocha, A., Hall, J.G., Rapanotti, L.: Design rationale capture for process improvement in the globalised enterprise: an industrial study. Softw. Syst. Model. **12**(4), 825–845 (2013). https://doi.org/10.1007/s10270-011-0223-y
19. Yoshikawa, H.: Systematization of design knowledge. CIRP Ann. **42**(1), 131–134 (1993). https://doi.org/10.1016/S0007-8506(07)62409-3
20. Takeda, H., Veerkamp, P., Tomiyama, T., Yoshikawa, H.: Modeling design processes. AI Mag. **11**(4), 37–48 (1990)
21. Tomiyama, T.: From general design theory to knowledge-intensive engineering. Artif. Intell. Eng. Des. Anal. Manuf. **8**(4), 319–333 (1994). https://doi.org/10.1017/S0890060400000998
22. Liu, J., Hu, X.: A reuse oriented representation model for capturing and formalizing the evolving design rationale. Artif. Intell. Eng. Des. Anal. Manuf. **27**(4), 401 (2013). https://doi.org/10.1017/S0890060413000395
23. Kimura, F., Suzuki, H.: Representing background information for product description to support product development process. CIRP Ann. **44**(1), 113–116 (1995). https://doi.org/10.1016/S0007-8506(07)62287-2

24. Burge, J., Brown, D.C.: Reasoning with design rationale. In: Gero, J.S. (ed.) Artificial Intelligence in Design 2000, pp. 611–629. Springer, Dordrecht (2000). https://doi.org/10.1007/978-94-011-4154-3_30

25. Shipman III, F.M., Marshall, C.C.: Formality considered harmful: experiences, emerging themes, and directions on the use of formal representations in interactive systems. Comput. Support. Coop. Work 8(4), 333–352 (1999). https://doi.org/10.1023/A:1008716330212

26. Horner, J., Atwood, M.E.: Design rationale: the rationale and the barriers. In: NordiCHI 2006, New York, NY, USA, pp 341–350 (2006)

27. Shum, S.J.B., Selvin, A.M., Sierhuis, M., Conklin, J., Haley, C.B., Nuseibeh, B.: Hypermedia support for argumentation-based rationale. In: Dutoit, A.H., McCall, R., Mistrík, I., Paech, B. (eds.) Rationale Management in Software Engineering, pp. 111–132. Springer, Heidelberg (2006). https://doi.org/10.1007/978-3-540-30998-7_5

28. Shipman, F.M., McCall, R.J.: Integrating different perspectives on design rationale: supporting the emergence of design rationale from design communication. Artif. Intell. Eng. Des. Anal. Manuf. 11(2), 141–154 (1997). https://doi.org/10.1017/S089006040000192X

29. Boehm, B., Kitapci, H.: The WinWin approach: using a requirements negotiation tool for rationale capture and use. In: Dutoit, A.H., McCall, R., Mistrík, I., Paech, B. (eds.) Rationale Management in Software Engineering, pp. 173–190. Springer, Heidelberg (2006). https://doi.org/10.1007/978-3-540-30998-7_8

30. Garcia, A.C.B., Howard, H.C.: Acquiring design knowledge through design decision justification. Artif. Intell. Eng. Des. Anal. Manuf. 6(01), 59 (1992). https://doi.org/10.1017/S0890060400002948

31. Myers, K.L., Zumel, N.B., Garcia, P.: Acquiring design rationale automatically. Artif. Intell. Eng. Des. Anal. Manuf. 14(2), 115–135 (2000). https://doi.org/10.1017/S089006040014 2027

32. Bracewell, R.H., Wallace, K.M.: A tool for capturing design rationale. In: The 14th International Conference on Engineering Design (ICED 2003), Stockholm, Sweden, pp. 185–186 (2003)

33. Bracewell, R., Wallace, K., Moss, M., Knott, D.: Capturing design rationale. Comput. Aided Des. 41(3), 173–186 (2009). https://doi.org/10.1016/j.cad.2008.10.005

34. Sung, R.C.W., Ritchie, J.M., Lim, T., Kosmadoudi, Z.: Automated generation of engineering rationale, knowledge and intent representations during the product life cycle. Virtual Real-London 16(1), 69–85 (2012). https://doi.org/10.1007/s10055-011-0196-8

35. Sung, R., Ritchie, J.M., Rea, H.J., Corney, J.: Automated design knowledge capture and representation in single-user CAD environments. J Eng. Des. 22(7), 487–503 (2011). https://doi.org/10.1080/09544820903527187

36. Mix, K.J., Jensen, C.G., Ryskamp, J.: Automated design rationale capture within the CAx environment. Comput.-Aided Design Appl. 7(3), 361–375 (2010). https://doi.org/10.3722/cadaps.2010.361-375

37. Rogers, B., Qiao, Y., Gung, J., Mathur, T., Burge, J.E.: Using text mining techniques to extract rationale from existing documentation. In: Gero, John S., Hanna, S. (eds.) Design Computing and Cognition '14, pp. 457–474. Springer, Cham (2015). https://doi.org/10.1007/978-3-319-14956-1_26

38. Liang, Y., Liu, Y., Kwong, C.K., Lee, W.B.: Learning the "whys": discovering design rationale using text mining - an algorithm perspective. Comput. Aided Des. 44(10), 916–930 (2012). https://doi.org/10.1016/j.cad.2011.08.002

39. Wang, H., Johnson, A.L., Bracewell, R.H.: The retrieval of structured design rationale for the re-use of design knowledge with an integrated representation. Adv. Eng. Inf. 26(2), 251–266 (2012). https://doi.org/10.1016/j.aei.2012.02.003

40. Peng, G., Wang, H., Zhang, H., Zhao, Y., Johnson, A.L.: A collaborative system for capturing and reusing in-context design knowledge with an integrated representation model. Adv. Eng. Inf. **33**, 314–329 (2017). https://doi.org/10.1016/j.aei.2016.12.007

41. Zhang, Y., Luo, X., Li, J., Buis, J.J.: A semantic representation model for design rationale of products. Adv. Eng. Inf. **27**(1), 13–26 (2013). https://doi.org/10.1016/j.aei.2012.10.005

42. Conklin, J., Selvin, A., Shum, S.B., Sierhuis, M.: Facilitated hypertext for collective sensemaking: 15 years on from gIBIS. In: HYPERTEXT 2001, New York, NY, USA, pp. 123—124 (2001)

43. Burge, J.E., Brown, D.C.: Integrating design rationale with a process model. In: Artificial Intelligence in Design (2002)

44. Poorkiany, M., Johansson, J., Elgh, F.: Capturing, structuring and accessing design rationale in integrated product design and manufacturing processes. Adv. Eng. Inf. **30**(3), 522–536 (2016). https://doi.org/10.1016/j.aei.2016.06.004

45. Pratt, M.J., Kim, J.: Experience in the exchange of procedural shape models using ISO 10303 (STEP). In: SPM 2006, New York, NY, USA, pp. 229—238 (2006). https://doi.org/10.1145/1128888.1128920

46. McCall, R.J., Bennett, P., Johnson, E.: An overview of the PHIDIAS II HyperCAD system. In: Reconnecting: ACADIA Conference Proceedings, St. Louis, Missouri. ACADIA. Washington University (1994)

47. Agouridas, V., Simons, P.: Antecedence and consequence in design rationale systems. Artif. Intell. Eng. Des. Anal. Manuf. **22**(4), 375–386 (2008). https://doi.org/10.1017/S0890060408000255

48. Tang, A., Jin, Y., Han, J.: A rationale-based architecture model for design traceability and reasoning. J. Syst. Softw. **80**(6), 918–934 (2007). https://doi.org/10.1016/j.jss.2006.08.040

Providing Sustainable Workforce for Care Services Through Citizen Collaboration

Sylvia Encheva[1(✉)] and Sharil Tumin[2]

[1] Western Norway University of Applied Sciences, Bjørnsonsgate 45,
5528 Haugesund, Norway
sbe@hvl.no
[2] SysIntPro, Postboks 589, 5501 Haugesund, Norway
sysintpro@live.com

Abstract. A solution to care services crisis by using current technology in which an incentive-based system is proposed. A method for trading care services using cryptocredit is suggested to facilitate a citizen to citizen collaboration. Based on blockchain technology, citizens can trade care services among each other.

Keywords: Sustainability · Care services · Citizen collaboration
Blockchain

1 Care Services

Kindness does not always get paid, except the promise of heaven. In the old time communities and more impoverished societies, people are more kind toward each other, perhaps due to necessity. There is a kind of breakdown in kindness in more modern and affluent societies of today. This state of affair can be seen in every major city of the worlds. The increasing trend in the cost of care services shows the mental attitudes that kindness is a commodity to be traded in a supply and demand free market. Currently, there is more demand than supply for kindness in the world. There is a crisis in care services [1]. Moreover, in the *World Population Ageing 2017* report by the United Nations [2], the rate at which older population of 60 years and above, is steadily rising.

There are many types of care, where among others are: age care, health care, child care, and social care. Child care is an investment work for the future, while age care is a payback work for the past. Such jobs do not provide the immediate profitable return to the society in general, except in the form of wages to the care workers.

Of course, most of the care services can only be done by trained professionals. The demands in care services keep on increasing, and the number of care professionals does not match these demands. Therefore, the cost of care services keeps on rising.

Y. Luo (Ed.): CDVE 2018, LNCS 11151, pp. 254–257, 2018.
https://doi.org/10.1007/978-3-030-00560-3_34

There are many types of care services, which can be given by non-professional care personnel. We are looking at the ordinary day to day assistance needed by the elderly, a child or any person that require care in one form or another.

We can list a few of the non-professional services here: (1) assisting elderly go to the bank, (2) bringing a child to and back from daycare centers, (3) taking an elderly person for a walk in the park, (4) helping a child with school work, (5) assisting an elderly with buying groceries, (6) helping elderly with meals, (7) assisting elderly with simple cleaning ups, (8) inviting the lonely for Chrismas dinner.

These are among many others that non-professional services nearly anyone can provide. In fact, these are the things most of us do every day. Most of us are offering these care services to our love ones, who are close by. The problems are with our modern and mobile society, those dear ones most of the time are far away.

2   Budi System and Budi Economy

We assume that most people are willing to help others if they get paid for their efforts. We introduce a cryptocredit for trading care among citizens called *Budicredit*, where a unit of *Budicredit* is a *budi*. "Budi" is also a Malay word which means kindness [3].

Care recipients pay for care services by *budi*s, while care providers will get pay in *budi*s. A *budi* is a care-credit and can only be used for trading care services. All transactions are recorded and controlled using a blockchain technology. All tradings are done online, supported by a framework of collaborative web-based clients and servers, collectively called a *Budi system*.

The *Budi system* is endorsed, and its core infrastructure is sponsored by the national government under the department of social security and social services. The whole *Budi economy* is supported and guaranteed by the federal government in such a way that will promote care providers and receivers to use the system from the entire ranks of nation citizens.

Every citizen has the right to participate in the *Budi economy* by buying and selling any care services not provided by the public or private care professionals. Initially, the department of social security and social services will create a fixed amount of *budi*s of *Budicredit* in direct relation to the number of population in the state. The *budi*s will be distributed to the citizens according to established rules, such as a part of a pension plan for retirees or a portion of a support for childcare support scheme. The amount of *budi*s in circulation and the minimum and maximum exchange rates for different kind of care services are regulated yearly by the ministery of social security and social services.

A citizen can freely transfer *budi*s to another, for example, a daughter can move some of her budis to her mother, useful for a student studying far away from home. *Budi*s belonging to a deceased person will be transferred to the immediate living relations. A *budi* cannot be exchanged for money, which makes the *Budi economy* simpler to control and will help prevent adverse side effects of speculation. Restricting *Budicredit* solely for trading care prevent it from abusive uses. *Budi*s awarded for child care cannot be used other than buying care services, unlike money when given for child benefits was used for other than childcare services. However, monetized *Budicredit* can help bringing businesses into *Budi economy*, which can be a good thing.

3 Blockchain

Blockchain technology could change the way we live our lives [4]. A blockchain is a trusted distributed ledger, containing records of transactions occurred in a business network sharing the same business processes. In finance, where customers, banks, insurers, regulators, auditors will all participate in the same business activities, as an example, of selling and buying properties. Without blockchain, different actors are currently keeping their copies ledger, which is expensive, inefficient, redundant and vulnerable. Separate ledgers may contain discrepancies which can only be resolved in a court of law. Blockchain provided the technology, first appeared in 2008, for supporting shared replicated and permissioned ledgers, enforcing different permissions for different business actors depending on a set of business rules and regulations. Blockchain ledgers will have these essential properties; ledger with consensus, provenance, immutability and finality. Before a transaction is put into the blockchain, all participants must agree to this change. Anyone can use the blockchain to track the history of all transactions. Once a transaction is made to the blockchain it cannot be changed at a later time in the future. Data in the blockchain is authoritative, and the blockchain contains the single source of truth about all transactions ever being done so far.

4 Proof of Concept

Bitcoin [5] is the first ever Blockchain application. It is a cryptocurrency with no central regulatory unit. A consensus is enforced in its algorithm by proof of work which is resource intensive. New coins are put into circulation by bitcoin miners given as rewards for calculating and inserting a new block of transactions into the Blockchain. *Budicredit* is different. Users of budicredits are uniquely identified, where else bitcoins users are anonymous. *Budicredit* does not use proof of work. Instead, different actors in the economy play different roles and are given a selective endorsement of rights in every transaction. *Budicredit*'s primary concern is in managing assets rather than cryptocurrency.

We propose using Hyperledge [6] as the blockchain infrastructure to implement our *Budi system*. Hyperledge provide four essential functionalities; (1) shared ledge, (2) smart contracts, (3) privacy, and (4) trust. Business terms are embedded in the transactions and timely and appropriately executed with the transactions. Users privacy is protected by ensuring appropriate visibility only to the participating parties. All transactions are done securely, authenticated and verifiable.

We also propose using this work as student projects, done collaboratively among students from different faculties. The *Budi system* will have two main components; (1) The user application, web-based and mobile app, (2) Hyperledge server installation. Engineering students will take the ICT part, while the economy students will work on the *Budi economy* part. Nursing students will concentrate on defining care services that could be provided by non-professionals. Students from teacher education will do user manual and design of a user interface. A working students' group will have students from different study programs. A test system will be used by the students where the services will be directly helping in their studies and their student life. Coursework in the form of a report, collectively written about their experience in designing, implementing and using the system, will be submitted by each group after a predifined study period.

5   Conclusion

The cost of care services is rising. The price of social benefits in many countries is not sustainable as more and more citizens are joining the rank of retirees. The tax-payers money supporting care services may not be enough in a few years to come. It is possible, with the help of current technological advancements to create social conditions where citizens collaborate in helping each other for typical day to day social care. The Budi system is meant to facilitate such social behavior, in general, by providing the incentive to those who are willing to give some help to others with payment of *Budicredit*. Credits earned while you are young and able can be used later in life when you are old and need little help. Broader public awareness of technology is crucial for success in such an endeavor. Technology when adequately understood and properly applied can create trust in the general public, in turn, a sustainable system of a citizen to citizen collaborative care services can be maintained. It pays to be kind.

References

1. ageuk.org.uk: Care in Crisis (2015). https://www.ageuk.org.uk/globalassets/age-uk/documents/reports-and-publications/reports-and-briefings/care--support/rb_14_care_in_crisis_report.pdf
2. United Nations: World Population Ageing 2017. ST/ESA/SER.A/397 ISBN 9789211515510 (2017)
3. Kim-Hui, L.: Budi as the malay mind. IIAS Newslett. **31**, 31 (2003)
4. Boucher, P., Nascimento, S., Kritikos, M.: How blockchain technology could change our lives. PE 581.948 ISBN 978-92-846-0549-1 (2017)
5. Nakamoto, S.: Bitcoin: A Peer-to-Peer Electronic Cash System. Whitepaper (2008). www.bitcoin.org
6. hyperledger.org: Hyperledger Overview (2018). https://www.hyperledger.org/wp-content/uploads/2018/03/Hyperledger-Overview_March-2018-5.pdf

Application of Apriori Algorithm in Meteorological Disaster Information Mining

Chunhui Wang[✉] and Boting Zhao

Fujian Meteorological Service Center, Fuzhou, China
563531822@qq.com

Abstract. With the progresses of meteorological informatization, large amounts of meteorological data were accumulated. For the better application of these data, this research introduced data mining and applied it to analysis meteorological disaster, which can extract implicit, and potential useful information from a large amount of data in order to guide agricultural production. Meteorological disaster data affecting tea production were analyzed based on Apriori algorithm in this research, and the strong association rules between meteorological factors and reduction rate of tea yield were found. The results showed that the reduction rate of tea yield is closely related to the daily minimum temperature in the germination stage. When the daily minimum temperature was less than 5 °C, the tea would be affected by the cold and freezing damage and the tea yield would decrease, the lower the temperature, the greater the cold and freezing damage.

Keywords: Data mining · Apriori algorithm · Meteorological disaster
Cold and freezing damage · Tea yield

1 Introduction

With the rapid development of modern information technology and the explosive growth of massive data, traditional small sample statistical analysis method couldn't meet the services demand. The excessive data and insufficient information placed us in the dilemma after the centralization of existing data. Using data mining technology to extract implicit, and potential useful information was an excellent way to solve this problem. In data mining, association rules can find interesting associations between data item sets in large amounts of data, therefore, association rules are suitable mining algorithms [1, 2]. The various algorithms of association rules and their superiority are favored by the industry, among them; the most classic algorithm is Apriori algorithm [3]. Though analyzing tea yield, disaster severity and temperature data collected from Anxi County of Fujian Province for nearly 30 years, this research used Apriori algorithm to find out the correlation between reduction rate of tea yield and daily minimum temperature and discovered the characteristics of cold and freezing damage of tea to provide decision-making basis for tea production in the region.

© Springer Nature Switzerland AG 2018
Y. Luo (Ed.): CDVE 2018, LNCS 11151, pp. 258–261, 2018.
https://doi.org/10.1007/978-3-030-00560-3_35

2 Apriori Algorithm

2.1 Algorithm Overview

The Apriori algorithm is the most classic algorithm in association rules [4], it is the priori knowledge of frequent item sets and uses an iterative method called layer-by-layer search [5]. Firstly, find all the frequent item sets by scanning the transaction record, and record the set as $L1$, then use $L1$ to find the set $L2$ of the frequent item sets 2, use $L2$ to find $L3$, and continue in such way until no more frequent K item sets can be found. Finally, find the strong association rules in all the frequent sets, thus the association rules that users are interested in are discovered. Let $I = \{i_1, i_2..., i_m\}$ be a set of all items [6]; let D be a set of all transactions (database); each transaction T is a set of some items, T is contained in I; each transaction can be represented by a unique $\subset$ identifier TID [7], and the association rule is represented as $R: X \geq Y$, where $X \subset I, Y \subset I$, and $X \cap Y = \emptyset$.

The support of the rule $X \geq Y$ in T is the percentage of the transactions containing $X \cup Y$ in T to the total transactions, and the mode larger than the given support is called the frequent mode.

The confidence of the rule $X \geq Y$ in T refers to the implication strength, that is, the probability that Y also appears in the number of transactions containing X in T [8].

The lift of the rule $X \geq Y$ in T refers to the ratio of the "probability of a transaction containing Y in a transaction containing X" to the" probability of a transaction containing Y". The lift reflects the correlation between X and Y in the association rules.

The mining issue of association rules is to find the association rule with the minimum support min_sup and the minimum confidence min_conf given by the user in the transaction database D.

2.2 Algorithm Flow

The specific Apriori algorithm is described as follows:
Input: Transaction database D, minimum support threshold min_sup;
Out: Maximum frequent K item set

(1) Scan the entire data set to get all the data that has appeared as a candidate frequent 1 item set. $k = 1$, the frequent 0 item set is an empty set.

(2) Mine frequent k item sets.
   a. Scan data and calculate the support of candidate frequent k item set.
   b. Remove the data sets with support below the threshold in candidate frequent k item set, and get the frequent k term set. If a frequent k-item set that is empty is obtained, directly return to the set of frequent $k-1$ item sets and take it as the algorithm result, and the algorithm ends. If a frequent k-item set that only has one item is acquired, directly return to the set of frequent k item sets and take it as the algorithm result, and the algorithm ends.
   c. Based on the frequent k-item set, link together to generate a candidate frequent $k + 1$ item set.

(3) Let $k = k + 1$, and go to setp2.

3   Application of Apriori Algorithm of Cold and Freezing Damage to Tea

3.1   Data Source

This research selects the daily minimum temperature data of 17 representative stations in tea-planting areas of Anxi County from 1987 to 2016 (February to April), and collects tea yield and disaster data for 30 years (1987–2016) in these areas. The yield data is from the Anxi County Statistical Yearbook, and the daily minimum temperature data comes from the Fujian Meteorological Information Center, and the disaster data comes from the Anxi County Meteorological Bureau.

3.2   Modeling Process

Data Cleaning. The original database contains tea yield data for the past 30 years from 24 villages and towns in Anxi County, and historical meteorological data from 17 representative stations, and disaster data of Anxi County. To facilitate data mining, we use regression analysis and principal component analysis to screen the data. For example, some of the raw data is shown in Table 1.

Table 1. Daily minimum temperature and yield reduction rate.

TID	A (daily minimum temperature)	B (yield reduction rate)
1	2.8	0.026
2	−2.3	0.093
3	0.3	0.059
4	3.4	0.012
5	0.7	0.056

Mining Association Rules. After the above data processing, the key to this step is to analyze and process the data using the Apriori algorithm. We set the minimum support *min_sup* to 20% and the minimum confidence *min_conf* to 50%. After using the Apriori algorithm program, some experimental results are shown in Table 2.

Table 2. Results of the association rule.

NO.	Rule	Support	Confidence	Lift
1	$A_1 \geq B_2$	31.6%	72.4%	1.8
2	$A_2 \geq B_3$	25.2%	60.6%	2.6
3	$A_4 \geq B_4$	20.0%	80.0%	3.5

Result Analysis. For the strong association rules obtained by mining, we can analyze the results. According to Table 2, rule 1 indicates that when the daily minimum temperature is lower than 5°C, the tea will be affected by cold and freezing damage and the yield will decrease; rules 2 and 3 indicate that the lower the temperature, the greater the extent of the cold and freezing damage to tea. Through the above mining rules, we can conclude that the impact of cold and freezing damage on tea is related to the daily minimum temperature. When the daily minimum temperature is lower than 5°C, the tea begins to be affected by the freezing damage, and the extent of the damage to tea is negatively correlated with the daily minimum temperature, the lower the temperature, the heavier the cold and freezing damage.

4   Conclusion

Association rule mining technology is a very useful tool. After studying of the association rules through Apriori algorithm, we apply this algorithm to the analysis of cold and freezing damage to tea. By preprocessing the relevant data, and then using the Apriori algorithm to mine the relationship between the daily minimum temperature and the reduction rate of tea yield, the association rules are finally generated. The conclusions drawn from the analysis of association rules can be used to guide future agricultural production and play a role in disaster prevention and mitigation.

References

1. Tao Guo, F., Daiyuan Zhang, S.: Research and application on association rules based on apriori algorithm. Comput. Technol. Dev. **21**(6), 102–107 (2011)
2. Yan Cui, F., Zhiqiang Bao, S.: Survey of association rule mining. Appl. Res. Comput. **33**(2), 330–334 (2016)
3. Bin Sun, F., Yanling Han, S., Guochao Feng, T.: Application of improved apriori algorithm in studying factors of soil reflectivity. Comput. Appl. Softw. **34**(7), 293–297 (2017)
4. Yuntao Zhang, F., Ling Gong, S.: The Principle and Technology of Data Mining, 1st edn. Publishing House of Electronics Industry, Beijing (2004)
5. Jiawei Han, F., Micheline Kamber, S., Jian Pei, T.: Data Mining Concepts and Techniques, 3rd edn. China Machine Press, Beijing (2012)
6. Yanqun Wang, F., Xianqiang Gao, S.: Application of apriori algorithm of association rules in information mining of corn yield. Hubei Agric. Sci. **55**(3), 736–739 (2016)
7. Wenjuan Qi, F., Jie Yan, S.: Association rules apriori algorithm in data mining. Comput. Syst. Appl. **22**(4), 121–124 (2013)
8. Qiao Li, F., Chunhua Yang, S.: Application of association rules apriori algorithm in teaching evaluation. Comput. Dig. Eng. **81**(6), 49–51 (2010)

Fish Swarm Based Man-Machine Cooperative Photographing Location Positioning Algorithm

Zelin Zang, Wanliang Wang$^{(\boxtimes)}$, Linyan Lu, and Yanwei Zhao

College of Computer Science and Technology, Zhejiang University of Technology,
Hangzhou, China
zangzelin@gmail.com, wwl@zjut.edu.cn

Abstract. This paper establishes a man-machine cooperation system to extract hidden shooting location information from the image data. The system extracts shadow position information (such as the estimated distance between the camera and the object) with the help of humans. Camera Imaging Model (CIM) is created with the knowledge of earth astronomy. This model maps latitude, longitude, and date factors to shadow space. Solar Projection Model (SPM) is established with the pinhole imaging principle. In the shadow space, a swarm intelligence algorithm, fish swarm algorithm, is used to minimizes the location error. The results show that the system can achieve effective extraction of picture depth information. Our algorithm can reduce the solution error to less than 20 km within 30 s.

Keywords: Video shooting point location · Fish swarm algorithm
Planning problem · Numerical calculation

1 Introduction

With the rise of the internet, pictures play an increasingly important role in media communication [13]. Following, people not satisfied with observing the photo's surface meaning, rather than finding the real and effective information from rich-original pictures. Such as the real shooting date and shooting location instead of the potentially deceiving label in the picture.

This kind of idea has plenty of surprising application. For example, analyzing the videos or photographs uploading by terrorist can help us determine their hiding location [1], Analyzing the videos or photographs evidence provided by the parties to the court can confirm whether the parties are lying [12]. Good effect always predicate the huge difficulty, establishing a Man-machine Cooperative system can make the completion above goals possible.

The relative movement between sun and earth is very exactitude and stabilize. Therefore, the shadow formed by the sunshine shooting on a fixed object will follow a very precise mathematical formula. Wu [14] conducted a preliminary review of this functional relationship. As shown in Fig. 1, with the changing

© Springer Nature Switzerland AG 2018
Y. Luo (Ed.): CDVE 2018, LNCS 11151, pp. 262–269, 2018.
https://doi.org/10.1007/978-3-030-00560-3_36

of sun's position, the shadow length has changed correspondingly. It is worth to point that the shadow change is different in different place.

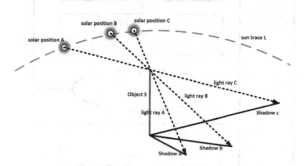

Fig. 1. The length and angle of the shadow changes with the change of the position of the sun

We build a mathematical model by using the principle of Small hole [10] imaging and geometrical optics [6] to describe the process from changing of sun position to changing of shadow length and finally to changing of Pixels in the image. Based on this mathematical model, an optimization problem is established. Finally, use the photo or video data to extract real latitude and longitude information.

However, computers do not perform well in recognizing cognitive information on pictures. For example, computers can hardly recognize the shadow of object. On this side, even the hot talking deep learning method [2] can't give a very accurate identification scheme. Therefore, the establishment of a man-machine cooperation system has become inevitable. The system makes the extraction of picture depth information more accurate by introducing the effective annotation of the position of the object, the light receiving surface and the length of the shadow.

2   Frame of Man-Machine Cooperative System

The man-machine Cooperative system is shown in Fig. 2.

The method is divided into 5 sections, which are pictures or videos input, camera imaging model, human-assisted, solar projection model and fish swarm algorithm. Pictures or videos input section take videos or continuously taken photograph into the system. Then it will output coordinate value of an obviously shadow-producing objects image and shadow of the corresponding object with the help of section human assisted (line a). Camera imaging model section takes the Pixels data from Pictures or videos input section and maps it into shadow space with the human set camera parameters (line b). Shadow space describes the changing nature of the shadow.

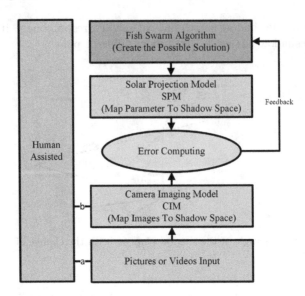

Fig. 2. Block Diagram of Man-machine CooperativePositioning of Photographing Location method

Human-assisted section help pictures or videos input section and camera imaging model section work better. Prepare the efficiency data through artificially set parameters and artificially selected object locations. Fish swarm algorithm section and solar projection model combine together with the form of feedback. Finding the best latitude and longitude solution by optimizing the operation again and again with fish swarm algorithm. The error computing process calculates the gap between the optimization process data generated by the SPM and the target data generated by the CIM, thereby returning the difference to the fish swarm algorithm as an information source for optimizing the fish swarm algorithm.

3   Mathematical Model of Positioning

3.1   Solar Projection Model

Solar projection model (SPM) describes the relationship between the shadow and other parameters (longitude($°$), latitude $°$, date(Nth day in this year), and clock(Mth minuit in this day)). The shadow length is closely related to latitude, longitude, date, and clock (minutes). The problem of shooting location can be transformed into the upper four-parameter-programming problem [5]. The optimal objective is shown in (1).

$$\min_{x,y,n} \ \mathrm{E} = \sum_{i=1}^{k} \left(f(x,y,n,t) - g(x,y,n,t) \right)^2$$

$$s.t. \quad 0 \le x \le 180.0 \quad 0 \le y \le 180.0 \quad 0 \le n \le 365 \quad 0 \le t \le 1440 \tag{1}$$

In (1), E represents the cumulative sum of shadow length errors. x, y, n and t represent the longitude, latitude, date and clock. $g(x, y, n, t)$ is the shadow length data extracted from the image. $f(x, y, n, t)$ represents the shadow length calculated from the x,y,n,t. The formula of $f(x, y, n, t)$ is shown in (2).

$$f(x, y, n, t) = L/\tan(\arcsin(\sin \alpha \sin y + \cos \alpha \cos y \cos \omega)) \tag{2}$$

Where α is the solar altitude angle, w is the solar hour angle. α denotes in (3).

$$\sin \alpha = 0.39795 \cos\left[0.98563\left(N - 173\right)\right] \tag{3}$$

and ω denotes in (4).

$$\omega = 15 * \left(T + (120° - x)/15° - 12\right) \tag{4}$$

Formula (2) is the ratio of the actual length of the rod and the height of the sun at the local clock. L is the actual height of the object of the image. Formulas (3) and (4) is the calculation formulas of the declination and solar hour angle.

3.2   Camera Imaging Model

In combination with the traditional camera model [7], this paper innovatively proposes a model that uses fewer parameters to estimate the change in shadow length.

Camera imaging model (CIM) describes the relationship between object shadow and the pixels in the image. Based on the assumption that the object can be estimated by the upright and distance, the coordinate transformation can be carried out. Shadow imaging principle in the camera shown in Fig. 3.

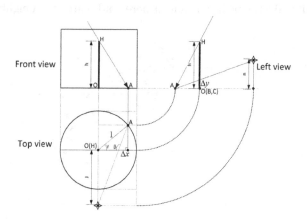

Fig. 3. Relative shadow length ratio from data image

In Fig. 3, J represents the distance from the camera to the object. n represents the height of the camera, L represents the length of the shadow OA. And γ

represent the angle of the shadow. The star represents the camera, OH is the object, HA is the sunlight, OA is the shallow which is the formulation of wood in sunlight shadow. Δx, Δy is the amount of change in the horizontal and vertical coordinates.

According to Pythagorean theorem, formulary is shown as (5).

$$
\begin{aligned}
T_{OA} &= \sqrt{(OA - \Delta x)^2 + \Delta y^2} \\
\Delta x &= \frac{l^2 \cos(\Upsilon)\sin(\Upsilon)}{J + \sin(\Upsilon)} \\
\Delta y &= \frac{l \cdot n \cdot \sin(\Upsilon)}{J}
\end{aligned}
\tag{5}
$$

The formula can be approximated as (6) :

$$
T_{OA} = \sqrt{\left(OA - \frac{l^2 \cos(\gamma)\sin(\gamma)}{J + \sin(\gamma)}\right)^2 + \left(\frac{nl \sin(\gamma)}{J}\right)^2}
\tag{6}
$$

4   Solution and Discussion of the Model

One kind of group intelligent algorithm, Fish swarm algorithm [8,15], is used to solve the problem.

Fish swarm algorithm is a kind of algorithm to imitate the cooperation strategy of fish. In nature, fish naturally gathers in the most food abundant areas.

This paper selects a group of shadow data of a straight rod (coordinate is 79.23°, 40.54°) as the original data. Try to find the most probable location using the fish swarm algorithm, and compares it with the common algorithm.

As shown in Fig. 4, artificial fish is distributed over the entire solution space before a relatively optimal solution is found. When one of the fish found a good solution, it will make the nearby fish near here, and search the neighboring place.

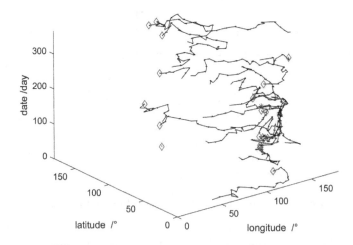

Fig. 4. The trajectory of fish swarm algorithm in solving the localization problem

In order to show the rapidity of the fish swarm algorithm to solve this problem, the algorithm is illustrated by grid search algorithm [3], greedy algorithm [11], two-step greedy algorithm [16], genetic algorithm [9], particle swarm optimization [4] and fish swarm algorithm.

The grid search algorithm is to be divided into grid search parameters in a given space, through all the grid traversal to find the optimal parameters. This method in the searching interval is large enough and step away from the small enough case can find the global optimal solution. The greedy algorithm is that in problem-solving, always seems to be made in the best choice. That is to say, not greedy algorithm considering the algorithm as a whole, can only get the local optimal solution in a certain sense. Two-step greedy algorithm combines the characteristics of greedy algorithm and grid search algorithm.

The results of different algorithms are compared in Table 1.

Table 1. Result of grid search algorithm, greedy algorithm, two-step greedy method, genetic algorithm, particle swarm optimization and fish swarm algorithm

Algorithm	L ($^\circ E$)	A ($^\circ N$)	D (day)	T_s (hour)	E_d (km)	Remarks
Grid search algorithm [3]	109.2	20.4	20/345	4.12	44.43	Steady but slow
Greedy algorithm [11]	29.2	46.8	20	0.05	75.77	Unstable but fast
Two-step greedy method [16]	109.2	20.4	20/345	0.32	14.43	Stable and fast
Genetic algorithm [9]	108.5	20.1	21/345	0.16	16.43	Unstable, sensitive to initial population
Particle swarm optimization [4]	107.4	21.9	20/347	0.1	30.43	Fast but large error
Fish swarm algorithm	109.19	20.37	20/345	0.01	25.36	Fast stable and less error

L: Denotes longitude; A: Denotes Attitude; D: Denotes Date
T_a: Denotes Searching time; E_d: Denotes Distance error

In this paper, the algorithms are divided into two categories: traditional algorithms (Including grid search algorithm, greedy algorithm, and two-step greedy method) and intelligent algorithms (Including genetic algorithm, particle swarm optimization, and fish swarm algorithm). The convergence rate of the traditional algorithms has been discussed in the reference. Generally speaking, the traditional algorithm is relatively slow. There is a great deal of uncertainty in the greedy algorithm, and the success of the search depends on its initial position. Although the two-step greedy method to a certain extent to improve the above two algorithms, in the performance and cannot achieve the desired state.

The application of intelligent algorithm can solve this problem very well. The effect is better than the traditional algorithm, but it all depends on the adjustment of the corresponding calculation parameters, and to a certain extent, affected by randomness. In three intelligent algorithms convergence error is small, but the search for a relatively long period of time, and can observe the sensitivity of the initial population, in the experiment that the different initial population is randomly generated, the convergence time gap is larger.

Particle swarm algorithm is better than the genetic algorithm in speed, but its accuracy has larger errors. After the adjustment of parameters, we found that this algorithm could enable it to reach the best level, both in speed and accuracy with fast, stable and small error characteristics, performance is better than all the algorithms, and the two to solve the problem of the intelligent algorithm. The algorithm can obtain the optimal solution to fish in 30 s.

The experimental results are shown in the Table 2.

Table 2. Sampling time and error table

Interval times	Attitude($A°$)	Longitude($A°$)	Mean linear error(km)
1	123.42	30.68	312.22
2	118.43	29.42	196.71
5	118.83	29.13	185.61
10	119.99	29.53	87.96
20	120.05	29.54	85.71
30	120.98	29.47	73.85
40	119.99	30.40	22.62

When the time interval is less than 10 min, the error of the system is larger, and the distance between the actual measurement point and the calculated location point is greater than 100 km. When the sampling interval is greater than 10 min, the positioning error is small, and the acceptable longitude is achieved. Therefore, the use of this method of inland areas should be as far as possible to meet the sampling time interval of more than 10 min of the four groups of data (length of data, photos, or video length greater than 30 min).

5   Conclusion

In order to solve the problem of extracting shooting location information from hidden image data, this paper establishes a man-machine cooperation system. The system completes the extraction of shadow locations in the image with the help of humans and uses camera model and geographic model to map all data into a shadow space. The results show that the system can achieve effective extraction of picture depth information. The algorithm can reduce the solution error to within 20 km within 30 s.

References

1. Beckman, J.: Comparative Legal Approaches to Homeland Security and Anti-terrorism. Routledge, Abingdon (2007)
2. Goodfellow, I.J., Bengio, Y., Courville, A.: Deep learning. Nature **521**(7553), 436 (2017)
3. He, D., Hong, Y.: An improved Tabu search algorithm based on grid search used in the antenna parameters optimization. Math. Problems Eng. **2015**, 1–8 (2015)
4. Kennedy, J., Eberhart, R.C.: Particle swarm optimization. In: IEEE International Conference on Neural Networks - Conference Proceedings, vol. 4, pp. 1942–1948 (1995)
5. Kumar, L., Skidmore, A.K., Knowles, E.: Research article modelling topographic variation in solar radiation in a GIS environment. World **11**(5), 475–497 (1997)
6. Munk, W.H., MacDonald, G.J.F.: The rotation of the earth: a geophysical discussion. The rotation of the earth: a geophysical discussion. In: Munk, W.H., MacDonald, G.J.F. (eds.) First Published 1960, 19+ 323 p. Cambridge University Press, Cambridge (1975)
7. Potmesil, M., Chakravarty, I.: A lens and aperture camera model for synthetic image generation. ACM SIGGRAPH Comput. Graph. **15**(3), 297–305 (1981)
8. Pythaloka, D., Wibowo, A.T., Sulistiyo, M.D.: Artificial fish swarm algorithm for job shop scheduling problem. In: 2015 3rd International Conference on Information and Communication Technology (ICoICT), pp. 439–444. IEEE (2015)
9. Qiu, M., Ming, Z., Li, J., Gai, K., Zong, Z.: Phase-change memory optimization for green cloud with genetic algorithm. IEEE Trans. Comput. **64**(12), 3528–3540 (2015)
10. Sturm, P.: Pinhole camera model. In: Ikeuchi, K. (ed.) Computer Vision, pp. 610–613. Springer, Heidelberg (2014). https://doi.org/10.1007/978-0-387-31439-6
11. Tang, W., Shi, Z., Wu, Y.: Regularized simultaneous forward – backward greedy algorithm for sparse unmixing of hyperspectral data. IEEE Trans. Geosci. Remote Sens. **52**(9), 5271–5288 (2014)
12. Vacca, J.: Computer Forensics: Computer Crime Scene Investigation. Charles River Media Inc., Wilmington (2005)
13. Varkey, P., Tan, N.C., Girotto, R., Tang, W.R., Liu, Y.T., Chen, H.C.: A picture speaks a thousand words: the use of digital photography and the internet as a cost-effective tool in monitoring free flaps. Ann. Plast. Surg. **60**(1), 45–48 (2008)
14. Wu, L., Cao, X.: Geo-location estimation from two shadow trajectories. In: Proceedings of the IEEE Computer Society Conference on Computer Vision and Pattern Recognition, vol. 114, no. 8, pp. 585–590 (2010)
15. Xiao, L.I., Yun, X.U.E., Fei, L.U., Guo, T.: Parameter estimation method based 2 on artificial fish school algorithm. J. Shan Dong Univ. **34**(60104009), 84–87 (2004)
16. Zang, Z., Xu, L., Li, J., Wang, H., Kang, X.: Video location positioning study based on two steps greedy algorithm. In: International Conference on Applied Mathematics, Simulation and Modelling (2016)

Designing an Anxiety Self-regulation and Education Mobile Application for High School Students

Caslon Chua$^{(\boxtimes)}$, Mathew Wakefield, Rachel Mui,
and Weidong Huang

Swinburne University of Technology, Melbourne, VIC 3122, Australia
{cchua,weidonghuang}@swin.edu.au,
{6724140,101448821}@student.swin.edu.au

Abstract. High school students often experience high pressure in relation to their learning and social activities, which can increase their worries and anxiety. Giving students access to relevant information and teaching them how to manage anxiety are important for their school performance and wellbeing. Given the wide use of smart phones, local community organisations have decided to develop a mobile application to help high school students cope with anxiety as part of a collaborative project with us. Developing applications for high school students requires thorough understanding of preferences and phone usage habits of this special user group. We followed a user centred and collaborative design approach involving target users throughout the design process and in this paper, we report the activities and findings of this project.

Keywords: Stress and anxiety · Collaborative design · Mobile application

1 Introduction

For an increasingly vulnerable population like teenagers, a significant barrier to education is stress and anxiety. According to a youth survey of 24,055 people aged 15–19 held by Mission Australia [2], "coping with stress" was one of the top three concerns held by young people in Australia, with over 40% of respondents either extremely or very concerned with coping with stress. In addition, the 2012–2016 Youth Mental Health Report by Mission Australia & Black Dog Institute [3] found almost one in four respondents met criteria for having a probable serious mental illness.

As part of an effort to address this issue, several local community organisations in Melbourne have begun a joint effort for the development of a mobile application (app) aimed at providing mental health support and education to high school students. The app is intended to be distributed through a local education network of 33 secondary schools in Melbourne's southeast suburbs, helping remove mental health concerns as a barrier to education. Potentially, the app's adoption will spread beyond this initial user base to more schools throughout Australia. More specifically, the app is intended to be used by school students to help them better understand issues of stress and anxiety and provide support through education and self-care. For example, students

© Springer Nature Switzerland AG 2018
Y. Luo (Ed.): CDVE 2018, LNCS 11151, pp. 270–275, 2018.
https://doi.org/10.1007/978-3-030-00560-3_37

may use the app to calm themselves during high stress periods such as exams, to discover their best selves and which coping methods work for them, as well as to encourage users to develop good self-care habits through regular engagement. To complement personal development, opportunities for social engagement with other users may also be a feature.

In this paper, we report on the design process of this app which is part of our collaborative project with the community organisations (client). We first describe the user centred approach [1] that we took for the app design. Then the results of focus-group studies and user testing and design examples of the app interfaces are presented. Finally, the paper concludes with a short summary and our future plan.

2 Method

2.1 Understanding Context, Users and Task

Literature on adolescents, anxiety, mental health apps, mental health treatment, and coping with stress were reviewed to understand the context. The understanding derived from the review of literature was used to develop a dimension upon which the app could be developed [4, 5]. Concurrent to the literature review, a competitive analysis of existing apps aimed at addressing anxiety were also reviewed [6–8]. The knowledge discovered from these sources was used to design a line of general enquiry for the first focus group held with secondary users.

The knowledge sourced from literature review, competitive analysis, and the first focus group were used to determine the client's exact position and desired development direction for the app. This determination also involved discovering the exact intention for the apps work flow and content.

2.2 Design and Validation

The design process was divided into two phases. The first phase involved getting user input to make design decisions about high-level design concepts relating to the app's structure, look and feel. The second phase involved getting user input to make design decisions about user interactions with the app's various activities.

To meet the objectives of the first phase, several independent design alternatives were formulated for various aspects of the app, which were taken to the second focus group. Comments and preference data were collected to determine the designs most suited for the general adolescent user group. The opportunity was also taken to further verify and validate the conclusions drawn from the first focus group to help ensure generalisability. This was especially important because the demographic makeup of the two focus groups were very different. The first group had a strong majority of males of an Asian heritage, whereas the second group was all female of an Anglo background.

To meet the objectives of the second phase, conceptual designs for the various tasks and activities specified by the client were made into interaction prototypes. Where possible the design team made alternative interaction styles for each activity. These prototypes were coded using web application technologies, such that the users could interact and use the various alternatives.

The interaction prototypes for the various activities of the app were then taken for user testing at a local school. Students attempted each activity on a mobile phone. Comments and difficulties with the interactions were noted. A menu design that was derived from the second focus group was also validated with this group via the use of an interactive prototype of the menu systems. This test also allowed for drawing more data about the naming of sections as users attempted to navigate the proposed app.

3 Results

3.1 Focus Group One

Due to space limitations, only high level results are presented. The same applies for the next three subsections. The first focus group was a group of six adolescents, mostly aged around sixteen years old. Five of the six adolescents were male.

The focus group was first asked about their general mobile app use and reasons for use. The group generally mentioned apps with specific goals and intentions in mind, and these tended to be quite specific and for immediate purposes. Examples were messaging apps, dictionaries, and photo apps (such as Instagram). These apps came up as favourites and were used for social reasons, convenience, and due to their mix of features. Ease of use, good organisation, and aesthetics were cited as what was liked about apps in general.

The next line of questioning related to the context of use in which adolescents used mobile apps. The group generally indicated that they use apps when they are not engaged in another activity. Usually when they are alone and bored. They also indicated that they will use an app when they have an immediate need (such as looking up a map when lost). They used all kinds of apps in during these times.

Regarding privacy the group viewed this as largely a question of self-regulation. Whilst the group certainly had privacy concerns, they saw most of these as simply a question of being sensible with what they shared and with whom. They generally indicated a greater tendency to share things in personal channels (such as messaging) than in open forums (such as social media).

3.2 Focus Group Two

The second focus group aimed to investigate user preferences for the apps structure and style. The focus group consisted of three fifteen-year-old girls from the same high school whom were recruited as a convenience sample. All the girls used phones with the iOS operating system.

The focus group began with some general questioning about the participants' use of apps anxiety management and self-improvement apps, as well the coverage of stress and anxiety topics at school. The group's initial responses to these questions were generally dismissive. However, with some further thought it appeared that they did have some exposure. This suggested that these topics were not of great importance to the group. For example, they initially indicated that they had not used anxiety management apps, but then later recalled using Smiling Mind as part of school. They also indicated not being too aware of mood and mental health topics, but then indicated knowledge of their being avenues for help for those who needed it, but that they did not need it themselves. This was further reinforced by comments about topics of stress and its management at school being boring and unengaging.

3.3   User Testing

The user testing session was conducted with two year nine students at a local secondary college. The students were asked to use various interaction prototypes to complete activity tasks. During the session, they were observed for any difficulties that they had in interaction and were encouraged to provide comments about the prototypes. For our discussion, we present the results of the Breathing Waltz activity here as an example.

The Breathing Waltz activity had the most number of prototype variants. These variants were divided into two general categories; passive and active. Passive variants involved an animation with instructions for the user to follow. The active variants involved animation plus user interaction via gestures. Active variants generally required the user to follow an on-screen animation with their finger as well as following instructions to breath.

Overall it was found that the active variants required too much attention to be done properly. The users were too focused on trying to complete the gestures with their fingers to be able to follow the instructions and do the actual breathing exercise. Two of the active prototypes that involved drawing a line on the screen with their fingers however were enjoyed. One involved a free drawing of a line and the other involved tracing a line that was charted out by the app.

The passive variants were generally better followed as breathing exercises, with the users doing the breathing. Of these variants an animation in which a linear gradient transition gave the appearance of moving up the screen for breathing in, changing colour at the top of the screen for holding the breath, and then moving down the screen was liked the most. The users stated that this was because it followed their expectations of breathing most closely. Another variant that used a radial gradient which grew, pulsated, and shrunk was seen as too intense, whilst another variant that involved a dial the rotated around and changed direction for in and out was seen as 'mesmerising' but did not meet their expectations for breathing in terms of its directions of movement.

3.4   Final Prototype Features

Based on the feedback from the client and users (focus groups and user testing), the prototype was further updated and improved. The latest version of the app is divided into seven sections including the front page as shown in Fig. 1. Each section may or may not contain additional sub-sections. Common features are explained as follows:

Quick access menu: the quick access menu will be visible on every page of the app, and is the primary means of app navigation.

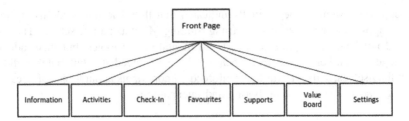

Fig. 1. App section overview.

Section menus: some sections with many items also have subsections to help organise the content. Both subsections and actual items will be presented in a card format. Cards when pressed will link to the subsection or content.

Section information: each section and subsection will have an information section. This information will be navigable to by an information icon on the top right corner of the page (see Fig. 2). The information will provide in-depth explanations of the purpose and aims that correspond with that context. This information is separate and different from any instructions that may be presented as part of an activity.

Fig. 2. Interface examples of the app prototype.

Notifications: many of the apps items (activities, information) will have a corresponding notification that may be switched on. These notifications will provide reminders to complete activities or to enact certain behaviours (e.g., drink water). Notifications will either be displayed on the app's front page or sent as device notifications. Front page notifications will be presented as a card.

Favourites: activities, information, and other in app content will be able to be added to Favourites by the user. All content sections with some exceptions will have the facility to be tagged as favourite.

4   Concluding Remarks

In this paper, we presented a design process experience of a mobile app that is part of our collaborative project with community organisations. The design process showed that requirements set by the client can be implemented with different types of inter-action. As such, it is quite important to obtain feedback from the target users and observe their interaction with the prototype. It was also found that what was perceived as plain English used in the navigation by the client, is interpreted quite differently by the user. This may be attributed to the different app experiences encountered by the user and the client which are from different age groups. In addition, interaction of active variants had been found to be more difficult to use by the users compared to passive ones.

The process of having focus group studies is extremely helpful, as this enabled the designer to capture candid feedback from the user and provides an opportunity for the user to contribute to the design in both interface layout and interaction. This resulted to having a more intuitive design that is based on interaction.

For the design examples, the colour pallet adopted was based on what the client is currently using in their website and corporate branding. Further investigation can be conducted on what is the best colour scheme for users facing stress and anxiety. Moreover, designing of appropriate icons may also be explored.

Finally, the design document that was produced from this design process is to be turned over to the development team as part of the requirements specification document.

References

1. Hartson, R., Pyla, P.: The UX Book: Process and Guidelines for Ensuring a Quality User Experience. Morgan-Kaufman, Burlington (2012)
2. Mission Australia 2017. https://www.missionaustralia.com.au/publications/research/young-people/746-youth-survey-2017-report/file. Accessed 21 Sept 2017
3. Mission Australia & Black Dog Institute 2017. https://www.missionaustralia.com.au/publications/research/young-people/706-five-year-mentalhealth-youth-report/file. Accessed 21 Sept 2017
4. Brown, D.K., Barton, J.L., Gladwell, V.F.: Viewing nature scenes positively affects recovery of autonomic function following acute-mental stress. Environ. Sci. Technol. **47**(11), 5562–5569 (2013)
5. McMahan, E.A., Estes, D.: The effect of contact with natural environments on positive and negative affect: a meta-analysis. J. Posit. Psychol. **10**(6), 507–519 (2015)
6. Renfree, I., Harrison, D., Marshall, P., Stawarz, K., Cox, A.: Don't kick the habit: the role of dependency in habit formation apps. In: CHI EA 2016, pp. 2932–2939 (2016)
7. Stawarz, K., Cox, A.L., Blandford, A.: Beyond self-tracking and reminders: designing smartphone apps that support habit formation. In: CHI 2015, pp. 2653–2662 (2015)
8. Huang, W., et al.: SMART: design and evaluation of a collaborative museum visiting application. In: Luo, Y. (ed.) CDVE 2015. LNCS, vol. 9320, pp. 57–64. Springer, Cham (2015). https://doi.org/10.1007/978-3-319-24132-6_7

Cooperative Decision Making
for Resource Allocation

Sylvia Encheva[(✉)]

Western Norway University of Applied Sciences,
Bjørnsonsg. 45, 5528 Haugesund, Norway
sbe@hvl.no

Abstract. This work aims at facilitating processes of cooperative decision making related to resource allocation in educational organisations. Different institutional units usually have a variety of ways to work, present earlier results, and evaluate what is important for the future. Thus even the involved parties generally agree on the main criteria governing their decisions, they still have to find a way to compare available data and to see to which degree any of the submitted proposals is going to contribute to realizing institutional goals. Employing a decision support system will decrease the amount of manual labor and probability for human error.

Keywords: Interval numbers · Cooperative decision making
Dependencies

1 Introduction

Resource allocation in educational organisations is without any doubt a very complicated task where both institutional and personal preferences have to be taken under consideration. Such a process involves a number of decision makers who's main responsibilities vary considerably. National priorities, university's goals, faculty's and department's policies are to be followed based on staff's professional interests and expertise. In a case of newly merged entities there are additional differences rooted in local cultures. To facilitate the work of personnel preparing guidelines for resource allocation we suggest application of decision support systems. This is clearly a multi person multi criteria decision making problem, [6,11]. A practical approach is shown in [13]. However, while the authors are focusing on implications related to decision attributes applying association rules we employ formal concept analysis in order to determine elements of larger sets of objects sharing certain attributes. Further on we propose use of a compensative weighted averaging (CWA) operator, [1,3] to overcome complications arising from inclusion of new elements and or deleting some of the old ones. Interval numbers, [12,14], are used to support systematic handling of data presented in intervals and originating from different sources.

Y. Luo (Ed.): CDVE 2018, LNCS 11151, pp. 276–279, 2018.
https://doi.org/10.1007/978-3-030-00560-3_38

2   Preliminaries

A different method for handling multi criteria decision making called 'The Analytic Hierarchy Process' (AHP) was introduced in [9]. One of the critics is that eventual changes of the original data may result in rank reversal. The method was further develop by a number of researches and is also used to support software based applications. Analytic Network Process (ANP) is a generalization of AHP accommodating to decisions with dependence and feedback, [10].

Interval arithmetic was introduced in [2] and presented as a formal system in [7,8].

In [15] an interval $A = [a_L, a_R], \{a : a_L \le a \ge a_R, a \in R\}$ is alternatively represented as $A = \langle m(A), w(A) \rangle$, where $m(A)$ and $w(A)$ are the mid-point and half-width (or simply be termed as 'width') of interval A, i.e.,

$$m(A) = \frac{a_L + a_R}{2}, \qquad w(A) = \frac{a_R - a_L}{2}.$$

The authors also list a variety of methods for comparing and ordering intervals and define an acceptability function

$$\mathcal{A} = \frac{m(B) - m(A)}{w(B) + w(A)}.$$

that can be interpreted as the grade of acceptability of the 'first interval A to be inferior to the second interval B'.

3   Resource Allocation

Merging organizations in higher education face a number of challenges during initial negotiations. Once the official work at institutional level is concluded it is time to deal with making agreements in all units supporting newly established organizations. Let's focus on a seemingly feasible task like the one of academic resource allocation at a faculty level. Some of the important issues in this case are subjects related, others are rooted in local cultures, another ones address staff related issues, and so on.

Our intention is to present a model facilitating cooperative decision making processes related to resource allocation in educational organizations. On yearly basis the total amount of resources for a faculty is clear due to the annual institutional budget. While most of the time long term goals for an organization are well formulated finding ways to join similar criteria for achieving a goal into one criterion can be quite challenging. Note that handling human differences is out of the scope of this work.

Assume the amount of resources needed to support Bachelor studies in a new faculty is known. Next question is how to distribute resources addressing other activities concerning graduate students, research, organizational development, etc. To the rest of this work we will refer to them as the following criteria:

- c1, master students supervision

- c2, PhD students supervision
- c3, personal career advancement or supporting other members career advancement
- c3, national project proposal development
- c4, international project proposal development
- c5, scientific publications
- c6, amount of hours per employee (refer to previous practice)

Note that the list above is by no means complete and it is intended to illustrate the approach only.

Relevant data collected from different departments (they could be previous institutes, sections, subsections) is organized in Table 1. In this example four departments (D1,D2, D3, D4) come up with descriptions of somewhat typical work tasks for their employees and the amount of time they usually have for completing these tasks. Some of the criteria are described as intervals while for others we use a scale from 1 to 5, where 5 is the best. Empty cells refer to lack of data. This could happen if f. ex. a particular department does not offer studies at a PhD level.

Table 1. Applicants' distances and similarities related to the best applicant

Departments	c1	c2	c3	c4	c5	c6
D1	(1, 3)	(1, 2)	2		2	20%–25%
D2	(2, 4)	(3, 4)	1	2	4	30%–40%
D3	(3, 6)		5		4	25%–35%
D4	(1, 2)	(1, 2)	4	2	4	20%–40%

After applying midt-point description of intervals [15] and assuming equal participation for the four departments we obtain an approximation based on the data in Table 1 are shown in Table 2, where D stands for a department.

Table 2. Approximation outcomes

Department	c1	c2	c3	c4	c5	c6
D	3	2	3	2	4	25%

Data presented in Table 2 can be used as a guideline for further distribution of resources. Another interesting question here is how to address criteria importance. Assigning weights to all criteria according to the degrees to which they contribute to achieving institutional goals might be beneficial. In some cases this could simply be necessary since previous organizational units do not necessarily have faced the same challenges.

Remark: Scaling rules, [5] assisting in unifying various data sets can be applied if needed. Interval number operations, [4] may be afterwards executed to decrease the number of options that need further attention.

4 Conclusion

Decision support systems appear to be very useful in many areas including resource allocation in educational organizations. However, substantial amount of preliminary work is required with respect to establishing common understanding about relevance importance of criteria incorporated in the system.

References

1. Aggarwal, M.: Compensative weighted averaging aggregation operators. Appl. Soft Comput. **28**, 368–378 (2015)
2. Dwyer, P.S.: Linear Computation. Wiley, New York (1951)
3. Emrouznejad, A., Marra, M.: Ordered weighted averaging operators 1988 2014: a citation-based literature survey. Int. J. Intell. Syst. **29**, 994–1014 (2014)
4. Ganesan, K., Veeramani, P.: On arithmetic operations of interval numbers. Int. J. Uncertain. Fuzziness Knowl.-Based Syst. Arch. **13**(6), 619–631 (2005)
5. Ganter, B., Wille, R.: Formal Concept Analysis: Mathematic Foundations. Springer, Heidelberg (1999). https://doi.org/10.1007/978-3-642-59830-2
6. Kksalan, M., Wallenius, J., Zionts, S.: Multiple Criteria Decision Making: From Early History to the 21st Century. World Scientific, Singapore (2011)
7. Moore, R.E.: Automatic Error Analysis in Digital Computation, LSMD-48421, Lockheed Missiles and Space Company (1959)
8. Moore, R.E., Yang, C.T.: Interval analysis I. Technical report, LMSD-285875, Lockheed Missiles and Space Company (1962)
9. Saaty, T.L.: The Analytic Hierarchy Process: Planning, Priority Setting, Resource Allocation. McGraw-Hill, New York (1980)
10. Saaty, T.L., Vargas, L.G.: Decision Making with the Analytic Network Process: Economic, Political, Social and Technological Applications with Benefits, Opportunities, Costs and Risks. Springer, Heidelberg (2013). https://doi.org/10.1007/978-1-4614-7279-7
11. Triantaphyllou, E.: Multi-Criteria Decision Making: A Comparative Study. Kluwer Academic Publishers, Dordrecht (now Springer) (2000)
12. Vidhya, R., Hepzibah, R.I.: A comparative study on interval arithmetic operations with intuitionistic fuzzy numbers for solving an intuitionistic fuzzy multi objective linear programming. Int. J. Appl. Math. Comput. Sci. **127**(3), 563–557 (2007)
13. Liu, W., Zhai, Y.: A new attribute decision making model based on attribute importance. Technol. Invest. **4**, 224–228 (2013)
14. Zhang, J., Wu, D., Olson, D.L.: The method of grey related analysis to multiple attribute decision making problems with interval numbers. Math. Comput. Modell. **42**(9–10), 991–998 (2005)
15. Sengupta, A., Pal, T.K.: On comparing interval numbers. Eur. J. Oper. Res. **127**(1), 28–43 (2000)

Iron and Steel Enterprises Big Data Visualization Analysis Based on Spark

Xiaojuan Ban$^{(\boxtimes)}$, Ben Wang$^{(\boxtimes)}$, Changxin Cheng,
and Salah Taghzouit

University of Science and Technology Beijing, Beijing 100083, China
banxj@ustb.edu.cn, ben_ben_wang@yeah.net

Abstract. Given the difficulty of browsing and analyzing big data via web browsers, using Spark technology, we took the big-data analysis of steel companies as an example to propose a framework for big-data visualization technology. We used HDFS for data storage, Spark for data analysis, Django for web systems, and ECharts for data visualization, ultimately providing a complete visualization solution. Using visualization, we realized price forecasting, sales analysis and production process quality traceability, help enterprises to make decisions and provide support for technological process improvement.

Keywords: Visualization · Industrial intelligence · Data analysis
ECharts · Spark

1 Introduction

With the surge of the data volume in the era of big data, iron and steel enterprises including other traditional enterprises have stored large amounts of both structured and semi-structured data through years of on information accumulation. These massive amounts of data have caused a gap in the data and the information islet [1]. To master the market trend, to improve the technological process and to carry out efficiency analysis, it is necessary to rely on the valid data analysis technique and visualization method. Big data analysis technologies are focused on exploring how to parse big data from the underlayer so that the data initially isolated in each department can be related and integrated. Data visualization is a means to explore how to express big data from the presentation level. It helps users explore complex relationships from vast amounts of data in a visual way and makes big data understandable. At present, the visualization of big data in iron and steel industry is faced with several problems described below.

- Data is complicated and scattered, and the degree of structuring is not high. Missing data and data errors often occur;
- The continuous industrial production process is difficult to trace back, and it is necessary to estimate the time point of each cycle of a batch (sample) by using an estimated production delay;
- Due to various reasons such as temperature, aging of equipment, type of sensor, and sampling period, it is difficult to ensure that the data collected by the sensor is consistent in time dimension.

Y. Luo (Ed.): CDVE 2018, LNCS 11151, pp. 280–286, 2018.
https://doi.org/10.1007/978-3-030-00560-3_39

To solve problems above, we study and design a novel visualization platform for big-data analysis of steel companies using Spark [2]. The main content of this paper is following:

Firstly, the architecture of the data analysis platform based on Spark, the critical technologies for implementation, and how to use ECharts to realize the visualization of data are introduced. Then the visualization of the intelligent decision analysis function is discussed.

2   Visual Data Analysis Platform Based on Spark

First of all, to visualize the data, it is necessary to build a data analysis platform for data integration, data preprocessing and data analysis, and lay the foundation for providing data interfaces. Then, a visualization system is built to realize the communication between data analysis results and visual components. Finally, the analysis results are displayed on the Web page visually.

2.1   Overall Architecture Design

The data visualization platform needs a stable and efficient data source and can adapt to the needs of timely queries. Big-data processing has several critical architectural layers, including data storage, resource managers, resource coordinators, computational frameworks, and data analysis. To achieve real-time and efficient visual display of real-time data query, we need to integrate the data resources of the steel plant information system and accelerate the data analysis speed. For this purpose, we have built a spark-based data analysis platform. The architecture hierarchy of the program is as Fig. 1 shown.

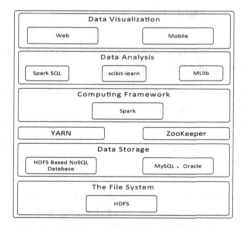

Fig. 1. Overall architecture design

2.2   Hybrid Integration of Multiple Data Sources

We use relational and non-relational databases to store data in a hybrid way. The sources of big data in the steel industry include the following three categories: the relational database data of many independent information systems, text document data, and related data on the external Internet industry chain. To ensure the efficiency of data processing, according to the actual requirements of the visualization, all relational databases are not completely migrated to HDFS for distributed storage [3]. Without affecting the actual production database usage, on the one hand, Spark is directly used to retrieve data from the backup relational database. On the other hand, necessary data is extracted and stored in the NoSQL database for distributed storage.

2.3   Data Analysis Based on Spark

The spark ecosystem takes spark as the core and RDD as the foundation to create a big data platform based on memory computing. Berkeley called Spark's entire ecosystem the Berkeley Data Analysis Stack (BDAS) [4] presented in Fig. 2.

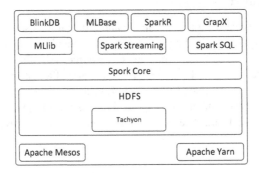

Fig. 2. BDAS structure diagram

Compared with other big-data technologies, especially MapReduce of Hadoop [5, 6], spark has the following advantages:

- Provides a comprehensive, unified framework for managing various data sets and data sources with different properties;
- Memory data sharing.

Apache Spark is a next generation batch processing framework that contains flow processing capabilities, which focuses on speeding up the run of batch workloads through a perfect memory computing and processing optimization mechanism. Since Apache Spark itself does not have a distributed storage system, it needs to provide similar distributed storage environment. Since Hadoop has been in the industry for many years, it has a whole ecology in all aspects and uses the HDFS file system to store data. It can be used for any data source compatible with Hadoop, including HDFS,

HBase, and Cassandra. We choose HDFS as a file system, integrate spark with Hadoop, retain HDFS, and use spark instead of MapReduce engine to calculate.

Shorter response time is one of the principal reasons for choosing spark. For memory batches computation, spark uses the model named RDD [7], namely the elastic distributed dataset (Resilient Distributed Datasets) to process data. On some issues, Spark will be several times faster than MapReduce.

In the visualization scheme constructed in this paper, data can be loaded from different sources into RDD for processing analysis and visualization.

2.4   Visual Layer Functional Design

The visualization system serves as a powerful tool for abstract information representation [8, 9]. It helps to discover the relationship between abstract information and reveal hidden features in the information. To better grasp the point information visually, we need to present the data in a variety of forms, including standard line charts, bar charts, scatter charts, pie charts, K-line charts, parallel visualization of multidimensional data. Coordinates and so on.

The visual hierarchy of the system is shown in Fig. 3. The system is divided into two parts, including the website background and the Web page front-end page. Among them, Django is used as a website background, and ECharts is used for front-end GUI display.

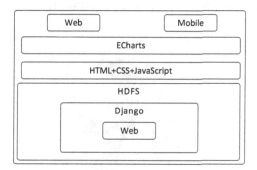

Fig. 3. Visualization layer hierarchy

Using Django is based on the following considerations: [10].

- Django is an open source web application framework written in Python that can use python's ecology to complete some preprocessing and analysis of small-scale data.
- Django is very convenient in setting up a web system, and it can be tested for security and robustness.

Users have real-time interaction requirements when viewing charts. For the same data, if we only want to display in a different way, we will search the database again and perform a series of data preprocessing and analysis. On the one hand, it affects the user experience. On the other hand, it is also a massive waste of computing resources.

We hope that after the data is loaded for the first time, it can independently perform some different forms of presentation. ECharts has an excellent support in this respect.

So far, the entire spark-based industrial big-data analytics platform visualization system has been completed. The next section will further introduce the use of visualization tools to realize steel price forecasting, sales analysis, and production process quality traceability to help companies make intelligent decisions and to provide support for process improvement.

3   Visualization of Intelligent Decision Analysis Function

3.1   Multi-angle Sales Analysis Visualization

The sales analysis consists of two parts, including spatial analysis and customer analysis. The two parts provide primarily the same conditions for the user interface, including: analysis content (total sales, total sales, return rate, the number of quality problems), start time, termination time, time selection basis (order time, delivery time Etc.), location range selection (World, China, Shandong).

The spatial analysis section shows the analysis results of steel in different spatial ranges. According to the different scopes of the selection, the world map, China map and Shandong map are displayed. The corresponding sales volume will be represented by the difference in color. This shows the comparison of regional sales.

In the client analysis section, pie charts and cone charts are used to show the trading volume of a customer on different steel grades (see Fig. 4).

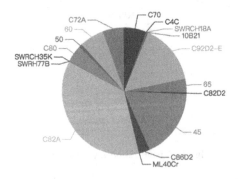

Fig. 4. Customer sales analysis pie chart: the total sales of customers

3.2   Multi-factor Multidimensional Presentation of Production Control

The production process control includes two parts: data statistics and quality traceability. The data statistics part is mainly based on the historical data of the production process. The raw materials, materials, alloys and various components of the product are statistically analyzed, and the standard deviation of the mean data and the judgment data are obtained. Normal distribution, etc. lay the foundation for the next step of quality traceability. The primary results of this part are mainly histograms and standard curves (see Fig. 5). It can be seen whether the content of a particular component is stable in the historical production process.

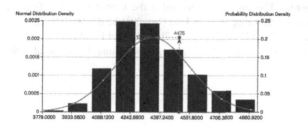

Fig. 5. Oxygen blowing probability and normal distribution

The quality traceability [11] section compares a new production data with historical data to determine the deviation ratio from the standard value, and to determines whether to trace it back. If quality traceability is to be performed, further association analysis and regression analysis are performed to determine the most likely causes of deviations from a given component.

This section uses a histogram of multiple coordinate systems based on the difference in metrics for different types of materials (see Fig. 6). At the same time, stopping the cursor on the bar chart will display the actual value of the material, the degree of deviation, qualitative judgments and other information. Click on the bar graph to display the normal distribution of the material, and the deviation of the material will be displayed in text form, and the similar reason is traced.

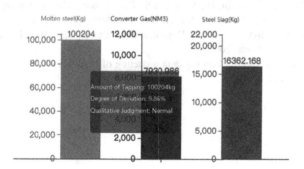

Fig. 6. Multi-axis display material composition

4   Conclusions

This article is mainly based on the data of multiple independent systems of steel companies and related data on the external Internet industry chain for data integration management. It provides users with three services including sales space, time analysis, price forecast trend distribution, and production process control. Features. Through a rich visual model and an excellent human-computer interaction environment, it provides support for enterprise practitioners in decision-making and process improvement, and it also gives new life and value to these slumbering industrial data.

Acknowledgements. The authors acknowledge the financial support from the National Key Research and Development Program of China (No. 2016YFB0700500), and the National Science Foundation of China (No. 61572075, No. 61702036), and Fundamental Research Funds for the Central Universities (No. FRF-TP-17-012A1), and China Postdoctoral Science Foundation (No. 2017M620619).

References

1. Yin, S., Kaynak, O.: Big data for modern industry: challenges and trends [point of view]. Proc. IEEE **103**, 143–146 (2015)
2. Zaharia, M., Chowdhury, M., Franklin, M.J., Shenker, S., Stoica, I.: Spark: cluster computing with working sets. HotCloud **10**, 95 (2010)
3. Shvachko, K., Kuang, H., Radia, S., Chansler, R. (eds.): The Hadoop Distributed File System. IEEE (2010)
4. Franklin, M. (ed.): The Berkeley Data Analytics Stack: Present and Future. IEEE (2013)
5. Shi, J., et al.: Clash of the titans: Mapreduce vs. spark for large scale data analytics. Proc. VLDB Endow. **8**, 2110–2121 (2015)
6. Dean, J., Ghemawat, S.: MapReduce: simplified data processing on large clusters. Commun. ACM **51**, 107–113 (2008)
7. Zaharia, M., et al. (eds.): Resilient distributed datasets: a fault-tolerant abstraction for in-memory cluster computing. USENIX Association (2012)
8. Chen, H., Chiang, R.H.L., Storey, V.C.: Business intelligence and analytics: from big data to big impact. MIS Q. 1165–1188 (2012)
9. Fiaz, A.S., Asha, N., Sumathi, D., Navaz, A.S.: Data visualization: enhancing big data more adaptable and valuable. Int. J. Appl. Eng. Res. **11**, 2801–2804 (2016)
10. Holovaty, A., Kaplan-Moss, J.: The Definitive Guide to Django: Web Development Done Right. Apress, New York (2009)
11. Liu, J., Qin, S.J.: Perspectives on big data modeling of process industries. Acta Automatica Sinica **42**, 161–171 (2016)

Visualization of Farm Land Use by Classifying Satellite Images

Xiaojin Liao[1], Xiaodi Huang[1], and Weidong Huang[2(✉)]

[1] Charles Sturt University, Albury, NSW 2640, Australia
xhuang@csu.edu.au
[2] Swinburne University of Technology, Melbourne, VIC 3122, Australia
weidonghuang@swin.edu.au

Abstract. Land use mapping is becoming increasingly important in agriculture. Nowadays, satellite visualizations of farmland are available. On the other hand, the machine learning techniques have been advanced rapidly. This paper comprehensively investigates the use of the recently developed machine learning techniques to automatize land use mapping. Our comprehensive experiments are reported. The results of comparison experiments have demonstrated the performance of the algorithms on land use mapping.

Keywords: Classification · CapsNet · CNN · Land use mapping
Data analytics · Visualization

1 Introduction

Since Google Maps are available, how to use satellite map visualizations of land for management and farming becomes increasingly important. The use of machine learning to identify the land use of satellite images reduces the intensive manual effort required and produces results within a shorter period of time. In fact, machine learning for land use mapping has been applied into different areas such as profitable and sustainable farming and grazing, seasonal crop mapping and monitoring, and prevention of Banana Bunchy Top Virus (BBTV) outbreak [1].

We have developed a system for land use. In particular, given a set of satellite imagery visualizations, the system uses different machine learning algorithms to produce classification outputs. We applied several important machine learning algorithms to land use, and comprehensively compared their performance by conducting extensive experiments.

2 Related Work

A large number of methods for classifying satellite images are available. These methods can be classified into four categories: template matching-based methods, knowledge-based methods, OBIA-based methods, and machine learning-based methods. Some methods are hybrids of these four categories [2]. The template matching-based methods, knowledge-based methods, and OBIA-based methods are built on

Y. Luo (Ed.): CDVE 2018, LNCS 11151, pp. 287–290, 2018.
https://doi.org/10.1007/978-3-030-00560-3_40

traditional techniques such as segmentation and classification. Using the eCognition Client version, Kasper Johansen [1] identified banana plants from satellite images with an accuracy of 79%–88%, and the average processing time of 13 min per 1 km^2 tiles. This is significantly faster than 73 min of manual interpretation [1]. Building on Fractal Net Evolution and following completely programmable workflows [3], the eCognition makes use of the Nearest Neighbor (NN) and the integrated fuzzy rule-based classification method [4]. In the geographic object-based image analysis (GEOBIA), pixels are grouped into uniform objects, which are then classified or marked and modelled [1, 2]. Decision tree uses a series of decisions that are based on the results of sequential tests for class label assignment [5].

So far, there are no reports on applying deep learning to the land use mapping. Our approach is different from existing ones.

3 Approaches

This work compares several promising machine learning (ML) methods from classic algorithms to state-of-the-art models. As one of the simplest of classification algorithms, k-Nearest Neighbour (kNN) searches for the closest match of the test data in feature space. SVMs have been extensively studied in the classification of hyperspectral images to deal with the Hughes phenomenon. Recently, CNN is a very successful method that has achieved breakthrough results in image recognition. The trained CNN can be considered as an extractor of features that has developed a nonlinear mapping based on the input images. CapsNet [7] was introduced by Hinton and his team in 2017. It is the-state-of-art machine learning algorithm. The approach has reduced error rates on MNIST by 45% and significantly reduces training set sizes. Results were claimed to be considerably better than a CNN on highly overlapped digits [6, 7]. The reason for choosing these approaches for land use mapping is that we take into account both their performance and the characteristics of land images.

4 Experiments

For experiments, we developed Python programs to implement the compared ML algorithms so as to process various satellite images and produce classification results. The main library includes TensorFlow-GPU & Keras, and OpenCV.

4.1 Datasets

We built the data sets by using the Wet Tropics Natural Resource Management (NRM) Region Map 2015. 10 typical classes of their high definition satellite images were chosen. We grouped images, converted them into grayscale, segment to 28*28 pixels images with labels, and then shuffled these images to form the dataset. The total size of the dataset was 102,222 images.

4.2   Comparisons Results and Performance

The same algorithm training for the different datasets can produce very different results, as shown in Table 1. From our satellite image test, kNN was not good at handling these sort of images as it only achieved 54% accuracy. It is obvious that compared to kNN, SVM had achieved much better results on the satellite image dataset.

Table 1. Performance comparisons of the four algorithms

Algorithm	kNN	SVM	CNN	CapsNet
Accuracy (MNIST)	97.04%	94%	99.06%	99.67%
Accuracy (satellite dataset)	54%	75%	93.70%	96%
Training time (seconds)	0.09	2.82	572	46530
Test time (seconds)	169	5.19	1.5	18
Prediction time (seconds)/km^2	395	1.14	0.72	52

With the satellite image dataset test: CNN used much more computing resources than kNN and SVM. The training for the 6 layers has taken CNN about 10 min with running 50 epochs. The validation accuracy rate achieved 93.68%. The CapsNet algorithm consumed even more computing resource. It used 13 h to run 50 epochs with the achieved accuracy of 96.82%. kNN and SVM used the minimum computer resource and time. The training could be finished in a few seconds. Figure 1 plots the accuracies of the four compared algorithms.

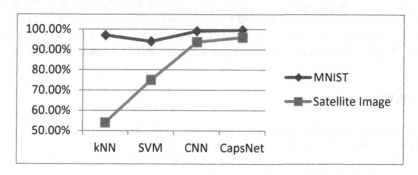

Fig. 1. Comparisons of the accuracy of the four algorithms

5   Case Study

In this section, we report a real-world example by using our system. These trained models used are those models with the best accuracy in each algorithm group. We also recorded the prediction time for each algorithm to go over 1 km^2 tile image. As the accuracy of the kNN model was almost unusable, we did not apply it in this test.

From Fig. 2, we can see that CNN performs best in identifying and marking banana plants. It is remarkable that its speed is also the best, with 0.72 s per square kilometre. The CapsNet algorithm has achieved the best verification accuracy rate. For these satellite images, the results of CapsNet is not the best, and processing time is much longer. This can be caused by the overfitting with the training dataset.

Fig. 2. The original image and output classified images

We applied a filter to remove noises from the output of CNN. As shown in the image on the right hand side of Fig. 2, the result is clear and the banana plants are perfectly marked.

In summary, we have presented in this paper our comparisons of the four algorithms, which are selected from both classic and newly developed ones, for classifying the satellite visualizations of land. In particular, we applied the newly proposed deep learning algorithms to land use mapping and validated their performance. From our experiments, we found that CNN and CapsNet have achieved the great accuracy on land use mapping. CapsNet, however, takes more computing resources and time than others. We plan to conduct experiments on different types of datasets for future work.

References

1. Johansen, K., et al.: Mapping banana plants from high spatial resolution orthophotos to facilitate plant health assessment. Remote Sens. **6**(12), 8261–8286 (2014)
2. Cheng, G., Han, J.: A survey on object detection in optical remote sensing images. ISPRS J. Photogramm. Remote Sens. **117**, 11–28 (2016)
3. Blaschke, T.: Object based image analysis for remote sensing. ISPRS J. Photogramm. Remote Sens. **65**, 2–16 (2010)
4. Ma, L., et al.: A review of supervised object-based land-cover image classification. ISPRS J. Photogramm. Remote Sens. **130**, 277–293 (2017)
5. Wieland, M., Pittore, M.: Performance Evaluation of Machine Learning Algorithms for Urban Pattern Recognition from Multi-spectral Satellite Images (2014)
6. Jean, N., et al.: Combining satellite imagery and machine learning to predict poverty. Science **353**(6301), 790–794 (2016)
7. Sabour, S., Frosst, N., Hinton, G.E.: Dynamic routing between capsules. In: Advances in Neural Information Processing Systems (2017)

Toward a View Coordination Methodology for Collaborative Shared Large-Display Environments

Yu Liu[✉] and Paul Craig[✉]

Department of Computer Science and Software Engineering, Xian Jiaotong Liverpool University, Suzhou, China
{Yu.Liu,P.Craig}@xjtlu.edu.cn

Abstract. Allowing multiple users to explore data together on the same large display has great potential to help people to work together and solve problems in a more effective and amiable manner. This paper looks at how we can coordinate views between multiple users on a large-display for a simple collaborative task. We compare split-screen and shared-screen methods in order to develop a better understanding of the relative advantages and disadvantages of these methods and outline a new view coordination method that could combine the advantages of both.

Keywords: Information visualization · Collaborative visualization

1 Introduction

People often benefit from being able to work-together to explore data in the same place and at the same time. For example, a group of friends may want to search tourist map to plan the holidays in a café, or a group of students might want to analyze financial data together in the library. Here, people work together on a common task to achieve their goal, and a co-located environment has the power to better facilitate information exchange and accelerate the pace of problem solving [1–3].

Large displays have become more affordable, more interactive and easier to connect to other devices. As a result researchers are now using this technology to support more collaborative activities [4, 5] and results indicate that multi-user large-display interfaces have great potential in this area. There are, however, issues that impede their adoption. One major issue we identified, in a short observational study looking at how people collaborated using mobile devices, was that users would often switch between individual and team-work during a collaborative task. This study explores further how people work this way and how split-screen and shared view interfaces accommodate this type of working.

2 Related Work

Previous work has proposed some solutions to the problem of managing multiple users have control over the same device. It has been suggested ranking users, which means the system would give privilege to some users and limit some users' access [6].

© Springer Nature Switzerland AG 2018
Y. Luo (Ed.): CDVE 2018, LNCS 11151, pp. 291–294, 2018.
https://doi.org/10.1007/978-3-030-00560-3_41

However, this method can only be used in very confined situations where there are clearly stratified groups like teachers and students or group leaders and other members. It also does not solve the problem of conflict between users of the same class.

Multiple view systems, using two or more different views to investigate data are also found to be quite powerful [7, 8]. These bring many benefits, including improving user performance and allowing users to discover unpredicted relationships in data [9] and have been widely used in many fields such as movie editing, TV and video surveillance as well as scientific research [7, 10, 11]. For example, they can be used to combine documentation of different scales, like a broad view of basic framework and a precise view of part of screen, reunifying them in a unique and synchronized view [9]. In this study we focus on view coordination for information visualization in a large display by conducting an observation study, in which two basic view coordination are tested.

3   Case Study

As a case study to test spit-screen and shared-screen displays and better understand how people explore data collaboratively in large display centric multi-device environment we conduct an observation study looking an interface for two users planning a trip around the world. This helps us to have a deeper understanding on how different users' attention shift between different screens, and each other, when they explore the data.

Our focus group for the study consisted of twenty participants all aged from eighteen to twenty-four. We used interactive world map application, which runs on a large wall mounted display and two mobile phones used for control. Groups of two users each are asked to explore the different parts of map based on their interests and where they want to plan their trip. Participants worked together with a partner to plan a trip around the world according to a certain theme and within a certain budget. The interface was operated in either split-screen mode or shares-screen mode with slightly different travel requirements (to visit natural wonders, landmarks, big cities etc.).

The shared-screen mode for the large display (see Fig. 1) presents the combination of the selections made by users. In particular, the combination is the smallest rectangle viewport which contains all the selections' areas. In split-screen mode (see Fig. 2) users have different views and the large display space is split in half using equal space for each view.

Based observations of ten pairs of users using each interface configuration for approximately ten minutes, we found that participants worked independently for approximately seventy-three percent of their time and together twenty-seven percent of their time. Unsurprisingly the shared-screen gained positive feedback for aspects related to teamwork, whereas the users considered that the split-screen worked better for independent working. The shared screen mode tended to work well when there was a significant overlap between the areas of interest of each user whereas the split-screen worked better when they looked at different areas on the map. So both types of display appeared to have its own unique advantage over the other.

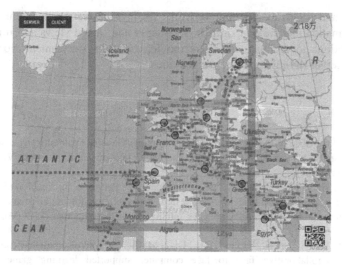

Fig. 1. The interface running in shared-screen mode. The red area is selected by one user and the green area is selected by another user. (Color figure online)

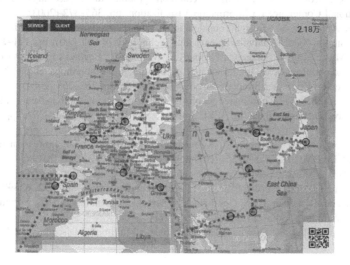

Fig. 2. The interface running in split-screen mode.

4   Conclusion and Future Work

We have developed and performed preliminary tests on interfaces with split-screens and shared-screens for information visualization. This used the scenario of users planning a trip around the world with a limited budget. Approximately seventy-three percent of the users' time was spent on independent working, where they preferred the split screen. Twenty three percent of the users' time was spent working together, where they preferred the shared view. Each of these views was found to have distinct advantages and disadvantages. Future work will involve the development of a new view coordination method that shifts between split and shared views according to the users' selections to facilitate the users moving between independent working and working together during collaborative activities.

References

1. Roberts, J.C.: State of the art: coordinated & multiple views in exploratory visualization. In: International Conference on Coordinated and Multiple Views in Exploratory Visualization, pp. 61–71 (2007)
2. Craig, P., Huang, X., Chen, H., Wang, X., Zhang, S.: Pervasive information visualization: toward an information visualization design methodology for multi-device co-located synchronous collaboration. In: Pervasive Intelligence and Computing (PICOM), pp. 2232–2239 (2015)
3. Craig, P., Roa-Seïler, N., Rosano, F.L., Díaz, M.M.: The role of embodied conversational agents in collaborative face to face computer supported learning games. In: 26th International Conference on System Research, Informatics & Cybernetics, Baden-Baden, Germany (2013)
4. Mei, C.C., Roth, S.F.: Visualizing common ground. In: Proceedings of IV 2003, International Conference on Information Visualization, pp. 365–372 (2003)
5. Heer, J., Agrawala, M.: Design considerations for collaborative visual analytics. In: IEEE Symposium on Visual Analytics Science and Technology, VAST 2007, pp. 171–178 (2007)
6. Morris, M.R., Ryall, K., Shen, C., Forlines, C., Vernier, F.: Beyond social protocols: multi-user coordination policies for co-located groupware. In: Proceedings of the 2004 ACM Conference on Computer Supported Cooperative Work, pp. 262–265 (2004)
7. Craig, P., Kennedy, J.: Coordinated graph and scatter-plot views for the visual exploration of microarray time-series data. In: IEEE InfoVis, Seattle, Washington, USA, pp. 173–180 (2003)
8. Craig, P., Cannon, A., Kukla, R., Kennedy, J.: MaTSE: the gene expression time-series explorer. In: BMC Bioinformatics (Highlights of BioVis 2012), July 2013
9. Mondada, L.: Video recording practices and the reflexive constitution of the interactional order: some systematic uses of the split-screen technique. Hum. Stud. 32, 67–99 (2009)
10. Koschmann, T., Lebaron, C., Goodwin, C., Zemel, A., Dunnington, G.: Formulating the triangle of doom. Gesture 7(22), 97–118 (2007)
11. Levine, P., Scollon, R.: Discourse and Technology: Multimodal Discourse Analysis (2004)

Spark-Based Distributed Quantum-Behaved Particle Swarm Optimization Algorithm

Zhaojuan Zhang, Wanliang Wang[✉], Nan Gao, and Yanwei Zhao

College of Computer Science and Technology,
Zhejiang University of Technology, Hangzhou 310023,
People's Republic of China
jenniferzhang19@163.com, {wwl,gaonan,zyw}@zjut.edu.cn

Abstract. For high dimensional and complex tasks, quantum optimization algorithms suffer from the problem of high computational cost. Distributed computing is an efficient way to solve such problems. Therefore, distributed optimization algorithms have become a hotspot for large scale optimization problems with the increasing volume of the data. In this paper, a novel Spark-based distributed quantum-behaved particle swarm optimization algorithm (SDQPSO) was proposed. By submitting the task to a higher computing cluster in parallel, the SDQPSO algorithm can improve the convergence performance.

Keywords: Spark · Distributed computing · Quantum optimization
Big data

1 Introduction

As real-world optimization problems become complex and large scale, and the serial optimization algorithms are time-consuming. Distributed optimization algorithms with the advantage of distributed computation have received considerable attention over the past decade.

A lot of work have been done to improve the optimization performance by distributed computing. Gong [1] proposed a comprehensive survey of the state-of-the-art on distributed evolutionary algorithms and models, where all the algorithms were classified into two groups, namely, the population-distributed model and dimension-distributed model. Cao [2] presented a distributed cooperative co-evolution particle swarm optimization algorithm using Spark to speed up the search process. Wang [3] implemented cooperative particle swarm optimization algorithm in parallel based on MapReduce platform. By partitioning the search space, MapReduce Quantum-behaved particle swarm optimization (QPSO) performs well for large scale problems [4]. Furthermore, the co-evolutionary quantum-behaved particle swarm optimization using MapReduce was proposed by Ding [5], which could obtain the global best solutions in a shorter time. Cristobal [6] tested the performance of different algorithms by implementing the multi-objective big data optimization with jMetal and Spark.

However, less studies have been done on distributed optimization algorithms using MapReduce and Spark. Therefore, a novel SDQPSO algorithm was proposed to save computational cost and avoid the curse of dimensionality.

Y. Luo (Ed.): CDVE 2018, LNCS 11151, pp. 295–298, 2018.
https://doi.org/10.1007/978-3-030-00560-3_42

2   The SDQPSO Algorithm

Based on the Spark platform, a Spark master and one or more Spark workers are included. In the SDQPSO algorithm, the whole decision space is divided into several subspaces, and a resilient distributed dataset (RDD) is created by several subspaces. Then each worker searches the local best solution on the RDD in parallel. Finally, the Spark master obtains the global best solution by analyzing the local best solution from all the Spark workers. The specific steps of the SDQPSO algorithm are as follows:

Step 1: Initialize the Population Parameters.

The initialized population parameters are uniformly distributed to different workers based on the Spark platform. In the SDQPSO, p_{id} denotes the best position of particle i at the d dimension. p_{id} is computed by

$$p_{id} = \mu p_{best} + (1 - \mu)g_{best}. \tag{1}$$

The local best position and the global best position are denoted by p_{best} and g_{best}, respectively. p_{best} and g_{best} are obtained by compared with the fitness value of each particle. where μ represents the weight between p_{best} and g_{best}.

$mbest$ is called the mean best position defined by the average of the p_{best} of all particles, which is given by the following equation:

$$mbest = \sum_{i=1}^{M} \frac{p_i}{M} = \left(\sum_{i=1}^{M} \frac{p_{i1}}{M}, \sum_{i=1}^{M} \frac{p_{i2}}{M}, \cdots \sum_{i=1}^{M} \frac{p_{id}}{M}\right), \tag{2}$$

where M is the size of population, d is the dimension of the searching space, the current position vector of the ith particle is represented by $X_i.p_i$ is the personal best of particle i.

Step 2: Each Worker Searches in Parallel.

Each worker calculates the fitness value of each particle at first. Then the fitness value of p_{best} is compared with the fitness value of each worker. If the fitness value of p_{best} is better than previous fitness value, the local best fitness value and other parameters of each particle are updated. Finally, the parameters are sent to the master. The position of each particle is updated by

$$X_{id}(t+1) = p_{id} \pm \beta |mbest_i - X_{id}(t)| \times \ln\left(\frac{1}{u}\right), \tag{3}$$

where $X_{id}(t+1)$ is the current position of particle, t denotes the tth iteration, u is the random number generated uniformly and distributed on $(0, 1)$, β is the contraction-expansion (CE) coefficient from 0.5 to 1.0. Equations (3) takes plus when a random number is greater than 0.5, otherwise it takes subtraction.

Step 3: Master Obtains the Global Best Solution of All Particles.

After the calculation of each worker is finished, the search results are sent to the Spark master. Then, master makes further comparisons of the fitness value of p_{best} and each particle. Finally, after the fitness value of g_{best} is compared with the fitness value of each particle to obtain the g_{best}, the parameters of particles are updated.

If the number of iterations or the requirements of accuracy is satisfied, stop running and output the global best solution. Otherwise, the *mbest* is recalculated according to Eqs. (2), and the updated parameters are sent to the workers. Repeat steps 2-3 until the termination condition is reached, then the entire parallel search process is finished.

3 Parallel Design for SDQPSO Algorithm

The parallel design for the SDQPSO algorithm is as follows: (1) Search space partitioning: the overall decision space is split into many partitions based on the Spark platform at first, which are stored into RDDs and distributed to the Spark workers. (2) Search in parallel: each worker starts on different subspace by different mappers independently, the search results are sent to the reducer of master. (3) Search results merging: reducer makes further analysis of the search results, and then the global best solution is obtained by comparing of the local best solution.

3.1 SDQPSO Algorithm Map Function

In the map function, the mappers receive the key/value pairs from the RDDs, the key is the ID of the subspace and the value is the dataset of subspace. Then, the mappers start to search independently on subspace, the position and the fitness value of each particle are calculated and updated. In addition, the parallel search process on the RDDs is implemented by the computing cluster, p_{best}, p_{id} and the fitness value of p_{best} are denoted as the immediate key/value pairs and are sent to the reduce function. Finally, the mappers output the p_{best} and the corresponding fitness value on different subspace.

3.2 SDQPSO Algorithm Reduce Function

In the reduce function, the reducer receives the immediate key/value pairs from the parallel search, which include the *ID* of subspaces, p_{best} and the corresponding fitness value. Then the local best optimal solution on different key/value pairs are selected from the mappers. Thirdly, the reducer merges the search results of different mappers to get the g_{best}. Finally, the *mbest* is recalculated according to Eq. (2), and the g_{best} and the global best solution are updated by the reduce function.

4 Experimental Analysis and Conclusion

In order to evaluate the performance of the proposed SDQPSO algorithm, we use 20 benchmark functions of CEC'2013 special session and competition on real-parameter single-objective optimization to test. All experiments are operated on a Spark cluster, the platform is Spark version 2.3.0, Hadoop version 2.7.3 and python 3.6.4.

The SDQPSO algorithm is compared with QPSO algorithm, the performances are evaluated in terms of two aspects. On the one hand, the indicators of optimization performances are the min value, the mean value, the max value and the standard derivation of all the benchmark functions. On the other hand, the running time of the SDQPSO algorithm at different population and dimension level of parallelism are discussed. Above all, the parallel search can increase the probability to obtain a better solution, and the SDQPSO algorithm with better global search ability and shorter time is suitable for large scale optimization problems.

Due to the optimization problems are complex and time-consuming when faced with big data, therefore, we proposed a novel SDQPSO algorithm to improve the convergence performance. The parallel design of the SDQPSO algorithm are mainly concluded as follows: firstly, the Spark worker searches the whole decision space in parallel, and then the local best solution of each worker is merged by Spark master. In the future, we can improve the performance of the SDQPSO algorithm from different scenarios, e.g., the different problem-decomposition strategies and the distributed models.

Acknowledgement. This work was partly supported by the National Natural Science Foundation of China (Grant No. 61379123, 61572438 and 61702456).

References

1. Gong, Y., Chen, W., Zhan, Z., et al.: Distributed evolutionary algorithms and their models: a survey of the state-of-the-art. Appl. Soft Comput. **34**(C), 286–300 (2015)
2. Cao, B., Li, W., Zhao, J., et al.: Spark-based parallel cooperative co-evolution particle swarm optimization algorithm. In: IEEE International Conference on Web Services (ICWS), pp. 570–577. IEEE, Washington (2016)
3. Wang, Y., Li, Y., Chen, Z., et al.: Cooperative particle swarm optimization using MapReduce. Soft. Comput. **21**(22), 6593–6603 (2017)
4. Li, Y., Chen, Z., Wang, Y., Jiao, L.: Quantum-behaved particle swarm optimization using MapReduce. In: Gong, M., Pan, L., Song, T., Zhang, G. (eds.) BIC-TA 2016. CCIS, vol. 682, pp. 173–178. Springer, Singapore (2016). https://doi.org/10.1007/978-981-10-3614-9_22
5. Ding, W., Lin, C., Chen, S., et al.: Multiagent-consensus-MapReduce-based attribute reduction using co-evolutionary quantum PSO for big data applications. Neurocomputing **272**, 136–153 (2018)
6. Barba-Gonzaléz, C., García-Nieto, J., Nebro, A.J., Aldana-Montes, J.F.: Multi-objective big data optimization with jMetal and spark. In: Trautmann, H., et al. (eds.) EMO 2017. LNCS, vol. 10173, pp. 16–30. Springer, Cham (2017). https://doi.org/10.1007/978-3-319-54157-0_2

Improving Word Representation Quality Trained by *word2vec* via a More Efficient Hierarchical Clustering Method

Zhaolin Yuan, Xiaojuan Ban$^{(\boxtimes)}$, and Jinlong Hu

School of Computer and Communication Engineering,
University of Science and Technology Beijing, Beijing 100083, China
b20170324@xs.ustb.edu.cn

Abstract. In traditional *word2vec* methods, hierarchical softmax algorithm uses the whole vocabulary to construct a Huffman tree and it trains each pair of words just in logarithmic time consumption. But due to the lack of consideration about cooperation of each word in the corpus, it will reduce the performance of language model and the trained word vectors. In this paper, we substitute a purely data-driven method for the original Huffman-tree method to rebuild the binary tree. The new construction method utilizes the semantical and syntactical cooperation of words to cluster the words hierarchically. The cooperation of words is reflected in the word vectors which collected from the initial Huffman-tree training procedure. Our methods substantially improve the performances of word vectors in semantical and syntactical tasks.

Keywords: Language models · Hierarchical neural network · *word2vec*

1 Introduction

A statistical language model is a probability distribution cover sequences of words based on the cooperation of context [10]. NPLM (Neural Probabilistic Language Model) is a kind of language model, adopting neural network algorithm to acquire the joint probability function [1]. Word vectors trained by Neural language models has promoted great development in NLP study [3], such as Dependency Parser [2] and Named Entity Recognition [4]. *Word2vec* is a typical and widely used word vectors training method which is proposed by Mikolov in [6]. The original NPLM has suffered the problem of slow training speed with the large size of vocabulary in each language. Mikolov introduced "Hierarchical softmax" method to approximate the full softmax. This method rebuilds the structure of the output layer into a binary tree so that training speed could be

The National Key Research and Development Program of China (No. 2016YFB070 0500), and the National Science Foundation of China (No. 61572075, No. 61702036), and Fundamental Research Funds for the Central Universities (No. FRF-TP-17-012A1), and China Postdoctoral Science Foundation (No. 2017M620619).

Y. Luo (Ed.): CDVE 2018, LNCS 11151, pp. 299–303, 2018.
https://doi.org/10.1007/978-3-030-00560-3_43

optimized in exponential magnitude. The original "hierarchical softmax" optimization adopts Huffman-tree algorithm to build a binary tree. It can be proved that Huffman coding is Minimum-Redundancy Codes.

In this paper, we propose a hierarchical clustering methods to build absolutely balanced tree for retraining the model. Through the word distributed representation trained by the original Huffman-man method, we rebuild a new binary tree to train the language model and word vectors again. According to the comparison between the accuracy on word similarity tasks of original vectors and the retrained version, our method improve the quality of word vectors efficiently in spite of consuming more training time.

2   Related Work

In most languages, the enormous output layer of the neural network due to the large vocabulary is a common problem in many neural probabilistic language models. In [1] Bengio firstly introduced NPLM and integrates the rare words whose $frequency \leq 3$ into a single symbol as a output node. The vocabulary size could be reduced to One-third of the whole of words. In [8], Pereira clusters the transitive verbs and its direct noun words by their frequencies in the corpus. McMahon implements a binary top-down form of word clustering which employs an average class mutual information in [5]. Morin improved the original NNLM by modifying the output layer into a hierarchical structure [7] through the expert knowledge. K-means algorithm is used to separate the words set into two part to get a hierarchical binary tree. Hinton adopted a data-driven hierarchical structure to improve the training speed of log-bilinear language model (LBL). A new binary tree can be constructed via the word vectors trained initially by estimating two gauss model through EM algorithm in each word split step. And the method supports that a single word can correspond to multiple leaf nodes in the tree.

3   Linear Split Method Based on PCA

Firstly, we build the binary tree, adopting the intrinsical Huffman tree-building method in *word2vec*, and proceed initial training in this tree. Next, we rebuild the tree according to word vectors obtained from initial training, and then proceed the second training on it. The split method of the word set is as follows: We assume that the initial vector for each word is x_i and the dimension of word vectors is d, we want to find a $d - 1$ dimensional hyperplane to separate the whole space into two parts. we use the PCA method to reduce the dimensions of all words to only one, the projected straight line is the normal vector of the desired hyperplane. And then we sort the projected values and find the median one to ensure the position of the hyperplane. Finally, using this hyperplane as the demarcation, words are divided into two parts equally or the left is one more than the right. The details are shown in Algorithm 1.

Algorithm 1. PCA-Tree Construction

Input: WordLists
Output: Root
1: **function** CREATPCATREE(WordLists)
2:     $root \leftarrow$ NEWNODE()
3:     **if** $WordLists.size = 1$ **then**
4:        **return** WordLists[0] as a leaf node
5:     **else**
6:        $W \leftarrow PCA(WordLists, components = 1)$
7:        sort $WordLists$ based on W
8:        $n \leftarrow WordLists.size$
9:        $root.left \leftarrow$ CREATPCATREE($WordLists[0 : \frac{n}{2}]$)
10:       $root.right \leftarrow$ CREATPCATREE($WordLists[\frac{n}{2} : n]$)
11:       **return** $root$ as a nonleaf node

---

4 Experiments

4.1 Experiments Description

The word vector was trained on English Wikipedia corpus with the size limited to 2.6G approximately and the Gensim [9] tool is used to complete the experiments. To compare the quality of word vector obtained from different vector dimensionalities and word vector models, we did a number of comparative experiments. We select Skip-Gram (SG) and CBOW models with vector dimensionality 100,300 to achieve four groups of experiments. In addition, to compare the training speed of two methods, we calculate the weighted average depth of leaf nodes in various trees separately according to the frequency of words in the corpus as the measuring standard of training speed. We evaluate word vector obtained from training adopting word similarity task put forward by Mikolov in [6].

4.2 Results

According to Table 1, we find that the quality of word vector obtained from training has improved greatly. Moreover, the effect of improvement is more obvious in Skip-Gram (SG) model. In addition, iterative training is done for ten times according to Human tree-building algorithm, we find the quality of word vector has not changed significantly although the frequency of training increased. It suggests that the experimental results using the tree-building methods proposed in this paper are affected by the binary tree itself, rather than the increase of the number of training iterations.

The average depth of leaf nodes in huffman method is **10.94** and the counterpart in PCA method is **18.9298**. The weighted leaf nodes depth obtained from Human tree-building method is smaller than the counterpart from balanced binary tree method. The new method of tree-building will increase the training time, about 1.7 times of the original training time. The experimental model is Skip-Gram (SG) and the dimension is 300.

Table 1. Accuracy in different models and algorithms tables.

Method	Dimension	Model	Semantic	Syntactic	Total
Huffman	100	CBOW	0.2645	0.4524	0.3671
PCA	100	CBOW	0.4502	0.5168	**0.4866**
Huffman	100	Skip-Gram	0.4414	0.4573	0.4501
PCA	100	Skip-Gram	0.6404	0.5207	**0.5751**
Huffman	300	CBOW	0.3941	0.5400	0.4738
PCA	300	CBOW	0.4299	0.5874	**0.5159**
Huffman	300	Skip-Gram	0.6172	0.5449	0.5777
PCA	300	Skip-Gram	0.6971	0.6000	**0.6441**
Huffman-10iters	100	CBOW	0.2842	0.4407	0.3697
Huffman-10iters	300	CBOW	0.3865	0.5465	0.4739

5 Conclusion

We use the data-driven method to train the word vectors based on the cooperative information obtained from original *word2vec* model. Although the new tree-building method will lead to the increase of the training time, the process can greatly improve the quality of word vectors and make it perform better in word similarity task. Furthermore, the improvement is more obvious in Skip-Gram (SG) model.

References

1. Bengio, Y., Ducharme, R., Vincent, P., Janvin, C.: A neural probabilistic language model. J. Mach. Learn. Res. **3**, 1137–1155 (2003)
2. Chen, D., Manning, C.: A fast and accurate dependency parser using neural networks. In: Proceedings of the 2014 Conference on Empirical Methods in Natural Language Processing (EMNLP) (i), pp. 740–750 (2014)
3. Collobert, R., Weston, J., Bottou, L., Karlen, M., Kavukcuoglu, K., Kuksa, P.: Natural language processing (almost) from scratch. J. Mach. Learn. Res. **12**, 2493–2537 (2011)
4. Sienčnik, S.K.: Adapting word2vec to named entity recognition (2015)
5. McMahon, J.G., Smith, F.J.: Improving statistical language model performance with automatically generated word hierarchies. Comput. Linguist. **22**(2), 217–247 (1996)
6. Mikolov, T., Chen, K., Corrado, G., Dean, J.: Efficient estimation of word representations in vector space, pp. 1–12 (2013)
7. Morin, F., Bengio, Y.: Hierarchical probabilistic neural network language model. In: Proceedings of the 10th International Workshop on Artificial Intelligence and Statistics (AISTATS 2005), pp. 246–252, March 2005
8. Pereira, F., Tishby, N., Lee, L.: Distributional clustering of English words (1994)

9. Řehůřek, R., Sojka, P.: Software framework for topic modelling with large corpora. In: Proceedings of the LREC 2010 Workshop on New Challenges for NLP Frameworks, pp. 45–50. ELRA, Valletta, May 2010
10. Wikipedia Contributors: Language model – Wikipedia, the free encyclopedia (2018). (Online: Accessed 9 May 2018)

Towards Collaborative Immersive Environments for Parametric Modelling

Adrien Coppens$^{(\boxtimes)}$ (iD) and Tom Mens (iD)

Software Engineering Lab, University of Mons, Mons, Belgium
{adrien.coppens,tom.mens}@umons.ac.be

Abstract. The Architecture, Engineering and Construction (AEC) industry started to integrate Augmented Reality (AR) and Virtual Reality (VR) solutions in Computer-Aided Architectural Design (CAAD) tools, but their use is mostly limited to visualisation purposes. Few of these tools propose the ability of advanced modelling directly within an immersive environment. To fill this void, we previously proposed a software bridge between Grasshopper, a popular tool for parametric architectural modelling, and the HTC Vive VR headset. This bridge allows to adjust parameter values and get real-time feedback on the corresponding parametric geometries from within a VR environment.

In this paper, we discuss how to extend that solution with support for live collaboration as design processes very often involve multiple collaborators. This requires addressing a variety of related challenges such as bandwidth and latency issues, conflicting intents, and virtual co-presence. We describe these challenges and presents ways to tackle them.

Keywords: Cooperative design · Computer-aided design
Virtual reality · Parametric modelling · Architectural modelling

1   Introduction

Architectural modelling started with paper drawings and scale models. Even though we still use those techniques, software-based tools have automated many design activities. While these tools are evolving rapidly, designers still rely on the classic mouse and keyboard combination, even if this does not seem appropriate to manipulate objects in 3 dimensions [1]. Augmented Reality (AR) and Virtual Reality (VR) components have recently started to be included in modelling solutions, but their use remains mostly limited to visualisation purposes.

Parametric modelling is a design approach where the designer defines a model using a series of instructions that can be seen as an algorithm or computer program. Grasshopper[1] is a popular parametric modelling tool that is distributed as a plugin for the Rhino3D modeller[2]. If offers a visual representation of that

---

[1] http://www.grasshopper3d.com.

[2] https://www.rhino3d.com.

© Springer Nature Switzerland AG 2018
Y. Luo (Ed.): CDVE 2018, LNCS 11151, pp. 304–307, 2018.
https://doi.org/10.1007/978-3-030-00560-3_44

algorithm in the form of some kind of data flow diagram. The algorithm is parametrised by sets of variables whose value can be modified by the designer.

As a first step in embracing VR technologies within the parametric modelling phase, we built [2] a software bridge between Grasshopper and the HTC Vive VR headset[3]. This solution allows designers to benefit from real-time interaction with Grasshopper models, as they can directly experience how their modifications to the parameter values impact the geometries. Figure 1 presents a schematic overview of the solution, and a video of how the tool works is available.[4]

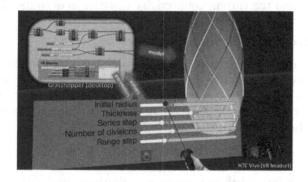

Fig. 1. Proof-of-concept of the proposed solution for VR interaction with parametric models.

The current version of our tool is limited in that it only allows users to modify parameter values of parametric models. There is a clear need to extend the tool with support for cooperative design, allowing multiple collaborators to communicate and interact with each other while designing or evolving their entire architectural models in a VR environment.

In the remainder of this paper we discuss the needs and issues with such collaborative design, and propose ways to tackle them in a VR-based environment.

2 Demands for and Issues with Collaborative VR-Based Design

2.1 User Location and Bandwidth

Depending on where the collaborators are located, the proposed solution should be different. If multiple designers share the same room, they will be able to talk directly to each other. When collaborators are geographically distributed, a Voice over IP (solution for distant communication) would be desirable, as far as this doesn't interfere with the direct communication between local collaborators.

---

[3] https://www.vive.com.

[4] http://informatique.umons.ac.be/staff/Coppens.Adrien/?video=CDVE2018.

Remote collaboration may be challenging if large amounts of data need to be shared over a limited bandwidth. This could lead to increased network latencies between collaborators, or between users and a shared server. If such connectivity issues arise, it becomes necessary to introduce the concept of Quality of Service (QoS) that is well-known in computer networks to define priorities. For instance, virtual co-presence could be sacrificed in order to keep the system as responsive as possible. The refresh rate of the co-presence feature can therefore be reduced (it could even be turned off in extreme circumstances). Dynamically adapting the software (turn on/off features and alter bandwidth allocation) depending on those priorities and the current connectivity situation is of course desirable.

2.2   Concurrent Modification Strategies

Conflicts may arise during collaborative design of parametric models. This is for example the case when different designers try to concurrently access and modify the values of the same or related parameters. Safeguards need to be put in place to avoid a frustrating user experience. A variety of different conflict handling strategies can be proposed, including:

- *Overwriting updates*: When the system receives a value update, the previous one is overwritten. This default behaviour is the most tolerant, but does not provide any safeguard to concurrent modifications. In addition, latency has to be minimal for this approach to work, otherwise the system appears to be ignoring user changes. This solution is acceptable if designers rarely modify parameters simultaneously, and if the rate of change is not too high.
- *Reactive locking:* Whenever a designer starts modifying a parameter value, his collaborators are notified (e.g., through some visual clue) and they can no longer modify that parameter until the first designer releases it. Conflicts could still happen due to latency, if another designer tries to modify the same parameter before receiving the "lock notification". In that case, the system should notify the user that his modification request was rejected.
- *Preemptive locking:* Preemptive locking is an even more conservative approach that prevents the previous problem from happening. By default, parameters cannot be edited. If a designer wants to modify a parameter value, he first needs to request access to that parameter (e.g. following an approach borrowed from computer networks [3]).
- *Privilege strategy:* Independent of the locking strategy, a mechanism based on user privileges could be put into place. Users with higher privileges might be granted the ability to take control of a parameter that is being modified concurrently by someone with lower privileges. In that case, the less-privileged user should be notified that he can no longer control the said parameter.
- *Parameter layers:* It could be useful to define different layers of parameters so that groups of users could get access to different sets of parameters. That would indeed reduce (or even remove if no parameters are shared) the concurrent modification problem. It would also be possible to lock an entire layer of parameters instead of individual ones but in that case, there would be more risks of conflict.

2.3 Related Work

To implement the above strategies, or even more "advanced" ones, we will rely on techniques and solutions used to resolve concurrency issues in similar contexts. For example, software transactional memory techniques have been implemented to control access to a shared memory at the software level [6]. Frameworks specifically targeted at collaborative applications have even been created and support similar concurrency control techniques [5].

However, as the number of collaborators (and therefore concurrent modifications) in collaborative architectural design is expected to be limited, the more elaborated techniques are likely to be overkill. A basic locking strategy seems to be the most reasonable option in a first phase, provided that an appropriate unlocking mechanism takes into account unexpected disconnections (as we do not want a lock to stay in place when the corresponding user is disconnected).

3   Conclusion

Our tool that brought parametric modelling into immersive environments, by acting as a bridge between Grasshopper and the HTC Vive, was initially only designed for single users. To extend upon it by adding collaborative capabilities, we faced challenges related to real-time collaboration. This paper presented those challenges and discussed potential options inspired from solutions to similar problems in other fields. We plan on further evolving our tool to allow multiple designers to make changes to the same parametric architectural model. To achieve this, we will develop more advanced mechanisms that take into account the impact of the changes on the semantics of the model. To do so, we will draw inspiration from software merging techniques such as the ones described in [4].

References

1. Chu, C.C.P., Dani, T.H., Gadh, R.: Multi-sensory user interface for a virtual-reality-based computer-aided design system. Comput.-Aided Des. **29**(10), 709–725 (1997)
2. Coppens, A., Mens, T., Gallas, M.-A.: Parametric modelling within immersive environments: building a bridge between existing tools and virtual reality headsets. In: 36th eCAADe Conference (2018)
3. Maekawa, M.: An algorithm for mutual exclusion in decentralized systems. ACM Trans. Comput. Syst. (TOCS) **3**(2), 145–159 (1985)
4. Mens, T.: A state-of-the-art survey on software merging. IEEE Trans. Softw. Eng. **28**(5), 449–462 (2002)
5. Munson, J., Dewan, P.: A concurrency control framework for collaborative systems. In: ACM Conference on Computer Supported Cooperative Work, pp. 278–287. ACM (1996)
6. Shavit, N., Touitou, D.: Software transactional memory. Distrib. Comput. **10**(2), 99–116 (1997)

Reviewing the Interaction Aspects of a Line of Electronic Brainstorming Social Interfaces

Peter Zelchenko[1]([✉]), Alex Ivanov[2], and Emma Mileva[3]

[1] School of Design, Shanghai Jiao Tong University, Shanghai, China
pkz@uchicago.edu
[2] School of Media and Communications, Shanghai Jiao Tong University,
Shanghai, China
alexivan@me.com
[3] Department of Linguistics, Simon Fraser University, Burnaby, BC, Canada
emileva@sfu.ca

Abstract. Electronic brainstorming (EBS) is one of the most widely studied topics in the fields of information systems (IS) and computer-mediated communication (CMC), but many questions remain as to what is the ideal virtual environment for generating ideas. We review several EBS interfaces originally developed and tested as part of our research over the past 10 years in studying the organization and management of the presentation of users and their content. This includes content spatial partitioning and marking for identifiability or anonymity, as well as certain related social, affective, and cognitive aspects of the user interface. We conclude by discussing the design trends and suggest that IS, human-computer interaction (HCI), and cognitive psychology will benefit from further coalition aimed at improving EBS interfaces.

Keywords: Cooperative user experience (UX) design
Electronic brainstorming · Multi-user interface design
Real-time user interactions · Anonymity

1 Introduction

According to some estimates, about half of a knowledge worker's time on the job is spent in meetings, and half of that time is wasted due to process losses [1]. Studies have found that companies spend millions on expensive groupware products that rarely get used [2]. Teams, whether co-located or distributed, prefer using instant messaging for their collaboration [3]. In China's workplaces, the freely distributed WeChat has almost entirely replaced the telephone (including cellular texts and calls), bulletin boards, and even most former e-mail discussions; yet it lacks many of the key functions that make GSS, including electronic brainstorming (EBS), useful to teams.

Many reasons underlie the low adoption rates of GSS in organizations. One is that these tools – although capable of increasing productivity – are not satisfying to use. As one CSCW expert pointed out in 2007: "While we are now seeing such systems augmented with video and other facilities, they tend to be unreliable, unimaginative, and awkward" [2: 141]. The importance of a well-designed graphical user interface in

© Springer Nature Switzerland AG 2018
Y. Luo (Ed.): CDVE 2018, LNCS 11151, pp. 308–316, 2018.
https://doi.org/10.1007/978-3-030-00560-3_45

the information systems (IS) field has been demonstrated by many studies (e.g., [4]), but its role in the GSS literature has been overlooked. To the user, an system acts like a "black box": its interface is the only thing that is tangible and meaningful [5].

In this paper, we retrospectively review several electronic brainstorming (EBS) interfaces originally developed and tested as part of our research over the past 10 years. The motivation behind these studies has been to develop EBS interfaces that, based on some theories of both social psychology and interface design, will prove satisfying to use. The level and kind of content anonymity, or the extent to which the contributions of EBS participants are identified, has usually been one of the key experimental manipulations. This has been implemented alongside other improvements to the user experience. We have already reported on these studies separately [6–11]. This is the first time that we survey these experiments as a group and observe trends as to the usability of the tested interfaces from an interface design point of view. Our own findings are based on over 50 synchronous group electronic brainstorming sessions conducted with student groups in Canada and China.

2   The Electronic Brainstorming Interface

Group support systems (GSS) have most simply been described as "interactive systems that support meeting processes, and aid in electronic brainstorming and voting" [12]. The original GSS prototypes were developed at the University of Arizona in the 1990's, meant for co-located corporate settings (often called "decision rooms"); since then, GSS usage has expanded to teams in geographically dispersed locations [13].

An important group task in organizations is brainstorming, a method of idea generation popularized by Osborn [14]. GSS for idea generation are called electronic brainstorming systems (EBS). Some EBS resemble the brainwriting method by Van Gundy [15], circulating individual ideas around workstations. Each participant initially receives the main question or problem and responds by inputting a brief idea. Each then sends this idea to a shared pool and gets a randomly drawn idea by another participant, then responds, sends again, and so on until all ideas have received at least as many comments as there are participants. More typical EBS interfaces show all ideas in one "shared" area of the screen, while another area is used for typing. The nature of comments varies with the rules, but there is usually some elaboration to – rather than a critical assessment of – others' ideas. Teams using EBS rather than face-to-face brainstorming are more productive, due to the ability of all participants to contribute ideas at the same time (parallelism) without fear of being judged (anonymity). Some systems by default do not identify participants' contributions, to prevent process losses due to evaluation apprehension. Anonymity has been shown to promote participation of timid individuals and expression of unpopular opinion [11].

Design research on EBS has been scattered. Some researchers have explored certain cognitive aspects of group creativity (for a survey, see [16]). One group has extensively explored engineering patterned modularity at the activity level in collaboration [e.g., 17]. Many have treated idea generation as central to simplified interface designs [e.g., 18, 19]. Dufner et al. [20] found that groups using a simple "list" feature for visualizing group convergence perceived the medium as richer and less ambiguous than did control groups. Aiken et al. [21] compared two EBS interfaces: pool vs. gallery writing, and generally found the latter to support better performance and satisfaction. Yet few have closely examined the visual organization and interaction aspects of the user experience, specifically how identity and content are visually described and depicted for balancing minimalist cognitive clarity and maximizing productive social dynamics.

Numerous novel EBS prototypes have been proposed in qualitative studies that lacked a rigorous empirical examination of the user experience. Of note is *Brainstorm* by Kratschmer and Kaufmann [22], whose color nodes allow each member to recognize his or her own ideation structure, and relate it to concepts that would be distant in his or her own cognitive network; also Reesink [23], presenting a node-link map application that allows consumers to externalize their perceptions of a brand.

Who knows I am here, and how do they feel about my input? A rich stream of empirical research has studied the effects of anonymity and evaluability in group collaboration environments [24–26]. At least two different kinds of anonymity have emerged [27]. *Process* anonymity (full anonymity) occurs when the real-life identity of participants cannot be determined. *Content* anonymity occurs in the absence of visual or textual indications linking content to a contributor. Related to anonymity is evaluability. Whereas conditions of identifiability are usually instantiated by labels, user names, icons, or avatars, evaluability stems from any feedback that relates participant or group performance to some subjective, objective, inter-group, intra-group, or external comparison standard. While not all of the studies shown here manipulated anonymity, it raises subtle interface and information architecture questions. In terms of identifiability, Jung et al. [28] randomly assigned predefined user names to group members in the experimental conditions, and these pseudonyms partially masked specific group members' identities while still maintaining links between individuals and their content. Evaluability may also, paradoxically, lead to *increased* productivity. The same study [28] also used a bar chart deliberately displaying the idea generation rates of each team member, which raised productivity even under anonymity.

Exactly how these kinds of conditions are represented to users is of interest in this article. Under this lens of affordances for social interaction in EBS user experience design, we examine a line of studies done over several years by our own labs.

3   Studies

3.1   Anonymous and Identified Ranking of Ideas

Our first experiment was conducted in 2008 with 126 second-year business students at a large Canadian university [7, 9]. Group size ranged from six to seven. The interface made use of basic information design principles. Studies have shown, for instance, that participants in collective decision-making tend to prefer a fully integrated, global view of the information [29]. The key feature was our graphical voting system, implemented via a small-multiple visualization. These have been shown to reduce the effort for pattern detection by displaying a large amount of data compactly [30, 31]. Figure 1 illustrates the anonymous and identified interface variations. Note that the sole design difference – and the sole condition of anonymity – is that votes in the small-multiple visualization for anonymous voting appeared as all black. This minimal design distinction responds to basic interface principles calling for consistency.

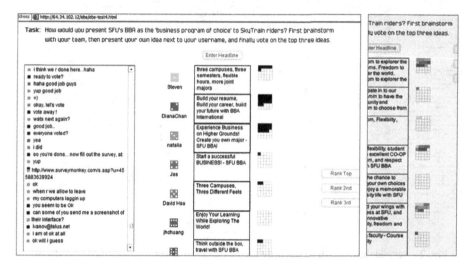

Fig. 1. First design [7, 9]. Pseudoidentities as dice; anonymous control voting treatment (left, all black vote tokens), identified treatment (detail at right, colored vote tokens). (Color figure online)

The main research question here was whether conditions of enhanced evaluability via the identified graphical voting treatment would lead to higher reported enjoyment and satisfaction with outcome. This turned out to be the case on the group level. However, predictably, on the individual level, participants whose ideas were not among the top three selections reported lower satisfaction than did their teammates whose ideas scored better. (For details, see [9].)

3.2   Anonymous and Identified Multiple Dialogs

A second experiment was conducted in 2008, with 30 second-year design students at a typical large Canadian university [10]. Group size was five. The interface here (Fig. 2) also made use of dice as social proxies. The difference was the lack of an evaluation phase, as we wanted to compare the effects of identifiability within idea generation. We drew on Dennis et al. [32], who compared a basic dialogue structure with a single chat window, to another layout with triple separate discussion sheets. We presented an identified chat dialog for five minutes. In the anonymous treatment, after this initial icebreaking, proposals, comments, and feedback were not identified. Members typed ideas in individual cells, similar to earlier designs. However, instead of a final voting phase, participants got more time to discuss each other's ideas in separate chat dialogs.

This study had a smaller sample of participants, but it included a discourse analysis that gave additional confidence to our findings. Both participation and cooperation were significantly higher with anonymous groups. Participants from both conditions

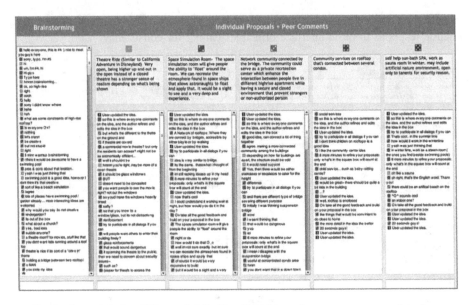

Fig. 2. Second design [10] tested fully identified (shown) versus anonymous interfaces.

reported problems with trying to follow all five chat dialogs, raising questions of focal attention and number of simultaneously active "chunks." This is one reason why the evolution of our interface design in later studies came to reduce chat influence. In fact, we decided to completely abandon the chat dialog format, as explained below.

3.3 Brainstorming for Less Individualistic Populations

The EBS interfaces developed for a yet later study [11] focused on idea generation as well, but in a more structured fashion than simple chat dialogs. We wanted to support an ideation process that was as close as possible to Osborn's original brainstorming technique [14], but with elements of brainwriting [15] and using a "gallery" format [33]. The latter would provide a more task-focused discussion.

As shown in Fig. 3, a grid layout was chosen for all groups in this study. This rationale was based on some prior studies [6, 9] that issued the same task using more conversation-based interfaces. Both EBS interface grids had two types of text boxes. Members would start off typing their new ideas in the top-row area, followed by commenting on each other's ideas below. All team members saw exactly the same view on their monitors. The interaction was synchronous, with virtually no lag between individual submissions. Simple changes in color-coding and partitioning of input by author created two vastly different group environments: the identified interface heightened identifiability, partitioning the shared space into four separate sections. The objective here was to instill a sense of ownership, recognition, even accountability. Using the same basic grid, the anonymous interface was nonpartitioned (pooled) and monochrome, each new idea occupying a subsequent column. As with identified, "elaborations" (comments) appeared below, only anonymously.

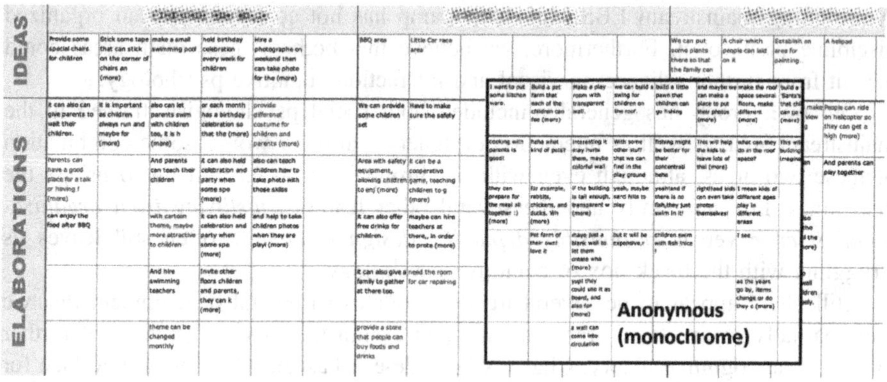

IDEAS

ELABORATIONS

Anonymous (monochrome)

Fig. 3. Design for [11]. Identified (shown) and anonymous (inset). Anonymous items and responses were all in a single color and also in a single pool. (Color figure online)

Brainstorming was originally designed for, and largely has thrived in the realm of, American corporate settings. Historically at least, these settings often emphasize open competition and reward strong personalities. In this study, we examined an East Asian female population. We were interested in whether and how a fully anonymous, pooled interface design would benefit less individualistic social types. It was felt that this might help maximize participation among those who might be more reluctant to join such an open activity. Findings included greater satisfaction from more reserved participants; in fact, it appeared that the anonymous interface may have had a strong damping effect on more zealous group members, a fact that may have helped to level the playing field. The anonymous interface itself also led to greater perceptions of ease of use, though aside from anonymity the sole distinction was that it was pooled. Thus, merely pooling versus partitioning may encourage participation by timid group members.

4 Discussion and Conclusion

Mainstream work in interactive EBS and its larger frame, GSS, has evolved in the past 20 years to emphasize detailed, step-by-step facilitation of EBS users and their content, through a set of orchestrated stages and with seven aspects considered essential [34]. This has culminated in a practice within traditional IS called *collaboration engineering*. It relies on object-oriented pattern-language software frameworks providing a rich menu of ways to shepherd the collaborative process, depending on the various inputs and problems [17]. Often, this process involves highly trained professional facilitators. The strength of the state of the art in this computer- and facilitator-prescribed line of development lies in its long heritage and a basis in IS; its weakness is that it lacks a strong foundation in modern interaction design. In contrast is the work by the many design, visualization, and technology engineers experimenting with new brainstorming and group process interfaces. These are rich in conceptual novelties and motifs, but they lack the social psychology and IS that has supported the mainstream discipline.

While citing mainstream EBS, this latter camp has not coalesced into an organized discipline of its own. Furthermore, we believe that both of these main areas could benefit from further reliance on visual and interaction cognitive psychology.

Our own group has generally included both social psychologists trained in the mainstream area, as well as interaction designers – in other words, some combination of these two areas, although even with our group it has been difficult to bridge the disciplines. For anonymity and the several other features, *justifying from organizational science* versus *responsibly deploying design metaphors* often still leaves us struggling with the black box of cognitive psychology.

Still, there appear to be several trends in our experimental development that we have partially justified via organizational and design theories, and that merit further evidence via cognitive theory. Chat has been de-emphasized as the main interface for EBS activity. EBS interfaces that emphasize free-flowing discussion – as is familiar in most scrolling chat-like applications and activities – invariably lead to a significant portion of non–task-related output. This proportion may be as much as 50% – incidentally also complicating conduction of studies with adequate internal validity. Generic chat is beneficial to break the ice or to reduce tension, but its casual nature can also invite distraction. Our designs evolved away from a central open discussion toward more spatiotemporally oriented, grid-like interface structures, with commentary appended to each item. Chat and spatial concerns may appear to be two separate matters; however, the grid made the ideation process more akin to brainwriting [16], and sidelining (and in one design eliminating) the generic chat window may have encouraged more focused discussion in each item's contextual commentary. We also tended toward instantiating items as individual screen objects, with varying levels of attentional focus. Finally, we increasingly used visualization techniques such as small multiples and iconization to reduce screen clutter and further encourage focus of cognitive resources.

The overall effect of these trends appears to be for us to have nudged the brainstorming *idea item node* conceptually and visuospatially toward center stage, and the item's place on the screen and its relation to other items are also evolving. Commentary and elaboration on an item; organizing and voting; and authors' and commentators' identities, have all been repositioned, both conceptually and visuo-spatially encapsulated and reduced. Anonymity and evaluation have become more granular extensions of the user- or even item-objects under certain conditions, rather than an assumption of the entire session process or product. Perhaps it is becoming clear that we might treat these and other assorted properties as an idea item's metadata. This is not limited to our own group's work: it is apparent in the more general trend toward brainwriting and mindmapping practice, as well as practice for mainstream IS (see, e.g., [35]). Whether and how the predominantly screen-spatial efforts of the first group fully reconcile with the elaborate process frameworks of collaboration engineering in mainstream IS, as well as its other prescriptions for practice, remains to be seen.

References

1. Roszkiewicz, R.: GDSS: the future of online meetings and true digital collaboration? Seybold Rep.: Anal. Publ. Technol. **7**(1), 13–17 (2007)
2. Greenberg, S.: Toolkits and interface creativity. Multimed. Tools Appl. **32**(2), 139–159 (2007). https://doi.org/10.1007/s11042-006-0062-y
3. Quan-Haase, A., Cothrel, J., Wellman, B.: Instant messaging as social mediation: a case study of a high-tech firm. J. Comp.-Mediat. Commun. **10**(4) (2005). https://doi.org/10.1111/j.1083-6101.2005.tb00276.x
4. Traktinsky, N.: Toward the study of aesthetics in information technology. In: Proceedings 25th International Conference on Information Systems, Washington, DC, USA, pp. 771–780 (2004)
5. Venkatesh, V., Ramesh, V.: Web and wireless site usability: understanding differences and modeling use. MIS Q. **30**(1), 181–206 (2006). https://doi.org/10.2307/25148723
6. Ivanov, A., Cyr, D.: The concept plot: a concept mapping visualization tool for asynchronous web-based brainstorming sessions. Inf. Vis. **5**(3), 185–191 (2006). Palgrave (McMillan). https://doi.org/10.1057/palgrave.ivs.9500130
7. Ivanov, A.: Satisfaction with web-based meetings for idea generation and selection: the role of instrumentality, enjoyment, and interface design. Ph.D. dissertation, School of Interactive Arts and Technology, Simon Fraser University (2009)
8. Ivanov, A., Schneider, C.: The effects of perceived visual aesthetics on process satisfaction in GSS use. In: 43rd Hawaii International Conference on Systems Sciences (HICSS), Honolulu, HI, pp. 1–10 (2010)
9. Ivanov, A., Cyr, D.: Satisfaction with outcome and process from web-based meetings for idea generation and selection: the roles of instrumentality, enjoyment, and interface design. Telemat. Inform. **31**(4), 543–558 (2014). https://doi.org/10.1016/j.tele.2013.12.004
10. Mileva, E.: Effects of anonymity: discourse analysis of conversation in electronic brainstorming. Unpublished MS, Department of Linguistics, Simon Fraser University (2009)
11. Ivanov, A., Zelchenko, P.: Electronic brainstorming environments for engaging East-Asian collaborative teams (in review)
12. Srite, M., Galvin, J.E., Ahuja, M.K., Karahanna, E.: Effects of individuals' psychological states on their satisfaction with the GSS process. Inf. Manag. **44**(6), 535–546 (2007). https://doi.org/10.1016/j.im.2007.04.005
13. Saunders, C., Ahuja, M.: Are all distributed teams the same? Small Group Res. **37**(6), 662–700 (2006). https://doi.org/10.1177/1046496406294323
14. Osborn, A.: Applied Imagination. Scribner, New York (1957)
15. Van Gundy Jr., V.: Techniques of Structured Problem Solving. Van Nostrand Reinhold, New York (1981)
16. Javadi, E., Gebauer, J., Mahoney, J.: The impact of user interface design on idea integration in electronic brainstorming: an attention-based view. J. Assoc. Inf. Syst. **14**(1), 1–21 (2013). https://doi.org/10.17705/1jais.00322
17. Briggs, R.O., De Vreede, G., Nunamaker, J.F.: Collaboration engineering with thinkLets to pursue sustained success with group support systems. J. Manag. Inf. Syst. **19**(4), 31–64 (2003). https://doi.org/10.1080/07421222.2003.11045743
18. Shipman III, F.M., Hsieh, H., Maloor, P., Moore, J.M.: The visual knowledge builder: a second generation spatial hypertext. In: Proceedings of ACM Conference on Hypertext, no. 1, pp. 113–122 (2001). https://doi.org/10.1145/504216.504245

19. Azevedo, D., Fonseca, B., Paredes, H., Lukosch, S., Janeiro, J., Briggs, R.O.: On the development and usability of a diagram-based collaborative brainstorming component. J. Univ. Comput. Sci. **19**(7), 873–893 (2013)

20. Dufner, D., Hiltz, S., Johnson, K., Czech, R.: Distributed group support: the effects of voting tools on group perceptions of media richness. Group Decis. Negot. **4**(3), 235–250 (1995). https://doi.org/10.1007/BF01384690

21. Aiken, M., Rebman, C., Vanjani, M.: Comment generation with three electronic brainwriting techniques. Acad. Inf. Manag. Sci. J. **10**(1), 11–29 (2007)

22. Kratschmer, T., Kaufmann, M.: Electronic brainstorming with graphical structures of ideas. In: European Conference on Information Systems, Gdansk, Poland, pp. 120–130 (2002)

23. Reesink, T.: Conceptual brand mapping: a web-based approach to collect brand knowledge and its interpretation using network analysis. In: Proceedings of First International Conference on Concept Mapping, Pamplona, Spain, pp. 305–308 (2004)

24. Jessup, L.M., Connolly, T., Galegher, J.: The effects of anonymity on GDSS group process with an idea-generating task. MIS Q. **14**, 313–321 (1990). https://doi.org/10.2307/248893

25. Kahai, S.S., Sosik, J.J., Avolio, B.J.: Effects of leadership style, anonymity, and rewards on creativity-relevant processes and outcomes in an electronic meeting system context. Leadersh. Q. **14**(4–5), 499–524 (2003). https://doi.org/10.1016/S1048-9843(03)00049-3

26. Pissarra, J., Jesuino, J.C.: Idea generation through computer-mediated communication: the effects of anonymity. J. Man Psychol. **20**(3/4), 275–291 (2005). https://doi.org/10.1108/02683940510589055

27. Lea, M., Spears, R., de Groot, D.: Knowing me, knowing you: anonymity effects on social identity processes within groups. Pers. Soc. Psychol. Bull. **27**(5), 526–537 (2001). https://doi.org/10.1177/0146167201275002

28. Jung, J.H., Schneider, C., Valacich, J.: Enhancing the motivational affordance of information systems: the effects of real-time performance feedback and goal setting in group collaboration environments. Manag. Sci. **56**(4), 724–742 (2010). https://doi.org/10.1287/mnsc.1090.1129

29. Barone, R., Cheng, P.C.H.: Representations for problem solving: on the benefits of integrated structure. In: Banissi, E., Börner, K., Chen, C., et al. (eds.) Proceedings of 8th International Conference Information Visualisation. IEEE, Los Alamitos, CA, pp. 575–580 (2004). https://doi.org/10.1109/IV.2004.1320201

30. Tufte, E.: Visual Explanations. Graphics Press, Cheshire (1997)

31. Chabris, C.F., Kosslyn, S.M.: Representational correspondence as a basic principle of diagram design. In: Tergan, S.-O., Keller, T. (eds.) Knowledge and Information Visualization. LNCS, vol. 3426, pp. 36–57. Springer, Heidelberg (2005). https://doi.org/10.1007/11510154_3

32. Dennis, A.R., Aronson, J.E., Heninger, W.G.: Structuring time and task in electronic brainstorming. MIS Q. **23**(1), 95–108 (1999)

33. Aiken, M., Vanjani, M.: Idea generation with electronic poolwriting and gallery writing. Int. J. Inf. Manag. Sci. **7**, 1–9 (1996)

34. Briggs, R.O., Albrecht, C.C., Dean, D.R., Kolfschoten, G., de Vreede, G.J., Lukosch, S.: A seven-layer model of collaboration: separation of concerns for designers of collaboration systems. In: Proceedings of International Conference Information Systems (ICIS), Paper 26 (2009). http://aisel.aisnet.org/icis2009/26

35. Kolfschoten, G.L., Briggs, R.O., Lukosch, S.: Modifiers: Increasing richness and nuance of design pattern languages. In: Noble, J., Johnson, R., Avgeriou, P., Harrison, N.B., Zdun, U. (eds.) Transactions on Pattern Languages of Programming II, vol. 6510, pp. 62–78. Springer, Heidelberg (2011). https://doi.org/10.1007/978-3-642-19432-0_4

Building Shared Design Rationale Knowledge Model for Collaborative Design

Jianhui Zhou, Jihong Liu[✉], and Yongzhu Hou

School of Mechanical Engineering and Automation,
Beihang University, Beijing, China
ryukeiko@buaa.edu.cn

Abstract. Aiming to provide a knowledge basis for product redesign and variant design in collaborative design situation, this paper proposed a method of building shared design rationale knowledge model to represent the design consensus about certain design issues by processing and integrating individual design rationale knowledge model. The feasibility of the proposed method is elaborated by the instance of the overall design process about certain aircraft.

Keywords: Shared design rationale · Design rationale · Collaborative design

1 Introduction

Design rationale knowledge model (DRKM) records the design thinking process of designers [1]. DRKM transforms the implicit knowledge into explicit and structured knowledge [2]. DRKM can be classified into coarse-granularity design rationale model (C-DRKM) and fine-granularity design rationale model (F-DRKM).

C-DRKM is mainly used to represent the design intents generated in product design process. C-DRKM is a kind of know-what knowledge, such as decision support ontology (DSO) [3]. F-DRKM is mainly used to represent the decisions and its justifications generated in product design process. F-DRKM is a kind of know-how and know-why knowledge, such as the ISAL (issue, solution and artifact layer) model [4], the ISAA (issue, solution and artifact argument) model [5], etc.

Shared design rationale knowledge model (S-DRKM) represents the design consensus about certain design issues. As the product research and development has the characteristic of redesign and variant design, the S-DRKM can be reused for future product design especially in a collaborative design situation. This paper proposed a method for building S-DRKM, aiming to provide a knowledge model for collaborative design.

2 Methods

As showed in Fig. 1, the method of building S-DRKM for collaborative design mainly contains four steps. Firstly, design teamers build C-DRKMs named as individual design intention. Secondly, high-frequency design intents were extracted and clustered

© Springer Nature Switzerland AG 2018
Y. Luo (Ed.): CDVE 2018, LNCS 11151, pp. 317–320, 2018.
https://doi.org/10.1007/978-3-030-00560-3_46

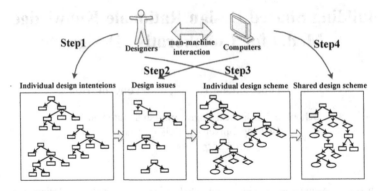

Fig. 1. Process of building S-DRKM for collaborative design.

into design intents sets, named as design topic blocks. Thirdly, design teamers replenish each design topic and build F-DRKMs, named as individual design schemes. Finally, S-DRKM, named as shared design scheme, will be generated by integrating all the individual design schemes. The S-DRKM represents the design consensus of the design teamers.

2.1 Building Individual Design Intention

Individual design intention represents the design intents about certain design issue of one designer. Taking the task of robot designing as an example, designer decomposes the task into some intent according to the requirements of the task.

Individual design intention is represented as the C-DRKM. The elements of C-DRKM include design intents and the semantic relations between design intents. The semantic relations include decompose-into relation and evolve-to relation. Decompose-into relation represents the hierarchical relations between design intents. At the same time, the evolve-to relation represents the transformational relation between design intents.

2.2 Extracting Design Issue Blocks

After the constructing of all individual design intentions were accomplished, design issue blocks could be extracted. Design issue blocks are the sets of design intents with high frequencies in all individual design intentions.

The high-frequency design intents are labelled automatically. Then the other design intents are clustered by taking the labelled design intents as the clustering center. The parameters of the method are the cohesiveness and coupling factor of cluster. Assuming g_i and g_j are the clusters and $W(d_i, d_j)$ is the weight of the relation between g_i and g_j, the cohesiveness(g_i, g_j) and coupling(g_i) can be computed as follows.

$$\text{cut}(g_i, g_j) = \frac{\Sigma\Sigma W(d_i, d_j)}{|g_i||g_j|} \tag{1}$$

$$\text{conhesiveness}(g_i, g_j) = \text{cut}(g_i, g_j) \tag{2}$$

$$\text{coupling}(g_i) = \text{cut}(g_i, g_i) \tag{3}$$

2.3 Building Individual Design Scheme

After the constructing of design issue blocks was accomplished, the design teamer should replenish each design issue block to complete more detailed design information such as design decisions and design justifications. As a result, the F-DRKMs are constructed. An F-DRKM includes design intent, design decision, design option, design justification and so on.

2.4 Generating Shared Design Scheme

According to the context and structure of individual design schemes, the method of data mapping was employed to match the elements between individual design schemes. Afterwards, the method of integrating individual design schemes was used to generate the shared F-DRKM, which named as shared design scheme. The string-level similarity and structure-level similarity degree should be computed when mapping the elements in shared F-DRKMs. The string-level similarity degree calculating method is showed as follows. Where Q is the number of sub-string both belong to e_i and e_j; R is the number of sub-string belongs to e_i but does not belong to e_j; S is the number of sub-string but does not belong to e_i and e_j; T is the number of sub-string neither belong to e_i or e_j; and λ is the harmonic coefficient.

$$\text{sim}_{\text{string-level}}(e_i, e_j) = \frac{\lambda Q}{\lambda Q + R + S + T} \tag{4}$$

The structure-level similarity degree calculating method is showed as follows, where m is the number of elements in F-DRKM that include e_i; n is the number of elements in F-DRKM that include e_j; k is the number of elements that has semantic relation.

$$\text{sim}_{\text{string-level}}(e_i, e_j) = \frac{k}{m+n-k} \bullet \frac{1}{k} \sum_{i=1, j=1}^{k} \text{sim}_{\text{string-level}}(e_i, e_j) \tag{5}$$

3 Validation

Taking the overall design process of certain aircraft as an example, 20 designers constitute the design team. As the consequence, the design teamers build 20 C-DRKMs at all. According to the frequencies of the design intents in the 20 C-DRKMs, 5 design issues blocks were extracted, including *general parameter analysis, select coefficients of space quality and fuel quality, select layout of aircraft, determine number and type of engine* and *determine parameters of wings*. On the basis of these 5 design issues,

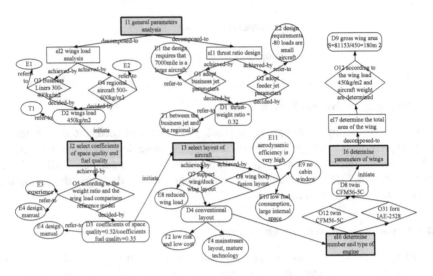

Fig. 2. The generated shared F-DRKM.

design teamers build 20 F-DRKMs included these 5 design issues. In the end, the shared F-DRKM was generated by integrating the 20 F-DRKMs. The generated shared F-DRKM is showed in Fig. 2.

4 Conclusions

This paper proposes an approach of building shared DRKM for collaborative design. The feasibility of the proposed method was verified by taking the overall design process of certain aircraft as an example. The future work will focus on the application of shared DRKM in product research and development.

Acknowledgement. This work has been supported by Project of National Science Foundation of China through approval No. 51475027 and No. 51575046.

References

1. Liu, J., Hu, X.: A reuse oriented representation model for capturing and formalizing the evolving design rationale. AI EDAM-Artif. Intell. Eng. Des. Anal. Manuf. **27**(4), 401–413 (2013)
2. Jing, S., Liu, J., Zhan, H.: A new design rationale knowledge evaluation method. In: International Conference on Computer-Aided Design and Computer Graphics. IEEE (2013)
3. Rockwell, J.A., Grosse, I.R., Krishmanurty, S.: A semantic information model for capturing and communicating design decisions. J. Comput. Inf. Sci. Eng. **10**(3), 1–8 (2010)
4. Liu, Y., Liang, Y., Kwong, C.K., Lee, W.B.: A new design rationale representation model for rationale mining. Comput. Inform. Sci. Eng **10**(3), 031009-1–031009-10 (2010)
5. Zhang, Y., Luo, X., Li, J., Buis, J.J.: A semantic representation model for design rationale of products. Adv. Eng. Inform. **27**, 13–26 (2013)

Achieving Cooperative Design Based on BIM Cloud Platform

Taian Xu[✉]

Zaozhuang University, Zaozhuang 277160, Shandong, China
tyanxu@163.com

Abstract. Through BIM cloud platform, this paper proposes a multi-party collaborative design approach including information integration and sharing. The approach is based on BIM technology and the co-management theory. We mainly investigate the BIM cloud platform and its application in design process. We believe that the approach can greatly improve the work efficiency and project controllability.

Keywords: BIM · Cloud platform · Collaborative design

The construction project is an organizational activity with multiple parties involved. Moreover, at all stages of the project's life cycle, there will be mutual transmission of the information flow. Thus, during the design process, if professional designers only consider problems from their own viewpoint, it will inevitably lead to the conflict of design schemes. Accordingly, to solve the contradictions among various professions in this process as early as possible, we need to ensure that all of the professional designers exchange information and reduce conflicts in due course, and we should also coordinate and manage the design process of each profession.

The emergence of BIM technology brings new ideas to the collaborative design of construction projects, for it not only realizes the transformation from pure geometric drawings to building information modeling, but also provides a new pattern that facilitates the changing from discrete distribution design to collaborative design [1].

Building information modeling (BIM) originated in the 1970s. In 1975, Chuck Eastman first proposed the concept of "Building Description System", which was regarded as the origin of the BIM. However, it was not until 2002 that the term "BIM" was explicated stated for the first time. Since then, with the establishment of BIM International Industry Standard, developed countries such as the United States and Japan have begun to research and promote the application of BIM technology.

The concept of BIM was introduced to China in ca.2004. In 2011, the research group based on Tsinghua University proposed the framework of BIM standard in China after referring to British and American national standards and combining them with the reality of the Chinese construction industry [2].

However, the current application of BIM technology in China mainly concentrates on its three-dimensional visualization, collision detection, optimization design and other features, its core value has not been fully utilized. In view of this, we try to realize multi-party collaborative design and information integration and sharing in this paper. The investigation is based on BIM technology and co-management theory.

© Springer Nature Switzerland AG 2018
Y. Luo (Ed.): CDVE 2018, LNCS 11151, pp. 321–325, 2018.
https://doi.org/10.1007/978-3-030-00560-3_47

1   The Architecture of the Server

There are mainly two models for distributed collaboration: (1) multi-site caching collaboration. Under this pattern, the system automatically distinguishes design files required by a profession according to the rule, and buffers them locally in advance, thus greatly improves the collaborative efficiency [3]. (2) Site-based collaboration. In this mode, there are different home sites for different professions or working directories of a project. Combined with the first kind of buffered collaboration, this mode could ensure the synchronization of project data between different locations is extremely fast.

In order to implement the distributed system, there can be multiple server arrangement frameworks. Here, we employed a hierarchical one. It has three levels.

The first level is composed by the main server of the group center which is set up in its machine room. The server mainly stores the integrative information of the group's personnel and the basic project information of various designing institutes, such as staff situation, public data of drafting standards and document template, etc. At this level, regular data push between different sites could be realized, thus ensuring the consistency of public data standards across the whole community and providing data validation supports for the project collaboration among various institutions.

The second level is composed by the central server of each design institute. This server stores the personnel information and the project information of this institute. In order to synchronize personnel, standard, project, server configuration and other related information, it keeps a scheduled contact with the group's central server [4].

The third level is composed by each project's central server. They are deployed on the ground, and can be divided into two parts: one is the regional center server, which mainly synchronizes with the information of the design institute's central server, and realizes the information localization [5]. The other part is to store project information and achieve project-level collaborative design between local and remote areas. All projects can work in the central server, and the participants do not need to log in the server of the group and institute center. Therefore, the advantage of this approach is that no matter how the network situation is, it will not affect the operation of the project's central server. In general, each design institute can set up several central servers based on different office locations.

2   Co-design Operating Mode Based on BIM Cloud Platform

As an operating platform, each participant can utilize BIM's function to manage knowledge, design, BIM (CAD import, model import), quality (quality analysis, red-coil note, approval and submission) and schedule. The stage of project designing is divided into three periods: scheme design, preliminary design, and construction documents design. The operation of each stage needs to be combined with the Platform's function, and all participants will complete the designing according to the contract.

During the scheme design phase, the designers draw the blueprint by collecting materials, and the BIM consultants establish corresponding models which contains complete design information of all schemes. After that, BIM consultants will check their accuracy and completeness. Next, the participants perform simulation and optimization of the blueprint based on the BIM model. In this period, they can put forward optimization suggestions and submit them to the owners as initial results. The owner will organize regular meetings, where the related parties will sign and confirm the results. Thus, the effectiveness of the results is ensured and could be used in the optimization of the design. The process is shown in Fig. 1.

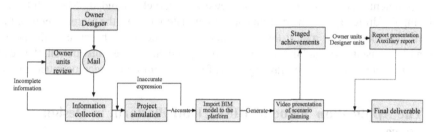

Fig. 1. Workflow in the design phase

The designer and the BIM consultant conduct two-dimensional and three-dimensional linage on the BIM cloud platform. The preliminary design phase mainly performs simulation analysis, but it must be based on the premise that the BIM model can correctly represent the design idea. The operation process is shown in Fig. 2.

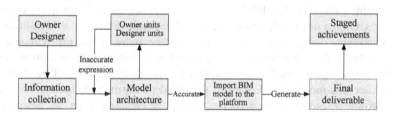

Fig. 2. Workflow in the preliminary design phase

The simulation analysis has a guiding role. For example, if there is a visual simulation of the distribution of the building's surrounding strata, it will be conducive to optimizing the construction and avoiding risks. Because by examining the three-dimensional model of geology, we can better anticipate problems that may be encountered during construction. From this perspective, the owner ought to complete all preparations before construction, so as to facilitate their communication and coordination in construction designing.

In the phase of construction drawing design, BIM consultants build the BIM model based on the design drawing. At the same time, they extract the amount of work to assist the owner in determining the tender price. By signing the contract, the contractors also establish a cooperative relationship with the owner, the designer and the consultant. During the design phase, the constructor will assist BIM consultants in the pipeline collision and integrated simulation optimization. Then the results are revised and improved together with the designer. In order to improve the quality of construction drawings, the constructor and the designer should work together to hand over the design and technology.

At the end of construction drawing design stage, the BIM consultants will cooperate with the owner and constructor to simulate the equipment installation process. For the owner, this method can better control the site and improve management efficiency. For the constructor, they can see the problems that may arise during the installation of the equipment before construction, so rework is largely avoided. Meanwhile, by reducing the difficulty of construction and saving material costs, the requirements of the owner and designer are met at the same time. For the designer, because of the simulation of the installation and the removal of the equipment before construction, they can detect problems in the design drawings, thus further optimization become much easier.

3   The Application Value of BIM Cloud Platform in Design Phase

In the design phase, the core idea of applying the BIM cloud platform is to manage collaborative projects. Compared with the traditional design stage, the application of BIM cloud platform had improved work efficiency and owner's satisfaction as well as project controllability.

At the design stage, the owners, designers, consultants and constructors are involved. For BIM models and the design effects they exhibit, all participants communicate with each other. The BIM cloud platform enhances work efficiency mainly in two aspects. On the one hand, by making use of the three-dimensional visualization of BIM technology, design intent and results can be more intuitively demonstrated. Through collision detection and deepening design, it also reduces the repetitive work in the traditional design stage. On the other hand, one can build a model by BIM technology. After this model is uploaded to the cloud platform, participating parties can quickly browse it, and mark the parts that need to be changed. Then, the designer and consultant modify the model accordingly. Later, the modified part will be marked again. All of the above operations can be accomplished on the platform, thus transforming the process of change in traditional design and greatly improving efficiency.

The owner reserves the right to audit the design achievement. At the design stage, the designer submits the drawings to BIM consultants who conducts model building afterwards. At this time, the owner can comment on the design results presented by the BIM model [6]. And the designer will modify it according to the owner's requirements. The modified design are displayed by the BIM consultant to the owner. This procedure is repeated until the owner is satisfied. During the application process of the BIM cloud platform, the owner can also put forward his own requirements and suggestions to the designer, and examine the design achievements. This will not only ensure the design quality, but also improve the owner's satisfaction.

The application of BIM cloud platform in the design phase has improved the controllability of the project, which is mainly reflected in cost and quality. In terms of the cost, BIM consultant will extract the detailed list of engineering quantities according to the model. In later construction, the owner will also control the project's investment cost based on the previous project schedule. The BIM cloud platform can simulate and analyze the construction environment of the project at the design stage, and it can also strengthen the management and control of the construction site, thus saving the cost. In terms of quality control, BIM consultant's pipeline collisions and integrated simulation optimization of the BIM model have eliminated design error to a large extent. Modifications such as design change and rework in normal construction have therefore been reduced, and the quality of project construction has also been greatly improved.

4 Conclusion

With the popularization of BIM technology, its application experience in the project life cycle will become more and more mature. This paper investigates the integrated application of BIM cloud platform in the design phase. Restricted by the progress of project construction, this paper cannot explore the application effect of BIM cloud platform on the project from the perspective of the whole life cycle, but intercepts its application in the design phase. In future research, if quantitative method are resorted to, the argument may be more convincing.

References

1. Wei, X., Yuandong, L.: The application of BIM collaborative design in the design preparation stage. Value Eng. **33**, 74–76 (2015)
2. Dong, D.: The theory and application of collaboration management system, pp. 126–129. Tsinghua University Press, Beijing (2013)
3. Jie, Z.: The application of 3D cooperative design in designing institutes [J]. Water Resour. Plann. Des. **04**, 58–62 (2014)
4. Hyunk, K., Sung, H.H., Jaehyun, P., et al.: How user experience changes over time: a case study of social network services. Hum. Factors Ergonom. Manuf. Serv. Ind. **25**(6), 659–673 (2015)
5. Ying, G.: The transboundary application and exploitation of "BIM" towards intelligent water conservancy. Water Resour. Plan. Des. **09**, 154–157 (2017)
6. Hui, L.: BIM data management based on standard data format of water conservancy and BIM ecological exploration of water conservancy. Water Resour. Plan. Des. **11**, 24–29 (2017)

Ecological Scheduling for Small Hydropower Groups Based on Grey Wolf Algorithm with Simulated Annealing

Yule Wang, Wanliang Wang[✉], Qin Ren, and Yanwei Zhao

College of Computer Science and Technology,
Zhejiang University of Technology, Hangzhou 310023,
People's Republic of China
yulewang1990@163.com, {wwl, renqin, zyw}@zjut.edu.cn

Abstract. An improved multi-objective grey wolf algorithm with simulated annealing (MOGWO/SA) is proposed in this paper. Compared with origin algorithm, the new multi-objective grey wolf algorithm has combined with simulated annealing algorithm optimization and the new leading wolf selection mechanism, which makes the algorithm with stronger global searching ability and faster rate of convergence. The diversity of non-dominated solutions and ductility of MOGWO/SA are also improved. Finally, MOGWO/SA are applied to the ecological optimal operation of small hydropower stations for both the maximum output of generated energy and the maximum assurance rate of ecological water requirement.

Keywords: Multi-objective grey wolf algorithm · Simulated annealing
Leader selection mechanism · Ecological scheduling

1 Introduction

Hydropower development is the objective demand and inevitable choice of human society, human development and social progress. Small hydropower, as the main rural hydropower, is clean and renewable energy which has an important significance for the energy supply in rural areas. After continuous development and utilization in recent years, small hydropower plays an irreplaceable role in the steady construction of rural electrification and rural economic development [1].

Ecological scheduling refers to the operation that meets economic and social objectives such as the power generation, flood control, navigation, water supply and the needs of river ecosystems. Traditional optimal operation of hydropower station aims to maximize the electrical power output [2] or the benefits of power generation [3] while ignoring the ecological needs of the ecological benefits, thus it makes many negative impacts on the fragile ecosystem such as the extinction of species and endemic drought. Symphorien [4] thinks the ecological operation refers to the irrigation scheduling of reservoirs which can meet both human demands on water resources and the water demand of the ecosystem.

© Springer Nature Switzerland AG 2018
Y. Luo (Ed.): CDVE 2018, LNCS 11151, pp. 326–334, 2018.
https://doi.org/10.1007/978-3-030-00560-3_48

Hydropower scheduling is an important engineering application for optimization aiming to gain more economic and ecological benefits. A lot of intelligent algorithms have been used in hydropower scheduling such as Particle Swarm Optimization [5], Ant Colony Algorithm [6], and Artificial Bee Colony algorithm [7]. Grey Wolf Optimization [8, 9], which is advanced in this paper, simulates the hunting behavior of grey wolf group, and is inspired by the hunting technique of them.

The remaining part of the paper proceeds as follows: Sect. 2 surveys the theoretical background of ecological scheduling for small hydropower groups and Multi-Objective Grey Wolf Optimization (MOGWO). Section 3 proposes the Simulated Annealing Strategy and new leader selected mechanism which is added in MOGWO. Experimental results on the convergence and coverage of the algorithm implemented are also given. The application of the new algorithm for small hydropower groups are presented in Sect. 4. Eventually, Sect. 5 draws the conclusions and proposes the future work.

2 Related Works

2.1 Ecological Scheduling for Small Hydropower Groups

Ecological scheduling for small hydropower groups is a multi-objective optimization. It needs to balance both economic objective and ecological objective.

The objective function to reach the maximum power output [5] is shown as follows:

$$f_1 = \max \sum_{t=1}^{T} \left[\sum_{i=1}^{I} K_i Q_i(t) H_i(t) \Delta t_i + \sum_{j=1}^{J} K_j' Q_j'(t) H_j'(t) \Delta t_j' \right] \tag{1}$$

T is the number of dispatch interval. I and J are the number of series power stations and parallel power stations. K is the coefficient of output of power station. Q is the power discharge, and H is the water head.

The objective function to reach the best assurance rate of ecological water requirement [10] is shown as follows:

$$f_2 = \max \left\{ W \sum_{t=1}^{T} \sum_{i=1}^{I} \frac{Q_{Di}(t)}{Q_{Ei}(t)} + \sum_{t=1}^{T} \sum_{j=1}^{J} \frac{Q_{Di}'(t)}{Q_{Ej}'(t)} \right\} \tag{2}$$

W is the assurance rate of ecological water requirement. QD is the downstream runoff of power station, while QE is the ecological runoff.

2.2 Multi-Objective Grey Wolf Optimizer (MOGWO)

The MOGWO algorithm [9] is inspired by the social leadership and hunting technique of grey wolves. The first, second and third best solutions are named as the alpha (α), beta (β) and delta (δ) wolves. The rest of candidate solutions are assumed to be omega (ω) wolves. In the MOGWO algorithm the hunting is guided by α, β and δ, and the ω wolves follow these three wolves in the search for the global optimum (target).

The MOGWO algorithm uses an archive to save or retrieve non-dominated Pareto optimal solutions obtained so far. During the course of iteration, dominated solutions will be elided and new non-dominated solutions should be added. If the archive is full, one of most crowded segment will be omitted.

This algorithm use a leader selection mechanism to get alpha, beta and delta wolves. The leader selection component chooses the least crowded segments of the search space and offers one of its non-dominated solutions as alpha, beta, or delta wolves from the archive by a roulette-wheel method. Then each search agent are calculated with the following formulas for the next iteration during the optimization.

$$\vec{D}_i = \left| \vec{C}_i \cdot \vec{X}_i(t) - \vec{X}(t) \right| \quad , i \in (\alpha, \beta, \delta) \tag{3}$$

$$\vec{X}_i(t) = \vec{X}_i(t) - \vec{A}_i \cdot \vec{D}_i, \quad i \in (\alpha, \beta, \delta) \tag{4}$$

$$\vec{X}(t+1) = \frac{\vec{X}_\alpha(t) + \vec{X}_\beta(t) + \vec{X}_\delta(t)}{3} \tag{5}$$

The vectors $\vec{A}$ and $\vec{C}$ are calculated as follows:

$$\vec{A} = 2\vec{a} \cdot \vec{r}_1 - \vec{a} \tag{6}$$

$$\vec{C} = 2 \cdot \vec{r}_2 \tag{7}$$

where elements of $\vec{a}$ linearly decrease from 2 to 0 over the course of iterations and r_1, r_2 are random vectors in [0, 1].

3   Multi-Objective Grey Wolf Algorithm with Simulated Annealing (MOGWO/SA)

3.1   Simulated Annealing Strategy for MOGWO

MOGWO is a novel multi-objective meta-heuristic algorithm which can provide competitive results in standard test problems compared to other well-known algorithms. However, in order to adapt MOGWO to ecological scheduling for small hydropower groups, new strategies is needed to help improve the performance of not only convergence but also coverage.

Simulated Annealing Strategy [11] can make a contribution to these problems. This paper proposed an improved MOGWO algorithm with Simulated Annealing, called MOGWO/SA. In MOGWO/SA, some dominated solution can be added into the archive in probability. There would be three different possible cases as follows:

- The new solution dominates one or more solutions in the archive. Then the dominated solution(s) in the archive should be replaced by the new solution.
- If neither the new solution nor archive members dominate each other, the new solution should be added into the archive.

- The new solution is dominated by one of the archive members. In this case, probability of acceptance is calculated as follows:

$$S(F, \lambda) = \sum_{i=1}^{N} \lambda_i f_i \qquad (8)$$

$$p = \begin{cases} 1 & S(f(y), \lambda) \leq 0 \\ \exp\left(\frac{-S(f(y), \lambda)}{T}\right) & else \end{cases} \qquad (9)$$

T is the annealing temperature which decreases over iterations. λ_i is weight factor of each objective.

3.2 Improvement of Leader Selection Mechanism

According to the weight factor λ_i, S can be calculated for each search agent by Eq. (8). Then the alpha wolf can be set to the member in archive with the biggest S value. While the other beta and delta wolves are selected by a roulette-wheel method as usual. In addition, the position formula of the search agent for next iteration is changed as follows:

$$\vec{X}(t+1) = \frac{\vec{X}_\alpha(t)}{2} + \frac{\vec{X}_\beta(t) + \vec{X}_\delta(t)}{4} \qquad (10)$$

3.3 Procedure of the Proposed MOGWO/SA Algorithm

The steps of MOGWO/SA is noted as follows:

Step 1.   Initialize the grey wolf population W_i (i = 1, 2, ..., n) and iteration t; Initialize a, A, C, T and weight factor λ.

Step 2.   Calculate the object values for each search agent.

Step 3.   Initialize the archive with the non-dominated solutions and start to find them.

Step 4.   Choose W_α by a roulette-wheel method and exclude alpha from the archive temporarily; Choose W_β by a roulette-wheel method and exclude beta from the archive temporarily; Choose W_δ by a roulette-wheel method and add back alpha and beta to the archive; Set t = 1.

Step 5.   Update the position of each search agent by Eqs. (3)–(7) and (10); Update a, A, C and calculate the objective values of all search agents.

Step 6.   For each search agent, find the solution in the archive which has the shortest Euclidean Distance with the search agent; Decide whether to add the search agent to the archive by Eq. (9) and add those chosen solutions to the archive.

Step 7.   If the archive is full, run the grid mechanism to elide one of the current archive members and add the new solution; If any of the new added solutions is located outside the hypercubes, update the grids to cover all the new solutions.

Step 8.   Calculate the S value for each solution by Eq. (8) in the archive.

Step 9.   Choose W_α as the solution with the biggest S value and exclude alpha from the archive temporarily; Choose W_β by a roulette-wheel method and exclude beta from the archive temporarily; Choose W_δ by a roulette-wheel method and add back alpha and beta to the archive; $t = t + 1$.

Step 10.   If $t <$ Max number of iterations then go to Step 5; Else stop the search and show the final archive of solutions.

3.4   Evolutionary Analyses of MOGWO/SA

In this section, some experiments with two classic and representative multi-objective algorithms (MOPSO [12] and MOEA/D [13]) have been adopted in order to evaluate the performance of the proposed MOGWO/SA algorithm. The number of population size and archive size sets to 100, and the maximum iteration sets to 200. Standard benchmark test problems are from representative UF suites [14]. The parameters of related algorithms are shown in Table 1.

Table 1. Parameters for MOPSO and MOEA/D

MOPSO parameter	Value	MOEA/D parameter	Value
Grid inflation parameter	0.1	Subproblems	100
Leader selection pressure parameter	4	Neighborhood size	10
nGrid	10	Mutation probability	0.5
c_1	2.05	Mutation distribution index	30
c_2	2.05	δ	0.9

The following three widely used metrics are adopted to perform the proposed approaches: Inverted Generational Distance (IGD) for measuring convergence, the Spacing (SP) and Maximum Spread (MS) for measuring the coverage [15].

IGD measures the distance between the true Pareto optimal solution and the closest obtained Pareto optimal solutions in the reference set. The lower the IGD value is, the better the performance of algorithm for approximating the whole Pareto front is.

SP measures the range variance of neighboring solutions in the non-dominated set by comparison with the solutions converged to the true Pareto front. A smaller value of this metric indicates a uniform distribution of solution in the non-dominated set as the solutions will be equally spaced. MS also measures the range variance of neighboring solutions in the non-dominated set. The higher the MS value is, the better the coverage of algorithm is.

Table 2. IGD metric results

IGD	UF1			UF2			UF3		
	MOGWO	MOPSO	MOEA/D	MOGWO	MOPSO	MOEA/D	MOGWO	MOPSO	MOEA/D
Average	0.0681	0.1096	0.1684	0.0395	0.0543	0.1101	0.2469	0.2825	0.2597
Median	0.0685	0.1185	0.1645	0.0396	0.0435	0.1081	0.2406	0.277	0.2603
STD. Dev.	0.0144	0.0396	0.0456	0.0048	0.0248	0.0096	0.051	0.0602	0.143
IGD	UF4			UF5			UF6		
	MOGWO	MOPSO	MOEA/D	MOGWO	MOPSO	MOEA/D	MOGWO	MOPSO	MOEA/D
Average	0.055	0.1224	0.0613	0.4946	1.9821	1.1623	0.6911	0.5827	0.6193
Median	0.054	0.1208	0.0616	0.4971	1.913	1.2038	0.7115	0.4956	0.6285
STD. Dev.	0.0044	0.0066	0.0019	0.133	0.4977	0.1214	0.15	0.2395	0.0497

Table 3. SP metric results

SP	UF1			UF2			UF3		
	MOGWO	MOPSO	MOEA/D	MOGWO	MOPSO	MOEA/D	MOGWO	MOPSO	MOEA/D
Average	0.0624	0.0090	0.0038	0.0548	0.0074	0.0083	0.0517	0.0069	0.0288
Median	0.0798	0.0099	0.0042	0.0878	0.0091	0.0096	0.0242	0.0077	0.0295
STD. Dev.	0.0814	0.0094	0.0042	0.0823	0.0089	0.0094	0.0073	0.0074	0.0276
SP	UF4			UF5			UF6		
	MOGWO	MOPSO	MOEA/D	MOGWO	MOPSO	MOEA/D	MOGWO	MOPSO	MOEA/D
Average	0.0046	0.0052	0.0048	0.0057	0.0060	0.0067	0.0021	0.0091	0.0063
Median	0.0052	0.0073	0.0058	0.0049	0.0053	0.0063	0.0023	0.0079	0.0069
STD. Dev.	0.0062	0.0073	0.0078	0.0022	0.0053	0.0011	0.0023	0.0134	0.0226

Table 4. MS metric results

MS	UF1			UF2			UF3		
	MOGWO	MOPSO	MOEA/D	MOGWO	MOPSO	MOEA/D	MOGWO	MOPSO	MOEA/D
Average	0.9992	0.6518	0.5229	0.9985	0.9211	0.8807	0.9999	0.6164	0.2423
Median	0.9994	0.6698	0.6013	0.9997	0.9255	0.8831	0.9999	0.6222	0.2317
STD. Dev.	0.0009	0.1832	0.1577	0.0033	0.0243	0.0053	0.0001	0.1004	0.1152
MS	UF4			UF5			UF6		
	MOGWO	MOPSO	MOEA/D	MOGWO	MOPSO	MOEA/D	MOGWO	MOPSO	MOEA/D
Average	0.9873	0.8208	0.8920	0.9518	0.2820	0.2950	0.8354	0.2770	0.0977
Median	0.9879	0.8213	0.8901	0.963	0.2894	0.2945	0.8528	0.2314	0.0001
STD. Dev.	0.0013	0.0129	0.0172	0.0486	0.0909	0.0329	0.0848	0.1072	0.1967

From Tables 2, 3, and 4, it shows that MOGWO has better performance of IGD and MS for almost every test function, and has better performance of SP for UF 4, 5, 6. Generally, MOGWO has high convergence behavior and superior coverage and has significant merits in solving multi-objective problems.

4   Applications of MOGWO/SA in Ecological Scheduling for Small Hydropower Groups

The experimental research in this section is based on the data of Lushui River Basin. The structure of small hydropower group in Lushui River Basin is shown as Fig. 1.

In this section, multi-objective optimization is held in order to reach both the maximum power output and the best assurance rate of ecological water requirement as Eq. (1)–(2) shown. MOGWO/SA is adopted to solve the optimization model. The scheduling period is one year while the interval time is a month. The number of population size and archive size sets to 100, and the maximum iteration sets to 200. The initial water level of reservoir sets to the actual water level in January. The results of optimization model with MOGWO above are shown in Table 5.

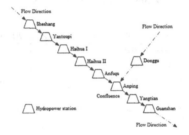

Fig. 1. Structure of small hydropower group in Lushui River Basin

Table 5. Results of multi-objective optimization of small hydropower group in Lushui River Basin

| No. | Small hydropower group | | Sheshang station | | Donggu station | |
---	Annual power output [10^3 kW h]	Ecological water requirement [km^3]	Annual power output [10^3 kW h]	Ecological water requirement [km^3]	Annual power output [10^3 kW h]	Ecological water requirement [km^3]
1	106463.247	242921.059	19541.893	189623.134	41846.692	153652.625
2	113601.856	206592.100	23346.709	96279.990	46225.584	105621.636
3	111397.676	225778.739	22441.897	113026.457	44270.669	109559.968
4	108076.277	236827.054	21858.198	119060.097	43518.034	112752.282
5	110426.474	235138.871	22142.760	118312.676	44152.598	112430.602
6	111701.550	211931.327	23190.303	99719.458	44503.072	106872.643
7	111578.621	216087.414	22708.104	106527.160	44402.929	107878.163
8	107668.114	239768.933	21532.780	127338.330	43432.832	115651.337
9	113126.863	207329.094	23270.528	99450.931	44973.538	105621.636
10	107053.670	240223.159	21195.293	131205.418	43398.015	116826.196

This optimization model with MOGWO/SA can provide more scientifically reasonable solutions for management of small hydropower groups.

5   Conclusions

The ecological scheduling for small hydropower groups is an important multi-objective optimization task for economic and society development. This paper presents an improved algorithm of MOGWO by using Simulated Annealing Strategy to receive solutions and improving the leader selection mechanism. The experimental simulation results indicate that MOGWO/SA has splendid global search ability and great performance in both convergence and coverage, which can effectively solve such a multi-constrains, non-linearity problem in small hydropower group scheduling.

For future study, we are going to investigate the application of this algorithm in different types of multi-objective optimization problems such as flow shop scheduling problem and logistics resources planning problem.

Acknowledgments. The authors would like to thank the anonymous reviewers for their constructive comments and suggestions. This project was supported in part by National Science and Technology Support Plan (2012BAD10B0101).

References

1. Han, D., Fang, H., Yan, B.: China's hydropower status in 2013. J. Hydroelectr. Eng. **33**(5), 1–5 (2014)
2. Yao, Y.-T., Zhang, H., Meng, Q.-S.: Optimized operation of Three Gorges and GeZhouba cascade stations based on maximum generating watt. Mech. Electr. Tech. Hydropower Stn. **33**(3), 87–89 (2010)
3. Li, C.-J., Chen, B.-S.: Study of long-term hydro optimal dispatching model of reservoir. Water Resour. Power **22**(3), 51–52, 60 (2004)
4. Symphorian, G.-R., Madamombe, E., van der Zaag, P.: Dam operation for environmental water releases; the case of Osborne dam, save catchment, Zimbabwe. Phys. Chem. Earth **28** (20–27), 985–993 (2003)
5. Wang, W., Li, L., Xu, X., et al.: Research on hydropower station optimal scheduling considering ecological water demand. In: IEEE Symposium on Computational Intelligence for Engineering Solutions, pp. 35–42 (2013)
6. Zecchin, A.C., Simpson, A.R., Maier, H.R., et al.: Parametric study for an ant algorithm applied to water distribution system optimization. IEEE Trans. Evol. Comput. **9**(2), 175–191 (2005)
7. Li, W., Li, Y., Ren, P.: Optimal operation of cascade reservoirs based on cloud variation-artificial bee colony algorithm. J. Hydroelectr. Eng. **33**(1), 37–42 (2014)
8. Mirjalili, S., Mirjalili, S.M., Lewis, A.: Grey wolf optimizer. Adv. Eng. Soft. **69**(3), 46–61 (2014)
9. Mirjalili, S., Saremi, S., Mirjalili, S.M., et al.: Multi-objective grey wolf optimizer: a novel algorithm for multi-criterion optimization. Expert Syst. Appl. **47**, 106–119 (2015)
10. Wang, Z., Cheng, L., Wang, Y., et al.: A multi-reservoir ecological operation model based on subdivision application of reservoir storage capacities. Adv. Water Sci. **25**(3), 435–443 (2014)
11. Li, J.-Z., Xia, J.-W., Zeng, X.-H., et al.: Survey of multi-objective simulated annealing algorithm and its applications. Comput. Eng. Sci. **35**(8), 77–88 (2013)

12. Li, L., Wang, W., Xu, X.: Multi-objective particle swarm optimization based on global margin ranking. Inf. Sci. **375**, 30–47 (2017)
13. Zhang, Q., Li, H.: MOEA/D: a multiobjective evolutionary algorithm based on decomposition. IEEE Trans. Evol. Comput. **11**(6), 712–731 (2007)
14. Zhang, Q., Zhou, A., Zhao, S., et al.: Multi-objective optimization test instances for the CEC 2009 special session and competition. Technical report, University of Essex, Colchester, UK and Nanyang technological University, Singapore (2008). Special session on performance assessment of multi-objective optimization algorithms, p. 264
15. Sierra, M.R., Coello Coello, C.A.: Improving PSO-based multi-objective optimization using crowding, mutation and $\in$-dominance. In: Coello Coello, C.A., Hernández Aguirre, A., Zitzler, E. (eds.) EMO 2005. LNCS, vol. 3410, pp. 505–519. Springer, Heidelberg (2005). https://doi.org/10.1007/978-3-540-31880-4_35

Design Rationale Knowledge-Integrated MBD Model to Support Collaboration Between Design and Manufacturing

Yongzhu Hou[1], Jihong Liu[1(✉)], and Gaofeng Yue[2]

[1] School of Mechanical Engineering and Automation, Beihang University,
Beijing, China
ryukeiko@buaa.edu.cn
[2] China National Institue of Standardization, Beijing, China

Abstract. To solve the complex and low efficiency problems of collaborative communication between design and manufacturing, this paper proposes a method for the construction of design rationale knowledge-integrated Model based Definition (MBD) model. Based on the above starting point, the product design knowledge sharing and design-manufacturing communicating mechanisms are proposed to support collaboration. A prototype system is designed and implemented to verify the effectiveness of the proposed method.

Keywords: Collaborative communication · Design rationale knowledge
Model based definition

1 Introduction

The traditional process of product research and development (R&D) includes product design, process planning and manufacturing. This traditional R&D process separates the link between design and manufacturing [1]. For example, repeated communication and confirmation with the upstream, which greatly reduces the R&D efficiency, are required [2].

The role of 3D model becomes more and more important after the introduction and application of MBD model [3]. The MBD model integrates all the product information and acts as a single data source. The geometric and technical information in the MBD model acts as the collaborative information that connects different R&D process. However, the geometric and technical information is only a design result. As the consequence, the downstream engineers could not understand the design rationale behind the design result. For example, whether the design can be adjusted, what is the scope of the design and why the design should be like this way. In this case, iterative communications between design and manufacturing, which is time-consuming and labor-intensive, relies on the form of networks and conferences. Aiming at solving this problem, this paper proposes a method for the construction of design rationale knowledge-integrated MBD model. The method helps to improve the comprehensibility of the MBD model and the convenience of collaborative communication.

© Springer Nature Switzerland AG 2018
Y. Luo (Ed.): CDVE 2018, LNCS 11151, pp. 335–338, 2018.
https://doi.org/10.1007/978-3-030-00560-3_49

2 Methods

2.1 Integration of MBD Model and DR

DR knowledge is used to expresses and records the design thinking process of designers [4]. The contents of DR include design intent, design scheme, design justification, design decision and design operation. This article uses the simplified DR knowledge to express the design thinking process of geometrical and technical information in MBD model.

Figure 1 shows the integrating processes of MBD model and DR. The processes are mainly divided into three steps. (1) Product designers, such as Designer A and B, express their own design knowledge K1 and K2 as DR1 and DR2 through a simplified DR knowledge model. (2) DR1 and DR2 were integrated with the geometric and technical information and become the Annotations in MBD model. (3) After the integrating processes, the annotations content were recorded through an XML file.

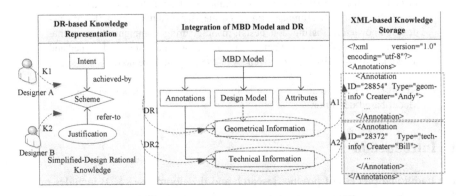

Fig. 1. Integrating processes of MBD model and DR.

2.2 Collaboration Mechanism Based on DR-Integrated MBD Model

The DR-integrated MBD model serves as the basis for collaboration between design and manufacturing. As shown in Fig. 2, the DR-integrated MBD model supports two collaborative mechanisms.

The design knowledge sharing mechanism means that the DR knowledge is shared among different stages of product R&D processes. When the DR-integrated MBD model enters the PLM system, the downstream engineers can directly carry out engineering problems through viewing and understanding of DR knowledge.

The design-manufacturing collaborative mechanism means that the collaborative communication is implemented through a feedback mechanism. This mechanism is used when the engineering problems cannot be solved directly by the using of DR knowledge. The downstream engineers can annotate the feedback information about specific geometric and technical information to MBD model through PMD system.

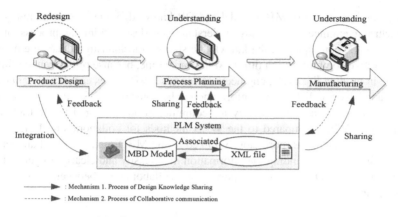

Fig. 2. Two mechanisms for collaboration.

Then the feedback information is also recorded in the XML file, by which the feedback information passed to other stages of the product R&D processes.

3 Implementation and Evaluation

The design and implementation of the prototype system was based on NX7.5. This article takes the MBD model of an engine centrifugal nozzle as an example. As shown in Fig. 3, the designer integrates the DR knowledge at ① for the first time. The downstream engineers views the DR knowledge at ② and perform corresponding engineering operations. The feedback could be annotated at ③. Then the corresponding engineers can view the communication information at ④.

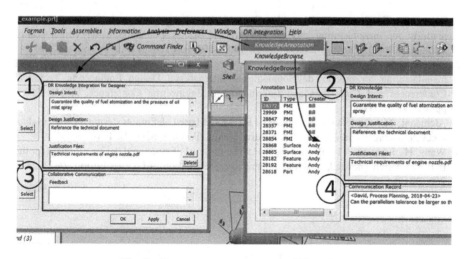

Fig. 3. Prototype system support collaboration.

After the integrating of MBD model and DR knowledge, the process planning and manufacturing engineers can easily understand the design thinking process of the designer. As the consequence, the knowledge sharing mechanism reduces the number of collaborative communication times. At the same time, because of the transmitting of XML file in product life cycle, engineers at various R&D stages can directly annotate, transfer and share collaborative information when necessary. So the collaborative mechanism provides an efficient way for communication compared to the traditional meeting form. When compared to the WEB methods for collaboration, design communication information is more closely linked to the MBD model. This characteristic makes engineers understanding the information more easily and clearly. In general, the DR-integrated MBD method supports the collaboration between design and manufacturing.

4 Conclusions and Future Work

This paper proposes an approach for the construction of DR-integrated MBD model to support the collaborative communication between design, process planning and manufacturing. The usefulness and effectiveness of the proposed method was verified by the prototype system. The future work will focus on the visualization of collaborative process, aiming to provide method and platform with characteristics of good interaction and easy operation for collaborative communication.

Acknowledgement. This work has been supported by Project of National Science Foundation of China through approval No. 51475027 and No. 51575046.

References

1. Pappas, M., Karabatsou, V., Mavrikios, D., et al.: Development of a web-based collaboration platform for manufacturing product and process design evaluation using virtual reality techniques. Int. J. Comput. Integr. Manuf. **19**(8), 805–814 (2006)
2. Sakamoto, H., Tsuneishi, T., Sakamoto, M.: Internet collaboration of 3D-CAD design and manufacturing for product development. In: International Design Engineering Technical Conferences and Computers and Information in Engineering Conference, ASME 2003, pp. 61–66 (2003)
3. Alemanni, M., Destefanis, F., Vezzetti, E.: Model-based definition design in the product lifecycle management scenario. Int. J. Adv. Manuf. Technol. **52**(1–4), 1–14 (2011)
4. Wang, H., Johnson, A.L., Bracewell, R.H.: The retrieval of structured design rationale for the re-use of design knowledge with an integrated representation. Adv. Eng. Inform. **26**(2), 251–266 (2012)

Author Index

Printed in the United States
By Bookmasters